magazines
THAT MAKE HISTORY

editorial**Sol90**©media

© 2004 by Norberto Angeletti and Alberto Oliva.
All rights reserved.
A record of cataloging-in-publication information is
available from the Library of Congress.
ISBN 0-8130-2766
Duty copy B-26717-2004

Editorial Sol 90
Av. Diagonal, 456, planta 5ª
08006 Barcelona. Spain.
www.sol90.com

The University Press of Florida is the scholarly
publishing agency for the State University System
of Florida, comprising Florida A&M University,
Florida Atlantic University, Florida Gulf Coast
University, Florida International University, Florida
State University, University of Central Florida,
University of Florida, University of North Florida,
University of South Florida, and University of
West Florida.

University Press of Florida
15 Northwest 15th Street
Gainesville, FL 32611-2079
http://www.upf.com

Florida A&M University, Tallahassee
Florida Atlantic University, Boca Raton
Florida Gulf Coast University, Ft. Myers
Florida International University, Miami
Florida State University, Tallahassee
University of Central Florida, Orlando
University of Florida, Gainesville
University of North Florida, Jacksonville
University of South Florida, Tampa
University of West Florida, Pensacola

Foreword

As the former editor of two of the publications (*People* and *Life*) described in this remarkable book, I can fully appreciate the energy, imagination, sleepless nights, and missed meals that went into developing these trailblazing magazines around the globe. They and the editors who launched them, or nourished their vitality into publishing middle age and even senior citizenship, have changed and, I think, improved democratic societies on two continents.

Many of the editorial techniques these editors used so successfully—through research, surprising details and anecdotes, face-to-face interviews, welcoming design, and lavish illustrations—are precisely the techniques the authors have used in putting this book together to tell the inspiring stories of eight world-famous titles.

If you love magazines, rely on them, believe they are essential to both your life and that of your nation, then this book is for you. Its editorial treats await.

Richard B. Stolley
Senior Editorial Adviser
Time Inc.

aBouT THe auTHors

Norberto Angeletti
(left)
and Alberto Oliva

Alberto Oliva studied journalism and communications at New York University and during his thirty-year journalism career has worked as a reporter for several Argentine publications (*Confirmado, Análisis,* and *Leoplan* magazines and the newspapers *Clarín* and *La Nación*) as well as United States bureau chief for Editorial Atlántida, publisher of such magazines as *Gente, El Gráfico, Conozca Más, Para Ti,* and *Billiken.* In this capacity he represented the company in New York at the Magazine Publishers Association and attended regular story meetings at *Time, Newsweek,* and *In Style* magazines. In 1999 he was named associate editor of *People en Español,* a Time Warner publication. He has also been a reporter for the same group's *Fortune of the Americas* and a reporter and editor for the Associated Press in New York, as well as content supervisor at Starmedia, an Internet portal. He is currently editor-in-chief of *Ser Padres,* published by Gruner and Jahr USA, a division of Bertelsmann. Oliva lives in New York.

Norberto Angeletti studied journalism and communications at the Universidad de La Plata in Argentina. He got his start in journalism in 1971 as a reporter for *Siete Días,* a newsweekly published by Editorial Abril, where he worked as a reporter, star writer, associate editor, and editor. In 1978 he was hired by the newsweekly *Somos* as associate editor, starting up the ladder at Editorial Atlántida. Over the years he became editor of the women's magazine *Para Ti* (1980–81), deputy editor of *Gente* (1981–85), founder and editor of *Conozca Más,* a science magazine (1988–93), and a member of the Atlántida editorial board (1993–96). During this period he participated in seminars on journalism at the Universidad de Navarra, Spain, and in research and development of new products in Germany, France, Italy, Spain, and the United States. In 1996 he was named senior editor at the Argentine daily *Clarín,* where he is responsible for developing promotional materials, such as books, videos, and one-shots. Angeletti lives in Buenos Aires.

The authors can be reached by e-mail at **http://www.magazineshistory.com.**

STaFF

maGazInes THaT make HISTorY

PUBLISHERS Editorial Sol 90 and University Press of Florida   **AUTHORS** Norberto Angeletti and Alberto Oliva   **DESIGN** Lisa Brande
LAYOUT Fabián Cassan, Marcela Noble Herrera and Lara Rodkevic   **ILLUSTRATIONS** Javier Basile
RESEARCH Danielle Raymond and Stephanie Chemla (France) and César Litvak (Spain)   **TRANSLATION** Susana Bellido Cummings
PRODUCTION Montse Martínez   **PROCESS ENGRAVING** Artes Gráficas Rioplatense (AGR)   **PRINTING** Gráficas Mármol, S.L.

HOW THIS BOOK came INTO BEING

This book took five years and two lifetimes to write—and this is no exaggeration or self-aggrandizement. The project embodies half a decade of research, production, and execution in Europe and the United States, and all the journalism experience of both our careers.

Unlike in our journalistic work, when we generally perform one or two tasks at a time, to conceive and produce this book required us to take part in each and every stage of the production line. We were researchers, librarians, reporters, writers, graphic editors, copyeditors, fact checkers. We even worked on the layout.

Our research took us to the Internet and European and American bookstores, as well as to magazine collectors' basements and attics, in search of books, documents, first issues, the historic original numbers of each publication we analyzed, and other old issues to illustrate each magazine's birth, evolution, and key elements. Much of this material had been sold out, was unavailable, or had prohibitive prices—hurdles that never impeded or impaired our efforts and enthusiasm.

As journalists, we had the privilege of interviewing the current or former editors of the magazines featured in the book: *Time*'s James Kelly and Ray Cave; *People*'s Martha Nelson and Landon Jones; *National Geographic*'s William Allen; Richard Stolley of *People* and *Life*; Jacqueline Leo of *Reader's Digest*; Stefan Aust and Joachim Preuss of *Der Spiegel*; Eduardo Sánchez, son of the founder and current editor of *¡Hola!*; and Alain Genestar and Patrick Jarnoux, the current top editors at *Paris Match*. Regarding the magazines' visual evolution, changes in graphic style, and in some cases redesign, we interviewed Walter Bernard, Milton Glaser, Roger Black, Mary Baumann, Connie Phelps, Guy Trillat, and the pioneer of infographics Nigel Holmes. Their comments, experiences, and advice are part of this book's backbone; they made and will make history, just like the magazines featured here.

This work aims to serve as a reference book in a market lacking in such titles and, more than a book, to be a key to the past of the magazines' future.

contents
magazines **THAT make HISTORY**

Introduction
THE CHALLENGE OF PUBLISHING magazines

INTRODUCTION

THE CHALLENGE OF PUBLISHING ma

Is there room for another magazine? How do we give ours freshness, originality, and reader impact? How will our concept stand out from the rest? Who is our target audience?

These questions, more pertinent today than ever, have come up again and again over the decades in the magazine market. They are the motivating principles behind the most resounding publishing successes. In order to answer them, publishers had to stretch their imaginations. This is how, from year to year, from product to product, from one novelty to the next, they found new formulas for the editing, writing, visual impact, and organization of the news. They confronted each new challenge and came out ahead.

Here, in *Magazines That Make History: Their Origins, Development, and Influence,* we set out to study and analyze in detail those publications that revolutionized the market—some of them because they made a niche for themselves and others because, even though they weren't the first in their sector, they created a new style, offered innovations, and generated a phenomenon that continues to be relevant in today's journalism.

These magazines are, in and of themselves, a reference manual. There is much to learn from their histories, how they dealt with their competitors, how they capitalized on opportunities, and how they are produced today. This applies to journalists and publishers as well as to communications professors and students. In this volume we will cover four sectors—news, general interest, dissemination of knowledge, and celebrity magazines—and these titles:

Time because, through its organization of the news, it gave rise to the newsmagazine sector

Der Spiegel because it brought investigative reporting and critical analysis to the newsmagazine, thereby making itself confrontational, polemical, and prestigious

Life because it was the first to tell its stories through photo essays and became the most popular magazine in the United States

Paris Match because it added to its written reportage the impact of news photography and became internationally synonymous with the general interest magazine

National Geographic because it is the world's leading publication for the dissemination of knowledge

Reader's Digest because its formula of condensed articles emphasizing practical information brought unprecedented success, with an international circulation now topping 23 million

¡Hola! because, thanks to a unique style with breezy news of public figures and royalty, it was fundamental to the development of celebrity magazines

People because its formula revolutionized celebrity journalism, adding human interest to stories that featured not only personalities but ordinary people under extraordinary circumstances

We know that this list is incomplete. Missing are women's magazines like *Vogue* or *Elle*, men's magazines like *Playboy* or *Interviú*, and business publications like *The Economist*, among others. They will be included in a second volume of this work. But we also know that the titles we have chosen for the present volume are incontrovertible. They are where they are. They made and make history.

Each chapter of this book serves two purposes. One focuses on the historical perspective: the magazine's launch, its innovations, its changes and evolution. The other, which we call "Keys for the Editor," deals directly with how each magazine operates today, its secrets, editorial meetings, cover stories, or, in the case of *Life*, why it ceased to publish at a point when it was selling 5 million copies per issue. With a practical and attractive design and graphic layout, this book attempts to exemplify to the maximum each publication's contributions, with reproductions of covers

and stories that today, seen from a distance, constitute outstanding material for general reference and for teaching and molding today's journalists.

Finally, this book is meant as a tribute to all those journalists, photographers, illustrators, designers, photo agencies, editors, and entrepreneurs in the industry who with their imagination and dedication create new news stories, and new success stories, every day. Today more than ever, it is worthwhile to quote Henry Luce, one of *Time*'s founders, who in 1938 said, "If I had to make my fortune over again ... you wouldn't catch me wandering off looking for gold mines–you'd find me peddling stock right now in a real genuine Newsmagazine. Good grief, in 1923 the basic premise of *Time* was that the newspapers were excellent and the magazines were excellent BUT. The more means of communication there are, the bigger that BUT."

This book begins precisely with him, and with his creation, *Time*.

28,5 %
191 102
10,9 %
73 225
17 275
11,1 %
74 753
5657
22,7 %
152 775
6,3 %
10,0 %
67 232
3166
788
3123
MILESTONES
MONEY IN MOTION
Kultur
Wirtschaft

newsmagazines

1 TIME
2 DER SPIEGEL

CHAPTER
1 TIME

In 1923 the launch of time revolutionized the magazine market worldwide. With it were born the newsmagazine genre and an endless series of innovative ideas that remain pertinent today. Here we take a look at its history and all its contributions, from the way it organized the news to its naming of the man of the year, and even the renowned red border of its cover. In closing, the chapter recounts a typical workweek at time today: how the magazine is written and edited, and what happens between the first story meeting and the cover's final touches.

THE TIME MODEL

**How the idea
originated. Its creators.
How they presented it.
The stories. The editing.
The keys to its success.
Its contributions to
journalism that
still apply.**

On March 3, 1923, with a run of 9,000 copies, a magazine called *Time: The Weekly News-Magazine* came out in the United States. The weekly, directed by two young Yale University graduates, Briton Hadden and Henry Robinson Luce, presented in thirty-two pages a new and original publication model that would go on to become what today is known worldwide as the newsmagazine. With an initial capital investment of $86,000 provided by a group of friends, Hadden and Luce and their magazine, *Time*, also planted the seeds of the most important and transcendent media and communications empires in the world.

But what was the great innovation that Hadden and Luce introduced into a magazine market that, as we shall see, was already saturated? The first and most outstanding attribute of *Time* was its organization of the news. The items were grouped in sections and were selected according to their level of importance. Thus in the magazine's first issue the selected news items occupied twenty-two sections, from the most extensive –National Affairs (six pages), Foreign News (five pages), Books, and The Theatre (about two pages each)–to the shortest, like Crime or Imaginary Interviews, each one column long.

But in addition to its organization of the news, *Time* offered its readers something more: it went on to interpret the news. It positioned the reader in every event, related it, put it into context. In a few lines *Time* summarized the week's developments in a given matter, interpreted them, evaluated them, and added its opinion. *Time* contributed more innovations than these, but the organization of the news items, their interpretation,

and the fact that it was a weekly that selected the most important events of that time span were the fundamental characteristics that gave birth to a sector that today includes hundreds of magazines throughout the world and attracts millions of readers.

This is why it's important to spotlight this magazine. Its history –how Hadden and Luce saw a chance to create a new product, how they wrote and edited the magazine, and how *Time* evolved up to the present–provides dozens of examples and tips for today's editors. The quotes and accounts in this chapter, and the one on *Life*, are heavily indebted to *Time Inc.: The Intimate History of a Publishing Enterprise*, which the company itself commissioned in the mid-1960s. The first two volumes of this three-volume corporate biography, which eventually covered the period from 1923 to 1980, were written by Robert T. Elson, who worked at Time Inc. for twenty-five years.

FIFTEEN CENTS

TIME

The Weekly News-Magazine

VOL. 1, NO. 1   MARCH 3, 1923

THE FIRST ISSUE. This was the magazine's first cover. The issue went on sale on March 3, 1923, with a print run of 9,000 copies. The image is that of Senator Joseph Cannon, a veteran of politics who was retiring from Congress at the age of eighty-six. Inside, under the headline "Uncle Joe," the cover article took up fifty lines in the National Affairs section. The photograph reproduced on this page is of a reprint issued in 1938.

BEGINNINGS. The first *Time* and the design of its two longest sections. The complete National Affairs text began on page 3 and Foreign News on page 7.

THE ORDER. These pages (2–3 and 4–5 of the first issue) show how the magazine was organized into sections, with stories distributed in three columns per page.

PHOTOS AND ILLUSTRATIONS. The photo shown here is one of six that *Time* published in its first issue, which included a total of twelve illustrations, including the cover drawing of Joseph Cannon. They were all printed in black and white, of course.

Page 6 — TIME — March 3

National Affairs

© Underwood & Underwood

SMITH W. BROOKHART
Iowa's new Senator says: "I have never owned evening clothes and never propose to."

POLITICAL NOTES

Senator Brookhart, Iowa, favors a studied informality in the matter of dress.

"If I am asked to the White House, or to attend any other state occasion, I shall go as I am, with cowhide shoes and the clothes I wear on the farm. If my constituents wish me to do so, I shall go to the extreme of donning overalls."

The shoes in question are of a breadth allowing free play to the legislative toes, and are a rich ochre in tint.

Senator Brookhart's advocacy of simplicity is applicable to every condition with which he may be confronted. He remarks further:

"I have never owned evening clothes and never propose to. I do not care for social functions and would prefer to remain away. If the occasion requires that I should be present I will go just as I am."

Washington hostesses have not yet

"Get vaccinated or stay home." Such is the gist of a note sent by Chile to the American Commission of Senators and Diplomats who plan to attend the Pan-American conference at Santiago de Chile this month.

Senator McCormick of Illinois remarked to a friend that he would rather write his Child Labor amendment into the Constitution than be a two-termer in the White House.

Until March 4 Senator Johnson of California is a "Republican and Progressive." He holds that official designation through the fact that he is still serving the term to which he was elected in 1916—when the Progressive Party still had an official existence in California.

Last fall Mr. Johnson was re-elected by a constituency exclusively Republican. A "plain Republican" he must be after March 4.

How to Make a Distinctive Product

Hadden and Luce observed to the letter the prime considerations that should apply when contemplating a new magazine: What's new about what we're proposing to our readers? What are the traits that set this new publication apart from the rest? Why would readers who already have a favorite magazine switch to ours?

These questions, still relevant today, constitute a true challenge to publishers' imagination, ability, creativity, and experience. They are also what make journalists and editors important. From their creativity new media products have emerged and will continue to emerge.

To be sure, unlike in the first decades of the past century, we now have reliable market studies that offer guidance regarding the public's tastes, preferences, and tendencies. But experience shows that marketing studies will never come up with the idea of what product to create. This is a job that only journalists and editors are capable of doing. And they do it in

their own right, not because a corporation imposed it. Once an editorial product is ready for release, marketing studies can pinpoint consumers' tastes and indicate whether it's necessary to make adjustments or strengthen certain aspects. But first the product must be imagined, defined, designed, created, and written. Each section, the photos, the impact of the covers, and so forth, must be analyzed, then worked and reworked constantly until the editorial team is fully convinced that it's the best publication they can present to the market.

Were Luce and Hadden fully convinced of their magazine's appeal when they presented it to the American public in 1923?

Actually, according to Elson, the two young men had begun to sketch out a news publication in 1918, when they were in their sophomore year at Yale. Strange as it may seem, the first conversations on the subject took place at Camp Jackson in South Carolina where, as members of the Yale ROTC unit,

they completed officer training in anticipation of being called to serve in World War I.

At the time, they referred to their idea as "that paper" and they considered it a dream for the future. After their military training, the two graduated from Yale and their paths diverged, though they always remained in contact, developing the idea for "that paper."

Luce first went to Europe and to Oxford, and then to Chicago, where he joined the *Chicago Daily News* staff as a cub reporter. Hadden went to New York, where he entered the world of journalism at the *World*.

But their paths would cross once more in 1921. The two young journalists were recruited by the *Baltimore News*, an offer they eagerly accepted because, aside from the experience, it meant a chance to work again on the project of their dreams.

For three months they dedicated all their free time to the project, a magazine that already had a name, *Facts*, though clearly this was not to be the final name.

JOHN F. KENNEDY, 1960   LEON TROTSKY, 1927   FIDEL CASTRO, 1959   DE GAULLE, 1947   MUSSOLINI, 1943   ROOSEVELT, 1942

WAS THERE ANY ROOM FOR ANOTHER MAGAZINE?

On February 6, 1922, having decided that their idea for a magazine was ripe and ready to be put to the test, Luce and Hadden resigned from the *News* and left for New York.

Hadden and the slightly younger Luce were not yet twenty-four. Ahead lay a huge challenge, particularly considering that they had no capital and no experience in business or finance. All they had was their idea for a magazine, their plan, their hopes and dreams. Would that suffice to persuade investors to support the project?

As if this weren't challenge enough, the American magazine and periodicals market was saturated. There were 2,033 newspapers, 14 in New York City alone, ranging from the all-encompassing *Times* to a new tabloid, the *Daily News*, soon to be the highest-circulation paper in the United States. On Thursdays 2,200,000 subscribers received the *Saturday Evening Post* at home, while a similar number of women were informed, entertained, and advised by the *Ladies' Home Journal*. In addition, for those interested in public affairs, there was the *Literary Digest*, a weekly with a circulation of 1.2 million copies and thirty-four years of experience. And there were other periodicals that commanded great loyalty from their readers, like the *Atlantic*, *Harper's*, *Scribner's*, and *Century*.

Was there really room for another magazine?
Today, given the number of publications that pack newsstands, this is a question that many editors and media entrepreneurs ask themselves. It's a question that, as we can see, isn't new at all. How did Luce and Hadden answer it?

FIRST: They started by identifying a segment that the American publishing market had not covered yet. The big cities had important newspapers, but a national publication was lacking.

SECOND: American citizens received a great deal of information—too much for the amount of time they could devote to reading.

THIRD: This information was presented in the raw, focused on what happened yesterday, without relating it to prior events. The news was not contextualized.

IN SUM: There was a market, a need, and an opportunity. The only thing missing was the correct vehicle to go out in search of those readers.

VLADIMIR I. LENIN, 1964   ADOLF HITLER, 1941   MAO TSE-TUNG, 1949   CHURCHILL, 1941

POLITICAL LEADERS. Democrats and dictators, moderates and extremists, of the right or center or left. For one reason or another, world leaders of every era were featured on the cover of *Time*. It is often said that if you put all the covers of the magazine side by side, you'd end up with an accurate snapshot of the twentieth century.

THE PROJECT

Once settled in New York, the two young journalists sat down to write the prospectus presenting their idea to potential financiers. They put special emphasis on forestalling the argument that there was no room for another magazine. Elson's book makes reference to the letter introducing the magazine that, at the time, no one imagined would become such a milestone.

That letter, transcribed almost in its entirety here, anticipates *Time*'s journalistic philosophy, identifies the segment where it would look to establish itself, and quantifies the potential readership that might be interested in the new product. Over the years this letter, besides being a historical document, has come to be considered a model of how to present new publications to investors. It read:

THE SECTIONS.
Music, Education, Religion, Medicine, Law, Science, Crime, The Press. These are just some of the twenty-two sections that made up the first issue of *Time*.

"

Although daily journalism has been more highly developed in the United States than in any other country of the world...

Although foreigners marvel at the excellence of our periodicals...

people in America are, for the most part, poorly informed.

This is not the fault of the daily newspapers; they print all the news.

It is not the fault of the weekly "reviews"; they adequately develop and comment on the news.

To say with the facile cynic that it is the fault of the people themselves is to beg the question.

People are uninformed because no publication has adapted itself to the time which busy men are able to spend on simply keeping informed.

"

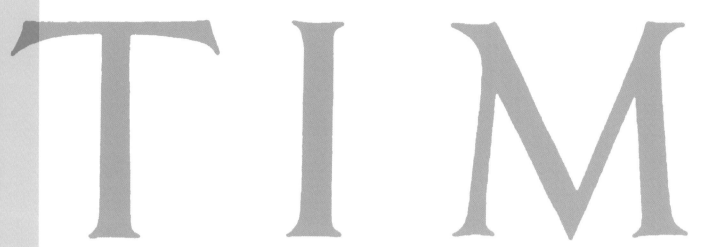

After laying the groundwork, Luce and Hadden prepared to launch their magazine, which they had already renamed. They had never really bought into the title *Facts*. It seemed "small" to them, inappropriate for such an ambitious project. They hit upon the new name just as they were writing the prospectus. One night, as he returned home exhausted, Luce happened to see an ad that said something like "*Time to Retire*" or "*Time for a Change*." Actually, he would recount years later, the word *Time* made such a strong impression on him that he didn't pay attention to the rest. And so it was that *Time* already bore its definitive name at its debut.

"*Time* is a weekly news-magazine, aimed to serve the modern necessity of keeping the people informed…

Time is interested—not in how much it includes between its covers—but in how much it gets off its pages into the minds of its readers…

From virtually every magazine and newspaper of note in the world, *Time* collects all available information on all subjects of importance and general interest. The essence of all this information is reduced to approximately 100 short articles, none of which are over 400 words in length (seven inches of type). Each of these articles will be found in its logical place in the magazine, according to a fixed method of arrangement which constitutes a complete organization of all the news.

Time, like all weeklies, differs from the daily papers in what it omits.

It differs from other weeklies in that it deals briefly with every happening of importance and presents these happenings as news (fact), rather than as "comment." It further differs in that it is from three to fifteen days more up-to-date than they.

The *Literary Digest* treats at great length a few subjects selected more or less arbitrarily from week to week. *Time* gives all the week's news in a brief, organized manner…

The *Digest*, in giving both sides of a question, gives little or no hint as to which side it considers to be right. *Time* gives both sides, but clearly indicates which side it believes to have the stronger position…"

E

Another difference between *Time* and the existing products was that *Time* would not have an editorial page. Nevertheless, at the end of their prospectus Luce and Hadden clearly established what their journalistic philosophy would be: "This magazine is not founded to promulgate prejudices, liberal or conservative. 'To keep men well-informed' –that, first and last, is the only axe this magazine has to grind. The magazine is one of news, not argument, and verges on the controversial only where it is necessary to point out what the news means." They immediately identified their potential readers:

"It is estimated that there are over 1,000,000 people in the United States with a college education. *Time* is aiming at every one of these 1,000,000.

But more than that, there are thousands and tens of thousands of men and women in the country who have not had a college education, but who are intelligent and want such an organized paper as *Time* to keep them posted on the necessary news...

Time should appeal to every man and woman in America who has the slightest interest in the world and its affairs. "

It took several weeks to write and polish this prospectus. Samuel Everitt, treasurer of the magazine and book publisher Doubleday, Page & Company, was one of the first to receive it. The proposal excited him. He promised to get Luce and Hadden in touch with investors and other publishers, and he gave them a bit of basic advice: If they wanted their magazine to succeed, they had to learn direct mail techniques. At the time, more than 50 percent of magazine subscriptions in the United States were sold in this way.

Not only did Luce and Hadden heed his advice, but they also took advantage of the list of subscribers to *World's Work*, a Doubleday publication, that Everitt made available to them, and did a rudimentary but efficient market analysis. They mailed its readers 7,000 copies of the prospectus introducing *Time*. The results were good: 6.5 percent responded accepting the product.

Now there was no more room for doubt. *Time* would be a hit.

TRIAL RUNS.
Before the launch, Luce and Hadden produced two practice editions to fine-tune the project. The logo presented in the second version used wider and heavier type. In the end a typeface of intermediate weight was used.

THE FIRST TIME

Astute observers, Luce and Hadden had noticed before anyone else that the United States had changed substantially after the Great War, as the first worldwide armed conflict was then called. The country's cultural center of gravity had shifted. A new emerging middle class, urban, often intellectual, and socially insecure, was beginning to enter the business world, to earn money, and to purchase goods. The consumer society had been born.

In the new era of the automobile, cinema, and radio, Hadden and Luce perceived the consumer's new appetite for movement, stimulation, variety, and novelty. Traditional information sources were no longer adequate. The newspapers were local and regional and, at most, offered fragments of national information. The magazines tended to be specialized, with an inclination toward bombastic phrases filled with empty words. Seldom was news presented as such. No one else had proposed the creation of a journalistic product that would include all the news on a national and international scale.

They chose New York as the headquarters for their publication for a simple strategic reason: it was the nerve center of the country. "But our magazine –they would say– isn't a New York magazine. On the contrary, it's intended to be read by the gentleman or lady from Indiana, Florida, Boston, or Chicago."

Indeed, in its first issue they ran an ad for subscriptions aimed not only at capturing readers but, above all, at defining the reader they hoped to attract. This was, they said, "the man who wants the facts–the man who wants to do his own thinking after he has the facts–the busy man." Did such a man exist? The response to their new magazine, they declared, showed that he did. "Who is he? Is he merely a distinguished citizen? Is he necessarily President of a great university? or an Ambassador? or a Magnate? or a Bishop? or a Member of the United States Senate? As a matter of fact the man was found in Ohio, among the lesser nobility. It is also true that he was discovered in flight to Florida. His twin-likeness was tracked down in Boston and the postmaster reported his alias–in Chicago."

The first cover, on March 3, 1923, featured Joseph Gurney Cannon, an eighty-six-year-old veteran senator who was retiring from Congress. The story, headlined "Uncle Joe," was fifty lines long, a little less than a column. The article, one of 125 that *Time* published in its first issue, appeared in the National Affairs section.

The other twenty-one sections that made up the magazine were Foreign News, Books, Art, The Theatre, Cinema, Music, Education, Religion, Medicine, Law, Science, Finance, Sport, Aeronautics, Crime, The Press, Milestones, Miscellany, Imaginary Interviews, Point with Pride, and View with Alarm.

ADVERTISEMENTS. The first issue included twenty-eight pages plus the four sides of the folded cover. The back cover and the insides of the front and back covers were reserved for full-page ads.

THE FIRST OFFICE. The magazine's first prototype was produced in a small office located at 9 East Fortieth Street in Manhattan. Luce (seated higher) and Hadden always explained that they set up their headquarters in New York because the city was the country's nerve center; the magazine, however, was not a New York magazine but rather a national one.

THE SLOGANS THAT SOLD TIME

The word Time, besides being impressive as a title and practical and simple for the design of a logo, also had enormous advertising potential. Throughout its history, the creative minds that came up with its slogans have played with it in different ways, depending on how they needed to reach the reader. Here are some of the slogans used from 1924 on.

"Time flies" 1924

"Time marches on!" 1932

"It´s time to get the facts" 1932

"It´s about Time" 1938

"Take Time, it's a brief" 1939

"Time to get it straight!" 1951

"This is the time to start reading Time" 1960

"Make time for Time" 1989

"Understanding comes with Time" 1994

SOURCE: TIME MAGAZINE

originality above all

Time's determination to set itself apart from other publications, and above all to show its own personality and character, reached levels seldom seen before. And it went well beyond the organization, the order, the selection, and the contextualizing of the news. A contents summary did not appear at the beginning of the magazine, as was customary in other publications. It appeared at the end, and in an unusual form: ranking the news.

On page 27, in a column under the heading Point with Pride, *Time* made up an imaginary character called the Generous Citizen. This gentleman selected the items that the magazine considered to be positive and organized them with pride in the following way:

Uncle Joe Cannon, retiring after weathering the Congressional storms of 50 years. (P. 2.)

Female efficiency, with Mrs. Mabel Willebrandt as acting head of the Attorney-General's office. (P. 4.)

The new touch of dignity added to Supreme Court procedure by Chief Justice Taft. (P. 4.)

The efficiency of the Chilean Department of Health, which demands that our delegates to the Pan-American Conference be vaccinated. (P. 6.)

Annual taxes of $90 per capita which England bears like a great nation, without grumbling. (P. 8.)

Fifteen of the articles contained in the issue were recommended this way.

WALT DISNEY
1954

CHARLIE CHAPLIN
1925

STEVEN SPIELBERG
1985

ORSON WELLES
1938

ARTISTS AND CREATORS. From psychoanalysis to the Polaroid camera, from the genius of Charlie Chaplin to George Lucas's special effects, the magazine knew how to capture on its covers all the phenomena and newsmakers of our times, whether from cinema, philosophy, literature, or art.

numbers

6,000
Initial subscribers to the magazine.

12,000
Peak newsstand sales between 1923 and 1927.

1922
Year before the launch, when Judge Robert Luce, cousin to Henry, sent a check for the cost of a subscription. He was the first subscriber.

23,000
Newsstand sales in the last three months of 1928.

1973
Year when, at the height of the Watergate scandal, *Time* urged President Nixon to resign. It was the magazine's first editorial.

4,100,000
Circulation in 1998, when the magazine celebrated its seventy-fifth anniversary.

PUTNAM BOOKS AND AUTHORS

Philip Guedalla

enjoys the distinction of having written the most lavishly praised book of the season. His

The Second Empire

claims the right to quote with proper credit nearly every laudatory adjective in the dictionary. Nobody seems to write quite like Guedalla these days.

Eventually You Will Own

The Outline of Science

4 volumes. $4.50 each

One thing that makes Eugene Bagger's

Eminent Europeans

such interesting reading is the feeling that these terribly important people he writes of so intimately are characters from a fairy tale. But, Mr. Bagger need not remind us that instead of magic wands, they are more likely to wave sticks of dynamite.

J. St. Loe Strachey's memoirs

THE ADVENTURE OF LIVING

"is the work of a frank, friendly, original and bold writer who has entertained very strong opinions and entertains most of them still."—The British Weekly.

* * *

Robert Keable's
New Novel

PERADVENTURE

which it is our great privilege to publish, is likely to cause more general and more serious controversy than either "Simon Called Peter," or "Mother of All Living". For in "Peradventure" Mr. Keable writes fearlessly and often startlingly, of a man's religious experiences, taking him through all the faiths in search of one which might prove satisfying. You can enjoy "Peradventure" as a novel, but its extraordinary treatment of a subject so often sidestepped will leave a deep and lasting impression.

* * *

Snowdrift
The Texan
The Promise
and now NORTH

just about proves that, book by book, James B. Hendryx's romances of the Northwest get better and better. North is the kind of book that once started, keeps you up all night.

The widespread attention and large audiences which Miss Maude Royden's lectures are attracting emphasize the need of reading her three recent books—

Prayer As A Force
Political Christianity
Sex and Common Sense

G. P. P.

Page 27

VIEW with ALARM

Having perused well the chronicle of the week, the Vigilant Patriot views with alarm:

Any attempt on the part of Washington hostesses to exploit Senator Brookhart as a curiosity. (See p. 6.)

The light heavyweight championship of the world, an honor tarnished in transit. (P. 21.)

The attempt of a partly blind youth to make money by a partly blind pig. (P. 19.)

Waste minds who lose themselves on *Waste Lands.* (P. 12.)

Bolivia, Mexico, Peru, who will be absent for their own reasons from the Pan-American Conference. (P. 11.)

Taller Japanese to be evolved by straphanging in Tokio's new subway. (P. 11.)

The anger of Popocatepetl. (P. 11.)

The bluntness of the American Minister to Peking. (P. 11.)

The skylines of old Italy—now to be broken for the first time. (P. 9.)

A difference in addition between the French and German totals of reparations made by Germany. (P. 9.)

Ireland at the throat of Ireland. (P. 8.)

A four to one vote to abolish the Wisconsin National Guard, recorded in the House of Representatives of that state. (P. 6.)

The primrose path along which Lady Nicotine is being invited to follow John Barleycorn. (P. 6.)

Fifty-one per cent of the population of Hawaii, who are Orientals. (P. 6.)

A billion dollars to be spent this year on their armies by the United States, England, France, Italy. (P. 4.)

Page 28

SUMMARY WITH COMMENTS. *Time* did not have a traditional table of contents, merely a listing of sections, but on pages 27 and 28, in columns called "Point with Pride" and "View with Alarm," it commented on news items and gave the page number where each could be found.

This highly original news index was complemented on page 28 of the first issue by a selection bearing the heading "View with Alarm." In it the Vigilant Patriot, another imaginary character, apprehensively pointed out fourteen items. Among them:

Any attempt on the part of Washington hostesses to exploit Senator Brookhart as a curiosity. (P. 6.)

The bluntness of the American Minister to Peking. (P. 11.)

Bolivia, Mexico, Peru, who will be absent for their own reasons from the Pan-American Conference. (P. 11.)

The light heavyweight championship of the world, an honor tarnished in transit. (P. 21.)

E BEATLES
67

SIGMUND FREUD
1924

LOUIS ARMSTRONG
1949

PABLO PICASSO
1950

EDWIN LAND
1972

GEORGE LUCAS
1983

144 Number of perpetual subscriptions in 1998.

8 Number of times Princess Diana and the Virgin Mary were featured on the cover.

55 Number of times Richard Nixon was featured on the cover. He holds the record.

1942 Year when reporter Melville Jacoby became the first *Time* journalist to die on the job. An airplane struck him on a runway in Australia during World War II. Since then, several *Time* reporters have died in the line of duty.

...llar price in 1929 of a ...rpetual subscription to ...e magazine. It was ...nsferable and inheritable ...d could not be cancelled.

1 Number of women featured on a *Time* cover in 1923. The lone female subject in that debut year was the actress Eleonora Duse.

1,000 Dollar price in 1998 of a lifetime subscription, nontransferable.

SOURCE: TIME MAGAZINE

In this way, by **evaluating the news**, *Time* not only provided a novel table of contents but also expressed to its readers the magazine's opinion of the news.

This aspect—the magazine's opinion—was present in every story it ever published. *Time* provided the news, various viewpoints about that news, and its own viewpoint. And it did so in all of its sections.

In the National Affairs section of the first issue, in an article on a monument that was planned in homage to black nannies, it remarked: "In dignified and quiet language, two thousand Negro women … protested against a proposal to erect at the Capitol a statue to 'The Black Mammy of the South,' …(seeing it as) 'the reminder that we come from a race of slaves.' This, of course, will rebuke forever the sentimentalists who thought they were doing honor to a character whom they loved… But that person's educated granddaughters snuffed out the impulse by showing that they are ashamed of her."

The Sport section was no exception to the rule. Noting the arrival in the United States of the Argentine boxer Luis Ángel Firpo, the magazine also gave its opinion of the opponent he would face in the ring. Bearing the headline "Firpo," the item stated: "Two hundred and thirty-five pounds of Luis Angel Firpo, pretender to the throne of Jack Dempsey, arrived in New York from his native Argentina. The immediate objective of Firpo's wanderings is a bout with the aged British heavyweight, Bill Brennan, at Madison Square Garden on March 14 under the aegis of Tex Rickard. If Brennan allows himself to be dispatched with the deftness and docility that has characterized his appearances before other young heavyweights, Firpo will be matched with Willard, Floyd Johnson, and—if fate favors him—with Dempsey."

The Books section was likewise marked by *Time*'s opinion, and not only in the reviews. In an aggressively antimodernist article, the magazine defended readers' rights thus: "There is a new kind of literature abroad on the land, whose only obvious fault is that no one can understand it. Last year there appeared a gigantic volume entitled *Ulysses*, by James Joyce. To the uninitiated, it appeared that Mr. Joyce had taken some half million assorted words–many such as are not ordinarily heard in reputable circles– shaken them up in a colossal hat, laid them end to end. To those in on the secret the result represented the greatest achievement of modern letters–a new idea in novels… the admirers of Messrs. Eliot, Joyce, et al. [contend]: Literature is self-expression. It is up to the reader to extract the meaning, not up to the writer to offer it. If the author writes everything that pops into his head… that is all that should be asked. Lucidity is not part of the auctorial task."

RARITIES. Several *Time* issues are greatly prized by collectors, among them those of May 14, 1956, with Marilyn Monroe on the cover, and October 27, 1975, with Bruce Springsteen.

FINANCE AND FISTICUFFS. Pages 20-21 of the first issue covered Finance, Sport, Aeronautics, and the first ad for subscriptions published in the magazine. The Sport section announced the arrival in New York of Argentine boxer Luis Ángel Firpo, who would later face Jack Dempsey for the world title.

THE Price OF OLD News

AL CAPONE   **JOE DIMAGGIO**

When *Time* celebrated its seventy-fifth anniversary in 1998, it canvassed New York's dealers in rare books and magazines to find out which back issues were the most coveted and how much collectors were paying for them.

It found that the first issue, with Joe Cannon on the cover, was the most desirable, fetching up to $1,000. This was followed, in order of price, by the issue with the legendary gangster Al Capone on the cover, published in 1930, and the issue featuring the popular baseball player Joe DiMaggio, from 1936. Each one went for $500 a copy.

The Marx Brothers issue (August 15, 1932) went for a little less –$300– and the one featuring Charles Lindbergh, the first Man of the Year, and the Bruce Springsteen issue (October 27, 1975) were worth $200. The same price was quoted for the Marilyn Monroe issue (May 14, 1956) and the issue with Vivien Leigh as Scarlett O'Hara in *Gone with the Wind* (December 25, 1939). On the other hand, issues featuring Sigmund Freud, Charlie Chaplin, and Adolf Hitler, Man of the Year in 1938, fetched only $150.

HENRY R. LUCE 1967

ERNESTO "CHE" GUEVARA 1960

JUAN AND EVA PERÓN 1951

The same order, rigor, and meticulous-
ness that Luce and Hadden had used to
lay the foundation of the magazine they
had just created were applied to its
everyday journalistic jobs. Before release,
the issue went through innumerable filters
—writers, researchers, copyeditors,
section heads, and editors. The news was
selected, enriched, condensed,
summarized.

One thing was clear: Everyone understood precisely the kind of journalism to
be produced. This precept, which surely
was not invented by *Time*, is one of the
fundamental principles to apply when
considering the launch of any new
publication. Before the reader can be
convinced, the members of the entire
editorial team must believe absolutely in
what they are doing, must be completely
passionate about their work, immersed in
it. Only then can they reach their readers'
minds and hearts, thoughts and emotions.
To use a sports analogy, editors, writers,
and reporters must all wear the team
colors, must live and breathe their
product with skill, effort, and dedication.
This is the sole way to ensure the
publication's success.

Time had clear principles. The
magazine should **report and interpret**
the news in a highly concise and
entertaining way. "The super concise
based on real events," was the key phrase
that guided writers. *Time* proposed, then,
to justify its title by giving readers what
was to become the century's most
precious commodity: time. And it did so
not only by reporting the news but also by
interpreting it for people who lacked
precisely that, the time or energy or
knowledge to do so for themselves, all in
an entertaining, attractive, and concise
way. The magazine was thus designed to
be read in no more than **an hour**.

Thursday. The workweek began on Thursday. On this day the writers in charge of each section met with the managing editor to offer their story ideas, which had been drawn from the world's major newspapers. Once the proposals were approved, the arduous task of seeking additional information for each item began.

That is where the **fact-checkers** came in. They did research in books, encyclopedias, and clipping files to provide all the data that would enrich the basic story.

Friday. The main articles were written on Fridays, but often were tossed out later. They had to be condensed as much as possible. A tight, telegraphic prose, which came to be known as *Time* style, was invented almost entirely by Briton Hadden. In "*The Times of Our Lives*," an article written to commemorate the magazine's seventy-fifth anniversary, *Time* editorial board member Lance Morrow quoted John Martin–a cousin of Hadden's who was one of the magazine's first writers and editors and its managing editor in 1929–33 and 1936–37–on the concise style. Martin remembered the "astonishing ease" with which

"Brit would edit copy to eliminate unnecessary verbiage. … If you wrote something like 'in the nick of time,' five words, he might change it to 'in time's nick,' three words… At all times he had by him a carefully annotated translation of the *Iliad*. In the back cover he had listed hundreds of words, especially verbs and the compound adjectives, which had seemed to him fresh and forceful."

Saturday. The process of selecting, eliminating, and rewriting stories continued on Saturday. The writers worked from morning to midnight to ready the text for submission to the editor in chief first thing on Sunday.

Sunday. On Sunday afternoon, the first finished articles were sent–first by express train, later by wire–to Chicago, where the magazine was printed. The magazine was finally put to bed between 8 and 10 p.m. on Monday, with the stories for the National Affairs and Foreign News sections. Until then the writers struggled over every

article, every sentence, every word. They looked for the exact synonym, the word that shortened the phrase as much as possible without losing its meaning, strength, or appeal. This was the style and the objective that the magazine's creators firmly enforced. Luce had written an internal memo about the need to work hard on every article. It read:

"The other day a fairly interesting item was written in 50 lines. I got fussing with it. Fuss. Fuss. Fuss. I fussed for an hour. At the hour's end I had in 30 lines every single fact which was in the 50 lines–plus one or two extra facts…

"This particular story was interesting enough for 30 lines; in 50 lines it was dull… [Writers] are supposed to have time enough and to be just as willing as the M.E. to sweat and swink until they have reduced 50 lines to 30–without losing a single fact."

THE NOVEL AND EFFECTIVE FACT-CHECKING SYSTEM

Time was also the pioneer of a strict fact-checking system. That system, imposed right from 1923, still applies today at all magazines of the group, from the most "serious," such as *Fortune*, to the most "frivolous," like *People*. Through this rigorous procedure the magazines have guaranteed to their readers the most accurate information, the most precise facts. It is a dependability pledge. Today they go so far as to submit draft copy to interviewees to make sure that their exact meaning is conveyed by the writers' stories.

When *Time* was born, this fact-checking process was carried out by the fact-checkers or proofreaders—or rewriters, as they were pejoratively referred to by the writers, who considered them their persecutors. The fact-checkers, who were mostly women, played the role of a newsroom within a newsroom and offered support and control. This fact-checking section was made up of cultivated professionals, some of them experts in linguistics, others in history, grammar, geography, or research.

Their work began as soon as the stories to be published were selected. In the first phase, they set out to search for any additional information that would add to the story. Later, as press time approached, their task became meticulous, obsessive, and even hostile to the writers. They worked closely together and, before the article reached the editor in chief, it had to go through the stringent hands of the proofreaders. They marked every confirmed word in the text and left a red pencil dot at every historical event, name, place, or date that the writer should go back and correct. As deadline approached, the exhausted writer—who had gone through shortening the text, looking for precise words that wouldn't make it less appealing—faced the assault the proofreader submitted him to.

And the writer had to pay heed to their instructions, which often meant going back and rewriting the story. If the slightest error slipped through to the final text, it was not the writer but the proofreader who was held responsible. Any adjective used inaccurately by the writer, any quote out of context, any physical description that didn't jibe with the photograph, exposed the fact-checker to a kind of trial during the weekly error meeting, in which the whole newsroom participated.

THE FIRST MAGAZINE TO DESCRIBE THE CELEBRITIES

This ordering, this segmentation, this brevity and rigor of text might give the impression of a product that was plain and boring, without personality or journalistic impact. Nothing of the sort occurred with *Time*. The magazine brilliantly played with the public's appetite. It turned the news into saga, comedy, melodrama.

Its style—just as Hadden intended—was Homeric. Behind every news story was a personage, and behind every personage a person, with virtues and defects, tics and mannerisms, a characteristic way of dressing and acting, long legs, ample waist, or round face. No effort was spared by the writers to adapt to this style in which the personalities were bigger than life.

From the very first issue, *Time* set out in earnest to describe the newsmakers. The debut cover story, when it talked about Senator Cannon's replacement, said:

"… On March 4 Uncle Joe will be gone, and Henry Cabot Lodge alone will remain to carry on the banner of the ideal. To the American people, however, the senior Senator from Massachusetts must perforce seem a little too genteel, too cold, too Back Bay to serve as an adequate trustee for the Old Guard tradition. They will long for the homely democracy of Mr. Cannon, so often expressed by those homely democratic symbols—Uncle Joe's black cigar and thumping quid."

In that same issue, *Time* described Senator Joseph Robinson (D-Ark.) as "a fighting Southerner who talks with his fists. Born with a red-headed temper, he soon acquired freckles. But years of law and politics have induced a certain amiability, so that he now enjoys fishing."

In its early years, *Time*'s novel form of describing newsmakers became an obsession with the reporters. Accordingly, Mexican president Francisco Madero was "wild-eyed," Minnesota senator Henrik Shipstead was invariably "the duck-hunting dentist," George Bernard Shaw was "mocking, mordant, misanthropic," and General Erich von Ludendorff was "flagitious, inscrutable, unrelenting."

This characteristic that distinguished *Time* from the other magazines of the day did not arise by chance. The idea was analyzed, discussed, and put into practice by the magazine's creators for a reason. Robert Elson points out that Luce never tired of repeating to his writers:

"No idea exists outside a human skull—and no human skull exists without hair and a face and a voice—in fact the flesh and blood attributes of a human personality. *Time* journalism began by being deeply interested in people, as individuals who were making history, or a small part of it, from week to week. We tried to make our readers see and hear and even smell these people as part of a better understanding of their ideas—or lack of them."

SCIENTISTS AND EXPLORERS. In its Science, Technology, Medicine, and Space sections, the magazine presented everything from the theory of relativity to the contributions of penicillin, the polio vaccine, and space and undersea exploration. And on various occasions the authors of these scientific achievements were recognized by being featured on the cover of *Time*.

MARÍA MONTESSORI
1930

PRINCESS ELIZABETH
1947

VIVIEN LEIGH
1939

CHER
1975

VIRGINIA WOOLF
1937

MARÍA EVA DUARTE DE PERÓN, 1947

THe scandaL aBOUT roosevelT's LeGs

These instructions, which came from management, were diligently carried out by writers. They called New Orleans mayor Thomas Walmsley **"buzzard-bald"** and Senator James Watson **"long-legged, large-paunched, small-eyed"**; Senator David Walsh of Massachusetts was "tall and stout. A double chin tends to get out over his tight-fitting collar. His stomach bulges over his belt."

The provocative picture captions –which *Time*'s editors considered one of the strongest hooks to draw the reader into a story–also tended toward disrespectful description verging at times on the hostile. For example, under a photo of the queen mother of Spain, who had just died, it said: "They took her to the Dump." The article explained that El Escorial–the monastery outside Madrid which is the burial place of Spanish monarchs, now a major tourist attraction–literally means "slag heap." The unabashed "*Time* style" earned the magazine subscribers and supporters, but also controversy.

One reader protested, "It matters not at all that Capone is sleek and fat, that Chiang is wasp-waisted… These persons' importance is in their relationship and effect on humanity [and]… does not arise out of physical characteristics." The editors printed the letter, with this dissenting response: "Physical characteristics are an inevitable concomitant of personality. And personalities are the stuff of which history is made. *Time*, historian, must continue to notice noses large and small, waists wasp or fat."

But the fiercest criticism faced by *Time* came when it wrote openly of President Franklin Delano Roosevelt's physical disabilities. In youth the American leader had suffered from polio, which prevented him from walking normally. The magazine, in a description of the president, made mention of his **"shriveled legs."** This phrase set off a firestorm. Until then the newspapers had never referred to the president's illness, nor had they shown him in a wheelchair. Indeed, there was an unspoken agreement among them not to do so. *Time*'s phrase thus elicited a double reaction: surprise and displeasure. Some readers were indignant. "How can you justify the utter

PRESIDENT ROOSEVELT.
The press had never made any mention of the illness that afflicted his legs. *Time* called him "the man with the shriveled legs." It was a scandal.

ARÍA CALLAS
956

MADONNA
1985

SUSAN SARANDON AND
GEENA DAVIS, 1991

MOTHER TERESA
1975

WOMEN. During *Time*'s first year only one woman, the actress Eleonora Duse, was featured on the cover. The following year there were three. The magazine is not noted for putting many women on the cover: there are seldom ten in a year. The record is held by Princess Diana and the Virgin Mary, each featured eight times.

cruelty?" asked one, while another demanded: "Who is your editorial writer so completely lacking in a sense of common decency and good taste?"

The scandal reached such proportions that the editors were forced to respond to their readers. They did so with a small editorial column in which they tried to justify the expression "shriveled legs," arguing that it was important not to ignore the illness: "*Time* conveys the full significance of a man, paralyzed in the prime of life, rising above what to another man might have been an insuperable hindrance and going on to high national destiny… Without stressing the subject, and certainly never with malice or disrespect, *Time* will continue to regard Mr. Roosevelt's legs as mentionable –unless a great majority of *Time* readers commands otherwise."

The controversy continued for some weeks, until the magazine itself put an end to it with an explanatory note: "No clear majority of readers 'commands otherwise.' Score of letters through last week: 238 con, 252 pro. This *Time* construes as a firm mandate to continue mirroring Nature."

But the scandal left its mark. Luce realized that, in their zeal to set their publication apart from the others, his writers and editors had gone too far in their descriptions, at times pushing the limits of personal offense. And this was doing his magazine no good. He addressed the issue in a memo to his writers. According to Elson's records, this is how he did it:

"No more cracks please about Mr. Gielgud's nose. (John Gielgud had been described as "a sensitive and intelligent Englishman of 32 with a nose the size of a hockey puck.") Long experience has taught us that what hurts people most is a reference to some physical characteristic–and this is also what readers most resent our saying about people in whom they have no personal interest… Any reference to any characteristic is peculiarly the responsibility of the M.E. This means that any writer who says a man has a nose as big as a hockey puck is putting the M.E. on a spot–because if the M.E. doesn't catch it, it is the M.E. who is peculiarly at fault–and the M.E. is apt to become annoyed with a writer who pitches him too many sour balls. Obviously this does not mean a ban on physical characterizations. What it does mean is that physical characterizations are to be given the first call on our best journalistic skill, sensitivity and sense of responsibility. Hereafter if a king is to look like a dentist or if anybody is to have a nose as big as a hockey puck, he will have it for *Time's* best considered reasons."

on each cover, THe Face OF THe news

Time's covers, and the newsmakers on them, were yet another publishing landmark that distinguished the magazine. From the beginning *Time* proposed to be an accurate witness to history, every week—to history as written in the news, but all the while following a fundamental principle of its identity: **People make the news, people are at the root of events, men and women are behind every story.**

This is why, from Joseph Cannon onward, the cover of *Time*—during its first four decades and, with few exceptions, thereafter—was always illustrated with a personality. On its covers marched a procession of presidents, dictators, captains of industry, generals, scientists, artists, writers, politicians, saints, revolutionaries, and athletes, the whole parade in step with Luce's enthusiasm for people of flesh and blood and with his journalistic philosophy that great men produce great events.

If today we were to cast our minds back and try to remember who were the main newsmakers of the twentieth century, we would surely find them all on *Time*'s covers: Marilyn Monroe, Al Capone, John Kennedy, Fidel Castro, Winston Churchill, Adolf Hitler, Mother Teresa of Calcutta, John Lennon, Princess Diana, "Che" Guevara, Joseph Stalin, Mohandas Gandhi—all of them, absolutely all of them, appeared at some point on the cover of *Time*.

THe Ten BeST SeLLerS

Tragedies, resignations, deaths of famous people, wars, and the hottest current events were the most profitable subjects for *Time*. Below are the ten issues that registered the highest newsstand sales in the magazine's history.

DATE	COVER SUBJECT	COPIES SOLD
09-14-01	9/11 Memorial Special	3,312,458
09-24-01	One Nation, Indivisible	2,023,987
07-26-99	JFK, Jr. 1960-1999	1,304,288
09-15-97	Diana Commemorative	1,183,758
10-01-01	Target: Bin Laden	841,165
09-08-97	Diana, Princess of Wales	820,060
08-09-74	Nixon Resignation (Special Issue-Ford)	564,723
12-22-80	John Lennon	531,340
08-02-99	JFK, Jr. Ask Not ...	519,896
03-09-84	Michael Jackson	500,290

SOURCE: *TIME* MAGAZINE

THe Ten WORST SeLLerS

The covers of *Time* can serve as a barometer that reflects the scant interest Americans have in reading about some topics. One such is international affairs. The list below shows the covers that sold the least at newsstands (as a percentage of circulation at the time of publication).

DATE	COVER SUBJECT	COPIES SOLD
10-10-94	Black Renaissance	100,827
08-22-94	Baseball Strike	101,125
05-17-93	Anguish over Bosnia	102,193
04-04-96	Nuclear Safety	108,900
06-10-96	Benjamin Netanyahu	109,300
03-29-93	Boris Yeltsin	109,365
06-03-96	Hope Returns in Somalia	111,170
12-21-92	In Defense of the Children	111,176
11-20-96	Bob Dole	112,310
10-24-94	U.S. Economy	113,041

SOURCE: *TIME* MAGAZINE

In 1998, on the occasion of the magazine's seventy-fifth anniversary, statistics were published on the newsmakers whose faces had occupied this important spot. The all-time record holder was Richard Nixon, who was featured fifty-five times. The numbers confirmed that in 1923 only one woman appeared on the cover, the actress Eleonora Duse, whereas in 1997 nine women were on the cover. The female figures who made the cover most often in the course of the magazine's history were the Virgin Mary and Princess Diana, at eight times each.

THE MOST CONTROVERSIAL COVERS

On more than one occasion, a cover article's slant or the choice of a controversial subject evoked complaints from furious readers. These are the ten covers that generated the most letters of protest and, particularly in the first four cases, the greatest number of cancelled subscriptions.

DATE	COVER SUBJECT	PROTEST LETTERS
1973	Last Tango in Paris	12,191
1980	Ayatollah Khomeini, Man of the Year	5,180
1966	Is God Dead?	3,500
1964	Sex in the United States	3,336
1989	The Gun in America	2,361
1996	Newt Gingrich, Man of the Year	2,283
1998	Monica Lewinsky and Bill Clinton	2,199
1963	Kennedy Assassination	2,182
1988	Who Was Jesus?	2,121
1997	Ellen DeGeneres	2,085

SOURCE: *TIME* MAGAZINE

RICHARD NIXON. He was featured on the cover of *Time* more than anyone else –fifty-five times– and was the subject of the first editorial the magazine published.

VIOLENCE. The cover about gun deaths generated a good deal of controversy among readers.

JOHN LENNON. His 1980 death in New York was a shock, which *Time* reflected on its December 22 cover. When the issue came out, it sold more than 500,000 copies at newsstands. Today it is the issue most coveted by collectors.

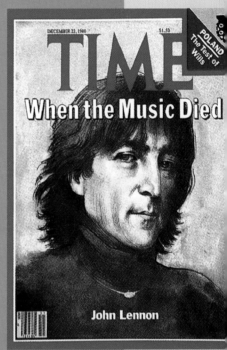

DIANA. She was featured on the cover of *Time* eight times. The issue that paid tribute to her after her death in 1997 ranks fourth among the highest selling issues.

another editorial innovation: the man of the year

As time went by, *Time* established itself more and more as a solid, dependable, influential newsmagazine. Its organization and its original writing won over readers and subscribers little by little. From the initial 9,000 copies printed in 1923, in 1927 *Time* had jumped to 6,000 subscribers and an average of 12,000 copies sold at newsstands. This figure rose even further in 1928, when sales reached 23,000 copies in the last three months of the year.

Along with commercial success, Luce and Hadden gradually began to achieve the goal they had set for themselves when they said the magazine should be judged by "how much of it gets off its pages into the minds of its readers." *Time* had organized into its stories the United States, the world, and their newsmakers. And it had transported these articles from outside, from wherever they took place, into the reader's mind, to his interior, where the news was transformed with reflection, entertainment, admiration, anger, or excitement.

Pursuing its editorial philosophy–order in the news, a context that aided the reader's comprehension, making sure that behind every item there was a personality and that the protagonist of the week's most important event illustrated its cover–in 1928 *Time* added another important link in its chain of journalistic innovations: "The Man of the Year."

This novelty was the clearest indication for Luce and Hadden of the degree to which the magazine had been able to penetrate "the minds of its readers." From that point on, *Time*'s Man of the Year would become an American institution: the naming created anticipation, wagers, and controversy. Guessing who would be designated turned into a national sport and, at the same time, a great intellectual challenge that forced people to reflect upon the year's positive events and who had been at the center of them.

Few know, however, how the idea came into being. In general, the last weeks of the year are a headache for magazine editors. Sales drop, readers have other things on their minds –the holidays, gifts, organizing family get-togethers–and cover subjects with strong appeal are hard to find. This season, fairly uninteresting from a journalistic point of view, tends to stretch into the first week of the new year. And what is true today was true in 1927.

It was in just such a season, at an editorial meeting where unattractive cover proposals were being discarded one after another, that the Man of the Year idea arose. It arose, in fact, as a way to correct an error in judgment. As it happened, in May of that year when Charles Lindbergh in his airplane *Spirit of St. Louis* crossed the Atlantic in a solo flight, *Time* had not recognized the feat on its cover. It had reported the event, but that was it. Then as the months went by, Lindbergh had become a national hero, with massive turnouts in every city that paid him tribute.

This long after the event, they wondered, how could they justify putting the image of Lindbergh on the cover? That's when someone in the meeting came up with the idea of crowning him as the man who had featured in the year's top news event. The proposal was met with enthusiasm. The Lindbergh cover appeared on January 2, 1928, and with it–by chance or stroke of brilliance or editorial whim–was born one of the longest-lasting journalistic successes and, indeed, one of the most imitated, as other media now designate Men of the Year, Women of the Year, Celebrities of the Year, the Scientist of the Year, the Athlete of the Year, the Soccer Player of the Year, and all the variations the press use every year to reward human endeavor.

PERSONALITY. On January 2, 1928, Charles Lindbergh was featured on the cover of *Time* as the first Man of the Year. In 1927 he had crossed the Atlantic in a solo flight in his plane *Spirit of St. Louis.*

PRESENTATION. *Time's* creators, Hadden (center) and Luce (left) in 1925, in Cleveland, during one of the presentations the magazine conducted.

HENRY LUCE. After 1929, when Hadden died, he headed up the magazine and the company. His success was such that even during the Depression he launched new magazines, like *Fortune* in 1930 and *Life* in 1936.

LUCE AND HADDEN: FROM TIME TO PCS

From different backgrounds, with opposing ambitions and even with divergent personal approaches to journalism, Henry Luce and Brit Hadden brought their geniuses together to create *Time*. Luce was born in 1898 in China, where his father, a Presbyterian minister and missionary, directed a small school for Chinese converts to Christianity. He grew up in a family with deep moral convictions, to which were added his unswerving ambition and endless curiosity. Hadden, in contrast, grew up in Brooklyn and was, to a much greater extent than Luce, a product of the American middle class. In 1929, six years after the launch of *Time*, Hadden died of a blood infection. He was thirty-one years old. Suddenly Luce found himself alone at the helm of the magazine. From that moment on, Time Inc. was his company and reflected his point of view, a vision that successfully interpreted the spirit of the times.

The company was so prosperous that even during the economic depression of the 1930s he was able to launch two new magazines: *Fortune* in 1930, and *Life*–the most popular magazine in the history of the United States–in 1936. By the end of World War II, Time Inc. was one of the largest and wealthiest publishers in the world. Luce headed the company until the mid-1960s. He died in 1967 at the age of sixty-eight.

Today, at the height of the cybernetic era, there are those who compare *Time*, the purveyor of news, with their personal computers. The print magazine from the outset performed the same function as the electronic machine now: it organizes information. Both creations came about in small places–*Time* in an office on East Fortieth Street in New York, the Apple personal computer in a garage in Los Altos, California. Both products were invented by a team of two people: the newsmagazine by Luce and Hadden, the home computer fifty years later by Steve Jobs and Steve Wozniak. Just like the ideas that dominate cyberindustry today, *Time* didn't generate information. The magazine set out to organize information so that curious people could access it in a fast, simple way. And isn't this exactly what people surfing the Internet are looking for?

As if this weren't enough of a parallel, today *Time* has merged with America Online, the largest Internet provider. In this way the little thirty-two-page creation that Hadden and Luce brought into the world in 1923 has become, in the twenty-first century, the largest communications group in the world.

all the men of the year 1927 1964

In 1927 with Charles Lindbergh, *Time*'s first Man of the Year, the magazine started a tradition that became a touchstone of world journalism. Occupying this important spot on its cover was considered a great honor, although more than once *Time* selected such infamous characters as Adolf Hitler, 1938 Man of the Year. Here are all the people or subjects the magazine selected over seventy-seven years, and why they were chosen.

 **1927 CHARLES LINDBERGH.** Popular hero who made the first solo flight across the Atlantic, in his plane *Spirit of St. Louis.*

 1928 WALTER CHRYSLER. Shook up the auto industry in Detroit when he bought Dodge and launched a new line, the Plymouth.

 **1929 OWEN D. YOUNG.** Businessman who presided over the second postwar reparations conference.

 1930 MAHATMA GANDHI. From a British prison cell in India, focused world attention on himself and the demands of his people.

1931 PIERRE LAVAL. With energy and vision, put France back at the center of world affairs.

 **1932 FRANKLIN D. ROOSEVELT.** President-elect of the United States at a time of unprecedented economic crisis.

 **1933 HUGH JOHNSON.** Chief of the National Recovery Administration, the government agency confronting the Depression.

 1934 FRANKLIN D. ROOSEVELT. Again Man of the Year, this time for having fervently battled the Depression.

 1935 HAILE SELASSIE. King of Ethiopia, fighting with all available means the advance of Italian fascist Benito Mussolini.

 **1936 WALLIS SIMPSON.** Divorcee who led Edward VIII to abdicate the throne and whose marriage rocked the British crown.

 **1937 GENERAL AND MADAME CHIANG KAI-SHEK.** Faced great danger with Japan's invasion of Imperial China.

 1938 ADOLF HITLER. Perhaps the most controversial choice in the magazine's history. In order to avoid tacitly supporting Hitler, the editors decided exceptionally not to use his face on the cover, but rather a lithograph by

Rudolph C. Von Ripper (who had been detained in Germany) showing naked cadavers hung on a Catherine wheel and, at bottom center, a tiny figure resembling Hitler playing a pipe organ.

 1939 JOSEPH STALIN. Signed a secret pact with Germany and opened the way to Hitler's war.

 1940 WINSTON CHURCHILL. Led the British as the main enemy of Hitler, whose armies had already overrun five countries.

 1941 FRANKLIN D. ROOSEVELT. Man of the Year for the third time, for his efforts to ready a reluctant United States to join the war.

 1942 JOSEPH STALIN. Again Man of the Year, this time for joining the Allied Powers after Hitler's betrayal and invasion of Russia.

 1943 GEORGE MARSHALL. Forged a professional army and directed the deployment of huge forces on two fronts.

1944 DWIGHT DAVID EISENHOWER. Commanded the Allied Forces that invaded France and crushed the Germans.

1945 HARRY S. TRUMAN. Rapidly asserted himself as Roosevelt's successor when few believed in him.

1946 JAMES BYRNES. First U.S. secretary of state to face a new, dangerous era –the Cold War.

1947 GEORGE MARSHALL. Again Man of the Year, this time as a diplomat who originated and directed the Marshall Plan for Europe's reconstruction.

1948 HARRY S. TRUMAN. Once again Man of the Year, reelected president by beating opponent Tom Dewey and inspiring the slogan "Give 'em hell, Harry!"

1949 WINSTON CHURCHILL. To *Time*, a "man in a class of his own" and Man of the Half-Century.

1950 THE AMERICAN SOLDIER. Named in homage to the American troops fighting in the Korean War.

1951 MOHAMMED MOSSADEGH. Prime minister of Iran who briefly led a government that attempted to oppose the West.

1952 QUEEN ELIZABETH II. Newly crowned queen, young and energetic, whose coronation ushered in a new era in Great Britain.

1953 KONRAD ADENAUER. Took the helm of a destroyed West Germany and pointed her toward the future.

1954 JOHN FOSTER DULLES. U.S. secretary of state who introduced the term "*brinkmanship*"–the art of pushing confrontation to the brink–into the Cold War lexicon.

1955 HARLOW H. CURTICE. Head of General Motors and prime example of businessmen who brought the United States a new era of abundance.

1956 THE HUNGARIAN PATRIOT. Emblematic participant in the first uprising against Soviet control behind the Iron Curtain.

1957 NIKITA KHRUSHCHEV. Premier of the Soviet Union as it launched its first satellite, *Sputnik,* and gained a surprise edge over the United States.

1958 CHARLES DE GAULLE. World War II hero now returned to power in France by Algerian crisis.

1959 DWIGHT D. EISENHOWER. Gathered the support of all NATO allies to confront the Soviet Union.

1960 U.S. SCIENTISTS. Homage to the American men of science who made remarkable advances during the year and fought against Soviet supremacy.

1961 JOHN KENNEDY. At age forty-three, won the White House by a narrow margin over Republican Richard Nixon.

1962 POPE JOHN XXIII. "Opened the windows" of the ancient church and touched off a revolution.

1963 MARTIN LUTHER KING. Black leader who with his dreams and words armed his soldiers and led the cause for civil rights.

1964 LYNDON JOHNSON. Newly reelected president of the United States, following a sweeping victory over Barry Goldwater.

1971 RICHARD NIXON. Leader who, during a complicated term, opened the doors to China, devalued the dollar, and stifled protest against the Vietnam War.

1965 GENERAL WILLIAM WESTMORELAND. General in command of ground troops in Vietnam.

1966 YOUNG GENERATION. Recognition of the twenty-five-and-unders, a generation that changed society and warned against trusting anyone over thirty.

1972 HENRY KISSINGER AND RICHARD NIXON. Masters of diplomacy who engaged in dialogue with the USSR about international tensions and visited Mao.

1973 JUDGE JOHN SIRICA. The judge who, in his search for the truth in the Oval Office, managed to untangle the Watergate case.

1978 DENG XIAOPING. Managed to govern a China plagued for many years by political instability.

1979 AYATOLLAH KHOMEINI. Another highly controversial choice. When *Time* named him Man of the Year during the hostage crisis in Iran, thousands of readers sent protest letters. The editors explained that his designation was meant not to honor him but to reflect the significance of his actions.

1967 LYNDON JOHNSON. The president who hoped to be the architect of social reform, but governed haunted by the Vietnam War.

1974 KING FAISAL. The Saudi Arabian king who supported raising oil prices in OPEC and caused turbulence in world markets.

1980 RONALD REAGAN. Won the White House as the American electorate swung to the right.

1968 THE APOLLO ASTRONAUTS. The men who participated in the race to reach the moon.

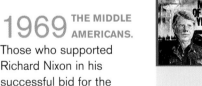

1975 AMERICAN WOMEN. At the peak of the women's rights movement, recognition of women who affirmed their equality and refused to take second place.

1981 LECH WALESA Leader of the Polish labor movement Solidarity and a newly severe critic of the Kremlin.

1969 THE MIDDLE AMERICANS. Those who supported Richard Nixon in his successful bid for the White House.

1976 JIMMY CARTER. The candidate who took advantage of his outsider image to reach the White House.

1982 THE COMPUTER. To *Time*, anticipating the personal computer revolution, the Machine of the Year.

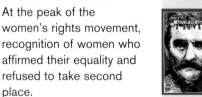

1970 WILLY BRANDT. Chancellor under whom West Germany embarked on a new Ostpolitik and a new dialogue with the West.

1977 ANWAR SADAT. Took a large, surprising political turn toward peace talks and later made a historic trip to Israel.

1983 RONALD REAGAN AND YURI ANDROPOV. Two leaders and a failed negotiation: deadlock over the stockpiling of missiles.

1984 PETER UEBERROTH. The man who turned the Los Angeles Olympic Games into a huge business.

1985 DENG XIAOPING. Abandoned Mao's leftist dogma and set about changing the Chinese model with free-market reforms.

1986 CORAZÓN AQUINO. Followed upon Marcos's hard times in the Philippines with a pacific revolution.

1987 MIKHAIL GORBACHEV. With "glasnost" and "perestroika," put an end to Soviet political and economic lethargy.

1988 THE ENDANGERED EARTH. *Time*'s initiation of a new era of environmental activism, eighteen years after the first Earth Day, with its recognition of Planet of the Year.

1989 MIKHAIL GORBACHEV. The reformist Soviet leader –called "revolutionary" by himself and "visionary" by *Time*– now named Man of the Decade.

1990 GEORGE BUSH. The two-faced president, confronting Saddam Hussein with one attitude and the weak domestic economy with another.

1991 TED TURNER. The man who revolutionized television news broadcasting through his cable network CNN.

1992 BILL CLINTON. Brought the White House back to the Democrats after twelve years of Republican government.

1993 THE PEACE-MAKERS YITZHAK RABIN, NELSON MANDELA, F. W. DE KLERK, YASSER ARAFAT. Four men in pursuit of a single goal: peace.

1994 POPE JOHN PAUL II. At seventy, still traveled extensively to express his conservative points of view.

1995 NEWT GINGRICH. The conservative who led a sweeping Republican victory in the United States Congress.

1996 DR. DAVID HO. AIDS treatment pioneer selected for helping lift a death sentence–for a few years at least, and perhaps longer– on tens of thousands of AIDS sufferers.

1997 ANDREW S. GROVE. Chairman of the microchip giant Intel, who guided the digital revolution.

1998 BILL CLINTON AND KENNETH STARR. Accused and accuser, president and prosecutor, in the Lewinsky case that was the news of the year.

1999 JEFF BEZOS. Amazon.com creator who revolutionized the commercial world with his Internet bookstore sales.

2000 GEORGE W. BUSH. And the final winner is . . . in the most controversial United States presidential election.

2001 RUDY GIULIANI. New York mayor, "Tower of Strength," who struggled hard and well to help Americans recover from the shock of the attack on the Twin Towers.

2002 CYNTHIA COOPER, COLEEN ROWLEY AND SHERRON WATKINS. Took huge professional and personal risks to blow the whistle on what went wrong at WorldCom, Enron, and the FBI–and in so doing helped remind us what American courage and American values are all about.

2003 THE AMERICAN SOLDIER. Swept across Iraq, conquered it in 21 days, and caught Saddam Hussein. They are the face of America, its might and goodwill, in a region unused to democracy.

The evolution of Time

In order to adapt to the changes imposed by society, the magazine reinvented itself constantly. Here are the most important textual and visual changes that it adopted.

In 1929 Hadden died from a bacterial infection that affected his heart. He was thirty-one years old. Luce then took on the editorship alone.

Two years earlier, however, the creators of the newsmagazine had left yet another emblematic mark on the editorial world: the cover's red frame. It was a graphic device that tended to enhance the central illustration. It was used for the first time in January 1927, on a cover featuring Britain's colonial secretary Leopold Amery. But in fact, the first attempts to add a touch of color to the cover dated back to 1926. In several editions that year—twelve in all—the cover had a wide stripe that ran along one side from top to bottom. In one issue the band was red, in

another it was green, and printed upon it was a brief index of the issue's stories. Finally, when they settled on a color the following year, it was red, and instead of the wide band they used a narrower border that framed the whole cover. Since then, the magazine has undergone changes and more changes, successive graphic makeovers and ample redesign, but *Time*'s red frame has remained intact and made history.

In 1929, in the issue that named the 1928 Man of the Year, the cover carried for the first time a color portrait, that of the automobile magnate Walter Chrysler. In 1936 *Time* published what was considered to be its first "frivolous" cover story (see overleaf). The German actress and Third Reich film director Leni Riefenstahl appeared in a provocative pose, showing off her skiing skills. Two years later, in 1938, a second heading was added to the cover inside a band that crossed at an oblique angle. It was used to announce, on a red background

that covered part of the *Time* logo, the magazine's fifteenth anniversary.

From the beginning, the magazine's cover portrait had a rococo-style border with wide vertical filigrees. These elements remained in place even after the appearance of the red frame, as a secondary internal device: the frame occupied the outside edges, while the rococo line work lay inside the vertical edges. But in 1940 the artist Ernest Hamlin Baker—author of the 1946 Einstein cover seen on the next page—introduced a new graphic device that emphasized the image of the person in this privileged position. Delicate, graduated lines framed all four sides of the main image, high-lighting the cover's central point and guiding the viewer's eye toward it. It worked as a frame inside the frame. This element was used for over a decade and later was succeeded by different-shaped ones—sometimes in white, sometimes in black or alternating—but always maintaining its function as a second frame.

TIME

THE WEEKLY NEWSMAGAZINE

COSMOCLAST EINSTEIN
All matter is speed and flame.

VOLUME XLVIII   (REG. U. S. PAT. OFF.)   NUMBER 1

THE RED BORDER. Since its introduction in January 1927, there has never been a cover without it. The first subject so framed was Leopold Amery (left). In those days filigrees still flanked the illustration. Later these were changed to fine lines (above). With time, even the logo changed, but the red frame remained.

Time and Group Journalism

Working for *Time* meant pride and prestige for its staffers. They belonged to a magazine that had revolutionized journalism, with original and innovative contributions. However, in the early 1930s some of the senior editors and section chiefs felt that *Time* needed to go further in its editorial strategy, that it should be more daring, that is wasn't enough to tell yesterday's news. *Time*, they submitted, was in a position not only to gather the news from the world's leading periodicals but to generate its own news stories. It should no longer be–and this was one of its competitors' main criticisms–a "re-write sheet."

Luce had warned of the self-criticism that the style he and Hadden had invented might produce in its writers. For this reason, in 1933 when the magazine was ten years old, he sent a memo to congratulate the writers, pointing out:

❝ *Time* is a re–write sheet. *Time* does get most of its news and information from the newspapers. *Time* is not only proud of the fact, but, in fact, the genius of *Time* lies in that fact...❞

❝ It takes brains and work to master all the facts dug up by the world's 10,000 journalists and to put them together in a little magazine.❞

He would repeat these phrases years later, when he again would tell his writers:

❝ In devoting ourselves to putting together 'the news,' we stoop to a task no weekly journalist has ever before stooped to and we render to hundreds of thousands of influential Americans a service greater than that rendered by any contemporary journalist–and the hell with the Pulitzer Prize!❞

❝ *Time* is even a better magazine today than it used to be... *Time* is heavy with information but it does not burst with information. Please don't hit me over the head if I say that at times *Time* gives the impression of being fat but not pregnant.❞

In 1929 *Time* opened its first bureau in Chicago and organized a network of correspondents to send information from different cities in the United States and Canada. But in the 1930s and 1940s, when the events that made the news became urgent and international, the magazine had to redouble its efforts: in 1945 it came to have 435 correspondents who reported from 33 regions of the world, writing their own stories. With the massive hiring of correspondents, the old complaints by writers and editors who wanted the magazine to create its own news instead of being a rewrite sheet were put to rest.

At the same time, a characteristic *Time* working style was born–or, rather, became international. This was group journalism. The term simply denoted a well-oiled and polished editorial process that precisely regulated the efforts of the correspondents, researchers, writers, and editors who worked on the magazine week after week.

Group journalism originated in one fundamental, key element: the correspondents. They wrote directly, in the full knowledge that their stories would not be printed as filed, but rather were to inform the editors. They presented copious reports and paid scant attention to length limitations or literary style. Their copy would always be rewritten and cut. For this reason, the dispatches produced mountains of detail, color, and quotes that would later be used by other writers to give *Time* articles their characteristic vitality.

The cycle of this journalistic method continued in New York. There group journalism reached its maximum expression, since the magazine's editorial production system required that each article be edited at least twice as it changed hands along the line: from the writer it went to the fact-checker, then to the senior editor, and the first phase ended on the desk of the editor in chief. Later, in an inverse process, the same article went back to the researcher or correspondent, who made one final revision to corroborate facts, then to the copyeditor, who made stylistic and syntactical revisions, and finally the article went back to the editor in chief, who cut or expanded it to fit its assigned slot.

Nevertheless, group journalism–a way of working that many journalism scholars consider a *Time* innovation–generated much controversy. Henry Luce, who had created it, denied doing so. "If I ever used that word in the old days, I soon quit it. *Time*'s method of journalism is highly organized–but a high degree of individualism has always been required–beginning with the absolutist authority of the M.E."

His executives defended the system. Noting that "*Time* has come under criticism by fellow journalists because its writers and editors in New York rewrote dispatches sent in by the correspondents," managing editor Otto Fuerbringer in 1959 wondered at his colleagues' consternation over "how all this collaboration can work… Quite obviously, *Time* believes that many minds are better than one."

Many writers criticized it. The editing system, as an article went through so many hands, condemned the writers to anonymity. In 1968 Andrew Kopkind, a former *Time* reporter, wrote in the *New York Review of Books:* "If reputation is a writer's capital, *Time* staffers can never invest."

Despite the system's detractors and defenders, *Time*'s editing process would remain unchanged for several decades. And it worked: it gave the magazine character, style, and personality.

In 1998, when the magazine celebrated its seventy-fifth anniversary, star writer Lance Morrow commented: "*Time*'s editorial process, which evolved over time, had a unique collective concentration of information, similar to a well-directed beehive." It was an arduous process of editorial polishing that sharpened and improved the article at every successive stage, or distorted it as it passed from hand to hand and from mind to mind. Morrow also points out that during the Vietnam War a disagreement over editorial policy–the Saigon bureau did not share New York's optimism about the war–finally led to a significant change in procedures at *Time*. "From that moment on, the edited stories began to be cabled back to the correspondents, whose comments and corrections were taken into consideration before they went to press."

Covers from 1926 with colored stripes, one red, one green, bearing an index of the stories included in the issue.

Cover announcing the fifteenth anniversary issue. For the first time, a band overlapped the logo.

First cover story with a "frivolous" theme, published in 1936. The skier is German actress and filmmaker Leni Riefenstahl.

In 1940, the inside filigrees were replaced by a patterned inner border and this in turn by another smaller frame within the outer red frame.

art and journalism on the covers

From the beginning, *Time*'s founders paid special attention to cover design. Both Luce and Hadden regarded the cover as the magazine's weekly letter of introduction to its readers. So the magazine created a special team to produce the detailed portraits of featured newsmakers through the years and, more than once, hired well-known artists for the task.

For instance, the French modernist Bernard Buffet did the 1958 Man of the Year portrait of Charles de Gaulle, Mexican expressionist Rufino Tamayo provided a portrait of his president, Adolfo López Mateos, and pop artist Andy Warhol illustrated the cover dedicated to American youth and, in 1984, the one featuring Michael Jackson. Marc Chagall was yet another famous artist showcased, as *Time* illustrated a cover story on him with a self-portrait. Recognizing the historical and artistic value of these portraits, the Smithsonian Institution's National Portrait Gallery in Washington keeps a permanent collection of some 1,800 paintings and sculptures used on *Time*'s covers. Madame Tussaud's Wax Museum in London has on view four papier mâché figures of the Beatles made especially by British caricaturist Gerald Scarfe for a 1967 *Time* cover.

But in addition to famous artists, there was a select group of illustrators whose inspired ideas and work were at the core of a constant evolution in the magazine's covers. Among these professionals, a trio known in New York press circles as the ABC trio of *Time* cover artists stood out in particular: Boris Artzybasheff, Ernest Hamlin Baker, and Boris Chaliapin.

Ernest Hamlin Baker. Baker was the first of the three to join *Time*, in 1939. It was he, as we have said, who introduced the cover's second, inner frame, but his most significant contribution was made along with editor-of-all-trades Dana Tasker in 1940 when they developed a new feature: the painted background behind the cover portrait. This consisted of a symbolic iconography that concisely put the person's life into context. For example, behind Henry Ford was an illustration that showed how the automobile had transformed the United States; behind Albert Einstein, the terrible mushroom cloud of an atomic explosion, along with the theory of relativity's equation $E=mc2$. The first of these portraits with symbolic backgrounds was of the German theologian Martin Niemöller. In his essay in *Faces of Time*, published in 1998, Frederick S. Voss described Baker's technique as "a very slow method that began by looking at photos of the person for hours under a loupe and then... he made a preliminary sketch, which Baker described as a 'facial map,' and he delineated the characteristics with complete detail... The result was a vibrant image, with an objectivity that was brutal at times."

HENRY FORD, 1941, by Baker

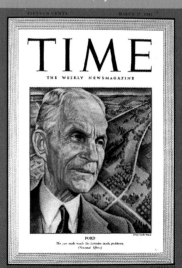

FUSION. Science fiction mixed with technology in the Artzybasheff style. From top to bottom, Admirals Osami Nagano and Karl Dönitz, 1943, and Buckminster Fuller, 1964.

Boris Artzybasheff. Working at the magazine from 1941 to 1965, Artzybasheff was chosen to come up with different-style covers, break the monotony, and surprise readers. Through his original and extravagant illustrations he achieved an attractive mix of the person's likeness and milieu, the story that merited the cover, and humor. He specialized in combining science fiction with technology. Admiral Osami Nagano's portrait in 1943 was superposed on the silhouette of a ship whose cannons formed the menacing profile of a human face; the head of Karl Dönitz, the Third Reich's naval commander, was turned into a periscope on one of his submarines. Artzybasheff created his most memorable cover in 1964, a year before his death: a portrait of Buckminster Fuller and his famous geodesic dome.

THELONIOUS MONK, 1964, by Chaliapin.

Boris Chaliapin.

Boris Chaliapin. The last of the ABC trio to join *Time*, Chaliapin painted in a realistic and striking style. His first cover, in 1942, showed a perturbing image of Jawaharlal Nehru under Gandhi's shadow. One of his most relevant cover works was his portrait of pianist Thelonious Monk, in which he captured in the hardness of the face what it meant to be young, talented, and black in the United States in the 1960s. In addition to his artistic attributes, Chaliapin was considered a master of speed. He was one of the illustrators most sought after by *Time* whenever the cover subject had to be changed at the last minute.

Artists and illustrators were not the only ones to leave their mark on *Time*'s covers. Other geniuses of the image achieved impressive covers with modern photographic and computer techniques. The editors' goals were always originality, surprise, a different angle reflected by the cover, so the reader would know that, even though other media had treated the same subject, no one would handle it the way *Time* did, no one else would offer that something extra. Among the top "technocrat" cover artists of the last two decades of the twentieth century, two stand out –Matt Mahurin and Gregory Heisler–as can be seen in the 1998 book *Time 1923–1998, 75 Years: An Anniversary Celebration.*

Matt Mahurin. The Sigmund Freud "puzzle," which falls apart like his reputation. A father rocking his child, whom he's just abused. A primitive man with a surprisingly modern face. A nuclear terrorist swallowing a radioactive missile. These memorable *Time* covers are the works of a master of image manipulation, Matt Mahurin. What's most amazing is that they are all actually portraits of the artist himself. A talented photographer, Mahurin used his self-portraits as the first step in creating each image. It's estimated that he has been on the cover of *Time* ten or twelve times, but always in disguise. In the first cover he did for Time, a 1983 article about domestic violence, Mahurin, barely twenty-three years old, posed with a doll; he later painted the image and altered successive copies of the photo until he achieved a sinister effect. For the story on Freud's lost reputation, Mahurin dyed his goatee white, dressed like the psychoanalyst, put on a false bald pate, and then altered the image with the computer to attain the puzzle effect. "The guys at *Time*'s art department," Mahurin would later say, "didn't recognize me. They asked, 'Matt, how did you do this? There are no color photos of Freud.'"

SELF-PORTRAITS. Domestic violence, 1983, and Sigmund Freud, 1993, by Mahurin, the photographer who used portraits of himself in the guise of his subjects.

BUSH, 1991, and **GATES,** 1994, by Heisler.

Gregory Heisler. Bill Gates, the wizard of software, appears on a 1994 *Time* cover personifying Prometheus, holding a burst of energy in his hand. Is it a digitally manipulated photograph? Absolutely not. The photo is the work of another kind of wizard: Gregory Heisler, whose unparalleled dexterity with the camera has turned him into the photographer *Time* calls on when special effects are needed. In the photograph, Gates holds a piece of polyester that creates a vivid glint, which the camera lens was able to capture at just the right angle. Heisler creates his special effects with the camera itself, not in the darkroom. One famous example: the photo of the 1991 Man of the Year, the two faces of George Bush. Instead of combining two separate photos with the computer, Heisler first opened the shutter while the president looked to the left, and then, on the same frame, he took the second shot while Bush looked in the opposite direction. Before the fifteen-minute session with the president, Heisler spent twenty-five hours in the studio with a stand-in for Bush, setting up the camera for the shots. The result was magic.

COVers: Great Illustrators for Great People

Time turned its covers into a newsmakers' gallery. More than once, the magazine invited famous illustrators to depict them at the exact moment that their lives became news. An exhibition of more than 1,800 of these works was held in 1998 at the National Portrait Gallery in Washington. Here are some of them.

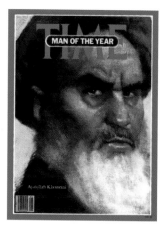

1980 Ayatollah Khomeini
ILLUSTRATOR **Brad Holland**

1990 David Lynch
PHOTOGRAPHER **Gregory Heisler**

1941 Rita Hayworth
ILLUSTRATOR **George Petty**

1951 American Fighting Man
ILLUSTRATOR **Ernest Baker**

1943 Admiral Karl Dönitz
ILLUSTRATOR **Boris Artzybasheff**

1984 Indira Gandhi
ILLUSTRATOR **Mario Donizetti**

1964 Buckminster Fuller
ILLUSTRATOR **Boris Artzybasheff**

1959 Dwight Eisenhower
ILLUSTRATOR **Andrew Wyeth**

1967 The Hippies
ILLUSTRATOR **Image Group**

1962 John F. Kennedy
ILLUSTRATOR **Pietro Annigoni**

1954 Ernest Hemingway
ILLUSTRATOR **Boris Artzybasheff**

1957 Kim Novak
ILLUSTRATOR **Robert Vickrey**

1984 Michael Jackson

ILLUSTRATOR **Andy Warhol**

1968 Robert Kennedy

ILLUSTRATOR **Roy Lichtenstein**

1937 Wallis Simpson

ILLUSTRATOR **Dorothy Wilding**

1969 Prince Charles

ILLUSTRATOR **Peter Max**

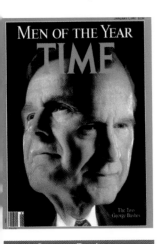

1991 George Bush

PHOTOGRAPHER **Gregory Heisler**

1958 Nikita Khrushchev

ILLUSTRATOR **Boris Artzybasheff**

1982 John Updike

ILLUSTRATOR **Alex Katz**

1964 Thelonious Monk

ILLUSTRATOR **Boris Chaliapin**

1981 Ronald Reagan

ILLUSTRATOR **Aaron Shikler**

1955 Frank Sinatra

ILLUSTRATOR **Aaron Bohrod**

1993 Bill Clinton

ILLUSTRATOR **C. F. Payne**

1946 Albert Einstein

ILLUSTRATOR **Ernest H. Baker**

THE SIXTIES, DECADE OF CHANGE

In late 1959 Otto Fuerbringer became the magazine's managing editor. He was the last of six managing editors directly named by Luce following Hadden's death. The others were John S. Martin (1929–33, 1936–37), John Shaw Billings (1933–36), Manfred Gottfried (1937–43), T. S. Matthews (1943–49), and Roy Alexander (1949–59).

The publication that Fuerbringer took over was, after almost forty years, still a weekly version of a newspaper that selected important current events according to a set method, arranging them by sections and completely organizing the news for the reader. According to Fuerbringer, this contract with the reader would remain in force. But he also maintained that *Time* should evolve and improve. In his opinion, "it had gone a little flat." To liven it up, he proposed to make changes both in the selection of the stories and in the way they were written. He meant to start slowly, but in May of 1960 change came with stunning swiftness. Forty hours before the issue's closing, the news arrived that an American spy plane had been shot down over the Soviet Union and its pilot, Francis Gary Powers, detained. The information caused a stir and a scandal around the world. *Time* rushed to publish a story based on Powers, cancelled the cover that had been printed for May 16, and substituted a black-and-white photo of the pilot. It was the first change

occasioned by a breaking news event, and it made readers feel the magazine was hot, alive, with-it, and ready to respond immediately to their needs. In the following years, last-minute developments would force cover changes, on average, about every three weeks. At the same time, color pages, which had previously been limited pretty much to the Art section, began to appear throughout the magazine. Stories were laid out so as to give the photos a larger, more central role. To this end *Time* popularized a design device that would be adopted by magazines worldwide, the "runaround," in which irregular lines of text ran around the image's outer contour, following its shape and highlighting it. In this way, the photo wound up delineated by the text, a fairly complicated technical feat for a time when typesetting was done mechanically.

The typography didn't escape change either. June of 1963 saw *Time*'s first-ever typographical update. A bolder typeface with a slightly larger body, called Times Roman, was introduced.

COVER CHANGE. Topicality ruled, and pilot Francis Gary Powers, captured by the Russians, became the cover story. This was the first time that breaking news forced a cover change. Inside, the article led the National Affairs section starting on a right-hand page and including a photo layout, rare for a *Time* news item.

CHAPIN'S MAPS. In 1938 *Time* tapped Robert M. Chapin Jr., who had worked at *Newsweek*. At the start of World War II he revolutionized the illustration world with his topographic maps. With an innovative technique based on the use of the airbrush and overlaying symbols and other devices, Chapin made maps attractive, informative, original, and eye-catching. "I try," he once said, "to capture the week's news, not just to produce a reference map like an atlas." His work could be found in most *Time* issues from the war years up to the 1960s, as when he was assigned to illustrate the shooting down of Powers' plane.

**WERNHER
VON BRAUN**
1958

YURI GAGARIN
1961

JOHN GLENN
1962

newsweek: the competition

Ten years after *Time* was launched, Newsweek, its first and main competitor in the American market, hit debuted on February 17, 1933. Its creator was Thomas Martyn, a former editor of *Time*'s Foreign News section, who proposed a publication "written in simple, unaffected English" in "a more significant format" with "a fundamentally sober attitude on all matters involving taste and ethics" in his prospectus. The *new magazine* also described itself as "the illustrated newsmagazine." Indeed, its first covers were illustrated with seven photographs, one for the most important event of each day of the past week. In fact, that was practically the only thing that set *Newsweek* apart from the competition. In other respects it was similar to *Time*, with the same format, the same way of organizing the news, and no particular difference in the writing.

In 1937 *Newsweek* merged with another publication called *Today*, edited by Raymond Moley, who replaced Martyn at the helm. The magazine's structure remained the same, much like *Time*'s. Both weeklies hit the streets on Monday, both showed Republican leanings, and both published their stories without bylines. Only the column signed by Moley gave *Newsweek* an edge over its competitors. In terms of style, the younger publication was considered the more serious, with a less affected and more straightforward writing style. In 1960 *Newsweek* was acquired by the *Washington Post*.

From then on, under the direction of Katharine Graham, the newspaper's owner and highly capable editor, the magazine began to achieve its own identity, wider editorial recognition, and sounder finances. Politically *Newsweek* has generally been considered closer to the Democrats than *Time*. Its current U.S. circulation is 3.1 million copies.

NEIL ARMSTRONG
1969

**THE RETURN OF
APOLLO 13**
1970

**SPACE SHUTTLE
CHALLENGER**
1986

SPACE AGE PIONEERS From the first rocket tests to the losses of *Challenger* and *Columbia*, the covers of *Time* have recorded, step by step, year by year, the important events in the conquest of space, including the 1969 high point when men first reached the moon.

TWO SECTIONS THAT MADE HISTORY:
MODERN LIVING AND THE *TIME* ESSAY

During the magazine's first forty years, the sections originally created by Hadden and Luce went through only minor modifications. Animals, Transport, and Personality came and went. Others were born and transformed over the years. For instance, Radio, which was launched in 1938, went on to become Radio & TV and then, in 1958, Show Business.

With Fuerbringer's arrival, as we have seen, the magazine began to modify its thematic sections in an attempt to keep up with the times. As a first step the emblematic Miscellany section–intact since 1923 and, in the view of many writers, the only amusing part of the magazine–was eliminated. The cut was hotly debated, but the thematic restructuring went on unhindered.

In March of 1961 *Time*'s two main sections were renamed. National Affairs became The Nation, and Foreign News was now called The World. That May the magazine's first new section came out, and its name clearly sent the message of up-to-the-minute-ness that the magazine wanted to offer its readers. This section was Modern Living–later, simply Living. As its editors remarked at the time, it was intended to cover "every aspect of how people, and Americans in particular, live –their cars, homes, travel, play, food, fads, fashions, customs, manners." At first the section generated suspicion, even from Luce, who considered it a bit "bland" and "frivolous" for the informative format the magazine should have. Nonetheless, three years later, in January of 1964, Modern Living produced one of the most controversial cover stories of the decade. "Sex in the Sixties" positioned *Time* as a magazine capable of tackling issues that were not political but of profound social import.

Another section created during that decade was World Business. Its goal was to report on Europe with its increasingly important Common Market, as well as the emerging economies of Asia and elsewhere. It first came out in 1962 and five years later was taken over by the existing Business section.

SECTION PREMIERES. *Modern Living* came out in May of 1961 in the issue we see pictured, with its cover, above. It was introduced in "A letter from the publisher" as the section that would reflect people's lifestyle: travel, cars, fashion, home, mores.

NAME CHANGE. In 1961 *Time*'s two main sections, National Affairs and Foreign News, changed their names: the first became The Nation and then Nation alone, while the second became The World. These modifications were related to other profound changes taking place in the subject matter.

Y-FIVE CENTS

APRIL 2, 1965

THE COMPUTER IN SOCIETY

TIME

VOL. 85 NO. 14

ESSAY. Essay was first published (above) in the April 2, 1965, issue. It was a two-page spread and its aim was to provide a deeper look at serious questions.

All in all, perhaps the most innovative section in terms of *Time*'s journalistic approach was its Essay. This feature debuted on April 2, 1965, marking a new era in the magazine's approach to the news. Essay did not fit into *Time*'s traditional organization of stories by section, but occupied its own, more extensive spot. On its launch date "A letter from the Publisher" described its aim: "Like the other sections of the magazine, Essay will treat topics in the news, but (except for the cover story) in greater detail and length. Essay will take a problem under current discussion and lay it bare. The new department will not treat a story or an issue when it is making the biggest headlines. That will be done in the appropriate section. Essay will come in later, when the problem is still far from settled but when second thoughts and greater reflection can be of particular benefit."

The section, created by Fuerbringer so the magazine could examine one issue each week in greater depth and without deadline pressures, also afforded the consulted experts a chance to express themselves more fully than in other sections. Essay–to Fuerbringer the title seemed "a nice, old-fashioned [word] to bring back"– was published that first time on two facing pages under the headline: "The U.N.: Prospects Beyond Paralysis." Subsequent issues would cover hotter, more controversial topics that hit closer to home, such as "Viet Nam: The Right War at the Right Time," "The New American Jew," or "The Pleasures and Pitfalls of Being in Debt." Ray Cave, *Time*'s editor during the 1970s, explained: "The important thing about this section was to say things that couldn't be said otherwise; to say the things that made readers think about something in a new way; to tell them about things they should know."

Essay, created in the 1960s, is still granted generous space and retains its relevance in the early years of the twenty-first century.

Until the mid-1960s, 99 percent of the covers of *Time* were illustrated with people, but on April 8, 1966, the cover bore only the stark question

"Is God Dead?" The controversy that this story generated–hundreds of subscribers even cancelled their subscriptions in protest–did not diminish the use of ideas, deeds, or phenomena as cover subjects.

Covers such as the one on the Pill in 1967 and photos of the Chernobyl disaster in 1986 or the San Francisco earthquake in 1989, among other subjects of social interest, focused on events more than on their protagonists.

Even the Man or Woman of the Year was at times replaced by fascinating objects or by events that generated great concern. In 1982 *Time* named the computer the Machine of the Year, and in 1988 the Planet of the Year was explored in the story "Endangered Earth."

Slowly *Time*, like any other living magazine, made changes. The Crime, Animals, and Aeronautics sections of the first era were replaced by more up-to-date ones like Essay, Behavior, or Notebook. As for the writing, it evolved notably. According to several *Time* editors, the magazine no longer set out to recapitulate or digest last week's news because their readers were already familiar with the majority of the items. In contrast, they put events into context to anticipate tendencies, communicate new events and points of view, tell the story behind the scenes, and explore the questions that others forget to ask.

As for design, *Time* worked to achieve the greatest visual impact and thereby brought important innovations to the magazine market as a whole.

THE redesign THAT CHANGED THE FACE OF THE magazine

THE REDESIGNED COVER. The new cover design by Bernard came out on August 15, 1977. But the changes had been made gradually. First the logo was changed: above left, the last cover with the "old" logo, with the image of Adolfo Suárez; above right, the first with the new *Time* logo. The following week, the corner flap was included with the headline and, four issues later (large photo), the cover with all the changes, including the titles in Franklin Gothic type.

"Whatever redesign is made, care must be taken to avoid a drastic change in character or personality, especially in a successful magazine. The editors want to make changes, but they also want them to pass unnoticed in order to avoid complaints. Their message is 'Help me, but don't hurt me,' or 'Change me, but don't touch me.' Whoever has subscribed to *Time* for twenty-five years believes that the product belongs to them and it is difficult to take the changes in stride."

This was the premise that Walter Bernard, of the New York design firm WBMG (from his initials and Milton Glaser's) used when *Time* called on him to redesign the magazine in 1977. How and why did they choose him? Partly because he had a brilliant background: Bernard had studied graphic design at the School of Visual Arts, had catapulted in the mid-1970s to assistant art director at *Esquire* magazine, and was soon art director at *New York* magazine under design director Milton Glaser, who would become his partner. Partly, too, because his proposal and concerns were the most persuasive to the *Time* editors. "A large part of my proposal," Bernard now remembers, "was simple and based on maintaining the organization and clarity of the publication. Neither the

editors nor I wanted *Time* to be a new magazine, rather that it continue to be *Time* but with a more modern and elegant look, with a visual and graphic style all its own."

Up to then, the magazine had been visually "retouched" over the years by the editors themselves with help from the art department. But Bernard turned the tables. He set up shop in the newsroom with his assistant Rudy Hoglund and worked there for three years, making changes and upgrades and explaining step by step the reason for each innovation, each new idea. "It is important," said the designer, "not only to conceive and execute the new design but also to make sure that the team understands the change, so that they can continue to apply the concept in the future —something that can take time and that in many cases requires individual analysis, story by story, article by article, case by case."

Bernard not only did an extraordinary job redesigning *Time*, but his contributions revolutionized the magazine graphic design business. The first issue with all the changes came out on August 15, 1977. A few weeks earlier, starting with the July 18 issue, Bernard had tried out the four now historic updates:

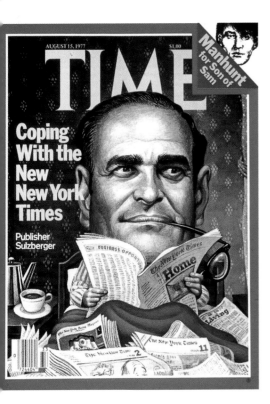

2 **THE HEADLINE TYPE**
For this Bernard chose Franklin Gothic, a font that not only would become "the voice of *Time*" but also would be used by many other magazines and periodicals.

3 **THE CORNERFLAP**
This ingenious "dog-ear" let readers know that, in addition to the cover story, there was another important story. When the editors complained that the type used on the flap wasn't positioned horizontally, Bernard told them: "Why don't you try something completely different, just once?" Bernard won the battle: the text was placed diagonally and the cornerflap is now a common feature of many other magazines.

AND THE LOGO KEPT ON CHANGING

In the 1990s *Time* undertook another redesign, mostly to update the work done by Walter Bernard. The publication would see its logo change for the third time in its history. This time Roger Black, another expert designer with an international reputation, was in charge. Black presented a simple proposal based on the two previous logos, the inaugural one and Bernard's later modification. "Luce's logo was very slight and Bernard's was very heavy," Black recalls. "I took something from each and built another combining the two." The new *Time* logo with its expanded characters was quickly approved and was first used in April of 1992 on a cover featuring Bill Clinton.

4 **VISUAL IMPACT.** The new layout, through a better use of images, photo series, and made-to-order graphics, gave the publication an eye impact unusual for newsmagazines of the time. The response was overwhelmingly positive, not only among *Time* readers but in the publishing world as well. It catapulted Bernard to the highest level of regard in the media business. In time Bernard would be called upon to redesign other important international publications, such as the *Washington Post*, Barcelona's *La Vanguardia*, and *O Globo* of Rio de Janeiro.

BEFORE AND AFTER. In presenting his proposal to the editors, Bernard took as his starting point previously published covers and stories. He made changes to the original (above) to show how it might have look if he'd edited it (below). His philosophy aimed at a lead page with strong graphic impact through in-house photo productions.

VISUAL IMPACT

In the first issue of 1978 *Time* named Anwar Sadat as Man of the Year. The article's impressive lead page, designed by Bernard, was probably the first time the magazine had published such a large photo. Another innovation was the filmstrip-like series of photos inside the magazine. The purpose of this device was to take a fairly boring subject, here a conversation between two seated statesmen, and draw the reader in.

THE SYMBOLS
OF NIGEL HOLMES

PICTOGRAMS. The revolver symbol was used in 1981 for a cover story on violent crime in the United States. The finger on the button is from a 1982 report on the dangers of nuclear war. The exploding oil barrel is from a 1980 cover featuring the Gulf War, and the guitar gave unity to an article on John Lennon's death.

As part of the new design, Bernard also proposed a series of changes for the inside pages. The purpose of most of them was to give the magazine greater unity and personality. Statistical graphics had become popular in print media, but they were mainly used to illustrate stories on the economy and, to a lesser degree, social issues. And the best use was not always made of them: at times their graphic style differed from the magazine's, and at others they were overly simplistic, monotonous, and limited to bar graphs. In *Time*'s case, there was another problem: some stories, particularly the longer ones like cover stories or essays, were interspersed with advertising, which made the articles look too strung out and segmented. Bernard thus proposed to give the magazine unity by giving it a new style of graphics. To achieve this, he suggested hiring an English designer named Nigel Holmes. It was an inspired choice.

With time, Holmes not only resolved some of *Time*'s internal design problems, he also created a whole style of symbols, pictograms, drawings, and illustrations, earning himself a reputation as the father of contemporary infographics. Educated at the Royal College of Art in London, he joined *Time* in 1978 and, as assistant art director, soon popularized a unique pictorial style of conveying statistical information.

This visual journalistic style, now known as infographics, found its maximum expression with Holmes at *Time*. It influenced and still influences an entire generation of graphic designers, journalists, editors, and publications, including newspapers. The infographics style, like the photo essay that we will examine in the chapter on *Life*, is one of those innovations created by magazines and then later adopted by large sectors of the daily press since the late 1980s in their race to make their products more magazine-like.

The task Holmes initially undertook at *Time* was to organize for readers the kind of extensive coverage that not only ran for several pages but often, in addition to the main article, involved other related stories. To accomplish this, Holmes used a small identifying symbol–later it would be called a pictogram–to link the various articles on one main subject. "The idea of doing a pictorial symbol for this purpose appealed to me," Holmes recalls in his book *Designing Pictorial Symbols*, first published in 1985; "it was not to be used decoratively (that is, just to dress up a page, as an art director's whim) but it had a real job to do, which was to let the reader see that a story had companion pieces related to it. For example, in our coverage of the chemical-plant disaster in India in 1984, there were six related articles. These included the news report, a think-piece about the terrible event, and four additional features: living next to similar plants around the world, the industry's own efforts in keeping the job safe, the question about whether it could happen in the U.S., and finally a look at the financial and business implications for the company concerned. The symbol was used six times, at the start of each new topic, but some of the articles were separated from a preceding one by advertisements. In all, the articles covered twenty-five pages, of which eleven were ads."

Although, arguably, all these separate stories could have been combined into just one, from a journalistic standpoint *Time* had its reasons and a style to maintain in consideration of its readers. By breaking a story into several sections, the magazine accomplished two objectives. In the first place, the reader received more information, organized in segments that were easier to handle and to read. In the second place, this system allowed the editor to assign various writers to develop different aspects of the story and thus to cover the news comprehensively –a particularly telling consideration when time is short. That is why, over the years, many periodicals have adopted this way of bringing together different aspects of the same news story, whether with pictograms or strips, repeated typefaces or colored banners.

INFOGRAPHICS
THAT SET TIME APART

MONSTROUS COSTS. Holmes gives teeth to a bar-graph representation of the Senate's excessive expenditures.

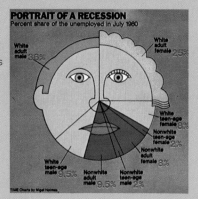

RECESSION. The classic pie chart becomes a clear and simple synthesis showing the distribution of unemployment by age, sex, and race.

PORTRAIT OF A RECESSION
Percent share of the unemployed in July 1980

White adult male 38%
White adult female 25%
White teen-age female 3%
Nonwhite teen-age female 2%
Nonwhite adult female 8%
White teen-age male 9.5%
Nonwhite adult male 9.5%
Nonwhite teen-age male 2%

TIME Charts by Nigel Holmes

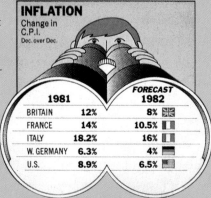

INFLATION. Binoculars bracket two tables that quickly show the reader the cost-of-living indexes in five countries.

INFLATION
Change in C.P.I.
Dec. over Dec.

	1981	FORECAST 1982	
BRITAIN	12%	8%	
FRANCE	14%	10.5%	
ITALY	18.2%	16%	
W. GERMANY	6.3%	4%	
U.S.	8.9%	6.5%	

PROSPERITY IN DECLINE. A double graph, its grid cleverly cast as lines of latitude and longitude, lends clarity to the global relation between inflation and growth.

PROSPERITY TRICKLES AWAY
Percent changes from previous year

1962   1972   1982 projected

INFLATION Consumer prices
GROWTH Real G.N.P.
Figures are for all 24 OECD countries

TIME Chart by Nigel Holmes

Holmes did not merely organize the news through symbols to give the magazine an identifying continuity. He went further: he interpreted the news. His pictograms, far from being just a decorative element, communicated the article's meaning to the reader. "I would speak with the editor and ask: What did he want to say with this element? Is it good or bad news? Later I sat down to think of the most appropriate way to express it in order to reflect the information accurately and in a visually agreeable way."

For a good example of Holmes's work style and the way he conceived and developed his symbols, let's consider the pictogram and infographic drawing he designed for the cover story of March 23, 1981. The story in question was published three months after John Lennon's assassination and was about violent crime in the United States. "Painted by Marshall Arisman," Holmes remembers, "the gruesomely powerful image of a deathmask-like face and a hand clutching a gun delivered an obvious message: violent crime in America really meant the proliferation of handguns and their involvement in the criminal loss of life and property. Thus, a hand clutching a pistol was all that was necessary to continue the message inside."

At the same time, Holmes had designed another group of pictograms to indicate four types of violent crime: a casket for murders, a hand with the female symbol for rapes, a money bag for robberies, and a hand with a knife for assaults. These symbols appeared on a map that showed the twelve most dangerous cities in the United States; the map itself took the form of a burglar's mask, with cold, shiny eyes.

The way his drawings could synthesize issues, the way he interpreted the news, and the way he worked as part of an editorial team were, taken together, the attributes that made Holmes one of the great pioneers of infographics—a style that he remembers as having been influenced by a series of educational publications called Patchwork, published weekly in England, that had a large number of explicative illustrations. Holmes claims that the objective was to interest the public in how things worked. He never worked for those publications but loved to look at them. His first job was in 1969, working for

Radio Times, a magazine with background stories and the BBC's program listings.

It was in this magazine that Holmes first began to publish his work during the 1972 Olympic Games. For each day of the games, he had to explain through illustration the main sports that would be televised that day: what the pole vault or a gymnastics event was all about, or how oxygen depletion affected runners. "The BBC commentators helped me a lot. They would tell me: 'Eight years ago a weightlifting champion could lift the equivalent of a small horse. Now he can lift a racehorse with its jockey.' So the pages of *Radio Times* would have drawings of weightlifters, dates and weights, but in place of the weights I put a horse on one side and a horse and rider on the other. The public loved it."

His first infographic pieces in *Time* appeared in the Economy section. Every week Holmes made his editors shudder, as they thought his illustrated statistics would interfere with the seriousness of their section. But an avalanche of letters from readers applauded the graphics, so useful in understanding business news, and the new style spread quickly to other sections. This visual style that combined information with photography or illustration, as Holmes himself defined it, should meet three objectives: "First, it should tell people what the idea is, what it is about. Then it should communicate the information, and lastly, it should tell people what that information means. When we proposed to do this type of work at *Time*, we assumed that it would be possible because the reader of a general interest magazine isn't specifically interested in, for example, the price of crude oil. Readers are interested in how that price will affect them. That is why, in our graphics, the interpretation is as important as communicating the information."

TWO CITIES. This graphic masterpiece, showing the cost of living in two cities, New York and Moscow, in 1980, is an example of what a comparative analysis illustration should look like.

DIAMONDS. A simple bit of information —the price of diamonds— becomes eyecatching with the witty recasting of the graph paper as a showgirl's fishnet stockings.

Time TODAY

How the editorial process works, from the first story meeting until the selection of the cover. The formula for writing in "*Time* style."

The weekly ritual begins on Monday morning at eleven, when a dozen people gather in the twenty-fourth-floor Conference Room halfway up the Time-Life Building in Rockefeller Center in New York. The group is composed of the managing editor, the deputy managing editor, the section editors, the chief of photography, and the art director. Only the managing editor wears a tie, but without a jacket; the rest are casually attired. Most of them have a cup of coffee from the second-floor cafeteria in one hand, and in the other a copy of the magazine that has just come off the press, a pencil, and a notebook. They sit down around the rectangular table with no specific seating

arrangement or order, except for the managing editor at the head. The mood is informal, even jovial. With large doses of self-criticism and humor, they compare the covers and main stories to those published by the competition at *Newsweek*, which a good 80 percent of the time coincide fairly closely with *Time*'s. However, both magazines give priority to verifying their information and the veracity of their sources over exclusivity. *Newsweek* was, in fact, the first magazine to learn that Bill Clinton was having a sexual relationship with intern Monica Lewinsky and that many of these encounters took place right in the Oval Office. Nonetheless, since the magazine didn't have time to check

its sources thoroughly enough to publish the article, it held off for a week, missing a scoop, but proclaiming in the following issue that its commitment to the truth and to its readers were of prime importance. At both *Time* and *Newsweek* the sacred journalistic slogan is **"Better late and right than early and wrong."** Anyway, neither of the two newsweeklies worries much about being first or about having the same stories because, in both cases, more than 75 percent of their circulation is by subscription, which in practice gives them a majority of guaranteed sales, whatever the cover story.

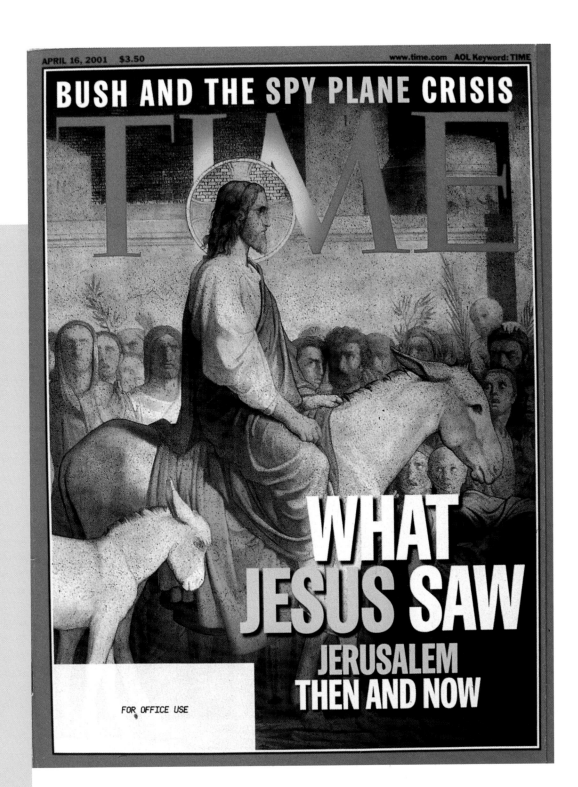

APRIL 16, 2001 $3.50

www.time.com   AOL Keyword: TIME

BUSH AND THE SPY PLANE CRISIS

WHAT JESUS SAW

JERUSALEM THEN AND NOW

FOR OFFICE USE

"SOFT" COVER. Today cover stories may be "hard news" (breaking current events) or "soft news" (subjects that can be treated at any time). In this issue, soft news beat out hard news: because of the likelihood that the spy plane story would not stay current, the editors chose the Jesus article for the cover.

FROM THE STORY MEETING
TO THE PREPARATION OF THE MOCK-UP

These meetings, called story or lineup meetings, began until a few years ago on Tuesdays (the week's last meetings were on Saturday night, when the issue was put to bed). However, today's high-speed journalism, spurred by globalization and the insatiable demand for freshness and immediacy—meaning that, like it or not, the aim of every news item is to outdate the previous one or the competition—has forced editors to move the meetings up a day to allow more time for research and in-depth coverage. "Before, TV and the wire services broke the news, the papers covered the story day-to-day, and the newsmagazines like *Time* put it in context and interpreted it," said a veteran editor of the magazine. "But today the lines between these roles have become blurred. Newspapers interpret and editorialize on the news. Cable television transmits breaking news live from the locale, with such drama that later photos seem stale. What is left, then, to set newsmagazines apart from other media? To dig deeper, to check the reliability of the sources, to put each story into historical or cultural perspective, to quote the leading experts on the subject so as to 'enlighten' the readers and fulfill the journalist's double duty of informing and educating the audience."

So **what is a lineup?** It is an inventory of story ideas for the issue gathered from the entire writing staff, including foreign correspondents, and often even from readers, who communicate their concerns to the editors by letter, fax, or e-mail. The section heads distill the suggestions, then offer the most appropriate, innovative, creative, or appealing ideas for consideration in these meetings.

The other editors orally approve or reject the choices, in either case explaining their reasons. The final judge of which stories will be selected and how much space allotted to each is the managing editor, although the relevant section heads tend to negotiate over the space assigned.

PREPARING THE MOCK-UP AND
MAINTAINING THE RHYTHM

From this group of selected stories, a **mock-up** or layout of the magazine is put together. Basically this is an organized list of the articles chosen, the number of pages assigned to each, and the distribution of advertising in the issue. This last task is performed by the editorial director along with the production chief, who generally attends the main weekly meetings, particularly when ads continue to arrive up until the last minute, forcing editors to cancel stories, postpone them, or cut back the space originally planned. The changes and variations in advertising space, like the rise and fall of news items as the week progresses, eventually result in several mock-up versions. Some weeks, an issue reaches its fifteenth version by the closing day.

The **mock-up** is to a magazine what the score is to orchestral music. It even has **"movements."** The first is the **"advance,"** so called because it closes early, normally between Wednesday night and Thursday noon. This folder contains what is called the **"back of the book"** or set sections, such as Art and Entertainment, Books, Letters, and Music, in addition to weekly columns and services like Health, Money, Technology, and Living. The second folder, called **"current,"** includes such sections as Nation, The World, Business, and Education, and does not close until Thursday or Friday so it can incorporate the most up-to-date information in its articles. The cover story usually is in the current folder, especially when the subject matter is related to breaking current events, in which case it closes on Saturday night. Otherwise, at times when news is slow and scarce, as tends to happen over long weekends or in summertime, the cover story may become part of the advance.

But the **layout** has its own **rhythm**. What does that mean? Every magazine has a tacit **agreement with readers** to maintain its identity. When readers buy a particular magazine, they know where to find the news. In the case of newsmagazines like *Time*, this reader agreement deals with the order of the sections, their set spot within the magazine. For this reason, great care is taken not to alter the rhythm of the layout. The stories may be longer or shorter, photos larger or smaller, but always within the same context, in the same order, with the same personality, with the same rhythm that respects this understanding with the reader.

Even when *Time* changes the layout rhythm to present a graphically spectacular piece or an exceptionally long text, it does so in an orderly manner and in a special location–usually in the middle of the magazine to set it apart and, at the same time, to signal to the reader that here is something special, out of the ordinary.

Nowadays *Time* publishes only four or five photo essays a year, and they are never longer than six pages. The idea for the essay can come from various sources: from the story meeting, from a photo agency, from a photographer who has worked for the magazine before. The less visual essays, in contrast, are chosen on the basis of the proposal's content and the way it's written. These are the work of "editors at large" –editors who aren't responsible for a particular section, generally special writers or former *Time* editors–who travel the world looking for ideas to develop and write for the magazine. In such cases the important thing is the quality of the text; the photos tend to be "pickups" bought from agencies.

THE CHAPTERS According to the magazine's editor, today *Time* divides its content into five large chapters. The first is the Notebook section, followed by articles grouped in the Nation, Education, Business, and World sections, then the main course, which is the cover story, and the service sections.

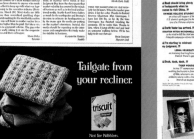

THE FIRST COURSE *Notebook* is the first of the sections to be placed in the mock-up today. It usually has five or six pages and is made up of small items that were developed over the week but don't merit longer treatment. They occupy boxes, columns, or half or whole pages.

The Lead Articles

In its usual sixty-four pages, the magazine today divides its content into five large chapters, within which sections and subsections share space. In terms of form, the pages of *Time* are not as structured and segmented today as they characteristically were for decades. In visual terms, the magazine's middle section—where the longer articles of two, three, or more pages are located—is surrounded, at the beginning and at the end, by fixed sections with short articles.

James Kelly, the magazine's first editor of the new twenty-first century, prefers to think of *Time*'s news selection as "a restaurant menu." The Notebook section, which occupies the first space in the layout nowadays, was created a few years ago as a kind of hors d'oeuvre. This "appetizer" includes three or four pages of subjects and personalities that, as Kelly puts it, "don't have enough content to justify a longer article, but whose information and journalistic coverage should fulfill two purposes: to be a news break and to be absolutely exclusive."

Set sections follow the appetizer with items that are each about two pages long and are the equivalent of

the "first course" on the menu: Nation, World, Business, Education. The "main dish" is the essay or cover story, invariably written by a select group of special writers.

Finally, the service items that are located at the back of the magazine immediately following the articles of the center spread have become the "dessert." These are aimed at providing the reader with very concrete, useful information, and basically focus on three subjects: Health, Money, and Technology.

According to Kelly, the "coffee" and "liqueur" of the menu would be the last two sections, one page each. The first is People, which generally includes four photos of as many personalities "in transition," such as weddings, baptisms, divorces, unknowns who are suddenly famous, or well-knowns who are changing the profession that won them fame or abandoning it altogether. These subjects were previously handled in a section called Transitions that no longer exists. The second of these last pages sometimes presents a *Time* Essay, "to make an interpretation or analysis, or to give an opinion on a topic of the week," and at other times a comic strip on

one of the week's news items "to add a light touch, a bit of humor to the news."

Kelly introduced one fundamental change in the magazine with an innovative section called *Time* in Depth, which is published once or twice a month and runs six to eight pages. The editor calls it "a piece of journalism written like an essay but researched in depth like a book." One of the most successful, published in 2001 under the headline "How Much Is a Life Worth?," analyzed the system developed by the United States government to calculate, in monetary terms, the loss of a family member, colleague, or friend following the terrorist attack that destroyed the World Trade Center on September 11 of that year.

THE ISSUE STARTS TO SHAPE UP

Some thirty or thirty-five people gather for the Monday meeting including, in addition to the top editors and section heads, some of their immediate subordinates, special writers and cover story writers, the chief of correspondents, and occasionally the production manager, who is in charge of the logistic organization of the edition. Unlike the regular Tuesday meeting, which lasts about an hour, the Wednesday meeting is held in the afternoon and can run more than two hours. It is there that decisions are made about future articles, known in the trade as "evergreens," that are not linked to the week's news event or newsmaker and therefore don't lose timeliness.

These articles, which function as "wild cards," tend to be written up to six months in advance and are ready to be inserted in an issue at any time, even to "rescue" a current story that for one reason or another is postponed or "killed." The Thursday meeting, on the other hand, is dedicated exclusively to the cover story and its options, and only the people involved participate. The Friday meeting focuses on the cover story as well, while the Saturday one, which only the top brass usually attend, has no schedule, lasting anywhere from fifteen to forty-five minutes, and is dedicated to settling particular issues or concerns the magazine's editor may have.

The flow of the workweek at *Time* requires that the staffers work Monday through Saturday. And during eventful weeks, like the uprising in Tiananmen Square in China, Princess Diana's death, the 2000 U.S. presidential election, or the attack on the Twin Towers, many of the editors don't even have time to go home to sleep and are forced to take turns catnapping on their office sofas. The only day of rest is Sunday, when the magazine is printed.

HOW an article is edited

The writing and editing of every article at *Time* follows strict procedures that have been refined over the years. For starters, the magazine prefers to have its own sources and to conduct its own interviews. At *Time*, neither "rumors" nor "talk around the water cooler" nor "speculation" are acceptable sources of information. Since the magazine is based on the premise that the journalist's role is to inform and educate, not to do public relations favoring or against something, and much less to pass judgment, three sources of information are usually required —one "for," one "against," and a third "independent"—as a way to guarantee the reader a balanced presentation. The instances of secondhand information taken from other media are few and far between, and in these cases the original source is always cited.

For any given article, the section head generally meets with the writer, a researcher, and one member each from the photo, art, and infographics and graphics departments. At this meeting the basic direction of the article is sketched out; the people to be interviewed are decided on, along with the delegation of such tasks to reporters or correspondents; the photos or graphics necessary to illustrate the article are defined, and appropriate professionals commissioned to produce them; the books and reference materials to be consulted are suggested. Though the photos and graphics follow their own path from that point on, all written materials finally come together to make up what is referred to as the "file," which includes transcriptions of the interviews, the vital statistics of every person interviewed (age, birthplace, profession, brief biography, marital status, names and ages of spouse and children), and the research notes on the subject.

A final text based on this material is then prepared—by a staff writer if it is a regular article, by a senior writer for a cornerflap or other important story, or by a star "cover story writer" in the case of the issue's main article. This same writer is in charge of coming up with the headline, the deck, and the photo captions that will accompany the article, even though the upper-level editors may later change them, with or without the writer's consent.

TEXT SUPERVISION

The article then goes to the editor, who will first see whether the text is written in *Time* style—something that has also has been refined over the years. Every editor's experiences and innovations in this regard have been gathered in the style manual, *Writing for Time*, by Jesse Birnbaum et al. *Time* style has three key aspects: the first is the "lede" (*Time*'s spelling) or lead, which may be a joke, a paradox, an anecdote, a foreshadowing, or just a statement that pulls the reader in; the second is the "billboard" with its clear statement of the subject; and the third is a "kicker" to wrap things up and link the ending to the beginning, whether with irony, a biting commentary, an exclamation, or even an apt quotation. The editor will then decide whether the text needs more quotes or interviews, whether it's balanced or tips toward one viewpoint, and whether it's clear and up to standard or needs to be amended by the writer or even sent back for a thorough rewrite. The editor's work also includes writing headlines, decks, and photo captions with a powerful enough hook to persuade the reader to read the article itself.

Continuing the editing process, the story is sent to the fact-checkers or researchers, whose job it is to verify all the names and data in the article. This is a meticulous and rigorous task that requires the use of two sources to confirm each fact. Once the article has been approved at this level, it goes to the proofreading department, which checks the spelling, grammar, syntax, punctuation, and house style. Then a

BEHIND THE SCENES

The average reader cannot fathom the checking and counterchecking process that a story must go through before publication. *Time* used to–and still occasionally does–hire ordinary readers selected at random to read stories before the magazine is put to bed to make sure that the articles are clear and easily understood by the average reader.

Another example of the much sought after editorial quality of the magazine and its emphasis on clarity is the special care devoted to cover images and illustrations. Several *Time* top editors concur that covers should not only provide the identity and sell the contents of the issue but also differentiate the product from the competition. Their goal is that the preparation and selection of the cover image should go beyond the news as covered by newspapers, cable television, or the Internet. *Time* currently looks for what its top editors call the "cover conceptual image," which is an ideal combination of journalism and artistic craft to convey the main idea of the leading story in each issue.

To achieve this goal, managing editor James Kelly has recently hired Arthur Hochstein as art director. Hochstein was trained as a journalist and even worked as a writer for the magazine before studying visual arts and design. The goal is to start both writers and art people thinking together about the cover illustrations very early in the editorial process.

"local" version of the article emerges: for the first time the actual story with photos and graphics is printed on paper. Each local must be approved by the research chief, the reporter, the writer, and the art, photography, and infographics departments as well as the editor in charge. Each responsible party signs the local, approving or, where necessary, correcting it. If the corrections are few or superficial, they are included and the process continues. But if they entail a content change, the text is sent back to the fact-checking department and the process has to start all over again. Only after all local versions are approved (generally there are two or three) is a "final" produced, showing what the page will look like in the finished issue. This final version must also be approved by the writer, the fact-checker, and the art, photography, and infographics people. The process ends, usually after two to four final versions, with the magazine editor's signature.

TION SECTION Today *Time* uses on certain issues, which it ndles in depth and at length, so t it now contains fewer articles than in its first seventy years. The first section always develops its most important story over several pages, treating it much like a cover story. This was the case with the issue shown above, in which the case of the airplane detained in China was the second cover story.

HOW TO WRITE an ARTICLE IN
"TIME STYLE"

Time's newsroom has a style manual titled *Writing for Time*, which was prepared by the magazine's editors for young, inexperienced reporters and journalism students. It provides good and bad examples of story leads, development, and kickers. As an example of a well-written article in *Time* style, below is part of a story by Valerie Marchant published on March 12, 2001, under the headline "They're Having a Ball." It is shown in segments to highlight the concepts of lead, billboard (or development), and kicker.

a **LEAD.** The lead is the story's "hook," an invitation to get into the article, so it should hit hard. "Cool… Really great!… Fun!… Funny… Nice… So good… These are definitely not the adjectives most parents today would use to describe the formal dance classes they attended as children. But they are the very words Grade 4 students at P.S. 127 in the Bay Ridge section of Brooklyn, N.Y., used last month to describe the first ballroom-dance class held at their school. In less than 45 minutes, these 9- and 10-year-olds had learned to dance the merengue, the first of 10 dances they would attempt in a 20-class session."

b **BILLBOARD.** This is the article's map, the paragraph that explains the reason for writing the article today. It is located directly after the lead. "The students at P.S. 127 are but a smattering of the tens of thousands of young people who are rapidly getting into ballroom dancing—practicing at their schools and at community and cultural centers, health clubs, dance studios, park programs and cotillions across the U.S."

c **KICKER.** To close the article, the kicker goes back to the beginning with something ironic or humorous, or simply something that will stick emotionally in the reader's mind. "The good news for ballroom aficionados –and anxious parents hoping their kids will find something wholesome to do and stick with it–is that this fad looks to have some legs. Many beginners are continuing to dance long after they complete their classes. They are discovering, as Ronnen Levinson says, that the 'world of ballroom is enormously complex, and there is always something new to explore.' Or as newly expert East Coast swing-dancer Brieanna Everts puts it, 'Once you start dancing, you just can't stop!'"

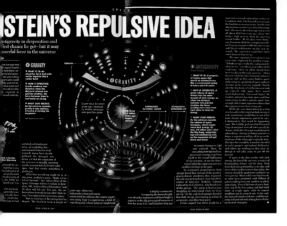

THE DESSERT After the cover story, the journalistic menu continues with shorter articles in the Science, Medicine, or Technology sections, followed by Movies, Television, Culture, and Health. This is what the editors called the "dessert." Two final fillips are the People section, dealing with celebrities, and an opinion column—or, in a more humorous vein, a cartoon strip—on an issue in the news.

d EXAMPLE OF A GOOD LEAD AND A BAD LEAD. Among the style book's tips, number 2E counsels writers never to start an article by narrating an event in the distant past, and gives a fanciful example: "Don't say, 'On the Fourth of July in 1960 the U.S. flag was raised for the first time at Fort McHenry, Md…' **Instead say,** 'Thirty years to the day after the U.S. flag was hoisted over Martha's Vineyard, the country's newest state…'"

e EXAMPLE OF A GOOD LEAD AND A GOOD BILLBOARD. "When Junichiro Koizumi was invited to Camp David one day last June, the Japanese Prime Minister brought along his baseball glove, and the two ball-playing leaders of the world's most powerful economies had a mutually admiring game of catch by the pool. This week, as George W. Bush flies to Tokyo, the first stop in a one-week Asian tour that includes Beijing and Seoul, he has to be wondering if it's time to play hardball." To follow this lead, *Time* described the purpose in the second paragraph: "There's no quick-fix option. The world's second-largest economy, Japan labors under the globe's highest level of public debt—140% of GDP. Across the nation, bankruptcies and unemployment are soaring. Practically everything else—stock values, consumer prices, confidence—is in free fall. The biggest crisis of all is the yen… Says Kenneth Courtis, Goldman Sachs Asia vice chairman: 'It is now really important to get Japan back on track economically, because their problems are about to become ours.'"

f EXAMPLE OF HARMONY BETWEEN A GOOD LEAD AND A GOOD KICKER. A *Time* article on the blackface singer Al Jolson had begun with "He always had a grating voice." The kicker used was "That night he found a job as a nightclub singer in South Chicago. He sang, and sang, and sang, night after night, until he lost his voice."

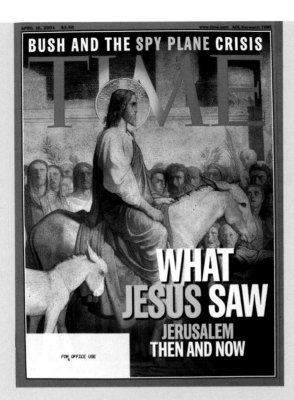

The cover story goes through the same double-checking process as other articles, but with different parameters. To begin with, *Time* magazine has a special team dedicated to the production and execution of these stories. Its mission is to come up with different journalistic takes on the calendar (Mother's Day, Easter, Christmas, the Oscars), seasonal themes (back to school, winter or summer vacations, Las Vegas: the second Hollywood), personalities (celebrities, leaders, innovators, or common people in uncommon circumstances), and current issues (children having children, children who murder children, new drugs that change lifestyles, the Latin American literary boom).

The writers in charge of preparing these articles are among the best in the world, and the cover

Jerusalem
At the Time of Jesus

By DAVID VAN BIEMA JERUSALEM

THIS WOULD HAVE BEEN HIS PATH. ACCORDING TO THE GOSPELS, IT WAS IN THE AREA OF Bethany and Bethphage that Jesus would have stayed each evening of the Passover holiday—on the far slope of the Mount of Olives, where his followers Mary and Martha lived and where he raised their brother Lazarus from the dead. During the festival it was a tradition and a necessity for pilgrims to spend the night on the outlying hills. Each morning Jesus would have set out again, over the top of the mount and then down its western slope to the great holy city below.

Today verses from the Koran waft from a dozen open windows in the town of Bethany. Islam regards Jesus as a great prophet, and Bethany's mostly Muslim residents are proud of its 2,000-year-old tradition. Just a few yards down a steep road from the tomb believed to have been Lazarus' is al Ozir Mosque, named for him in Arabic; a few yards up is a Greek Orthodox church honoring Mary and illustrators are also the best of the best. Even though the team prepares these and other articles months in advance, they also need to be prepared in case such a story should jump onto the cover at the last minute—as happened with the April 16, 2001, issue of *Time*.

In version 6 of the mock-up for this issue, the story featured on the cover was the American spy plane that had to make an emergency landing in China. Since the subject was a real-life international political and espionage thriller between two superpowers, and since the event had commanded the attention of the public and the press all week, a dozen pages were allotted to this cover story. Things followed their course until the late hours of Friday, when the editorial staff went home to await the crucial decisions that the White House would make by Saturday morning. But these decisions were postponed and there was nothing new to report on Saturday, which raised the specter of fresh news breaking on Monday morning just hours before the magazine would hit the newsstands. By midday Saturday the editors decided to change the cover story to one on Jerusalem, which had not appeared in the mock-up but had been finished in December of 2000. Their initial choice, "Bush and the Spy Plane Crisis," was merely granted a secondary cover headline and relegated to the interior, while the Jerusalem story, which had been bounced from mock-up to mock-up for the past four issues, became the final cover story.

THE MAIN COURSE. That is what the editors call the cover story, for it is the most important dish on the journalistic menu of each issue. Such stories range in length from eight to twelve pages, and there is a special team to produce them. Shown here is an example from 2001, when the cover story was an article on Jerusalem, a so-called evergreen story (ready to publish at any time) that had been finished four months earlier.

TIME BEFORE AND AFTER THE TWIN TOWERS

Though *Time* was created to be at the epicenter of the news, until the brutal terrorist attack on the Twin Towers on September 11, 2001, the magazine had been consistently moving away from "hot" news. Competition from cable television, the Internet, and the persistent avalanche of information accompanying globalization had left the magazine with fewer and fewer coverage options. *Time*, like many other information magazines, would thus decide to direct its journalistic focus toward popular culture and service-related subjects to capture its readers. In the 1960s, few could have imagined that *Time* would come to regularly publish cover stories like "The Power of Yoga," "How to Raise a Superchild," "What Jesus Saw," or "The New Thinking on Breast Cancer."

However, the events of September 11 abruptly changed all this—at least for a while. During the following months, *Time* went back to concentrating on "hard news," devoting its cover stories to war developments in the United States (anthrax) and beyond (Afghanistan). This not only led the magazine to reach its all-time worldwide circulation record —5.2 million copies sold, 4 million of them in the United States—but also turned 2001 into the year the magazine had its highest-ever newsstand sales, breaking the previous record set in 1982.

Since the attack, although it might seem from the outside that *Time* was gradually going back to "soft news" instead of breaking news, "the magazine tries," as Kelly said, "to maintain a balance between news and service items in order to keep ourselves up to date and attractive in a changing world." To criticism that it no longer publishes long articles on Russia, China, Japan, or other countries, Kelly responds: "The only way *Time* would publish a story on Russia or China is if it would be memorable; if not, it's not justified."

A SPECIAL ISSUE. After the September 11 attacks, *Time* came out with a special fifty-two-page issue that is, from beginning to end, a consummate example of stripped-down editing. On the cover a single photograph (by Lyle Owerko of the Gamma agency) shows the instant when the second plane crashed into one of the Twin Towers in an explosion of fire, smoke, and debris. No headline. Just the logo and a small caption giving the date. Inside, the first two-page spread has a page-and-a-half black-and-white photo and the Letter from the Publisher. The next has four half-page photos (by Robert Clark of the Aurora Agency) showing, step by step, the last few yards of the second plane's attack on the tower. Only on the following spread, overlaying an impressive photo, is there finally a headline— enormous by *Time* standards— reading "Day of Infamy."

From this point onward for the following two dozen pages, the issue presents an extraordinary combination of images —explosions, fear, soot, destruction, solidarity, tears—all in a sequential manner, all maintaining the rhythm and relating the action as if the magazine had become a movie. Then, beginning with a double-page graphic, there unfolds a twenty-page section of news, analysis, and opinion, creating a perfect balance with the impact-laden photo spreads that went before. On the back cover, the cinematographic finale to the story: a photo of the Statue of Liberty and, in the background, shrouded in dense smoke, almost impossible to see, a few Wall Street buildings. Without words, the photo says it all.

PHOTOGRAPHERS. The remaining photos reproduced here from the *Time* special edition were taken by Spencer Platt (Getty Images), Suzanne Plunkett, Gulnara Samiolava, Doug Mills and Tom Horan (AP), James Nachtwey (VII for Time), Angel Franco, Justine Kane, Ruth Fremson (New York Times), Harry Zernike, Timothy Fadek, and Jules Naudet (Gamma).

TIME FACES NEW CHALLENGES

Whatever the topics or the competitors or the type of news (hard or soft), *Time*'s editors knew, as Kelly said when we spoke with him in mid-2002, that "we have to maintain a stable relationship with the reader, seven days a week. Internet and cable television could disrupt this relationship. So every week we have to decide how and where we are going to battle our competitors. But it is also crucial to decide when and why we're not going to give them a fight."

That is why the magazine's leaders count on a strategy that, in the first place, gives readers what they want to know and what they need to know. This, in some ways, echoes Luce's original idea of creating a magazine that would "give the reader what he needs to know in 45 minutes' reading time." Still, editor Kelly thinks that, since the current purpose of the news is to make other news obsolete, *Time* must try not to offer the obvious; as a weekly, it would just lose newsworthiness competing with agencies, newspapers, and cable or Internet news. "If we are forced to offer the obvious, whether it is breaking news or something crucially inevitable that includes death and destruction, then we are left with no other option than

to do it. But the way to set ourselves apart from all our competitors is to give a different angle to the coverage and do it in depth." Thus the second rule in *Time*'s current strategy: Depth over breadth–in other words, fewer stories but handled in depth, as opposed to many superficial stories. "Since we have six days to investigate an event or person, this allows us to have depth, a luxury that the rest of our competitors cannot enjoy for lack of time," says Kelly, adding, "Curiously, in founding the magazine, Luce emphasized breadth over depth, but the times have brought us to creatively reverse that concept."

MAN OF THE YEAR TODAY. The Man of the Year issue is almost completely dedicated to that theme. That's what happened with the January 7, 2002, issue when Rudy Giuliani, mayor of New York during the Twin Towers disaster, was featured on the cover. Time dedicated some forty pages to him. A year earlier, the thing same happened when the Man of the Year was President George W. Bush. This is a new way of focusing on subjects "in depth" to set the magazine apart from the competition.

PERSON OF THE Y

Photograph for TIME by Gregory Heisler

According to Kelly, the future challenge for the magazine will be to maintain a balance between **breadth** and **depth** in journalistic coverage; that is to say, the correct balance between what the reader in a changing world wants and needs to know.

Today, eighty years after its creation and with an American circulation of some 4 million copies, it is estimated that on average every copy of *Time* is read by five people, which means that the magazine is read by no less than 12.5 percent of the U.S. adult population.

Today, as the twenty-first century takes its first steps and as the Internet and an overwhelming proliferation of other sources of information compete with traditional graphic media, it's worth recalling once more Henry Luce's phrase from 1938: "If I had to make my fortune over again, and there were no *Time*, you wouldn't catch me wandering off looking for gold mines–you'd find me peddling stock right now in a real genuwine Newsmagazine. Good grief, in 1923 the basic premise of *Time* was that the newspapers were excellent and the magazines were excellent **BUT**. The more means of communication there are, the bigger that **BUT**…"

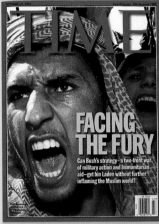

DEPTH OVER BREADTH. Whether they are breaking news events or human interest stories like those on these covers, today *Time* prefers to publish fewer stories but to treat them in depth.

CHAPTer 2
Der SPIEGEL

CHAPTer 2
Der SPIEGEL

Der SPIEGEL, THE German WEEKLY THAT WOULD make ITS mark BY INCORPORATING INVESTIGATIVE REPORTING INTO a newsmagazine, was Launched on January 4, 1947. SINCE THEN Der SPIEGEL (THE mirror) HAS DISTINGUISHED ITSELF BY PUBLISHING numerous exposés WHICH, BEING CORROBORATED, Have earned IT an UNMATCHED CREDIBILITY and PRESTIGE. DISCUSSED Here are ITS MOST NOTABLE INVESTIGATIONS, ITS WORK STYLE, and ITS EDITORIAL PHILOSOPHY.

Der SPIEGEL: THE POWER OF INVESTIGATIVE reporting

Founder Rudolf Augstein called his magazine "democracy's cannon" and focused its editorial strategy on investigative reporting. Here we follow its history and its best-known cases.

"Dad, what sounds better, Der Spiegel or Das Echo?" The German journalist Rudolf Augstein was nervously pacing about his house in Hanover as he pondered, that cold winter morning of 1946, the best name for the brand-new publication he had just been appointed to edit.

"Der Spiegel," his father answered. And that was the name finally given to what today is one of Europe's most important newsmagazines and, certainly, the world's most prestigious periodical of investigative reporting. The proof is in its numbers: it sells, on average, more than a million copies a week and it circulates in more than 150 countries despite the fact that German is not as widely spoken as English.

In the beginning, *Der Spiegel* was an offshoot of a newspaper called the *Hannoversche Nachrichten*, which published eight pages of text four times a week and for which Augstein worked as deputy editor. "People grabbed the newspaper out of each others' hands," Augstein would later write archly. "Wrapping paper was scarce at that time." The newspaper was published by the British occupation forces, which governed one of the four zones into which the World War II victors had divided Germany. "Three British soldiers, Major John Chaloner and Staff Sergeants Harry Bohrer and Henry Ormond, wanted to reintegrate the defeated Germans into the world community," Augstein said. "We were the instrument they came up with to do it."

The three hit on the idea of starting an Anglo newsmagazine directed by the British. They didn't want to follow the *Time* model, but rather that of its U.K. imitator, the *News Review*. Its name would be *Diese Woche* (This Week). "They translated some articles for us and told us: 'Something like this, with the factual information woven into a story and with special emphasis on personal details: age, tie, hair color —got it?'" Augstein recounted. "That's how we started, that's how they started us out."

Getting the magazine ready wasn't easy, however, in the somber Germany of the fall of 1946. Early in November, while the city of Hanover faced the harsh postwar winter, the magazine's staff experienced the hectic atmosphere of launch night in the Anzeiger Building. "I helped the British with everything I could," the magazine's first editor recalled later, "but it all seemed to be built on a foundation of sand." It was true: there were no top-notch reporters, there was no guarantee they could be paid, and nobody knew for sure where the main office or the presses would be located because they, along with paper and phones and furniture, had yet to be acquired. As Harry Bohrer put it later in a column in the magazine, "We began without the proverbial blessing from on high."

4. JANUAR 1947

DER SPIEGEL

PREIS
1
RM

1. JAHRGANG · NR **1**
ERSCHEINT JEDEN SONNABEND

MIT DEM HUT IN DER HAND —
WIRD MAN EIN BEFREITES LAND. ÖSTERREICHS GESANDTER Dr. KLEINWÄCHTER VOR DEM WEISSEN HAUS SIEHE „AUSLAND"

DER SPIEGEL'S FIRST ISSUE. The first issue of *Der Spiegel* appeared on Saturday, January 4, 1947. The cover bore the headline "With Hat in Hand" and featured a photo of the Austrian envoy to Washington, Hans Kleinwächter. The issue had a print run of only 15,000 copies. It had just twenty-five pages in black and white, plus a two-color cover printed on the same stock, and two folios set aside for ads. The price was 1 Reichsmark.

FROM ENGLISH TO GERMAN. *Diese Woche* (This Week) magazine was based on the British weekly *News Review*. It was Germany's first newsmagazine. Englishman Harry Bohrer would say years later: "We wanted to create a lively paper that could say a great deal in a few words, tell a good story instead of offering comments."

But *Diese Woche* was published against all odds and with a 15,000-copy run. Harry Bohrer would later explain in detail the magazine's original philosophy: "We knew there had never been anything like it in Germany. We wanted to create a lively paper that could say a great deal in a few words, tell a good story instead of offering comments. We wanted to show real people, not official portraits. And above all we wanted to write about real people —not necessarily about the remarkable similarity between a nobleman and a farmer in their underpants, but about their human desires, ambitions and weaknesses, which are just as important to the history of the world as their philosophies of life. We wanted to give many viewpoints, and not worship any idols. Frivolity was not our aim, but we did not like stupid solemnity."

In historical hindsight it's interesting to note that this precursor of the main magazine of sociopolitical analysis in today's Germany was, back then, very ingenuous politically. The young team in charge of *Diese Woche* alternated between naïveté and pure ignorance. "I didn't even know what a union was," Rudolf Augstein conceded, "until Harry Bohrer lent me a book that explained it." To Augstein, who leaned toward the arts, anything to do with economics was a great mystery. "But somebody had to write the articles in German or, at least, copy them from the British newspapers—which were the only ones around, by the way," Augstein the editor would later explain. "And they'd chosen the wrong person in me. I had no choice but to hit the occupation forces hard, thereby earning the magazine a well-deserved yellow card." Unwittingly, Augstein was giving the

FIRST NEWSROOM.
Rudolf Augstein in 1947, in the magazine's first newsroom in Hanover (right). Earlier, in 1946, a group of young Germans, along with British occupation officers, edited the weekly *Diese Woche*, forerunner of *Der Spiegel*.

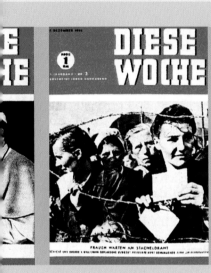

SIX. That is how many issues of *Diese Woche* were published. The magazine's critical and nonconformist tone created conflict with the French, Russians, British, and Americans. The British decided to shut the magazine down and authorize publication of a new title.

publication the critical and nonconformist tone that would later become a celebrated trademark of international journalism. Contrary to expectations for a publication that came out under the auspices of the military government—which should automatically make it an official organ of the British government—*Diese Woche* turned out to be exceptionally independent, bold, and irreverent, not only toward Great Britain but toward the other occupation forces in Germany. "The Russians, Americans, French, and British complained so much about this British paper that the end was

imminent," Augstein would later say. In the meantime, the British Foreign Office covered its flank by forcing the magazine to subject itself to a censor in Berlin, which sometimes delayed its publication a week. "Suddenly, an order came down from the Foreign Office that we had to get rid of the new magazine by turning it over to the Germans, who had to get a new name for it within two hours," Bohrer explained. *Diese Woche* had lasted barely six weeks and already it had to be buried, almost without a funeral. This was on the cold morning in 1946 when Rudolf Augstein was sleepless.

"The British hesitated over who would keep the magazine going when it was in German hands," he would recount later. "It had to be someone without other responsibilities. Since there was nobody else available, they gave the job to me, though I was only twenty-three. That's how the German paper *Der Spiegel* was born overnight, greeted by its more-or-less involuntary founders."

THE FIRST ISSUE.

Germany had five pages, Foreign News six, and Economy two. Six pages were devoted to the arts, including coverage of two new movies, one about Field Marshal Rommel, the other starring Marlene Dietrich and French actor Jean Gabin.

Der SPIEGEL's FIRST Issue

The first issue of the brand-new magazine was published on Saturday, January 4, 1947. It cost one Reichsmark, but it sold for more than fifteen marks on the black market since its paper ration was enough to print only 15,000 copies. It contained just twenty-five pages of articles and two ads, all in black and white, plus a cover printed on the same stock. The names of four editors were given on the masthead (Rudolf Augstein, Willi Gerberding, Roman Stempka, and Hans J. Toll), but listed under the heading of "correspondents" were the names of thirty-eight men and women. Although he actually played the role of publisher and managing editor, Rudolf Augstein's name appeared only as a "writer" at the top of the masthead and at the bottom of the editorial page, where it said, "Edited by Rudolf Augstein, under temporary license PR/ISC600PR of 1 January 1947."

Its emphasis on particular subjects and its editorial slant can be gleaned from the index. Five pages were devoted to national politics under the heading "Deutschland" (Germany), a section that would become a regular one. Six pages headed "Ausland" (Foreign Lands) focused on international politics, including the cover story about the diplomat Hans Kleinwächter, Austria's envoy to the White House. "Wirtschaft" (Economy) was allotted two pages but, interestingly, six pages were set aside for arts and entertainment, chiefly because of the release of the movies *Five Graves to Cairo*, in which Field

Marshal Rommel was portrayed by the revered German actor Erich von Stroheim, and *Martin Roumagnac* (U.S. title: *The Room Upstairs*) with Jean Gabin and the German diva Marlene Dietrich, idolized by the public since the wartime era of hunger and destruction. A section titled "Personalien" offered a list of the week's most notable celebrities, along with a couple of lines on each person, somewhat like *Time*'s "Transitions." It was a sort of counterpart to the opening "Panorama" section, which published short news items from various countries, but centered on issues rather than personalities. Altogether, the magazine included twenty photos, plus three cartoons and two maps, in eight two-page spreads.

The cover portrayed the diplomat Hans Kleinwächter, the Austrian envoy to the White House. The headline: "With Hat in Hand." The subhead: "They Will Be a Liberated Land." Inside, the cover story bore the headline "Viennese Active, But Only within the UN Framework." The lead summarized the article: "Austrian foreign policy is on the move. The foreign minister, Dr. Gruber, is a tireless diplomatic traveler on behalf of his country. With Dr. Kleinwächter (see cover) in Washington and Norbert Bischoff in Moscow, Austria occupies two very important positions once again. Austria demands the restitution of its sovereignty, a campaign that is supported by the United States and Great Britain. The United States' declaration leans in that direction:

Austria shall be seen as a liberated country and not as an old foe."

In the "Germany" section, only a simple box was devoted to this notice: "After six weeks, *Diese Woche* says goodbye. Its goal, to be a mirror of events, was much applauded and very well received. The British authorities have decided that the publication should continue exclusively in German hands. *Diese Woche* is ceding its place to *Der Spiegel*. The publishing house and editor bid their colleagues farewell, extend their thanks, and wish them much luck at *Der Spiegel*." Oddly, Augstein would later say: "None of us believed in the future of the publication, but we were conscious that they'd placed in our hands an instrument with which we could do something for the future. Even though it was impossible for us to live up to *Time*'s maxim–that is, to give the impression that the magazine was written by one person for one other person–in our small group, this phrase ruled: "We want to write what we'd like to read in another magazine if we didn't have this one." For us, political convictions took precedence. As the years went by, and as it fed on its own success, this broadened. The principle of not holding back, of not subjugating ourselves to any given authority, not even when it came to our friends, was ironclad. This dogma has made *Der Spiegel* great and will continue to help it grow."

WHO was rudolf augstein?

He earned the distinction of being named Journalist of the Century by *Medium* magazine. He is an international press icon for leading for many years the publication that paved the way for global newsmagazines. In his first period, however, Rudolf Augstein was indecipherable, an enigma.

People around him wondered if he was weary or cynical by nature. Did he have a physical problem, perhaps? Nothing of the sort. His wide forehead and glasses gave him the air of a perpetual graduate student. Even when he put on some weight and walked with a bit of a stoop, he still looked like an

AUGSTEIN IN ACTION. When he took charge of *Der Spiegel,* young Augstein was twenty-three years old. "Since there was nobody else available," he would later say, "they gave the job to me."

intellectual and irreproachable man. Whenever his physical appearance was mentioned, he modestly said that he regretted not being able to boast a better image.

Rudolf Augstein was born in Hanover on November 5, 1923, the sixth of seven children. His family was fervently Catholic, despite living in a Protestant area. Rudolf was raised the traditional Catholic way and concedes that this marked his whole life. Probably this education was also at the root of his reaction against the Church, since he started questioning the faith at fourteen or fifteen. Young Rudolf, however, was not only a Jesuit school altar boy but also a member of the Catholic youth organization Neu-Deutschland.

Instead of going to a regular local elementary school, Augstein attended a small one-room Catholic institution with eight students and two teachers. Four years later, his parents sent him to high school at Kaiserin Auguste Viktoria Gymnasium, on the other side of town. He was at the head of his class most years and also, most of

the time, class president. One of his teachers said, "Rudolf was the best student in the history of the school." His favorite courses: German and history. He especially loved to recite poetry. His idol then: Bismarck.

Father Mertens, a Jesuit priest who took a paternal interest, engaged the boy in profound discussions that influenced his views on everything from the deficiencies of National Socialism to the music of Wagner. While other lads dreamed of driving a locomotive, young Augstein wanted to conduct an orchestra.

From the time he was a young man, Augstein was a passionate defender of justice, dedicated to what is nowadays called social criticism. Though his friends between ten and fourteen joined the Jungvolk branch of the Hitler Youth, the Catholic high school student did not, even when it became mandatory. While they met on Saturdays sporting their brown shirts, Augstein and other young friends preferred to go to school. After great pressure was exerted on his school principal and parents, Rudolf ended up joining the Hitler Youth when he was fourteen, but he did his best to evade the drills and ideological training. He joined a puppet theater group that made its

own marionettes and wrote its own scripts. Rudolf was assigned to play the female roles, speaking in falsetto. Even in his seventies he could still recite long passages of these plays.

Later, in the fall of 1941, he worked a few months as an apprentice at the *Hannoverscher Anzeiger*. During the last days of World War II, in which he served for three years, Lieutenant Augstein virtually became a deserter. He ended up getting wounded, but while retreating. Grenade shrapnel blew open the lower part of his right arm. Wearing civvies (Hitler was now dead) and a sling on his arm, he made his way by bicycle to Offenbach, where his older sister and her husband lived. A few days later he went to Hanover to his parents' house, arriving six weeks after the surrender. His desire to go back to school had to wait: the University of Göttingen was still closed. To keep busy, Augstein considered returning to journalism. Major John Chaloner and Captain Ralph Kingsley of the British forces' Information Control Unit had the task of interviewing applicants for press vacancies. When, after a questionnaire and interview, Augstein got to the practical exam with photographs and proofs of print columns, Chaloner was surprised by

his attitude. "He looked at me with a smile, as if I were an idiot, although I thought this a particularly useful part of the test." As requested, Augstein pasted up a sample page of headlines, text, and photos. When Chaloner asked, "You think this is funny, do you?" Augstein diplomatically answered, "Oh no!" Later Augstein called this test a "puzzle" with no other purpose than to steer off undesirable candidates. Augstein passed—and the positive impression he made on Chaloner was reinforced when he found out they'd been born on the same day. Augstein got a job with the *Hanoversches Nachrichtenblatt*, a newspaper edited under the auspices of the military government. It came out four times a week as a four-page publication, limited by the critical paper shortage. A year later, he worked for six weeks at the *Neuer Hanoverscher Kurier*, also overseen by the British. However, it was in his naming as editor in chief of *Diese Woche* that the shared birthday with his interviewer benefited Augstein. During a decisive conversation between Chaloner and Bohrer about the selection of newsroom personnel, the major pulled out his personal notes and said, "This one right at the top, under 'A' –Rudolf Augstein. He

did well on my test." He added, "He was born on the same day as me, so he must be all right!" There's a word for that in German: *Schicksal*. It means fate.

John Chaloner probably described Augstein best: "With his smile and his appearance he struck me as rather like Peter Pan, who never grew up and never wanted to, and that's something I still see in Rudolf Augstein. It is also one of the things that make him so attractive to women –all women love the little boy in the man." In addition to being nice, he was brave: the first open letter from Augstein in *Der Spiegel* was of transcendental importance to his future. With it, the editor started his own personal dialogue with readers. Later on, Augstein would become the only *Der Spiegel* spokesman, just as he was the one to define its political leanings.

THE SPIEGEL STYLE

DER SPIEGEL IN HANOVER The magazine's first home (above), before moving to Hamburg. Below, the morgue and part of the art department. On the righthand page, some of the international figures who were featured on the cover in the early years.

Using an ingenious and increasingly sophisticated editing system, with different-colored paper for the different sections (articles on economic subjects, for instance, had to be turned in on green paper), Augstein designed a style for the magazine's stories that was demanding and precise in both form and content. Sometimes even the most experienced and expert editors felt their stomachs churn when, first thing in the morning, they once again found in their pigeonholes articles that had been edited by Augstein or executive editor Hans Becker and finally rejected. They then had to study the reasons given on the attached sheet.

Sometimes Rudolf Augstein would rewrite articles that had already been published, simply to show what they should have been like. Once he edited an article about an American general from top to bottom, and several editors posted the revised version prominently on the wall as a reminder.

After the initial push by John Chaloner and Harry Bohrer, along with Augstein's frequent lectures and examples, it was Hans Detlev Becker who made sure that the magazine maintained a clear, sober style and impeccable grammar. A scholarly analysis of *Spiegel* style quoted by early *Spiegel* staffer Leo Brawand found:

"As a rule, the story comprises five phases with several changes of tense:

1. **Lead-in** (present)
2. **Chief character or most important news item** (present)
3. **Flashback to background material** (often with several changes of tense and location);
4. **Up-to-date development** (present) **and**
5. **Summary or pointed conclusion** (present)

In any case, the editors made clear to *Der Spiegel* reporters that they were not to follow the *Time* model of covering all sorts of subjects. It's often said that when you read *Time*, you practically don't need any other news source to keep up with the events of the week. "In Germany, thank God," Augstein said, "no well-informed reader will content himself with nothing but *Der Spiegel*; our readers will see at least one daily paper… so the magazine shouldn't try to cover the daily news unless it can do so more informatively, with greater breadth and clarity… consequently, it must dig deeper… it will often try to feature some complementary aspect of an event whose basic details are well known, something that casts new light on the problem, and we always feel we have an obligation to print something

DWIGHT EISENHOWER

1950

MARILYN MONROE

1953

EVA PERÓN

1947

'new' and 'original' in every issue."
In an environment in which both journalistic style and the spoken language were still governed by deeply rooted tradition, the magazine's writers often were hard put to fill this demand for prose that was at once lively and original. Leo Brawand recounts: "For instance, Ludwig Erhard, heading the economic administration of the British and American Zones, raised his eyebrows when, at the end of a long and technical interview, I asked him what he had had for lunch. Erhard momentarily hesitated, and then said, 'Fried eggs.' The writer now had an opening for his article, which in almost confidental terms informed the reader that Erhard had enjoyed a plate of fried eggs at midday, but had found it harder to digest a phone call from Adenauer in the afternoon. This example is the essence of the *Spiegel* style.

"The editorial team was making progress: the colour of people's ties soon featured less frequently in our articles, as did 'piercing gazes.' Cheap jokes about names were banned too. And finally, there was a general agreement that it was not in principle newsworthy if a member of parliament had a mistress—but it was if he failed to turn up in time for an important vote because he had spent the night with her."

MARSHAL TITO

1951

MAO TSE TUNG

1950

PRINCE CHARLES

1952

THe newsroom
STYLe BOOK

In 1949 a sort of office task force was established to put into writing, for the first time, the new publication's principles on style and content. Many are still in effect. Written in Hanover, the so-called Spiegel Statute is referred to by the editorial top brass to this day as they set out to train a new generation of journalists in "house style" or to root out some imperfection that might have crept in. It begins, "Der Spiegel is a news magazine. Therefore it must:

Be topical, have a high news content. It must also offer details about news items different from those given in the daily papers—i.e., more personal, more intimate, with more background material—and they must be written up in different ways too.

Be interesting, which means:
a) recognizing important topical issues with a sure journalistic instinct: those issues that can be instantly assumed to affect, interest, and concern a large circle of lay people with normal interests.
b) presenting these issues in a way which will hook these normal lay readers, seizing their attention and making them read to the end of a story easily and with pleasure. (A *Spiegel* story that has to be read twice to be understood is not a *Spiegel* story.)
     There were three other key precepts.

1. "Nothing interests people as much as people, so all *Spiegel* stories should have a high level of human interest."
2. "*Der Spiegel* thinks poorly of blind respect."
3. "*Der Spiegel* must show where the weight of the argument lies." Also, a sidebar called on the magazine to "avoid all clichés, commonplaces and cheap popular usages, and try to find its own cogent, brief and precise phraseology. Anything contrived is to be avoided."

In terms of style, the main legacy of the British was the lead, which was considered vitally important and was a prime subject of the task force's debate. A bad lead in a story written by a correspondent was mentioned: "The Reverend Jürgen Kaulitz, of the Lutheran Church in the former state of Brunswick, will shortly be going to the Lüneberg Higher Administrative Court to appeal against a judgment in the Administrative Court of Brunswick which, if upheld, would rob the churches of several West German Länder of the potentially profitable chance to use state coercion in squeezing money out of those Federal citizens who have made a formal declaration of their withdrawal from church membership in a local court."

SUBJECTS OF ALL SORTS. Like the good newsmagazine it was, *Der Spiegel* dealt with a wide range of subjects, although it always gave political news more space. Until the late 1950s, just about all the main stories were illustrated with a newsmaker's image on the cover.

MOSHE DAYAN
1955

FRANCISCO FRANCO
1952

CASTRO AND KHRUSCHEV
1962

ADOLF EICHMANN
1961

MARLENE DIETRICH
1951

CHARLES DE GAULLE
1952

The editors at the time felt that the aforesaid lead, with its spate of names and information, would confuse readers and deter them from reading on. They suggested, instead of this endless introduction, a lead that could pique readers' interest and better accomplish its purpose: "Protestant housewife Meta obeyed her non-denominational husband Kurt and sued her church."

The phraseology and word coinages of *Der Spiegel* made their way not only into everyday speech but also into the dictionaries. The magazine's concise style, the custom of mentioning people's age after their names, the transposition of subject and predicate ("Said Adenauer," for instance), and the line that closed the magazine's interviews ("Thanks for speaking with us") are now tools widely employed by print and broadcast journalists after having been in common use by the American press for years.

Those who opposed Augstein and Becker during the talks still agreed, without question, that the magazine should expose abuse and explain its nature clearly. What they didn't like was the use of malice and contempt in making those revelations. But there was growing consensus that the magazine should focus on showing the shady side of events and newsmakers –the other side of the coin–because there were many official publications, and indeed nonofficial ones, that showed only positive aspects. A balance was needed. The result was that Augstein and Becker started, little by little, to get rid of those who didn't follow their guidelines.

an irreverent magazine that challenged the establishment

"Democracy's cannon." During the magazine's early years, that was Rudolf Augstein's favorite phrase to define the course he wanted his publication to follow. "Perhaps we were looking excessively for objective news subjects, objective news stories," he explained then. "But, little by little, I started to realize that there could and should be news that wasn't too objective and that we had no reason to cast this aside–quite the contrary."

On that premise, *Der Spiegel* set out on the path of investigative reporting, with a way of doing things and a style that set it apart from other magazines in Germany and throughout the world. Often four, five, or more reporters and correspondents were assigned to a single story, unearthing facts and events that had been covered up by those involved. Each issue's main subject became the cover story, which was handled in detail and in depth. The magazine's current

editor, Stefan Aust, summarizes its style in these words: "*Der Spiegel* is characterized by its careful and trustworthy investigations. We try to focus, above all, on politically and socially relevant news, and a great deal less on entertainment." The product is a magazine that offers plenty of background information, a balanced mix of long and short articles, bylined pieces that express incisively the writer's position, and a detailed presentation of the cover story.

However, it wasn't an investigative story that caused the magazine's first run-in with the establishment. In an article about the abdication of Queen Wilhelmina of the Netherlands, they happened to make jocular remarks about the departing queen's parsimony and the new queen's "solid substructure." The royals were deeply aggrieved. The Dutch government protested to London, claiming lèse-majesté and demanding the Hanover

journalists be punished. England, which by then was the occupation power by virtue of being a victor, used the opportunity to slap down *Der Spiegel* and try, perhaps, to muzzle it. The magazine was ordered to shut down for two weeks. In the October 16, 1948, edition, Augstein informed his readers of the ban and wrote: "We regret the fact that we were found guilty without being given a hearing… As for us, we will happily sacrifice these two issues of *Der Spiegel* as a modest offering on the altar of our native Western Europe."

A publication that didn't bow even to royalty was sure to stir the emotions of Germans living under occupation. The magazine, its nonconformist nature, and its influence were all growing apace. Its network of correspondents already covered London, Paris, Rome, and Vienna. In addition, the first multipart articles published in *Der Spiegel*–one was a series about

DER SPIEGEL

DAS DE   RICHTEN-MAGAZIN

BERÜCKENDER SCHURKE

German officers imprisoned in the Soviet Union titled "I Want to Be Shot"–grabbed readers' attention, as did smaller critical pieces on current affairs closer to home. Circulation increased with the magazine's popularity curve. From the initial print run of 15,000, sales rose during the days of monetary reform in mid-1948 to some 60,000 copies, and by the end of 1950 circulation had reached 100,000.

In 1950 *Der Spiegel* touched off the first big scandal resulting from this direction and style. The magazine soared nationally on the wings of accusations that Bonn's selection as provisional capital of the new republic was achieved by bribing members of Parliament to vote against Frankfurt. The members of the first German Bundestag had already made their decision and Parliament had started to work out of Bonn when the magazine caused a sensation on September 27,

1950, with an article titled "Federal Capital: Clever Folk Keep Quiet," quoting informants who said companies had paid some two million Deutschmarks to buy the votes of more than a hundred members of Parliament, who were bribed with amounts that ranged between 1,000 and 20,000 marks.

Sleepy Bonn, a city tucked behind the seven hills on the banks of the Rhine, started for the first time to awaken from its lethargy thanks to *Der Spiegel's* revelations. The appointment of a commission of inquiry by the Chamber of Deputies soon after the news broke allowed the magazine to keep the story alive. The commission was even officially named the Spiegel Commission. It subpoenaed Rudolf Augstein, but he refused to reveal his sources, citing the right to journalistic confidentiality. The commission held its own sessions for a month and determined that, beyond any doubt,

several members of Parliament had been bribed to vote in favor of Bonn as the capital and that, therefore, *Der Spiegel's* report was true. The hearing in Bonn encouraged the offending members to offer their resignation. None did, though the affair left a persistent stench of corruption in Bonn that was damaging to the image of democracy.

THe scandalous spiegel affair

While *Der Spiegel* took journalistic aim at the government, forcing it to make changes, the publication was going through internal transitions. In 1951 the magazine's co-owners, Gerhard R. Barsch and Roman Stempka, left the publishing company. Hamburg publisher John Jahr took over half its stock and became, along with Rudolf Augstein, a partner in Spiegel Verlag. A corporate maneuver forced the magazine to move its editorial headquarters from Hanover, its home and also the home of Germany's ancient kings, to Protestant Hamburg. But circulation was so high–121,202 copies a week–that the decision didn't cause any major upheavals.

The real upheaval came on October 10, 1962, when the magazine featured on its cover the image of the Bundeswehr's inspector general Friedrich Foertsch and, inside, an article headlined "Ready to Defend Ourselves?" about NATO maneuvers.

The magazine was charged with treason, defamation of the state, and corruption, and on the night of Friday the twenty-sixth, a few hours before the week's issue went to bed, the police broke into and took over the *Spiegel* newsroom and the publishing-house offices in Hamburg. This act, unprecedented in the brief history of the Federal Republic of Germany, boomeranged, throwing the coalition and the government into crisis and, according to political commentators, shaking the foundations of the state.

Nobody tells it like David Schoenbaum in his book *The Spiegel Affair*: "Swiftly and wordlessly the men entered the building where *Der Spiegel* had its offices in Hamburg and headed purposefully toward the elevators. The doorman Wilhelm Mugge, who wasn't used to such eruptions, assumed something bad was happening and ran after them to try to stop them. 'This is none of your business,' the leader of

the group told him and closed the elevator door in his face. The story unfolded at a rapid pace. On the sixth floor, the eight people didn't wait to be announced to editor-in-chief Claus Jacobi but went straight into his office. First, they introduced themselves: Inspector Karl Schutz and Criminal Investigations Officer Gerhard Boeden, both from the Federal Bureau of Criminal Investigation, the Bonn security group. 'The charge is treason,' they told the editor in chief as he glanced at the search warrant. '*Der Spiegel* must be vacated right now,' they added."

It was a little after 9 p.m. on October 26, 1962. Almost two dozen *Spiegel* writers were still working on issue number 44 of that year. Jacobi had heard correctly: They all had to leave because the offices were being closed down. "I have a superior to answer to, and I can't send the staff home just like that," Jacobi managed to say. Indeed

"TREASON." That was the charge the German government lodged against *Der Spiegel* following a story on NATO maneuvers. Augstein was thrown in jail (near right), the editorial offices taken over by the police (center). This case stirred the public, which had come to trust the magazine's integrity since, a decade earlier, its allegations of bribery in the Bonn selection case had been upheld (far right).

Augstein, the magazine's publisher and editor, had already left the newsroom, but that wasn't enough to deter the raiders. A few minutes later, Hamburg police vans pulled up in front of the publishing house and nearly three dozen police officers invaded *Der Spiegel*. Then the criminal brigade burst into the hallways of the editorial offices. *Der Spiegel* had been taken over and, in a few minutes, the whole building was under police control.

The police searched everything after sealing the doors with crime-scene tape. They finally detained Johannes K. Engel and Claus Jacobi—which was no feat because neither put up a fight. Writer Conrad Ahlers, the author of the cover story that had prompted the police raid, wasn't in the building, but the police managed to capture him in Spain, where he was working on another story. The publisher Rudolf Augstein, for whom an arrest warrant had also been issued, spent the night at home in Hamburg, but the next day he turned himself in at the Central Police Station, to Prosecutor Siegfried Buback's office. Prosecutors informed Augstein and the other arrestees of the reason for the raid: "published information that made reference to important matters related to the country's defense in such a way that it endangered the existence of the Federal Republic and the security of the German people—more precisely, a cover story about Defense Minister Franz Josef Strauss's military policy. Several *Spiegel* correspondents," the document said further, "have been detained provisionally on suspicion of treason, falsifying public documents, and active bribery."

Throughout the night and the next morning the questions mounted. Was the nation's welfare really endangered? Or was this rather a matter of silencing an organ of the press that went up against the power of the state?

a SYMBOL OF THE FreeDOM OF THE Press

"It could have been the end," essayist Hans Joachim Schops would write several years later in an anniversary issue. "*Der Spiegel* was blocked and its immediate future was at risk. No more issues would have been published if there hadn't developed in Hamburg a solidarity movement that the public prosecutor's office hadn't counted on."

Immediately after the takeover, the newsrooms of *Die Zeit* and *Stern* offered asylum to their *Spiegel* colleagues. *Constanze* magazine made room for those displaced and the *Hamburger Echo* cleared whole hallways for use as emergency quarters. Desks and typewriters were made available, as well as a staff cafeteria. Hamburg businesses that were not associated in any way with the press offered rooms and facilities. Thanks to their help, the work could go on, albeit on a limited basis. Researchers didn't have access to their valuable files and ran to libraries to fact-check the stories. Chaos reigned in the reporters' emergency lodging, and in the newsroom as well. Behind every writer was a police officer; access doors had to remain open; talking on the telephone was forbidden. Officers also escorted copyboys as they took manuscripts to the printing plant.

It was a very difficult night for both raiders and raided. However, *Spiegel* photographer Frank Müller-May managed to slip off and capture on film the entry of the police into the newsroom. "What are you doing here?" an officer asked him nervously. "I'm taking some very nice pictures of you," he responded with a touch of sarcasm. And a writer, fearful that the photographer's camera might be confiscated, said emphatically: "He's a great photographer. His subjects always come out very well." The officer ordered the camera confiscated, but in the reigning confusion Müller-May managed to salvage the roll of film. The following day, an assistant smuggled it out of the newsroom in her bra. An independent lab developed it immediately and the magazine's top brass heard in jail –where they would be detained for 103 days–that the photos were excellent. These would furnish the cover of more than one issue. "The photo of Augstein being led in handcuffs to the prosecutor's office would become an international symbol of an assault on the freedom of the press," the essayist Schops would say. To make things even worse for the government, issue 44 of *Der Spiegel* punctually hit the newsstands, with Rudolf Augstein featured on the cover. Though 700,000 issues had been printed –200,000 more than usual–it sold out in a couple of hours.

On May 13, 1965, as expected, the Supreme Court's Third Chamber rejected the government's suit. "The famous forty-one state secrets," the opinion summarized, "have turned

UNFOUNDED ACCUSATIONS. The Supreme Court rejected the government's accusations, Augstein and his staff were absolved, and the defense minister was forced to resign. *Der Spiegel* brought down the Adenauer government.

PROTESTS. The German public rallied behind the magazine. *Der Spiegel's* credibility increased, and so did its circulation.

into a grand fiasco. The great treason trial is without merit." By this decision, Augstein and all his correspondents were absolved and what started out as "an attack on justice" culminated in the political death of those who had provoked it. When it came out that the government charges were baseless, Franz Josef Strauss, the German defense minister deeply implicated in the case, was forced to resign. The conflict prompted the collapse of the Christian Democrat government of Konrad Adenauer.

From that point on, *Der Spiegel* would forever become a symbol of the freedom of the press and of the role of the fourth estate as watchdog over the government. The public, who at first had sent socks to Augstein's jail cell so he wouldn't freeze to death, sent an endless number of encouraging letters urging *Der Spiegel* to "continue its work as the people's defender" or taped *Der Spiegel* covers to their cars' back windshields. "A powerful

and staggering giant like the new Germany, to which we thought we'd taught the fundamentals of postwar democracy, has just given us an unforgettable lesson on democracy," said a *Los Angeles Times* editorial. And Rudolf Augstein would later write in the magazine's fiftieth-anniversary issue: "Government power lost the halo of infallibility, perhaps forever." People of all political leanings were united in recognizing that government doesn't have the right to do everything and that, when it incorrectly believes that it does, it must be stopped. The rule of law and the German parliamentary system were strengthened thanks to the magazine article and its unleashing of the *"Spiegel* affair." The magazine's growth and influence seemed unstoppable.

From that point on, *Der Spiegel* became Hamburg's and Germany's preferred newsmagazine, gradually gaining a level of importance that even its own newsroom and editor did not expect. According to political science professor Otto Kirchheimer, in its role of true opposition, *Der Spiegel* didn't give the government any respite and, in a way, would always keep a sword over its head, since this was not only the most exciting chapter in its history, but it gave the magazine a degree of popularity that would surely contribute to its economic momentum later. And it did, because the scandals that *Der Spiegel*'s investigations would provoke were just starting. Over the next forty years the magazine would continue "uncovering scandals" and "watching" government's moves. Among them:

PAYOFFS. The Flick case broke in 1982 when the magazine accused this consortium of buying off politicians to avoid paying millions of marks in taxes.

The Flick case. With the cover headline "Bribery or Government Service," *Der Spiegel*'s issue number 48 in 1982 revealed the details of an unprecedented affair in which the government was involved: The Flick consortium had paid politicians several millions in bribes from its slush fund and hidden the fact from the tax authorities. Flick expected to save several hundreds of millions of marks in taxes that way. To cap matters, Franz Josef Strauss, leader of the CSU (the Bavarian wing of the Christian Democrats), was part of a group of Flick advisors. According to the tax investigators, Flick was suspected of making "false statements about administrative practices" in the purchase of an interest in W. R. Grace, the American construction materials company. The company's purchase entailed a tax break. The German company argued that the investment in the United States would be good for the German economy and, therefore, should receive tax benefits. *Der Spiegel*'s investigation revealed that the Flick Group had offered illegal donations worth millions to key German politicians to "launder" income on which it never paid taxes. After the exposé, Friedrich Karl Flick, heir to Germany's largest industrial fortune, was forced to pay 450 million marks in back taxes. The case also had repercussions in other countries, among them Spain.

CONVICTED. In the aftermath of the magazine's allegations, the courts sentenced Friedrich Karl Flick, heir to Germany's largest industrial fortune, to pay 450 million marks in back taxes.

The case of ministers Lambsdorff and Matthöfer. "Flick money?" That was the question hanging over the heads of cabinet ministers Lambsdorff and Matthöfer on the cover of issue 9 in 1982. The accompanying cover story suggested that the impact on public opinion was disastrous. Indeed, the official investigation resulting from *Der Spiegel*'s cover article exposing two of government's central figures was a new blow for the governing coalition. Barely fifteen minutes before leaving for France, where the Thirty-ninth French-German Summit would take place, Secretary of State Manfred Lambsdorff, chief of the Bonn chancellery, was informed by prosecutors that they would indict him on charges of corruption. Soon after, during the trip to Paris, an in-flight call to the official plane delivered the rest of the news: finance minister Hans Matthöfer was suspected of illicit enrichment and was also under investigation. The Flick consortium had earmarked money for Matthöfer, who was officially involved in the company's requests for tax exemption on two billion marks from the sale of Daimler-Benz stock to Deutsche Bank.

JUSTICE STARTS AT HOME

As *Der Spiegel* uncovered scandals that rocked the German and the international world of journalism, the magazine also underwent internal changes. After co-owner John Jahr yielded equal shares of his interest in the company to publisher Richard Gruner and Rudolf Augstein in 1962, Gruner decided to sell his to Augstein, who ended up as the publication's sole owner. But in 1971 Augstein in turn sold one-fourth of this stock to the Gruner und Jahr publishing company.

Then in 1974, in a move that was almost unprecedented in the international publishing industry, Rudolf Augstein decided to give half of his company to his employees. "From this moment on," he said in the speech announcing his decision, "the responsibility, the shared decisions, and the right to profits are part of the working conditions and set the editorial climate. I must tell you, nowhere else has the idea of a company's workers becoming its owners been implemented so thoroughly."

Nevertheless, it seems that in 1989 Rudolf Augstein wanted to reverse this decision, though ultimately he did not. Just before turning seventy the owner-editor, in an interview with four of his young staff members, was asked specifically why he had considered this option. He answered: "I had my doubts. I wasn't sure if we weren't hurting ourselves too much in that way. I thought we should be more flexible than others. Often, we should choose to accumulate reserve funds instead of distributing earnings. Naturally, my colleagues are a little hard of hearing   in this regard."

"But then, do you mean to say that you regretted your generosity?" fired back one of the journalists.

"At times I regretted it, but I no longer do," he said. "We are somewhat less flexible than others, but the staff's greater dedication compensates for that."

FROM POISON GAS TO INDUSTRIAL ESPIONAGE

The Neue Heimat case, involving a nonprofit credit union directed by union leaders who got rich through shady deals, was also uncovered in 1982. The power of *Der Spiegel* and investigative reporting were evident once again.

The Neue Heimat Case. With a cover photo of Albert Vietor ("King Albert" as his cohorts called him) and a cover story headlined "Well Camouflaged in the Forest of Firms," *Der Spiegel* revealed how this nonprofit credit union that was attached to the labor unions had long been working chiefly to benefit itself. Vietor and his closest collaborators took advantage of the charitable organization's tax breaks to conduct personal business and build an apparently impregnable empire. The Neue Heimat management team and board members did ever-increasing private business in the guise of running companies founded and managed by the charitable organization. On their tax returns the owners of shares claimed the high cost of construction as losses, so they frequently paid no taxes on earnings. In six cover stories and dozens of follow-up articles, *Der Spiegel* unveiled the freewheeling lifestyle of the union leaders, which would wind up changing the German labor movement forever.

The Poison Gas Case. With a photo of Jürgen Imhausen on the cover and the story "Poison Gas Factory: The Evidence Is In" inside, issue 3 of 1989 earned *Der Spiegel* yet another investigative journalism award. To be sure, when inspectors from the city of Freiburg's finance office examined the books of the Imhausen chemical company in the nearby city of Lahr, they found no indication that the German company had participated in the construction of an illegal Libyan plant, as the magazine had reported. Instead, the company's owners produced photos and documents that clearly showed construction of a pharmaceutical plant in Hong Kong. With the director of the company's auditing firm at his side, manager Jürgen Hippenstiel-Imhausen spoke of "unfounded, but grave, suspicions." He demanded a retraction by the magazine. However, Imhausen's brazen performance was in vain. New investigations by *Der Spiegel* and the prosecutors established that the German chemical company had indeed built a factory in Hong Kong, but only as a screen to do other types of business. In fact, in an underhanded way, the Lahr firm had sent Libya's President Gadhafi a system that was probably intended to produce chemical warfare materials, just as the publication had said. Offenburg prosecutors therefore indicted the Libyan suppliers for violating foreign trade laws. An issue that at first seemed no more than a divergence in evaluating intelligence reports ended up as a real scandal. And the accusation about the poison gas acquired a huge political dimension, since the federal government was put on the spot and the country's image was damaged.

DER SPIEGEL

Der Giftgas-Skandal

Gaddafi-Partner imhausen

POISON GAS.
In 1989 the magazine caused a great stir when it published its investigation of a German company's construction of a poison gas factory in Libya. *Der Spiegel* thereby solidified its leading position in investigative journalism.

The GM-Volkswagen Case. Early in 1993 automotive industry engineer José Ignacio López de Arriortúa "Superlópez," along with some of his closest colleagues, left the American giant General Motors in Detroit for Volkswagen in Germany. The new employees brought along a score of cardboard boxes full of GM and Opel documents. Some of the documents contained secret details of GM's plans for a small vehicle called the O-Car. Also, on the hard drive of a Volkswagen computer, documents unexpectedly appeared with specifications for a VW assembly plant in Spain that were, for the most part, identical to a GM project titled Plant X. *Der Spiegel* investigated, gathered information, and published several cover stories so reliable that the Hamburg Regional Court concluded in its ruling, "There is no reasonable doubt that the *Spiegel* stories have been of extraordinary public interest and utility." López and his employees were found guilty. They submitted their resignations in November of 1996.

DER SPIEGEL

Der Skrupellose

VW-Manager López unter Verdacht: Industrie-Spionage

Kinderkrebs durch Atomkraftwerke

ESPIONAGE.
In 1993 José Ignacio "Superlópez" and his team moved from General Motors to Volkswagen. *Der Spiegel* proved through its investigations that they'd stolen industrial secrets. López and his employees were forced to resign in 1996.

Investigation and error

In issue 35 of 1985, *Der Spiegel* made one of the most notorious mistakes in its investigative reporting history. It was the Kurt Waldheim story and its claim about the Austrian diplomat's Nazi past. The magazine published a cover photo of a young Waldheim offering the Nazi salute, and a story headlined "We Austrians Vote for Whomever We Please." It said: "The man who wants to be elected president of Austria on May 4 has discredited himself and his country in the eyes of the world. Kurt Waldheim, who was U.N. Secretary General for many years, has effaced from his record precisely that period of his life in which he served in Hitler's Wehrmacht 1 in the war against the Balkan partisans. When Waldheim was attacked by Jewish organizations for that reason, the old anti-Semitism resurfaced: Austrians don't want anybody to awaken them from their fiction. It's a strange country, an impossible country. It's really Germany, though it's called something else. It's a country of disconcerting contradictions–the country of Mozart and the Mozartkugeln, of intensely green lakes and Sachertortes, the country from which came demoniacal Adolf Hitler to destroy Germany and devastate Europe, and from which came Kurt Waldheim to diplomatically assume his post as U.N. Secretary General and help the world keep going."

But the magazine had made a mistake: While the cable message that was the basis of the charge that he was in the Wehrmacht had allegedly been found in Yugoslavia by someone who claimed to be a historian and guaranteed the document's authenticity, it proved to be a forgery. *Der Spiegel* had been taken in and had to apologize to Waldheim. In doing so, Augstein said: "My writers were not the source but the messengers of a bad piece of news."

THE SPIEGEL PHILOSOPHY

The principles behind the magazine's investigative reporting. Its cover stories. Its best-selling issues.

Der Spiegel's past and present have a constant—the lack of marketing studies. Its working premise is different from other magazines: "You can't ask people what they want and, based on those comments, concoct a magazine, for the simple reason that people only know what they want after you've delivered it to them," deputy editor Joachim Preuss told the authors at *Spiegel* headquarters in Hamburg. "Of course we're always open to ideas from all sides. The good thing is that after all these years of earning a reputation as a sociopolitical investigation magazine that uncovers the truth, if there is something to denounce, people call *Der Spiegel* first."

Although the magazine's newsroom has approximately 220 writers, only 10 percent of them are normally assigned to "investigative reporting." This score or so of journalists work in teams of five or six, depending on the article and the beat. "They are the people that give adrenaline to the magazine," said Preuss. "But when nothing unusual happens, they may do stories on education, schools, the water in Germany, even if they're not the sociopolitical subjects that have made us famous." At one point the magazine considered creating a special investigative team, but later discarded the idea because everything would be unfairly concentrated in that elite group. "Then we decided that the whole company would be one big investigative pool. That's why in general the most important investigations, and the cover stories in particular, are done by maybe twenty people, who are never the same ones," Preuss added.

Der Spiegel must sometimes pay for information, but this is not a frequent occurrence. And if it can't be avoided, the editors first take every precaution.

"The offering party's information and motives must be kept strictly at arm's length," said editor Stefan Aust. "When that doesn't happen, errors lie in wait. That's why, in the case of particularly serious stories, first we firmly establish who we got the information from and under what conditions. It's painful to admit that sometimes we don't want to get involved because it's too risky, too dirty." One example: A few years ago a source showed up at the newsroom with information about a sting organized by Germany's intelligence service involving contraband plutonium—a case that would lead to a parliamentary inquiry. That day editor-in-chief Aust called all investigators and writers in and forced them to reveal all the sources they had talked to for the article. Only when it was clear how they'd obtained the information did they start to write the cover story, which was very widely read. "Only with that degree of certainty," Aust summarized, "can risks and possible lawsuits be minimized."

THE POWER OF INVESTIGATION. The journalistic reputation of *Der Spiegel's* investigations was once again reinforced in 2001. In the November 26 issue, the magazine published an extensive article about the terrorist cell that had planned part of the Twin Towers attack from Hamburg. The cover story was later the basis of a book, which is considered the best investigative work on the subject in Europe.

THE magazine TODAY:
HOW ITS DESIGN EVOLVED

It can be stated with certainty that, of the top magazines in the international market, *Der Spiegel* was among the last to modernize its visual style. The Hamburg weekly has appeared in full color only since 1997. Until then, apart from ads and the odd exception, both news and photos were printed in black and white. It has been widely suggested that the change was influenced by the advent of *Focus*, a Munich-based magazine that hit the German market in 1993 with a modern and arresting visual style. Highly successful, *Focus* became a direct competitor of *Der Spiegel* in the newsmagazine sector—and for this reason will be analyzed in depth in the next volume of this study.

In any case, *Der Spiegel* was always rather reluctant to make design changes. Part of its personality is having always placed especial emphasis on writing, investigation, and content. Over the years, almost until the end of the 1990s, its cover stories were laid out in dense blocks of text. Starting to read one was like entering a long tunnel, in which the reader would pass through the subject's various hypotheses before finally arriving at the journalistic synthesis of the story.

Seldom was the text broken up by a subhead or box–a characteristic that, except for the lightening lent by the color photos, the magazine retains to this day. "We think that readers must take their time reading the cover story," said Preuss, the deputy editor. "It's an article that tells a story, and the allure is the story itself, independent of whatever is added to it. People are prepared to read us, particularly if the material is interesting and has context."

The first redesign of the magazine goes back to 1955, eight years after it was born, when its cover was modified. The red stripes across the top and bottom gave way to a border in the same red that has framed the whole cover ever since. Twelve years later, the magazine started using the photogravure printing process, and its size became somewhat smaller. **Then in 1971–that is, nearly twenty-five years after it debuted– the first notable changes to the inside pages were made.** The most significant one, at least visually, was to stretch the headlines over two or three columns, using a more prominent and heavy type. Until then all articles, from the most insignificant

to the most important, had had one-column headlines within the box of text. But these were not the only novelties in issue number 20 of May 10, 1971. The editors also introduced slugs and, more particularly, leads–the small chunks of text below the headlines that summarize the most salient aspects of each article.

New changes took place in 1989, with more space allowed between the lines and with Franklin Gothic type used for the headlines. Broadly speaking, those were the chief design modifications in the magazine until late 1997. Then, **in addition to color, innovations in the order and organization of the news were made.** Nowadays all the main sections–Germany, International, Economy, Media, Society, Culture, Science and Technology– start on a left-hand page and include an internal "cover" of sorts with brief items, thus offering readers an overview before proceeding to the main articles. Besides setting the sections apart, these pages give the layout an appropriate balance, since they alternate short items with the longer stories that follow.

Der Spiegel is one of the publications that have undergone the fewest design changes throughout their history. Here are illustrated its most notable ones.

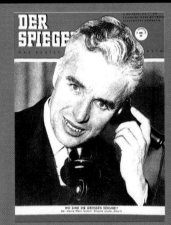

1955

New cover design, including the red border (instead of two bands in that same color) and a new typeface.

1967

Photo-gravure printing and, starting with this number, a slightly smaller size.

1971

First noticeable changes inside: The headlines were now spread over two or three columns and set in heavier type. Slugs were introduced, and also a lead briefly describing the subject of the article.

1989

More space between the lines of text, a new typeface, and more prominent headers. The Franklin Gothic font was now used in the headlines.

1997

The most conspicuous change: The whole magazine was printed in color, and each section started with a small "cover" with short news items.

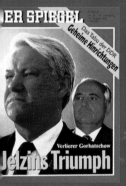

THE CORNERSTONES OF
THE SPIEGEL PHILOSOPHY

Der Spiegel's main editorial guidelines can be found in Die Spiegel-Titelbilder, 1947–1999, edited by Hans-Dieter Schütt and Oliver Schwarzkopf, a compilation of the publication's principles, rules, ideas, and philosophy established by the magazine's previous editors in chief as well as the current editor, Stefan Aust. Here is a summary of the most important:

We don't play politics; we just follow it critically. At times, particularly during the first days of the socialist-liberal coalition, the magazine was accused of being too close to the government. Regardless, Der Spiegel was ahead of other organs of the press when it came time to erode Willy Brandt's image. This is not to say that the publication is now more right-wing than before, since its ideological positions in the 1970s and 1980s have become irrelevant. The fact that Spiegel recently devoted an issue to successful young businesspeople doesn't mean it's moved to the right either, but rather that globalization is effacing the already diffuse national borders. In almost six decades, Der Spiegel has faced off against seven chancellors with differing political ideologies, from Konrad Adenauer to Gerhard Schröder, and has had problems with all seven. Helmut Kohl accused the magazine of "reflecting Hamburg's gutter more than reality." Adenauer advised the public: "Don't read it anymore; save your time and joie de vivre." Helmut Schmidt, on the other hand, spoke of "Augstein's journalistic genius, as well as his passion for freedom and justice" but conceded that "his sarcasm and cynicism are exaggerated." In any event, Augstein set the magazine's political tone in 1947 when he said, "Der Spiegel is a liberal newsmagazine and, when in doubt, a leftist one."

The good and the beautiful of this world do not interest us. "Those who want to find pure entertainment, beautiful models, or handsome men will never find them in this magazine. We try to reflect reality. During thrilling times, the magazine contains more politics. The fall of the Berlin Wall, German reunification, the collapse of the Soviet Empire, Kosovo, the Gulf War, the al-Qaeda terrorist cell that operated in Germany—these are priority matters. When there is no breaking news, as tends to happen in summer, we go for **issues** such as retirement, housing, education, taxes. Certainly the content of a magazine such as Der Spiegel strongly focuses on the subjects debated by society. During political times, there are more political subjects. The art of journalism comes to the fore when nothing is going on: that's the time to think up something that will have an illuminating effect on the public. The art of political coverage is not about reacting to a scandal or an electoral campaign or a war, because that must be done anyway. The art is to continue being political when the thinking and public debate about social reality are oriented toward softer issues."

Sources, sources, sources. That's an inviolable maxim at Der Spiegel. "We cannot tolerate things like 'An important party leader said' or 'according to an official source,' because the reader may wonder whether it's an anonymous quote or a quote from the writer or one of the interviewees in the guise of a 'reliable source.' We always ask ourselves: Where's the document or the report that this information comes from? You start with the premise that it isn't enough to believe someone, no matter how authoritative or knowledgeable or

powerful. If questions arise, you must be able to prove what is being stated, checking with an opposing source and an independent one. That's the key to the magazine's credibility, because this is linked to another of *Der Spiegel's* maxims: **Precision above promptness.** In several stories after September 11, even though we had good information and we ran the risk of other publications scooping us, we decided to postpone publication until we could verify the accuracy of the facts and the credibility of the sources."

We are a watchdog and investigative entity. "Our magazine's basic philosophy is that we can help to change something that hurts society or that isn't going well or that is corrupt. However, despite the desire to participate and shape politics, this must be only an indirect and secondary role for the magazine. We must never use journalism as an instrument of power because, if we do, we'll sacrifice its power to bring about change. Vanity and self-importance can cost us our role as watchdogs and incorruptible analysts. We mustn't confuse exposing things with changing the world. Effectiveness is a function of credibility. When we describe the weaknesses of a nuclear plant, our story is more effective if we haven't taken an opposing position from the outset. We must not deliver opinions but rather investigate, uncover, and clarify facts for readers, so that they can then come up with their own opinions on the subject. We must be realists yet skeptics, nonconformist militants."

invincible spiegel?

Of all the magazines researched for this book, *Der Spiegel* particularly caught our attention with one statistic: the number of publications that were launched to compete with it but failed. Some say that more than fifty magazines fell to the "Hamburg juggernaut." The authors have managed to find close to twenty titles, which means that almost methodically, every two-years-plus, a magazine was launched to compete with *Spiegel* in the newsmagazine sector and lost. Quite a record. Below, some of those magazines and the time they managed to stay afloat.

Kritik der Zeit (Critic of the Times), from June 1950 to May 1951.
Bonner Hefte (Bonn Files), from September 1953 to November 1956.
Mix, from December 1954 to January 1955.
Das Neue Journal (The New Journal), from December 1956 to May 1962.
Plus, from November 1959 to January 1960.
Kontinent (Continent), from March 1961 to August 1961.
Aktuell (Current), from July 1961 to September 1962.
Zeitung (Newspaper), from April 1964 to August 1965.
Deutsches Panorama (German Panorama), from February 1966 to May 1967.
Profil (Profile), from 1966 to September 1968
Dialog, from February 1970 to June 1973.
Puls (Pulse), February 1985 to October 1987.
Tango, from September 1994 to June 1995.
Ergo, from October 1994 to August 1996.

SPIEGEL VS. THE CHANCELLORS

"*Der Spiegel*'s image as a leftist magazine was always a cliché propagated by those who wanted to counter the magazine's influence on public opinion," said media expert Klaus Bolling. The best proof that *Der Spiegel* was and is independent, that it didn't and doesn't answer to any political power, can be found by examining the relationship between the magazine and Germany's seven chancellors over six decades. Many critics maintain that age is making *Der Spiegel* more tolerant, but the evidence indicates the opposite. For instance, when the magazine did a cover story on Helmut Kohl under the headline "The Eternal Chancellor," Rudolf Augstein objected that the interviewee wasn't "particularly sophisticated," leaving it to be inferred that he also wasn't very ambitious or smart. Still, Augstein honored him as the "unity chancellor" in the magazine and outside it, which proves that along with the criticism came praise when he considered it well deserved.

In any case, Kohl always preferred to grant interviews to other, less caustic magazines rather than to *Der Spiegel*, which seemed more aggressive. Just like former chancellor Konrad Adenauer, Kohl accused the magazine of "reflecting Hamburg's gutter more

than reality." At another point, when the then mayor of Vienna, Helmut Zilk, showed Helmut Kohl a *Spiegel* issue during a television program, the chancellor offered this opinion: "Its readers can go to hell. What a waste of money." Nevertheless, the chancellor congratulated the *Spiegel* editor on the magazine's anniversary with this portentous phrase: "That you are able to disseminate your political opinion broadly is a most valuable asset, which I am willing to defend with all my strength."

The magazine's fate was never more intertwined than with Konrad Adenauer. "No other head of state in Bonn challenged *Spiegel* as much as Adenauer," Klaus Bolling wrote. "No other chancellor made Augstein, the thinker, feel as provoked… Augstein adored him and despised him. He suffered from him, physically, and at the same time had strong emotional ties to him." Augstein even described Adenauer's presidential candidacy as "an extravagant coronation act," although he privately compared Adenauer to Winston Churchill and Franklin D. Roosevelt. But it was obvious that the magazine editor could never forget that Adenauer and his defense minister, Strauss, were the ones who'd jailed him for the NATO

maneuvers story. As for Adenauer, he generally put up with the magazine's hostility with dignity. *Der Spiegel* proclaimed for years that Adenauer "had to go," and after he won the parliamentary elections in 1953 with an absolute majority Adenauer said in an uncharacteristic outburst: "There's no way I'd read that dirty, self-destructive magazine."

Despite being just as critical of Ludwig Erhard, *Der Spiegel* never was as hard on him as with Adenauer. And then, with Chancellor Willy Brandt, *Der Spiegel* had what many call "a very special relationship." In 1969 Augstein celebrated the political unity that Willy Brandt was inaugurating, with the joyful expression "The government we were waiting for." The reason was that the chancellor and the magazine had similar views on normalizing relations with Eastern Europe. Brandt's motto "Leftist and Free" inspired many young writers at the magazine. And his slogan "To dare to be more democratic" had an impact in the newsroom itself. "There was a genuine, albeit unstable, relationship between us," Augstein would later say regarding the chemistry between Brandt and *Der Spiegel*. Yet when the chancellor started to lose power, *Der Spiegel* published a cover with the headline "The Monument

ADENAUER. During his administration *Der Spiegel* was charged with treason, and in 1953 he said of it: "There's no way I'd read that dirty, self-destructive magazine."

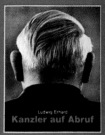

ERHARD. The magazine was more benevolent to him than to Adenauer. However, he was not spared criticism by *Spiegel* and its editorial position, which kept its distance from power.

Crumbles," which led Brandt to call it a "shitty magazine."

On the other hand, former chancellor Helmut Schmidt complained in his memoirs about "the inclination of *Spiegel's* writers to destroy any public figure, from behind the anonymity of the authors, who have a taste for very sardonic jargon." Augstein helped Schmidt out when his administration went through particularly tough times, but *Der Spiegel* didn't hesitate at all to openly oppose him. So when his political fortunes began to founder, the magazine came up with a cover montage with his face in place of Bismarck's and the headline "Let's Throw the Pilot Overboard."

But since he was as courteous as he was brave, Augstein would say ten years later: "I would venture to say that Helmut Schmidt was one of the ten most important national leaders we've had in the postwar period." In turn, with time, Schmidt would also be conciliatory toward Augstein in his memoirs: "He has a passion for freedom and justice… For that he must be praised despite his sarcasm and cynicism, in which he occasionally rejoiced."

BRANDT. Among the most praised chancellors for his position of negotiating with East Germany, he still became angry with the magazine from time to time and had cross words for it.

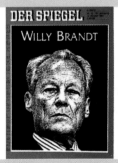

KOHL. One of the chancellors most irritated by the magazine, he accused it of "reflecting Hamburg's gutter more than reality" and said, "Its readers can go to hell. What a waste of money."

THE magazine's spirit

A normal cover investigation ranges between ten and fifteen pages. "In ads for the magazine and in our interviews with other media, we recommend that the public take its time reading it because that's where we throw all our investigative and illuminating efforts," deputy editor Joachim Preuss told the authors. *Der Spiegel* does not, as might be expected, have a special team to investigate or write these stories. "It all depends on the subject itself," Preuss explained. "The people who are trained to do an investigation on education are completely different from those who can come up with an article about, let's say, terrorism or China."

At a time of "zap journalism," a term editor Stefan Aust coined to describe "a reader who has the TV remote in one hand and the cell phone in the other," *Spiegel's* editors emphasize that its cover stories must reflect its role as an organ of criticism with a "politically recognizable" investigative mission. "We must put on the cover what those involved don't want exposed," said Rudolf Augstein. "But we must do investigative journalism, not witch hunts." However, when there are no "hot political issues," the covers assume the viewpoint of "critical observers of social reality." Although its critics claim *Spiegel* practices "machine-gun journalism," the traditional internal directive for the cover story is "do not keep quiet, do not subjugate yourselves to any authority."

In recent years, so as not to become rigidly dogmatic or give the impression of always writing the same story, the cover reporting has provided plenty of historical context. "For instance, when the cover is devoted to the Middle East," Joachim Preuss added, "we'll try to give the war a Biblical focus to be different, to set ourselves apart from the rest. So we'll have to delve into the Bible, explain what the Holy Land is—that is, we go looking for other roots to the conflict, beyond the merely cosmetic ones. If we do an investigation on education, we'll go back in time to analyze what schools were like in previous decades, or when and why education reform in Germany started."

ISSUES. When political, economic, or international affairs are not featured, social issues take over the cover. *Der Spiegel* doesn't publish frivolous material on its cover.

INVESTIGATION. On November 26, 2001, *Der Spiegel's* reportage (right and left) featured its investigation of the terrorist cell that planned part of the Twin Towers attack out of Hamburg. These cover stories usually take up ten or fifteen pages of the magazine.

The best indication that historical research works, that readers don't find it heavy, dates to early 2002. A cover story recounted Germans' suffering when they had to escape from Russia after World War II. "After talking for fifty years about what we Germans had done wrong and criticizing ourselves and painting ourselves inside and out as persecutors, this time we went on to explain why, historically, we had also been persecuted by the Russians," said the deputy editor. "The story idea came from something Günther Grass wrote," Preuss explained, "but the magazine dug deeper into the idea, consulting historians and experts on the subject. The response we received was impressive."

THE TOP 10 BESTSELLERS

ISSUE	COVER SUBJECT	COPIES SOLD
38/2001	The Terror Attack	1,446,000
04/1991	The War for Peace	1,312,000
39/2001	The Terror Network	1,312,000
06/1991	Before the Inferno	1,307,000
35/1991	Yeltsin's Victory	1,307,000
42/1992	Willy Brandt	1,302,000
05/1991	Germans and War	1,282,000
02/1993	The Shameless Society	1,277,000
08/1991	The End of Saddam?	1,257,000
03/1991	Decision in the Gulf	1,254,000

Cover on the attack on the World Trade Center in New York. This was the issue that sold the most copies in the history of the magazine. The events that have the greatest impact on Germans have to do with terrorism and wars.

THE FACE OF THE FUTURE

Although one of Rudolf Augstein's maxims was that a political publication such as *Der Spiegel* must be in opposition, he explained: "But we believe we must do it only 51 percent of the time. In other words, you can't survive on opposition alone, particularly when you can't offer recipes for solutions. It's true that we can't cast aside our critical character, because we're an entity that's committed to investigation, and that sometimes you might take a rather rude tone. But it's also true that if you have nothing to say, it's better not to write at all."

Building on its great tradition and journalistic accomplishments, 2001 was in many ways an extraordinary year for the Spiegel Group. Despite the tense economic situation and the September 11 terrorist attacks, the magazine's circulation went up, although ad volume declined.

Der Spiegel's issue number 38 in 2001, headlined "The Terror Attack: War in the Twenty-first Century," marked a new sales record with 1,446,000 copies. Paradoxically, there were many ad cancellations and, for the first time in years, sales and profits fell below the

previous year's. In this complicated environment the Spiegel Group's expansion into new markets, such as television and the Internet, were successful, particularly considering that the classical publishing business was facing tough competition. But beyond the general economic stagnation, *Der Spiegel's* journalistic prestige was recognized once again when on November 26, 2001, it published an investigation into a terrorist cell that, from Hamburg, had planned part of the attack on the Twin Towers. This cover story later was the basis of a book that critics considered the best European investigative work about the members of the group behind the attack.

Thus was confirmed what the magazine had written in 1997, in the fiftieth anniversary issue: "In 2,649 issues, 414,120 pages, and 1,793,966,873 copies sold, 3,677 staffers, among them 734 writers, 10 editors in chief, and one publisher were witness to Western Germany's history." The Hamburg newsmagazine, as it is called by those who don't want to mention its name, has at least made a spot for itself in the Bonn Hall of

History. The magazine was born in a war-devastated country whose residents, subjected first to Nazi censorship and then to the occupation forces, were captivated by the investigations and denunciations of a magazine that was nonconformist and irreverent toward the establishment.

In 2000, the young *Spiegel* journalists interviewed Rudolf Augstein and asked him to define his and the magazine's success. He answered: "A bit of being, a bit of seeming, a bit of luck."

"In what order?" the interviewers fired back.

"At any rate, no more seeming than being."

"And luck?"

"Yes, luck is also necessary. I had it, and it was no small amount."

CONTEXT. The editors say that, aside from current events, historical subjects are the ones that work best with the public. *Der Spiegel* always tries to offer readers a historical context, even in news stories.

From anonymity to Bylines

From the outset, Rudolf Augstein preferred *Der Spiegel's* articles to appear without bylines. It was the same idea *Time* had: to give the impression that the magazine was written by one person for one other person.

It was Stefan Aust, the current editor, who dared to go against this strong tradition. In his first fortnight as editor, he ordered a test issue with the authors' names under each article. The opposing argument had always been that, in general, several writers worked on a story, although they suddenly realized that wasn't really so. The premise was that if a long story was signed by only one person, it would damage *Spiegel's* aura as a powerful writing machine with great investigative and analytical capacities.

Despite strong resistance, inroads began to be made into anonymity. Some authors and columnists were excellent, and still are, but some injustice also resulted. "A sort of second-class society emerged," Aust explained. "Some remained loyal and obedient, writing wonderful articles but languishing in anonymity. Others, who for the most part came from other publications, made sure their contracts guaranteed them a byline. Finally, one day we decided to break with tradition altogether. Some thought it would be the end of the world. But it wasn't."

CHAPTER
3 LIFe

LIFE, WHICH WAS TO BECOME THE MOST POPULAR MAGAZINE IN THE UNITED STATES, THEN LOSE THAT POSITION AND DIE AWAY, WAS FIRST PUBLISHED ON NOVEMBER 19, 1936. WITH IT BEGAN A WHOLE NEW ERA IN THE NEWS AND GENERAL INTEREST SECTOR. AFTER LIFE, THE WORLD WAS SEEN IN A DIFFERENT LIGHT. AFTER LIFE, JOURNALISM SHOWED THE FACTS IN A DIFFERENT WAY. THIS CHAPTER EXPLAINS WHAT DEFINED THE MAGAZINE'S STYLE AND HOW A PHOTO ESSAY WAS PUT TOGETHER. IT ALSO ATTEMPTS TO EXPLAIN WHY, AT A TIME WHEN SALES STILL SURPASSED 5 MILLION COPIES, LIFE CEASED TO PUBLISH.

THE MAGIC LIFE STYLE

With the photo essay, the magazine imposed a new language that revolutionized the world of journalism. Here are its beginnings, and its formula for success.

In February of 1936, after spending two months in Cuba with his new wife, the former Clare Boothe Brokaw, Henry Luce returned to New York and quickly gathered his most trusted associates. His proposal was a forceful one: They absolutely had to start a photojournalism magazine, and they absolutely had to handle it in the strictest secrecy. Although he had been thinking about a photo magazine for a long time, it's rumored that it was his bride–a journalist and playwright, former editor of *Vanity Fair*, and Luce's wife since November of 1935–who really encouraged him to relaunch the project.

It's also true that several factors fed Luce's imagination and prompted his decision to publish the new product. The first factor was that sensibility that sets editors apart and makes them shine, that allows them to detect a niche of opportunity where others see nothing. At Editorial Atlántida–founded in Argentina in 1918 and an icon among Spanish-language magazines, with such titles as *Para Ti, Billiken, El Gráfico*, and *Gente*–many remember founder Constancio C. Vigil telling editors, "You must be able to see under water." That was why he'd given his company the name *Atlántida*. "It was chosen as a beacon to lead the way. In a place where others see only fish, we must be able to see the Lost Continent." And in *Life's* case, Luce was able to see beyond the fish. He detected, thanks to the development of the cinema during the first decades of the twentieth century, the enthusiasm generated by stories told in images. He also detected that images had become familiar and were attracting people more and more every day; that the public already had an educated eye and wanted to see and know more. He definitely detected that a magazine that showed news stories the way

people were used to seeing them at the movies, in sequence and within context, was needed.

The second factor was a techno-logical advance of the mid–1920s, as the miniature photo camera and 35-millimeter film came into more frequent and professional use. (See "The Leica and the Birth of Photojournalism" overleaf.) Its advent gave rise to an enthusiastic genera-tion of photographers and a conta-gious passion for photojournalism.

The third factor that propelled *Time's* leader to embark on his project was another technological advance, this time in the area of printing: the development by Donnelley & Sons Company, the Chicago printers whose presses were used by *Time*, of a quick drying ink that ensured high-quality, high-speed photogravure printing on glossy paper. This was an impressive step forward in the art of printing and marked the unfolding of a new concept in the publishing industry, a concept of which *Life* was a prime exponent.

LIFE

NOVEMBER 23, 1936 **10** CENTS

THE FIRST COVER.
The photo, taken by
Margaret Bourke-White, is
of a dam in Montana. *Life's*
first issue consisted of ninety-six
pages, cost ten cents, and had a
print run of 466,000 copies, which
quickly sold out.

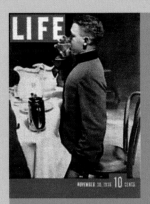
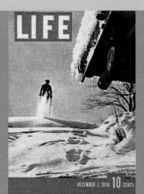

WEST POINT
NOVEMBER 30, 1936

SKIING
December 7

CANTERBURY
December 14

BABY CARRIAGE
December 21

AMERICAN BALLET
December 28

THe Leica anD THe BirTH OF PHOTOJournaLism

Time's birth in 1923 coincided almost exactly with the appearance in international journalism of a phenomenon known as photojournalism. And this phenomenon–which would later lead to the launching of innumerable magazines with popular appeal, particularly after the birth of *Life*–had its origin in one of the most important technological developments in the publishing industry: the emergence of the *miniature camera*. This diminutive, easy to use, and portable device soon became the photographers' faithful companion. Until then, they had been forced to carry heavy and inconvenient equipment from one spot to the next in their search for news. The *Ermanox* was one of the first miniature cameras used by photographers. Introduced in 1924, it used glass plates and a big lens and could work under low-light conditions. However, the camera that led to a true revolution in journalism was the *Leica,* also launched in 1924.

The Leica actually changed journalism's optics. In fact, this camera almost did away with the static and formal tradition that was typical of news photography up to

then. In Germany, one of the great cradles of photojournalistic innovation, critics baptized this fast evolution in capacity and technique with the term Foto-auge or photographic eye: *photography as mechanical vision.* They claimed that photography had ceased to be a mere contemplation of objects and could now subtly emphasize, through the photographers' eyes, their point of view and perception.

According to the 1995 book *Eyewitness: 150 Years of Photo-journalism* by Richard Lacayo and George Russell, the Leica was never intended for use by professional photographers. It was invented in 1913 by Oskar Barnack, an designer at the Leitz optical works in Wetzlar, Germany, who was also an amateur cinematographic buff. He originally conceived of the Leica as a small, relatively uncomplicated device for testing 35-mm movie film, but he soon realized it had greater potential. World War I interrupted the camera's development, but in the 1920s Barnack returned to his innovation. Loaded with a spool of 35-mm film that was linked mechanically with the camera shutter, the Leica allowed a

photographer to shoot rapidly and repeatedly from eye level. The images captured on film could then be magnified in the developing process and ordered in a sequence resembling action. This miniature camera also benefited, in its conquest of photojournalism, from the perfecting of extremely fast film, which allowed users to record sequential images in a hundredth and then a thousandth of a second. To this was added a complementary innovation: the invention of the flashbulb in 1925.

With all these advances, the idea emerged that photography, particularly action photography, could be viewed as a representation of what the photographers themselves saw. So the act of taking photos became a progressively more intuitive activity, an inspiration of the moment. Photographers–photojournalists–gained prominence; they were not limited to recording an event, but rather contributed their creativity, spontaneity, and experience.

It was in Germany that photo-journalism first took shape. According to Lacayo and Russell, the publication *Berliner Illustrirte Zeitung*

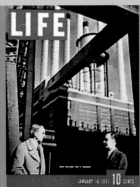

SIDENT ROOSEVELT
ry 4, 1937

JAPANESE SOLDIERS
January 11

HENRY AND EDSEL FORD
January 18

LION SCULPTURE
January 25

(BIZ) came out in 1929 with what is considered to be its first true photo story: the silent existence of the Trappist monks at the monastery of Notre Dame de la Trappe, done by the Hungarian photographer André Kertész, a master at capturing the drama of everyday scenes. The German *BIZ*–then edited by Kurt Korff, who later, as we shall see, would join *Life's* ranks–was one of the first publications in the world to devote two to five pages of photographs to a single subject.

Another German, photographer Erich Salomon, who is considered a photojournalism pioneer, surprised the industry in 1928 with his "stolen pictures." With a miniature Ermanox, the wellborn Salomon moved freely in European diplomatic circles and discreetly photographed summit meetings to which lesser mortals had no access. The tabloid *Graphic* of London dubbed him the "candid camera." The photos he took in Berlin's criminal courts, where cameras were banned, also became famous. Hiding his Ermanox underneath a bowler in which he had made a hole for the lens, he created quite a stir with his images of the trial

of a police killer. His reputation and fame grew dramatically, and his devotees and imitators multiplied. In the United States, for instance, a photo of Ruth Snyder's execution by electric chair in 1928 became a photojournalism landmark. Its author, photographer Tom Howard, had gone into the execution chamber with a hidden miniature camera tied to his ankle.

Like other German Jewish photographers, Salomon was forced to leave Hitler's Germany. *Life* offered him work in the United States, but he declined and decided to stay behind with his Dutch wife in The Hague. In 1940, when Hitler invaded the Netherlands, Salomon was arrested. He died in Auschwitz in July of 1944.

PIONEERS. Tom Howard took the first "stolen shots" of an electric chair execution. On the right, Kertész and his images of the Trappist monks.

YESTERYEAR'S CELEBRITIES.
Little by little, the emerging movie industry and its stars started to alternate with military and political issues and personalities on the magazine's cover. Here are some of the famous female Hollywood stars who were featured between 1939 and 1955.

BETTE DAVIS 1939

KATHARINE HEPBURN 1941

SHIRLEY TEMPLE 1942

LAUREN BACALL 1944

JUDY GARLAND 1944

"DUMMY." Seven weeks before the launch, 15,000 copies of a prototype issue were printed without a title to maintain secrecy. This is how Luce presented the magazine to advertisers (above). Below, a cover of the publication from which the name *Life* was bought.

CONFIDENTIALITY :
THE FIRST KEY TO SUCCESS

Everything was ready. Everything was set. It was all there: the printing technology, suitable cameras, photographers eager to learn and demonstrate their skills, a world to be shown, and people eager to see it, to know it, to marvel, to be touched.

In the world of New York journalism, there was a buzz about the need for a photo magazine. But what kind? With what format? With what content? With what editorial approach?

Time magazine wasn't removed from this climate. The top staff also knew that if a competitor found out about their project, it could beat them to the streets, snaring the novelty and the business. So they proceeded with absolute discretion and caution.

Under the Luce team's plan, *Time* was to be used as a screen to cover up the development of the new product. Their concealment strategy was justified: they had to face threats from *Newsweek* and other possible competitors. The excuse of improving the photos in *Time* was perfect. As related in *Time Inc.: The Intimate History of a Publishing Enterprise,* in 1934 the newsmagazine tapped Daniel Longwell as special assistant to the managing editor, John Billings. According to what Luce told the staff, his task was "to introduce more pictures… in a unique *Time*-like manner."

A year later in 1935, when the photo budget increased, Alfred Eisenstaedt arrived from Germany and joined *Time's* staff. Eisenstaedt was one of the best European photographers. He'd worked for the Associated Press and other agencies, in addition to doing a *Time* cover during the Ethiopian war.

As *Time* started using more photographs, an associate was assigned to Longwell: thirty-four-year-old Harvard graduate Joseph J. Thorndike Jr., who, like his boss, was interested in the new art of photojournalism. Joining them as an advisor was Kurt Korff, the former editor of *Berliner Illustrirte Zeitung* and one of the most renowned photo editors in Europe, who had also been expelled from Germany for being Jewish. This team, under journalist John S. Martin, made up the Experimental Department charged with coming up with a new publication.

However, all these hirings generated suspicion that *Time* was "up to something." Rumors circulated not only within the company but also outside.

Something had to be done, so Luce and his men decided to use this strategy: first, to speed up the project; second, to continue using *Time* as a screen; and third, to handle the rumors with a statement. To quiet the staff, this memorandum was circulated within the company: "The current activity on the 51st floor may give rise to the query, what's up? Something is up, and until further notice it should be considered an office secret. The Experimental Department is working on the idea of a picture supplement for *Time.* The less said about it, the better."

No matter. As work continued, it became harder and harder to keep it secret. The project's evolution generated needs that required the services of other companies in the world of journalism, like getting photos and finding out about their availability in the future, once the magazine was launched. Undoubtedly, this could attract the attention of the competition's editors. To avoid this and keep the project secret, *Time* came up with a complicated business screen. First, it signed an agreement with the Associated Press (AP) to use all its photo services. Then, through its subsidiary Pictures Inc., Time Inc. became the sales agent for AP photos not destined for use in newspapers. Of course, Pictures Inc. did not intend to sell photos. Its true goal was to get in touch with national and international agencies without generating sus-picion about the project and to make sure that the new magazine's editors had unlimited access to news photos from all available sources.

Of all of *Life's* contributions to the publishing industry, this is perhaps the first one that editors must keep in mind when they start a project: confidentiality. It doesn't ensure the product's success later on, but it is the beginning, the first signal, the first light that indicates within the company that whatever is in the works is being taken seriously. In addition, confidentiality acts like a pact, an alliance that strengthens the spirit of the small group in charge of the work, and it makes its participants feel important, as if they make up a select team chosen from among the best of the staff to meet the next financial and editorial challenge the company faces. On the other hand, the secret means great responsibility for all those who share it. It forces them to offer their best on behalf of the project: creativity, effort, desire for success. Those who are part of this pact feel that the success of what they are involved in is linked to their own success and professional growth.

But selecting such an outstanding team to develop a new editorial formula isn't easy. Generally speaking, secrecy and confidentiality and a low profile are not among our qualities as journalists when it comes to talking about our work. Our passion for our profession leads us to talk plenty about ourselves and what we do or did or will do, as if we were the news. That professional defect has been accentuated by the advent of television and the excessive urge to be in the limelight that afflicts newscasters. So it falls to the editor to bear the responsibility of assembling a team that is professionally qualified and, at the same time, able to keep things under wraps.

For this reason, to maintain secrecy, some media enterprises now develop their new projects in separate buildings, cities, even countries. This would have been considered excessive in 1930, as were the presentation Time Inc. made of its new product and the secrecy it kept about the magazine's real name. In a meeting with potential advertisers, *Time* presented a publication called *The Show-Book of the World,* with a line at the bottom of the page that said: "Actual name will appear on Vol. I, No. 1."

VIVIEN LEIGH 1946

GINA LOLLOBRIGIDA 1951

AUDREY HEPBURN 1953

RITA MORENO 1954

GRETA GARBO 1955

The selection of the name generated controversy within the company, and rightly so. In a first message to editors, the title *Dime* was suggested (after the proposed newsstand price of the new magazine). This was rejected because of its similarity to *Time* in both spelling and pronunciation. The words *Scene, Seen, Pictures,* and others were also tossed around. Finally, at the suggestion of Luce's wife, *Life*, a name used then by a magazine of humor and art criticism with a circulation of 70,000, was selected. *Time* bought the title for $92,000 and kept its last issue on the newsstands until the day before launching its new publication.

Although still unnamed, *Life* was introduced by Luce himself to the potential advertisers' market. The publisher had been working on a prospectus throughout June of 1936, while the members of the Experimental Department carried on with the difficult task of coming up with the impressive product they sought. In the last paragraph of the document, *Life* already anticipated enthusiastically the spirit, purpose, and new service it would provide to its readers:

> ❝ To see life; to see the world; to eyewitness great events; to watch the faces of the poor and the gestures of the proud; to see strange things–machines, armies, multitudes, shadows in the jungle and on the moon; to see man's work–his paintings, towers and discoveries; to see things thousands of miles away, things hidden behind walls and within rooms, things dangerous to come to; the women that men love and many children; to see and to take pleasure in seeing; to see and be amazed; to see and be instructed."

> ❝ Thus to see, and to be shown, is now the will and new expectancy of half mankind."

PRESENTATION.

Page 2 features a photo, highly symbolic, of a baby being born, with the caption *"Life Begins."*

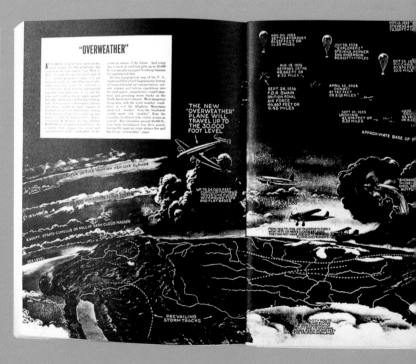

ILLUSTRATION.

A two-page spread on the upper atmosphere exemplifies a type of explanatory illustration used in almost every issue.

❝ To see, and to show, is the mission now undertaken by a new kind of publication . . . hereinafter described."

Luce also made reference to the timing and the window of opportunity in which the magazine hit the market. Although thousands of photos could be seen every week, until then no magazine had set out to become a compendium of "the cream of all the world's pictures." That would be the main goal of *The Show-Book of the World*, which also promised to search the world for the best photos, to edit them taking form, history, and drama into consideration, and to publish them on high-quality paper to attain a "complete and reliable record."

Also, according to the prospectus, the magazine's content would be centered on two key elements:

1 "The biggest news that is best recorded by the camera."

2 "Some subject of major current interest and significance." This element would be one of "Revelation taking you intimately into the life of a famed personage, be it Shirley Temple or the Pope; or intimately into the inner workings of a celebrated institution, such as The Jockey Club, The Japanese Army, Alcatraz, Vassar...."

In all, the magazine would offer between forty and forty-eight pages of editorial material, along with some twenty pages of ads. An estimated two hundred photos per issue would be published which, along with the most important issues, would record "the shifting mores and fashions," theater premieres, and Hollywood movies. Finally, the prospectus made a promise that, in time, became a true challenge for all who worked on the magazine: "that while *Show-Book* readers will usually know what to expect they will never be quite sure that they will not get a whacking surprise."

PHOTO NEWSCAST
"Life on the American Newsfront" was the name of the section that, through photos, recorded events taking place around the country.

And it was a whacking surprise.
Volume 1, number 1 of *Life* magazine was launched on November 19, 1936, as a ninety-six-page wonder, a publishing innovation that informed and entertained with joy and enthusiasm. Its photos exuded a sense of immediacy that was unprecedented in the media world. With a ten-cent newsstand price, the entire run of 466,000 was immediately sold out, and news dealers called desperately asking for more copies. The symbolic second page was titled "Life Begins" and showed a newborn held by the ankles above the text "The camera records the most vital moment in any life: Its beginning...."

that Northwest city, they didn't hesitate for a minute to run it in the first issue and in a way quite different from what was initially envisioned.

It so happened that Bourke-White, who had joined the company in 1929 as a *Fortune* photographer, was assigned to take pictures of the Montana dam for a spectacular article in *Life* about America's vigorous and growing industrial sector. Since she was a master at such tasks, it was expected that her talent would produce a terrific study. Indeed it did. Young Margaret fulfilled expectations and produced a spectacular architectural photo for the cover, but the rest of the images she took to portray the daily lives of workers and their families surprised everybody,

This play on words was the lead-in to the first issue. The cover featured a photo by Margaret Bourke-White that showed, below the *Life* logo in white letters on a red ground, an image of Fort Peck Dam in Montana. The photo introduced the issue's main story on pages 9 to 17 about one aspect of the New Deal, President Franklin Delano Roosevelt's plan to counter the Depression. The editors had intended the story for an issue down the road, but when they saw Bourke-White's work on

particularly her editors, who created with them a new human-interest cover story that showed how a Wild West city was built. It was the beginning of the *Life* style. But it was more: it was the beginning of a new type of magazine story that soon would be called the photo essay, a way of seeing and capturing and showing reality that filled, and still fills, thousands of pages in publications throughout the world. In 1983 Time-Life Books published a book titled *Photojournalism* that qualifies

Bourke-White's article in the first issue of *Life* as a milestone: "She made her cover, but she also stayed on to record something else. Around Fort Peck had sprung up a cluster of shanty settlements with their false fronts and dusty rutted streets, their tough migrant workers and scruffy taxi dancers thronging the bars on Saturday nights. Here was something that Americans had not seen for many years—a glimpse of the frontier suddenly reopened. The *Life* editor in charge, John Shaw Billings, spotted the potential in Bourke-White's pictures—the take, in photojournalists' jargon. And in that first issue of *Life* he laid out the first photo essay in the

photos of the most important events around the country. Another double-page story titled *Overweather* showed a map of the upper atmosphere where commercial airlines hoped someday to fly. A standout among the regular sections, giving character to the magazine every seven days, was The President's Album, a sort of visual diary of the chief executive's weekly activities; *Camera Overseas*, an international photographic news report; and *Life Goes to a Party,* which took its cameras to the first of many galas it would record in its pages through the years—this one in honor of the British ambassador to France.

The approach was clear: with *Life* and its cameras, readers could go

production of *Victoria Regina,* the new Broadway hit, and learned intimate details about Helen Hayes, its star, through her photo album. Film was also featured in the first issue with *Camille,* starring Greta Garbo and Robert Taylor. Elsewhere in its pages were the epic of a one-legged man who had climbed the steep crest of a mountain, an article about life in the Soviet Union, and a two-page spread of blowups detailing the habits of a lethal insect, the black widow spider.

THE FIRST ESSAY. This is how Life published the photos taken in Montana by Margaret Bourke-White. In nine pages there emerged the unknown human face of a city that grew along with the construction of a dam. Thus was born a new type of journalistic narrative, which would later be known as the photo essay.

form known today—organizing several subelements within an overall theme."

So the inaugural issue already possessed the tone and style that would become a magazine trademark. Its layout followed the beat of the news and events, mixing superb photo pieces with regular sections that offered intriguing, surprising photos. After the cover story came the first of these sections that readers would regularly encounter: *Newsfront,* a selection of

where they'd never gone, see what they'd never seen, cross boundaries and borders. In this first issue, two of the pages took readers to a school in Chinatown, and five pages took them to exotic Brazil; from above, they saw for the first time the country house and love nest of Edward VIII and Wallis Simpson, saw impregnable Fort Knox, saw Rockefeller Center and the NBC radio antenna; four pages took them to Kansas, to painter John Curry's house; they got a backstage look at the

THE newsroom setup

Life organized its staff along the same hierarchic lines that *Time* magazine had instituted thirteen years earlier; that is, the newsroom was divided into several departments: music, books, film, theater, arts, religion, nature, sports, science, fashion, editorials—seventeen main departments in all. In turn, these departments were grouped into divisions in such a way that film and theater, for instance, fell under entertainment, while art and religion were under culture. Each division was headed by an editor and a researcher, with assistant editors and researchers reporting to them.

Beginning: The week's work started to take shape when each department sent the section editor a summary of proposed stories, a list of completed articles, and a progress report on pieces in the works.

Mock-up: Next, each section editor met with the chief editor to produce a mock-up for that week's issue, page by page. It had to have a certain balance, a rhythm, a sequence that held the reader's interest, with strategic pauses between the peaks of excitement. Thus if the main story ran long, as a memoir or a scientific article might do, lighter subjects were sought to leaven the issue. Or if a news story was very stark and had hard-hitting photos, the science or education or religion department followed with something to soften its edges.

Current Events:

The news department was responsible for gathering newspaper clippings that could possibly lead to a story and sending each to the appropriate department. If the section was interested in a subject, the researchers in that department would send it to the chief of national or foreign news, who in turn would assign the work to *Life's* correspondents around the globe.

Photography: For *Life,* unlike its older sister *Time,* the core of the magazine was the photo department. Its editor was in touch with all the photographers who worked for *Life.* He handed out their assignments. He served as their liaison with the editorial departments. His job was to provide guidance to the photographers, set out in detail the coverage requirements, and keep tabs on their work and whereabouts. He then selected the material for each story and, at press time, sent the photos to the art department for its editor to lay out. The writers entered the process later, composing the text for all the photos on special yellow paper that showed the exact number of characters and lines that text should have. Next, researchers verified every word and, if the meaning seemed correct, placed a red dot on top of each. Further, to check the accuracy of its contents, *Life* retained a variety of experts, such as historians, geographers, educators, and psychologists.

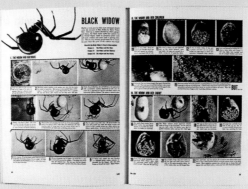

VISUAL IMPACT. Looking at the various two page spreads of *Life's* first issue juxtaposed, one can appreciate the magazine's graphic power. Until that time no publication had used photo layouts in such an organized way, leading the reader's eye. The issue included four color pages and made a great splash.

one Team anD one OBJecTive: PHOTOJournaLism

Its innovative organizational structure did not in itself ensure the magazine's success. The corporate history *Time Inc.* talks about the editorial difficulties the magazine faced initially. For the first editors, most of whom came from *Time,* mastering the art of photo editing wasn't easy. Nor was it easy to find a way to tell a visual story in a thorough and coherent way with a beginning, a development, and an end. The European photo magazines and the Sunday papers' rotogravure sections made no effort to link one photo to another. *Life* had to. That was its strength. Its success depended on how it presented the stories.

How were these challenges overcome? By attacking on several fronts. The marriage between text and image in a newsmagazine was a new and difficult one. John Billings remembered: "Most of the first editors and writers on *Life* had worked on *Time,* and they instinctively brought over their favorite words and rhythm of *Time* writing. As managing editor, I sought to eliminate all traces of the so-called '*Time style* ' and to develop a fresh literary form, clear, simple and factual, which would blend smoothly with the predominating pictures." The difference in styles was rooted in function. While in *Time* the text was the most important element and carried the substance of the article, the sole role of text in *Life* was to accompany the photographs, which conveyed the core story. In one way, this made writing for *Life* more complicated, not less. The format required that all captions fit perfectly within a set space, forcing writers not only to create spare and direct prose but to do it in a prescribed number of characters.

Still, those obstacles could be overcome. Not so with the lack of photos. At first *Life's* editors had thought the photo news services would provide their raw material. They were wrong. In any given week, they found, the agencies produced a bare handful of distinctive images—for instance, one car accident looks a lot like the next—and rarely did these photo services offer a sequence of pictures that told a coherent story. *Life* needed much more. It needed photographers who combined a mastery of the art and technique of the camera with the mentality of a reporter. It needed professionals who could capture a news story in photos with a beginning, a development, and an end.

Therefore, the recruiting and day-to-day directing of the photo staff ended up being a job almost as important as the managing editor's. For that job, in 1937 *Life* hired Wilson Hicks, the Associated Press photo editor. Hicks stayed until 1950, and in those thirteen years he molded a whole generation of photographers, many of whom attained fame. After he came on board, the quartet of original staff photographers, Bourke-White, Eisenstaedt, Thomas McAvoy, and Peter Stackpole, were augmented by such talented professionals as Hansel Mieth, Carl Mydans, John Phillips, W. Eugene Smith, and William Vandivert. On the freelance side, the fine work of Robert Capa, Fritz Goro, Wallace Kirkland, and Walter Sanders graced the pages of *Life* during its first year.

The trio of Billings, Longwell, and Hicks was responsible for the successful development of the *Life* photo formula that Henry Luce himself named the "photographic essay." Luce first applied the term to a piece Alfred Eisenstaedt did on Vassar. His photo sequence of the women's college, Luce said, left "mountains to be written about Education in general and Vassar in particular. It is not an account of Vassar. It is a delightful essay on Vassar. But it is vital. It does communicate. Both to those who know about girls' colleges and to those who do not, it tells something about Vassar and Education and America and Life in 1937. And it tells the kind of thing that only the most skillful (and now obsolete) literary essayists have hitherto managed to tell in words."

LIFE

INDOOR TENNIS AT VASSAR

FEBRUARY 1, 1937 **10** CENTS

HISTORIC COVER. In issue number 11 of January 2, 1937, the cover story featured the women's college Vassar. Here for the first time Luce defined *Life's* photographic style as The Photo Essay.

THE STORY. The photos were the work of Alfred Eisenstaedt and, according to Luce's encomium, the sequence "tells the kind of thing that only the most skillful (and now obsolete) literary essayists have hitherto managed to tell in words."

THE SEQUENCE. The article occupied eight pages, organized thematically. It showed an overall view of the college, the dorm rooms, the study halls, the fun times, and the fashions the girls wore at school.

LIFE'S PHOTO essay formula

In 1965 the Museum of Modern Art in New York organized a major show titled *The Photo Essay.* Before *Life,* this term was unknown. But what exactly is a photo essay? What is its method? Is there a formula? Characterized by many experts as one of the most complex end products in photography, the essay is based primarily on organization. This organization attempts to take several related photographs on a particular theme and array them within a structure, transforming a collection of individual elements into an extensive and complete look at the subject, and endowing it with more depth and coherence than a single photo or several shots scattered through a paper could ever achieve. Putting the essay together requires the skills of several people: editors, photographers, and designers. The subject itself may be anything–an idea, a person, an event, a place– and the organization may be chronological or topical. The key is to make the photos together form a whole that enriches the viewer's understanding of the subject.
In *The Magazine in America, 1741–1990,* one of the most meticulous and important studies of the history of U.S. magazines, authors John Tebbel and Mary Ellen Zuckerman refer in chapter 17 to *Life's* formula:
"The picture essay was a new and different method of communication, one which took first place in the nation's visual life until the coming of television. Editors learned that pictures could be used in several ways. They could stand by themselves or be used with captions and texts in various combinations, with the text subordinate. The point of photojournalism was to communicate, the photograph not necessarily being used for itself alone…. In *Life*, according to Stephen Heller, the picture story was described as an "act," a reference borrowed, no doubt, from the theater. It implied that the magazine was a stage. And so it was…. *Life* went even further than the European journals to institutionalize the photographic essay by allowing greater page runs…. *Life* responded well to the needs of 20th-century men and women for concise visual information…."

Surely one of the best and most detailed explanations of the photo essay belongs to Caroline Dow, a journalism professor at Flagler College in Saint Augustine, Florida. In 1979, at an annual meeting of the Association for Education in Journalism and Mass Communication in Houston, Dow presented an exhaustive study that began by pointing out that "*Life* distinguished itself by providing readers with a system of visual reporting that anticipated and planned the coverage of events."

She noted that, although *Life* had been envisioned as a magazine that, after a meticulous selection process, would make use of photographs previously published in other media, the weekly soon used up the available photos and news. It then started generating its own stories and photos. The result was what *Life* called a "mind-guided camera," a photo formula that grew out of three concepts:

1 Group Journalism. All the professionals who had had their initiation at *Time* magazine were well accustomed to its particular sort of teamwork.

2 Condensed style. Also characteristic of the *Time* system, and of the mindset of those who'd worked there, was the emphasis on a condensed news format.

3 Documentary approach. The favored work style was that of Roy Stryker, who had been director of documentary photography for the Farm Security Administration. Stryker believed that, before going out on a shoot, photographers should immerse themselves in the subject so they could understand the people or events they were photographing.

These three concepts, then, oriented the approach called the "mind-guided camera," which basically was a cooperative project between editors and photographers who decided to do a story, researched the subject, and prepared a shooting script. This script was designed to help the photographer understand the types of photos needed, their purpose, and the tone of the piece. Obviously, the script could not anticipate what would occur onsite, but it served as a guide that the photographers themselves could build on, which generally meant shooting many more frames than originally envisioned. As Dow put it, "*Life* elevated the photograph to an equal partnership with words."

MARILYN MONROE. First featured on the cover on April 7, 1952, as portrayed by Eisenstaedt, Monroe later occupied the same spot on ten other issues, sometimes with a new flame (photo 2, with Yves Montand), sometimes alone or with other actresses (photo 4, with Jane Russell). Five of the Monroe covers were published after her death.

THE 1950s. Sophia Loren was one of the European actresses selected most often for the cover of *Life*. She was first featured on August 22, 1955, then at least five more times. Americans were captivated by her distinctive style, and the magazine reflected that on its cover. She continued to appear there through the 1960s.

THE 1940s. Rita Hayworth was an icon of American cinema in the 1940s. She was first featured on the cover of *Life* on July 15, 1940 (upper left), and several other times through 1947 (left). Back then, before television, *Life* was one of the publications that gave the most space and prominence to Hollywood stars.

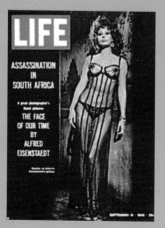

THE MAKING OF THE SHOOTING SCRIPT FOR A PHOTO ESSAY

Professor Caroline Dow studied the process the magazine followed and pointed out that "the essence of the *Life* method was that a photographic feature had to be defined in words first. Then the idea was researched. When the idea or experience was clear to everyone, a script of possible scenes would be prepared and approved." After the section editor approved the list of photos to be shot, a photographer and writer were assigned to the job, which they would carry out as a team. "The specific *Life* scripting formula," she added, "has not been published. Perhaps it was not considered necessary to record it because it was so well understood by those who practiced it." However, Dow analyzed the way in which Robert L. Drew, the weekly magazine's first bureau chief in Detroit, taught the formula in his workshops between 1949 and 1951. Dow took oral histories from workshop participants and combined them with documentary research to discern just what *Life's* photo essay formula was all about.

Her analysis reveals a list of eight types of photos that had to be on the rolls of film shot by photographers after researching the news value of the story undertaken. Here are the eight types of photos that made up the scripting formula:

1 An introductory or "overall" photo, usually a wide angle, often an aerial.

2 A middle-distance or "moving in" shot—a sign, a street, a building.

3 A close-up, usually hands, face, or detail.

4 A sequence or how-to shot.

5 A portrait, usually with an evocative background.

6 An interaction shot of persons conversing or action portrayed.

7 The signature picture—the decisive moment, the one picture that conveyed the essence of the story.

8 The clincher or "goodbye" shot signifying the end of the story.

"By thinking about the picture story in these terms," Dow concluded, "a photographer would prepare himself to see a story. Prethinking, or previsualizing a story, encouraged a photographer to shoot different views and angles of the same scene. The event was more likely to be covered in greater depth since the photographer, having run through the obvious pictures, was prepared to see the unusual or unique picture as well as to recognize the signature shot when it happened, even though it might not be what was planned."

This formula, ideal in theory, led to practical complications and frequently generated friction between editors and photographers. As the Time-Life book *Photojournalism* noted, the editor shaped the photographer's story "by deciding which pictures he would use, and how he would use them: large, small, in sequences; for dramatic effect or for information, to inspire humor, anger, curiosity, disgust…. This set up a great tension between editor and photographer—the one clamoring for better, more exciting, more 'sequential' and meaningful pictures, the other moaning that his best creations were discarded or subjected to a constricting layout. In a sense, both were right: the layout of the pictures had become nearly as important as the pictures themselves."

COUNTRY DOCTOR

THROUGH WEEDS GROWING RANK IN AN UNKEMPT DOORYARD, DR. ERNEST CERIANI OF KREMMLING MAKES HIS WAY TO CALL ON A PATIENT

HIS ENDLESS WORK HAS ITS OWN REWARDS

PHOTOGRAPHS FOR LIFE BY W. EUGENE SMITH

The town of Kremmling, Colo., 115 miles west of Denver, contains 1,000 people. The surrounding area of some 400 square miles, filled with ranches which extend high into the Rocky Mountains, contains 1,000 more. These 2,000 souls are constantly falling ill, recovering or dying, having children, being kicked by horses and cutting themselves on broken bottles. A single country doctor, known in the profession as a "g.p." or general practitioner, takes care of them all. His name is Ernest Guy Ceriani.

Dr. Ceriani begins to work soon after 8 o'clock and often continues far into the night. He serves as physician, surgeon, obstetrician, pediatrician, psychiatrist, dentist, oculist and laboratory technician. Like most rural g.p.s he has no vacations and few days off, although unlike them he

has a small hospital in which to work. Whenever he has a spare hour he spends it uneasily, worrying about a particular patient or regretting that he cannot study all of the medical journals which pour into his office. Although he is only 32 he is already slightly stooped, leaning forward as he hurries from place to place as though heading into a strong wind. His income for covering dozen fields is less than a city doctor makes by specializing in only one. But Ceriani is compensated by the affection of his patients and neighbors, by the high place he has earned in his community and by the fact that he is his own boss. For him this is enough. The fate of thousands of communities like Kremmling, in dire need of "country doctors," depends on whether the nation's 22,000 medical students, now choosing between specialization and general practice, also think it is enough.

CONTINUED ON NEXT PAGE 115

THE BEGINNING. Smith's photo, together with the headline, quickly shows the task that Doctor Ceriani performs. It is considered a photographic summary and a good example of an introduction to a photo essay.

THE DEVELOPMENT. Over four double pages, the story shows the newsmaker and his hectic humanitarian work. They express the full range of the life of a country doctor.

THE END. The town, his house, a break— the photos bring the story back to the main character and his measured satisfaction in a job well done. It's the final frame, as in the movies.

"country doctor": an exemplary photo essay

On September 20, 1948, *Life* published a photo story that made history. Titled "Country Doctor," it visually recounted a day in the life of a general practitioner in rural Colorado. The article covered eleven pages and was considered the best example of a photo essay during the magazine's early years. Indeed, with time, the story became entrenched in people's imagination. If you said "country doctor" in the 1950s in the United States, you were talking about the man photographed by *Life*. Many people didn't even remember his name, but they did remember the concerned and concentrated face pictured in the magazine. If the story had great impact among readers, it had even more in the publishing world. It showed a new way of "working" subjects, of following them and sharing their lives to get exceptional photo results.

This story had two main characters: Dr. Ernest Ceriani and photographer W. Eugene Smith, who managed to convey with his images the moving work that a medical professional did in a rural town day after day. When the story was reported, Ceriani was thirty-two years old and had just settled in Kremmling, Colorado, a small town with 1,296 residents spread throughout the area's ranches.

The presentation of the story shows clearly how to do a photo essay with beginning, development, and end. On the first page, the opening photo introduces readers to the subject, Ceriani, walking across the fields wearing a hat and carrying the traditional black bag, on his way from one house call to the next. In this image the photographer manages to show readers the occupation of the story's main character (the bag, and the jacket and tie, backing up the headline), the mobile nature of his profession (striding, professional tools in hand), and the vast and desolate area he served (weed-grown ground, brooding sky)–definitely an opener that summarizes it all. The four double page spreads that follow take readers to the heart of the article, showing the diverse, hectic, and overwhelming job of a country doctor. Smith depicts the moments in which Ceriani delivered a baby, treated two accident victims, and worked on a child's dislocated elbow, all within the same morning, and then in the afternoon did a round of house calls to check on several patients, including an elderly man on his deathbed. In those eight pages Smith develops the subject and does so full-speed-ahead, with an avalanche of images of great reader impact. Then comes the end, with a calm and relaxed double page spread that offers a panoramic view of the town center, a photo of the doctor's family at a local parade, a shot of the doctor's house-hospital, and a splendid finishing touch: a full-page photo of Ceriani, dressed in scrubs and wearing a white cap, leaning on the kitchen counter with a cup of tea in his right hand. A hard day at work has come to an end. Ceriani embodies, and Smith conveys, the image of a task accomplished. In a book about his work called *Let Truth Be the Prejudice*, Eugene Smith said he took photos of the doctor day and night, delivering babies, comforting patients, and binding wounds as well as in moments of relaxation for the eleven-page spread. "I spent 4 weeks living with him. I made very few pictures at first. I mainly tried to learn what made the doctor tick and what his personality was, how he worked and what the surroundings were. I had to wait for actuality instead of setting up poses. I simply faded into the wallpaper and waited." "By fading, by being in the background," Smith explained, "I was able to catch expressions and emotions. I moved quietly and did not open my mouth. The doctor was terrific, a grand fellow, which leads me to say that on any long story you have to be compatible with your subject as I was with him."

This zealous work by Eugene Smith was no accident. It was one of many essays he shot for *Life* over the seven years he worked at the magazine: 322, to be exact. In 1948 alone he photographed 31 stories like "Country Doctor," quite a praiseworthy feat if you keep in mind that Smith had to spend many hours getting to know the people he was about to portray. His main goal was to get natural and spontaneous images that, at the same time, had symbolic significance. Smith was also a prolific war photographer. In three years in the Pacific he covered thirteen island invasions including Tarawa, Saipan, Guam, Leyte, and Iwo Jima, and went aloft on bombing raids over Tokyo and Eniwetok. Wounded in Okinawa, he spent two years recovering before returning to *Life*. He retired from the magazine after a disagreement over the way the editors used his photos for an essay on Dr. Albert Schweitzer's humanitarian work.

THE WORLD OF LIFE

Actresses and actors, princes and princesses, presidents, works of art, memoirs, writers, wars. Events and people seen through *Life's* particular editorial style.

"

There was magic in *Life.* What magic? By definition, magic is indefinable….

"The magic of *Life* is obviously connected with the magic of pictures…. There are many aspects to this magic. One of them is that a picture will invite my attention to a subject which otherwise, at any given moment, I would ignore. Today I may not be in a mood nor feel the need to read the finest article about the Prime Minister of Britain but I will stop to watch him take off his shoe and to look a little more closely at his face and to wonder what manner of man he, and the British, are….

"I think if we are to mount up again, it has to be on the wings of picture-magic." (Henry Luce, 1958)

And his photographers did fly, just as they had in the magazine's early days. They flew to take readers to an intimate world, inside the White House, inside the Hollywood studios, inside the homes of the famous and the palaces of royalty. They showed another face of celebrities, with and without makeup. They saw and showed a unique world.

In her 1968 book translated as *Photography and Society,* the Franco-German portrait photographer Gisèle Freund analyzed from a psychological standpoint the magazine's thematic approach and the reasons for its success. In the chapter "American Mass Media Magazines," Freund wrote: "Like his Presbyterian forebears, (Henry Luce) wanted to educate the masses. His magazine's success was based on thorough study of mass psychology. Man is above all interested in himself: any human and social condition affecting his own life will move him. When conditions are miserable, he must be given the hope of a better future. From such reasoning flowed the nine pages on the New Deal program in Montana, which promised work for a large group of poverty-stricken people. The pictures of children struck a sentimental chord, while the photographs of the President symbolized the father-protector. The lives of actresses and movie stars showed that talent would always be rewarded; and the *Life* reader was taught that science performs miracles. The adventures of a one-legged man filled the need for sensation; the photographs of Brazil, the taste for the exotic. Finally, the garden party photographs of aristocrats brought the lives of the elite into everyone's home.

"The world reflected in *Life* was full of light and had only a few shadows. It was ultimately a false world, one that inspired the masses with false hopes. It is equally true, however, that *Life* popularized the arts and sciences, opened windows onto hidden worlds, and in its own special way educated…."

"*Life* was enormously successful and was read by the masses."

Could Luce have had this reasoning in mind when he launched *Life* in 1936? It is undeniable that in the 1940s, 1950s, 1960s, and even later, the magazine was known worldwide. It began a news-and-general-interest publishing sector characterized by the spectacular visual nature of its articles. And in the United States alone its circulation topped 8 million.

LIFE

U.S. MISSILE SCRAMBLE
WHAT WE DO—AND TRY TO DO—TO RECOUP

EUROPE'S HIGH-BORN SWEATER GIRLS

SOUTHERN EDITOR'S R.I.P. FOR DIXIE

ELIZABETH TAYLOR AND DAUGHTER, LIZA TODD

NOVEMBER 4, 1957 **25** CENTS

REG. U.S. PAT. OFF.

ONE MORE FOR LIZ TAYLOR. The cover of November 4, 1957, was the third of twelve in which *Life* featured Elizabeth Taylor, this time inspired by the birth of Elizabeth Frances, her daughter with husband Mike Todd. She was the woman with the record number of *Life* covers. Besides celebrities, the cover also featured topics in the news, politicians, military men, discoveries, and works of art.

ornado

Flipping for Ivan

Musical Feat

Show Stoppers

To See Life
... TO SEE THE WORLD;
TO EYEWITNESS GREAT EVENTS

CATCHING THE MOVING BODY

Ballerina Patricia McBride gave a private performance for Gjon Mili in 1962. Using the staccato flashes of stroboscopic light, Mili illustrated in a five-part series on the human body the range of movement permitted by the shoulder socket.

THINGS HIDDEN BEHIND
AND WITHIN
THINGS DANGEROUS TO C

IMPRESSIVE PHOTOS. Storms, shows, spectaculars, and space--these photos, compiled from a special fiftieth anniversary issue, are a clear example of the way Life reflected events as they happened, in original productions, or captured with special lenses. Its double-page spreads were the stage on which photography showcased its works.

LIFE and its magic stage

Its subject matter was unlimited. The magazine could tackle topics ranging from the contents of small boys' pockets to a multichapter series on Western civilization or the world's religions. It had stand-alone photos and photo essays, big names and no-names, memoirs and investigative stories. Among the many topics that *Life* took to its temple, its stage, were actors, accidents, storms, presidents, art, the human body, teenagers, royalty, space, housewives, budding stars, children, animals, works of nature, how-to information, what people wear, the gravity of war, the craziness of fashion. *Life* took a look at the world, took a look at its country, its people, and showed the extent of human feelings as nobody had before.

Tebbel and Zuckerman, in *The Magazine in America,* mention a phrase by Ralph Ingersoll, considered one of *Life*'s creators: "Pictures are for rich or poor, without regard for race, class or creed or prejudice, speaking the same language. . . . You use one vernacular to a truck driver, another to a bank president. But the truck driver and bank president will stand shoulder to shoulder to watch a parade. Only in the subject of pictures will their interests draw apart." Ingersoll was a Time Inc. executive during 1935 and 1936, when the *Life* project was developed. When it was launched and became a great hit, he felt cast aside by Luce, who took the helm. Ingersoll then quit and sued, claiming intellectual property rights. Controversy aside, *Life's* photos had universal appeal and spoke to all levels of society in a way that words could not. And its photographers won unprecedented fame. Such was the case of Margaret Bourke-White. According to Tebbel and Zuckerman, "She exemplified all that was glamorous about it, and her work struck responsive chords among readers. Her curiosity, her determination to get to the heart of a situation with her camera, her endless fascination with machines, wars, cities, and people–all these were reflected in her pictures and found a resonance among those who saw them."

The range of the works of *Life* photographers often surpassed the limits of traditional reporting. The special look they fixed upon a particular event or personality turned the photos themselves into news. Any survey must mention W. Eugene Smith's photo essay on the country doctor. Or Gjon Mili, an electrical engineer who abandoned his profession to become a photographer, did pioneer work with strobe lights, and took incredible shots that froze the poetry of movement in a split second. Another standout was Dmitri Kessel, who captured in color the majesty of Europe's cathedrals. Or Nina Leen, who with her measureless love for animals produced some of the most touching series on the subject. Or Fritz Goro, with his extraordinary capacity to capture and illustrate developments in the world of science. Other photographers remarkable for combining news and human interest were Lisa Larsen and Cornell Capa. Larsen's portraits were distinguished by their exceptional warmth, while Capa, brother of the well-known Robert, did touching essays on such subjects as the maltreatment of mentally retarded children or the five missionaries killed by indigenous people in Ecuador. All of them helped to create "the magic of the *Life* style."

BIOGRAPHICAL ALBUM. Jackie at 23; John Lennon at 24 and Frank Sinatra at 27 with their first wives and firstborn children; Brooke Shields at 13, Jane Fonda at 22, and Marlon Brando at 24; a trio of well-known people in rarely seen situations: Fidel Castro in pajamas, Desmond Tutu at breakfast, Margaret Thatcher painting; Princess Diana nodding off during a performance.

Private Life

One of the magazine's keys to success was taking readers everywhere, even the most private and reserved places. That curious eye went into palaces, homes, and bedrooms to capture unique and memorable moments of well-known people in rarely seen situations. Over the years, many of these photos used at the time to illustrate news events became true biographical albums that showed unseen aspects of famous people or recorded unforgettable moments in their careers. In 1986, to commemorate its fiftieth anniversary, *Life* published a special edition of 400-plus pages under the title *Half a Century of Life in America.* Several of its photos are reproduced here. They provided a peek at Princess Anne and Prince Charles of England in 1956 when they were six and eight years old, and examined the Buckingham Palace classrooms; at the first Beatle son, Julian Lennon, when he was two; at Frank Sinatra in 1943 having breakfast in his New Jersey home with his wife and three-year-old daughter Nancy; or at Jacqueline Bouvier sunbathing during a July 1953 visit with the Kennedy clan at Hyannis Port two months before her wedding.

This "magic of the *Life* style" was so strong, so appealing, that few refused to appear on the stage of its pages. Here is how Tom Griffith, a veteran *Time* journalist who later became managing editor of *Life*, described the phenomenon: *"Life,* with its success, gathered around itself a high-spirited staff, full of talent, cock-sure of itself, and to those of us on *Time* magazine, riding the same elevators to a different floor, enviably glamorous. Starlets, not yet able to get nationwide attention on television talk shows, would do anything to get on the big cover of *Life*…. Studios would delay release of their films if *Life* would promise them a spread; Broadway musical producers assembled their casts in full costume for expensive "photo call" rehearsals in hopes of coverage. *Life*'s attention was just as important to major political figures, and to generals in wartime, who gave its photographers, artists and correspondents special status. Margaret Bourke-White witnessed the German shelling of Moscow from the rooftop of the American embassy, and Harry Hopkins [FDR's confidant and troubleshooter] was happy to be the courier who took her pictures back to New York."

THE PRIVATE LIFE OF A LEGEND

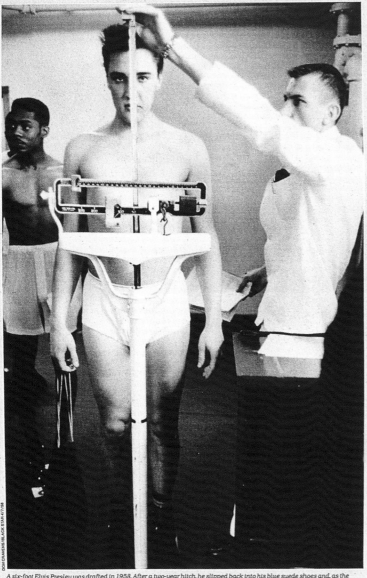

A six-foot Elvis Presley was drafted in 1958. After a two-year hitch, he slipped back into his blue suede shoes and, as the grandest greaser of them all, sold 500 million records with a voice as sweet and powerful as raw honey and white lightning.

INTIMACY. Clark Gable dancing with Marilyn Monroe; the weight and height of Elvis Presley; Caroline Kennedy's wedding. The magazine took readers into their idols' private worlds.

*T*he dizzy blond was a sensation even as a walk-on—with that shape, who needs a script? Astoundingly, Marilyn Monroe was even more fascinating when her roles allowed her comic genius to emerge, and she could spellbind millions the way she lit up her dance partner Clark Gable.

SURPRISE PHOTOS. Fred Astaire with his dancing shoes; Pablo Picasso with a saber; Albert Einstein undergoing a study of his brain; comedian Bob Hope backstage.

TROUPER OF THE LIGHT FANTASTIC

OFFSTAGE

COSMIC MIND AND COMIC GENIUS

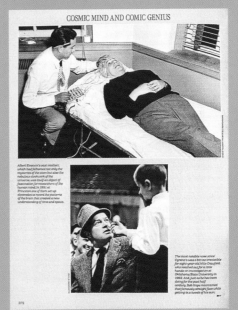

1947   1956   1961   1961   1962

LIFE's special eye

For *Life's* editors the first priority was keeping their readers well informed. But it was important, too, that the information be visual and be conveyed in an easy, clear, and, above all, interesting way. So most of the stories were first conceived from the graphic point of view. What mattered was getting the photos. No photo, no article. This mindset made editors sharpen their wits and focus all their creativity to come up with images, to connect them, to give them continuity, to view stories as sequential or linked. In this, *Life* led the way: over the years, its formula of "creating" news was imitated by many publications around the world.

Among the most memorable images of daily life published by *Life* were the group photos that became a trademark of the magazine. These images featured, in 1957, the fifty assembled aspirants to the Miss America title, in 1961 the fourteen best arms in the NFL, and in 1971 the 1,500 people it took to run Disney World in Florida on a given day –an image replicated ten years later when 5,000 people were needed.

Revisiting important stories or personalities over the years through photos also became a classic feature of *Life*. For its tenth anniversary in 1946, it came up with a report on the people who had figured in the first edition. Its readers were thus able to see what had become of the baby photographed in the delivery room in 1936. Later, in another anniversary issue, the magazine returned to Kremmling, Colorado, to check on Ernest Ceriani, the famous "country doctor" from 1948.

The magazine's photographic eye had no blinkers and scrutinized every last detail of the habits of the men and women of the time. Thus it brought onto its stage, into its pages, daily subjects so simple that it took a little thought even to recognize that they might be news. The different types of saunas, the right way to shave, step by step, or how to smoke without looking bad–these stories were photographed and edited in such a way that it was impossible to pass over them. Out of insignificant subjects, *Life* got impressive photo sequences. Its articles created customs, trends, fashion. For instance, in a 1945 article that described what movie stars carried in their purses, *Life* showed the need for purses with more room. Months later, after World War II and the shortage of materials was over, the purses created by designers became larger than ever.

1964

THE LIZ TAYLOR ALBUM. The first cover with her image came out in 1947. From then on, Liz was ever present: when she won the Oscar in 1961, when she turned forty, with Richard Burton, as Cleopatra in her best-known movie. Her twelve covers are a record.

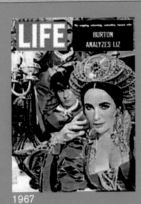
1967

1972

famous LIZ

"Producing *Life,* Luce was heard to say, **was like putting on a Broadway show every week.**" Right from the first issue with its scenes from *Camille,* the magazine made movies, and movie stars, one of its bastions. Elizabeth Taylor, for instance, was featured a dozen times on the cover and hundreds of times inside. Readers were able to see her when she was fifteen years old, when she fell in love and got married, when she played Cleopatra, at home with her children, in bed, in her living room, being kissed or crying. In the magazine's eyes, Liz was The Woman in Hollywood. She had even more covers than Marilyn Monroe, who took the spot eleven times, five of them after her death. But the magazine didn't focus on just these two. From Rita Hayworth to Meryl Streep, every movie star one can think of was willing to pose for *Life:* men and women, the famous and the not-so-famous, the eternal and the ephemeral. The magazine also devoted considerable coverage to the filming of the greatest box-office hits of the day: *An American in Paris, Oklahoma, The Ten Commandments, Doctor Zhivago.* Just as important were the lavish spreads on royal weddings and baptisms and engagements, or the adventures and amours of the rich and famous. But always through a different lens, with a particular and intimate focus, making readers feel a privileged part of the scene.

STAGED EVENTS. *Life* photographed the assembled Miss America candidates, and the massed employees of the new Disney World; it delved into famous people's purses. When it turned ten (cover, far left), it interviewed the boy whose birth was featured in the very first issue of the magazine and took him a cake.

LIZ THE MOTHER. This report's left-hand-page opening shows Liz with husband Mike Todd introducing their daughter Liza, her third child. The magazine always kept abreast of her artistic and domestic vicissitudes.

LIZ AND MIKE'S TINY COVER GIRL

LIZ AT FIFTEEN. Shot at the beach in 1947 by Bob Landry, this image was part of a cover story published on July 14 of that year. Taylor was fifteen.

LIFE LOOKS AT THE HUMAN BODY

In the magazine's first issue, under the headline "Life Begins," *Life* published an image of a newborn in the delivery room. In time this photograph not only epitomized the beginning of the magazine, it pointed the way to investigative photojournalism—the discovery and evocation of the human body. Never before had a general interest and mass circulation magazine presented such a topic in such a manner. Besides being a pioneer in coverage of the atom, laser beams, geophysics, and space, *Life* paid special attention to medical science, sending journalists to clinics, labs, and operating rooms everywhere news was in the making. Thus the magazine kept its readers abreast of the advances taking place in the world of medicine, whether in general research or new treatments.

Putting these stories together wasn't easy. It was necessary to win the trust of doctors and patients, who generally were unaccustomed and even reluctant to have their pictures published. And at first, the same thing happened with readers, who complained more than once about articles that were "too strong" for their taste. Such was the case in 1938 with "The Birth of a Baby," which reproduced some frames of a film produced by the American Committee on Maternal Welfare and endorsed by professional organizations that included the American College of Surgeons. Before publishing it, *Life* assured subscribers that the story, unprecedented for a general interest magazine, was conveniently placed in the center of the issue so it could be taken out if parents wanted it kept from their children. But no degree of prevision was enough. The magazine was banned in thirty-three cities, and the authorities confiscated thousands

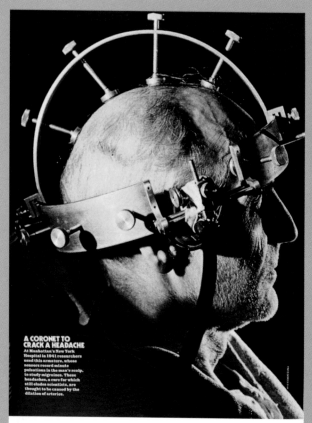

HEADACHE HELMET. Photographed at New York Hospital in 1941 during research on the origin of migraines, this crownlike contraption incorporated sensors that monitored pulsations. The photo had great impact.

FIRST BABY. The photo published in the magazine's first issue was a foretaste of reportage to come. Over time, *Life* devoted many pages to shots that its photographers would get in delivery rooms, laboratories, and research centers.

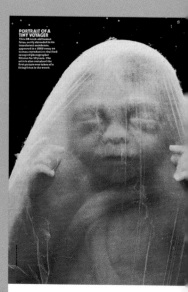

LIFE IN UTERO. This groundbreaking photo of a twenty-eight-week-old fetus inside the womb was the work of Lennart Nilsson, who specialized in medical photography.

of bales of copies. Although many readers backed this publication, there were some that condemned it without further thought. Among them was a reader from Caldwell, New Jersey, who wrote that she was dumbfounded by the story, which she considered a great affront to everything that constituted good taste and a true betrayal of all womankind. The subject went on to become one of those with the most repercussions in *Life's* history.

Regardless, the magazine continued to cover medical advances. Also in 1938, photojournalist Hansel Mieth captured with the camera the first images of a giant machine that helped four polio victims breathe: the "iron lung." Three years later, in 1941, the magazine witnessed a newsworthy experiment at New York Hospital: the placement of an armature on a man's skull with sensors that tried to discover the origin of migraines.

But in 1965, twenty-seven years after "The Birth of a Baby" led to scandal, *Life* published the most impressive and best-known photo essay in history, which included a photo of a live fetus inside its mother's uterus. This was a story about human reproduction done by photographer Lennart Nilsson, who worked the subject for ten years. To achieve the photo of a twenty-eight-week-old fetus, Nilsson, a medical photography expert, was aided by a scanning electron microscope. This device was used by Nilsson to explore and photograph areas in the human body that had never been seen before, and to come up with other astonishing shots—for instance, the first photos of red blood cells, at 10,000 times their true size, which *Life* published in 1970.

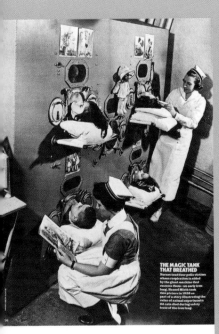

ARTIFICIAL LUNG. This 1938 photo shows how this giant machine helped four polio victims breathe. The photographer was Hansel Mieth.

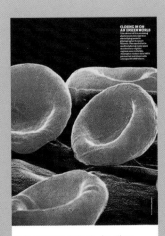

RED BLOOD CELLS. Another feat by Nilsson was this image of red blood cells, photographed through a scanning electron microscope and published in *Life* at 10,000 times life size.

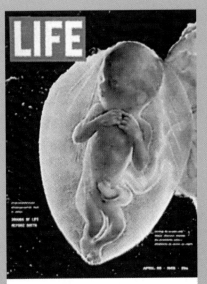

LANDMARK COVER. The first images of a fetus in its mother's womb were published in the April 30, 1965, issue. Photographer Nilsson worked on the human reproduction story for ten years.

1942. December 28
Raphael's Madonnas

1944. December 25
Christmas Art

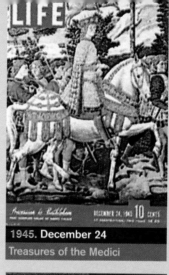

1945. December 24
Treasures of the Medici

1948. December 27
The Art of Giotto

1953. December 28
The Great Churches

1954. December 27
The Art of Brueghel

1956. June 4
Civilization

1956. October 1
Ancient Egypt

LIFE LOOKS AT ART AND CULTURE

At first *Life* was almost exclusively a photo magazine. Words took a decided backseat. That is, perhaps, why the most important editorial question in 1938 was whether *Life* should include whole written stories. Some editors were opposed, arguing that this would go against the basic concept of a magazine devoted to photography. However, they were confronted by a solid argument from the advertising agencies: the contention that *Life*, being a magazine that could be read quickly, didn't hold on to readers long enough for them to be adequately exposed to the ads. This approach overlooked the fact that both captions and text blocks in the magazine represented a substantial amount of reading material. Luce himself thought

that the advertisers' argument was false but had to be accepted. He decided then that each issue would include at least one lengthy article. The first was a biographical piece on James A. Farley, president of the National Democratic Committee, written by journalists Joseph Alsop and Robert Kintner. Over the long term, this was a wise decision for the magazine's future and stature, since it allowed it to publish the work of important authors, or the memoirs of international figures such as Winston Churchill, Harry S. Truman, and the duke of Windsor.

Life took the same special care with prose as it did with photos. It had to be written skillfully and therefore required top-notch writers. One of the most versatile and productive was Robert

Coughlan, who had joined Time Inc. as an apprentice writer at *Fortune* magazine in 1937, after graduating from Northwestern University. In 1943 he went to *Life* and was text editor for six years. Other members of the writing team were John Thorne, who distinguished himself by the poetic touch he gave to photo essays; Robert Wallace, who wrote sentimentally and with a great sense of humor; Maitland Edey, who was famous for writing about the white-footed mouse; Ernest Havemann, who was a good general writer; and Earl Brown, the first black writer on the staff, hired on the strength of a memorable article on Joe Louis.

Life also offered writers a unique spot in the magazine. In the 1940s and 1950s it published the writings of some of the

49. December 26
e Sistine Chapel

1951. December 25
The Art of Tintoretto

THE GREAT SERIES They were published sequentially and their goal was to acquaint readers with the great masterpieces and legacies of the past. Special series on the Egyptians, Greeks, and Romans (right) were produced, among others. Hemingway's *The Old Man and the Sea* appeared in *Life* in its entirety before it was available in bookstores.

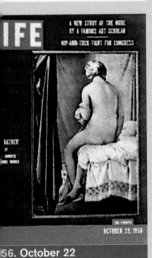

56. October 22
des in Art

1961. December 15
Chartres Cathedral

PAINTINGS AND ARTISTS. The magazine was a pioneer in the mass dissemination of Renaissance masterpieces. Its Christmas issues, which generally were characterized by art reproductions, became a publishing staple of the month of December

most important English-language writers—Evelyn Waugh, Graham Greene, Alan Moorehead, Robert Penn Warren, Carl Sandburg, James Michener. In 1952 *Life* did something that the world of journalism had yet to do when it published a book, *The Old Man and the Sea* by Ernest Hemingway, in its entirety, in a single issue, before it came out in hard covers. And in the late 1960s and early 1970s, it ran several long pieces by Norman Mailer.

The magazine's extended series were particularly memorable. They were arranged in careful sequence and, through the use of impressive photographs, aimed to bring readers close to the great masterpieces of art and the high points of our cultural heritage. The first series was

"The History of Western Culture." This was soon followed by the spectacularly successful "The World We Live In." Published in thirteen parts from December 1952 to December 1954, it was the cooperative effort of a large team of leading photographers and artists and 255 consultants. The circulation department, which had reacted coldly when the series were announced, was surprised to find that every time the series' illustrations made the cover, they increased newsstand sales, which disproved the theory that "only pretty girls sell magazines."

For its part, art had a prominent place in the pages of *Life* from the very first issue. It has been estimated that between 1936 and 1972 the magazine spent around $30

million to reproduce masterpieces and was the first mass circulation publication to show the great works of the Renaissance in full color. For instance, in 1949 it sent photographer Frank Lerner to Rome to reproduce Michelangelo's frescos in the Sistine Chapel, which were published in the Christmas issue that year. Several years later these photos, along with others in the files, were enlarged, framed, lit, and exhibited in art museums and galleries in the United States and other countries, in addition to being shown in Time Inc.'s Reception Center. These shows had a great turnout and the Sistine Chapel photos became part of the Vatican pavilion at the New York World's Fair in 1964–65.

Churchill's memoirs

BEGINNING
IN THIS
ISSUE

The Second Volume of

WINSTON
CHURCHILL'S
WAR MEMOIRS
"Their Finest Hour"

FEBRUARY 7, 1949 20 CENTS
YEARLY SUBSCRIPTION $6.00

As soon as the war ended, new fighting erupted, this time in the media. The battle was over who would land the memoirs of the great war protagonists. Without a doubt the most sought-after, the most pursued, the "star" memoirs were Winston Churchill's, particularly after it became known that he'd started to write them. The press put so much pressure on him that he, on behalf of the trust set up for his heirs, sold the unwritten memoirs outright to his friend Lord Camrose, owner-editor of *London's Daily Telegraph.* So it was not Churchill but Camrose that *Life* had to deal with. But the magazine wanted the top prize, and it pressed on, patiently and decisively playing all its cards.

In early 1946 Luce had visited the British leader at Chartwell, his country home. Luce, as volume 2 of *Time Inc.* recounts it, "admired his host's paintings and Churchill asked him to choose one for himself. Luce was delighted with a landscape of the grounds but offered a mild suggestion: Wouldn't it be enlivened by the introduction of a few more sheep in the foreground? The artist, far from being offended, said he would be happy to oblige." A few months later the painting crossed the Atlantic to Luce's house, with a note from the artist: "I hope you will admire the sheep. They are certainly a great improvement upon the two miserable quadrupeds which first figured in the landscape." Luce wrote back and took the opportunity to press, albeit elegantly and cautiously, the issue of the memoirs: "….the picture delights me. It hangs on my office walls and is the first and only picture there. I look forward to living pleasantly with it for many a year and expect my son to treasure it and carry it safely into the 21st century. How brightly then will burn the fame of its author, when civilization will have known

that it was saved by his efforts and by his eager love for all that is not barbarous."

Besides *Life,* other American publications were pursuing the memoirs, including the mighty *New York Times.* To resolve the matter, Camrose traveled to New York, first making clear that the memoirs would go to the top bidder and that the bidding for U.S. serial rights alone, sold separately from book rights, would begin at $1 million. In the end, the *Times* and *Life* joined forces to produce a winning bid of $1.15 million, with *Life* kicking in $750,000 and the *Times* the other $400,000. In return Churchill would produce five volumes, between 750,000 and a million words.

The agreement was signed in June 1947, but first several hurdles had to be overcome, most of them generated by the author himself. Churchill didn't want to bother with a contract and would have been happy with a simple letter of agreement. Obviously, this wasn't quite enough for the American media executives. Luce himself had to intercede and justify his employees' insistence on a contract. He wrote to Churchill: "The delays have often put a considerable tax on our mutual patience….Part of the fault may lie in the character of the American nation which Burke found to be contentious and litigious. The British seem to have maintained a happy custom over many years of doing things by gentleman's agreement or by letter." Finally a contract was executed, but not before several unusual issues were resolved. One was Churchill's rejection of a clause that precluded him from writing for any other magazine; Winnie protested that he didn't want to lose his freedom. He also managed, during the years of writing, to get *Life* and the *Times* to pay for six winter vacations in Morocco or on the Côte d'Azur. One of the most delicate

COVERS AND MEMOIRS. Although they were the most promoted ones, Churchill's memoirs were not *Life*'s first. Edward, Duke of Windsor, started the series in 1947. General MacArthur also published his.

THE MOST AWAITED.
Churchill's *War Memoirs* were begun on April 19, 1948. The second part (photos) came out in the issue of February 7, 1949.

MEMOIRS TIMES THREE.
Churchill in 1946 was already being pursued by *Life* for his memoirs. The duke of Windsor, shown with his wife Wallis Simpson, published the second part of his account in 1950. Former President Truman's memoirs appeared in 1955.

questions was what would happen if the British statesman died before completing his memoirs. In the course of contract negotiations, *Life* publisher Andrew Heiskell and Julius Adler of the *Times* went to Chartwell to discuss the terms. Churchill interpreted this as a pretext to check up on his health. As *Time Inc.* tells it, "he put on a great show of health and vitality, jumping up on couches to pull pictures off the walls and leading his guests on a very strenuous walking tour of the grounds." As he saw them to their car, he tapped his chest and said, "The body is sound, the body is sound."

Life started publishing Churchill's *War Memoirs* in the April 19, 1948, issue and printed excerpts from the six volumes intermittently until 1953. These weren't the magazine's first memoirs, but they were the most heavily promoted. Earlier, on December 8, 1947, *Life* had begun publishing the early memoirs of Edward, duke of Windsor, three installments titled "The Education of a Prince." Later came General MacArthur's memoirs, President Truman's, and many others. Unquestionably, such memoirs were a *Life* trademark and created a broad readership, which would not otherwise have been reached, for the writings of people with something important to say.

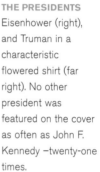

THE PRESIDENTS Eisenhower (right), and Truman in a characteristic flowered shirt (far right). No other president was featured on the cover as often as John F. Kennedy –twenty-one times.
The first was in 1957, when he was senator (top row, second from left). His wife, in turn, was on the cover nineteen times.

THE FAMILY ALBUM

JOHN-JOHN AND CAROLINE AS BABIES. Both were cover subjects. John-John was also featured on his first birthday. The Kennedys fascinated the public.

THE MURDER AND THE MEMORIAL

SEQUENCE. After the shock wave caused by the 1963 assassination, the magazine devoted three consecutive covers to the event and issued a special memorial edition.

Ever since its inaugural edition, in which the feature The President's Album first appeared, the magazine had devoted special attention to the chief executive's image. In 1936 the editors said that the section would be a sort of visual diary that would emphasize the personality at the center of the nation's life. The same thing happened with its cover: from Franklin Delano Roosevelt on, none of the men who occupied the White House was left out. John F. Kennedy made the cover the most times, twenty-one in all, while his wife, Jackie, was featured there nineteen times. Of the other presidents, Dwight D. Eisenhower appeared twenty times, Richard Nixon fifteen times, and Lyndon B. Johnson thirteen. All of them, without exception, were photographed inside the White House. And unlike other publications, Life went out of its way to show in its photographs the personalities of its subjects, with all their qualities and quirks, their manners and mannerisms. In other words, they did it "in Life style."

The magazine did its first presidential cover in 1937, and from then on it showed all aspects of Franklin Delano Roosevelt: resolute, informal, and, above all, confident. Confidence was the main trait of Roosevelt's administration, a trait he even managed to transmit to the nation in wartime through his radio programs, the "Fireside Chats."

Of course, Life photographed him during these broadcasts, during his family gatherings, and even in his private study. One man was behind the presidential photographic style that made its debut with Roosevelt: Tom McAvoy, one of four photographers on the magazine's original staff. At a time of formal photos with magnesium lights, McAvoy set the norm of unposed coverage within the presidential residence, a tradition continued by all his colleagues thereafter. Harry Truman was featured playing the piano or dressed in one of his florid Hawaiian shirts. Dwight Eisenhower, after his heart attack, came out in pajamas with the phrase "Much better, thanks." Johnson and Nixon, Reagan and Carter, each was captured in photographs that portrayed his personality as well as his position and the problems he faced.

But none of the presidential couples attracted Life's attention as much as John F. Kennedy and his wife, Jacqueline. Between them, they were on the cover forty times. Life started to feature them together there in 1958, two years before John became president. Their first cover after the election, published on November 21, 1960, showed them radiant in victory. In addition, Jackie showed under her coat the curve of advanced pregnancy. Four weeks later, on December 19, the couple was on the cover again with their brand-new baby, John-John.

The following year, in 1961, the Kennedys were on six of the fifty-one covers. They appeared on January 27 in the inauguration issue, and in the issues reporting the trip to Canada, the trip to Paris, the trip to Berlin. Jackie was featured by herself in one issue that showed the renovated White House, while her son John was on the front on November 24 to mark his first birthday, a day when he was photographed for a Life exclusive in the presidential mansion's nursery.

There was a reason for such devotion to the presidential couple and its clan: John Kennedy was the first president since Teddy Roosevelt in 1901 to bring children into the White House. This, together with the young couple's attractiveness, generated an unprecedented fascination by the public, and Life interpreted it better than anyone else. When Kennedy was assassinated in 1963, the magazine devoted four consecutive issues to the event. Even later, when Life had gone from being a weekly to a monthly, the Kennedys continued to be cover material: in 1983 there was an issue on the twentieth anniversary of the president's assassination; in 1984 Caroline and John-John were on the cover of an issue about presidential children, and Caroline was on the cover once again in September 1986 in her bridal gown.

UNDER FIRE

COMBAT COVERAGE ACROSS FIVE DECADES OF WAR

The way to report a war is to get terrifyingly close to the action. LIFE staff members have accepted extraordinary risk in doing just that through every major conflict and many minor ones since the magazine began. Hungarian-born photographer Robert Capa once said, "If your pictures aren't good enough, you aren't close enough." In July 1936 he was in a trench near Córdoba with Loyalist troops during the Spanish Civil War when a machine gun opened up on his position. As one of the Loyalists was shot, Capa snapped this picture, and LIFE ran it the following year. A dispute among historians of photography as to whether or not this image was staged remains unresolved; nonetheless, it has come to stand as the very essence of combat journalism.

During WWII 21 LIFE photographers spent 13,000 man-days overseas—about half the time on the front. Five of them were wounded. In wars since, three died in combat: Capa and Larry Burrows were killed in Southeast Asia in 1954 and 1971; Paul Schutzer died in the Arab-Israeli war of 1967.

What drove these people go into battle for a story? words that spoke for his colleagues, W. Eugene Smith, who survived 12 Pacific invasions before he was badly wounded during the 13th, said, "The belief, the try, a camera and some film—the fragile weapons of my good intentions. With these I fought war."

LIFE UNDER FIRE

"If your pictures aren't good enough, you're not close enough." These witty words belong to none other than Robert Capa, the most noted war photographer of his times. In July 1936 Capa, who was born in Budapest and whose real name was Endre Ernö Friedmann, was in the trenches near Córdoba with Loyalist forces during the Spanish Civil War when a machine gun opened fire on his position. A bullet killed one of the Loyalist soldiers and Capa took a photo that *Life* published the following year. Although historians still debate whether the picture was posed, the image by Capa has become the paradigm of war photojournalism.

This image, in addition to other superb ones published by the magazine, turned *Life* into a visual reference source on the wars that followed. During World War II alone, twenty-one of the magazine's photographers worked 13,000 hours abroad, almost half of the time at the front. Five of them were injured. In subsequent wars, three died in combat: Capa and Larry Burrows died in Southeast Asia in 1954 and 1971

respectively, while Paul Schutzer was killed during the Six-Day War between Arabs and Israelis in 1967.

During World War II there was practically no place that was not covered by *Life* photographers. The man responsible for that was Wilson Hicks, the magazine's executive editor, who handled photography assignments and who had witnessed the workings of the British pool system, under which correspondents took turns covering the news. Hicks realized that if *Life* could get accepted as a member of a similar news system, it would have an edge over other magazines in the matter of transportation. The army and navy accepted the idea and created a pool made up of the three main photo agencies and *Life*. The pictures taken by its members were available to the media as a whole, but the newspapers hadn't mastered the concept of photo sequences. *Life* was the only one that could use them to present a coherent panorama of war shots.

The *Life* photo team was made up of such big names as W. Eugene Smith and Margaret Bourke-White (who was

in Moscow during the Nazi bombings and was the first non-Russian woman to visit the Soviet front) and other risk takers including Eliot Elisofon, who landed in Casablanca and was the first to record war action in Tunisia; David Scherman, who covered the Normandy landing; Bernard Hoffman, who flew in a B-29 in the first bombing of Japan; Dmitri Kessel, who parachuted into Nazi-occupied Greece; William Shrout, who covered the Pacific theater and was seriously injured in the Solomons; Robert Landry, who worked the Pacific and Europe, with Libya in between; Frank Scherschel, who added work in the Arctic to the major theaters; Ralph Morse, who survived six hours in Pacific waters holding up a wounded officer after a torpedoing off Savo and, as pool photographer on V-E Day, recorded the German surrender; John Phillips, who covered the fall of Austria and Czechoslovakia and three times crossed enemy lines in Yugoslavia to join Tito's partisans; John Florea, who shot the marines' invasion of Tarawa from planes off aircraft carriers; Peter Stackpole, who covered the Funafuti

and Tarawa battles and lived through the last Japanese banzai attack on Saipan; George Strock, whose shot of three marines floating on the shoreline of Buna, New Guinea, was the first photo of American dead to be passed by the censors.

However, no war photographer was more noted and celebrated for his images than Robert Capa. A free-spirited professional, he had already had three stints with *Life* (was fired twice, quit once) when, in North Africa in 1943, he asked to rejoin the magazine's staff. Hired by wire, he was soon with the 82d Airborne parachuting into Sicily. On D-Day Capa was again in the vanguard, among the men heading ashore in sector "Easy Red" of Omaha Beach. There his camera recorded the disembarkation under

intense fire at first light that gray day. He captured men throwing themselves against the waves amidst the obstacles placed by the enemy, the landing craft that sank, and the bodies of their comrades. Capa took 106 shots of "Easy Red," but only a handful saw the light. A London technician, rushing to develop the film, forgot to watch the dryer, and the heat ruined the emulsion. The surviving eight were published by *Life* and, in the words of *Time Inc.*, "were so vivid and dramatic that to this day they are definitive of the terror and confusion of D-Day."

Capa's professional skill and personal sensibility earned him the affectionate regard of his colleagues. After he photographed a group of women in Naples weeping for their dead sons in October 1943, J. R. Eyerman, a veteran

of assignments with both the Atlantic and the Pacific fleets, said, **"You have to let yourself feel–that's why Capa is so respected as a war photographer; he's got a heart way out to here. That picture of his in last week's *Life* [the Naples mothers] is one of the greatest pictures of the war. Capa knew how they felt; he got the candid shot before they knew he was around. Being a good photographer is not a matter of being on hand, clicking a shutter and putting in a plate–that's just getting a record; it's seeing through the eyes of the people at home and controlling yourself so you can be receptive."** Robert Capa died in 1954 when he stepped on a mine in Thai Binh while covering the war in Indochina.

THE FACES OF WAR

While each photo captures an instant, an opportunity, and each has its documentary value, some stand out because they have behind them a story that frames them and makes them exceptionally memorable. Among the myriad photos published in *Life* were several that thus transcended the bounds of journalism. One was the shot taken by the AP's Joe Rosenthal on February 24, 1945, showing the marines raising the American flag on Mount Suribachi on Iwo Jima. Interestingly, when the photo arrived

at *Life*, managing editor Daniel Longwell refused to publish it because he thought the scene looked faked. He wired a correspondent on Iwo to ask how and when it had been done, and was told that, while the AP shot didn't record the first flag raising–that event had been staged by the marines themselves for the corps magazine–Rosenthal had found a larger flag and had the act repeated. Finally, three weeks later, after the photo had appeared in *Time* and many other media, *Life* decided to

run it. As Longwell later put it, "the country believed in that picture and I just had to pipe down." The country did indeed believe in the photo: it would later be reproduced on 3.5 million posters, fifteen billboards, and 137 million stamps. Moreover, in 1954 President Eisenhower dedicated at Arlington National Cemetery an enormous statue exactly replicating the scene.

Other war photos published in *Life* also made history. *Time Inc.* recounts: In its September 17, 1945, issue *Life* carried pictures of the

AMPHIBIOUS ASSAULT VEHICLE 1944

U.S. AIR FORCE 1941

AIR ATTACK 1941

CHANNEL DEFENSE 1941

NAVY NURSE 1941

U.S. NAVY 1940

THREE MOMENTS. The first photo of dead American soldiers allowed by the censors, taken by George Strock in New Guinea. The celebrated image by Eisenstaedt of the sailor kissing the nurse. And the moment when American marines raised the American flag on Iwo Jima, by Joe Rosenthal.

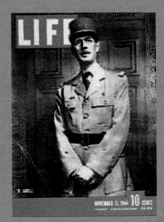

GENERAL DE GAULLE 1944

GENERAL EISENHOWER 1944

BENITO MUSSOLINI 1939

surrender ceremonies on the battleship *Missouri*. On November 5 twenty-two Japanese emerged from the jungles on Guam and surrendered to a passing G.I. truck driver. They did so by handing him a copy of the September 17 *Life* which they had picked up from a rubbish pile. Attached was a note: "We had been lived in this jangle from last year, but now we known by this book that the War end."

It was not only at the front, however, that *Life's* photographers were able to show off their camera skills. After Pearl Harbor the government imposed restrictions on the press and banned non-American photographers from traveling abroad as correspondents. Such great *Life* photographers as German-born Alfred Eisenstaedt had to stay in New York. Many readers would be thankful for that. Eisenstaedt was the creator of a memorable and touching photo essay published by the magazine on April 19, 1943, titled "Penn Station," which showed the anguish of farewell as the troops departed for war. However, the most memorable Eisenstaedt photo is the one often called "V-J Day in Times Square." It shows a jubilant sailor hugging and kissing a nurse amid thousands of people gathered on the streets of New York to celebrate the long awaited victory over Japan. This classic shot, first published in *Life*, embodies the American public's joy and relief at the end of World War II. Years later Eisenstaedt said, "People tell me that when I'm in heaven they will remember this picture."

IMA

BRITISH ROYAL AIR FORCE 1940

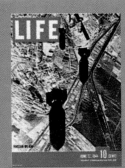

GERMAN SOLDIER 1940

BOMBS OVER EUROPE 1944

IN NORMANDY 1944

CAPTIVE NAZIS 1944

INDIVIDUAL ESSAY.
In one variant of the *Life* approach, the camera focused on a single person's life and work, with the aim of transmitting feelings and emotions.

THE PRIVATE LIFE OF
Gwyned Filling
THE HOPES AND FEARS OF COUNTLESS YOUNG CAREER GIRLS ARE SUMMED UP IN HER STRUGGLE TO SUCCEED IN NEW YORK

HER DAY BEGINS WITH A FRANTIC RACE AGAINST THE CLOCK

GWYNED IN ACTION.
In twelve pages McCombe visually related the life of a young woman in New York trying to make her way in advertising.

SOMETIMES HER LIFE IS LIGHT AND GAY...

. . . AND SOMETIMES SHE CRIES

THE RESULT. An exemplary essay, it transmits feelings through images that capture dreams, fantasies, difficulties, sweet and bitter moments.

ITS SPECIAL WAY OF LOOKING AT PEOPLE

Alfred Eisenstaedt, the legendary German photographer and pillar of *Life* since issue number one, once defined photojournalism as the act of finding and capturing **"the most eloquent moment."** But to do a photo essay, the reporting style imposed by *Life*, photojournalists also need a wide range of traits and talents including a natural eye for narrative, intuition, drive, good timing, emotional self-control, and, above all, great sensitivity. This last was one of the essential qualities that enabled *Life* photographers to do touching and eloquent reports on people's lives, and a prime example of this style was British photographer Leonard McCombe. The Time-Life book *Photojournalism* recounts when and why McCombe joined *Life*:

" **McCombe's responsiveness illuminates the first of his picture essays to appear in *Life*, a story he shot as a young British photographer in Berlin at the end of World War II. In the aftermath of hostilities, thousands of German refugees were pouring into the Berlin railroad station on top of boxcars, sick, starving, unwanted, –and totally unnoticed by most press photographers. McCombe documented their plight in photographs, which he sold first to the London picture weekly *Illustrated*. Henry Luce spotted them, pronounced them the year's best, bought them for the October 15, 1945, issue of *Life* magazine, and ordered that McCombe be hired immediately. McCombe, then 22, became the youngest photographer on the *Life* staff."**

As the book shows, McCombe's work for *Life* turned out to be crucial to its photo essays. When the war ended, the nation was eager to return to normal, and therefore demanded stories about the lives of regular people. McCombe's special skill was precisely his ability to get close to people, following in their wake all day until they forgot about his presence and started to expose for the camera their problems, sorrows, and joys. So the photo essay *Life* published under the headline "The Private Life of Gwyned Filling" is recognized as one of the most representative pieces of its genre. The twelve-page report took as its subject a young woman who was embarking on an advertising career in New York. Depicting her daily life with its bitter and tender moments through images of great emotional impact, the story transmitted the young woman's sweetness and sensibility as she tried to make her way in her profession. The essay touched readers, and McCombe's style gave rise to a whole school of photo essay subjects with their main focus on ordinary people.

ITS SPECIAL WAY
OF LOOKING AT PLACES

The flexibility of some *Life* photographers was admirable. They went from covering a war to photographing a school full of kids or describing with their cameras the tranquil life of a rural village. McCombe was a trendsetter who looked for different, more evocative and meaningful perspectives in any kind of scenario. And he always tried to find the human angle. That is what happened in 1969 when he was assigned to do a story on a Massachusetts day care center subsidized by a private company. The editors thought the story should highlight the importance of this cooperative effort between industry and government. But when McCombe arrived at the center, he found something totally different. The company was facing economic difficulties and had stopped contributing funds; that is, the reason for the envisioned story was no longer there. The photographer then did a photo essay of his own devising that focused on the remarkable bond between the children and their teachers, a relationship that was renewed daily at their gathering point, the day care center. The story reflected in human terms why the school in itself was an important social institution. It is significant because it showed another way in which *Life* approached a photo essay: not through a single person, as in the case of Gwyned Filling, but through a group of people gathered in the same space or spot, and interconnected at the same time by territorial and sentimental links.

   W. Eugene Smith was another photographer who tackled the *two classical types of essays:*

individual, in which the images focus mostly on one person, *and general,* where the mood of the piece is set by several people photographed together, as if they were subtopics. The man behind "Country Doctor" did memorable general photo essays, such as the one published in 1951 under the title **"Spanish Village."** The scene was Deleitosa, a place in Extremadura in western Spain, and Smith's images of the villagers were extraordinary, full of stark realism and emotion. Spread over ten pages were seventeen photographs that featured the doctor, the priest, Franco's Civil Guards, farmhands, women working in the fields, a baptism, a communion, a funeral, and the village school. All these portraits, these little individual stories, came together in a general photographic act that attained high emotional impact and reflected the way of life of a Spanish village at that time. The ten pages of photos were augmented by captions and an introduction, short but eloquent. Since those lines are a clear example of how to write the text accompaniment to a *Life* photo essay, they are transcribed here as published. Under the title "Spanish Village" was the subtitle "It Lives in Ancient Poverty and Faith" and the following story:

   "The village of Deleitosa, a place of about 2,300 peasant people, sits on the high, dry, western Spanish tableland called Extremadura, about halfway between Madrid and the border of Portugal. Its name means "delightful," which it no longer is, and its origins are obscure,

MEN AT WORK.
This is the way *Life* saw the residents of an Extremadura village through seventeen photographs.

SMITH IN
DELEITOSA.
Titled "Spanish
Village," this story
was done in 1951.

though they may go back a thousand years to Spain's Moorish period. In any event it is very old and *Life* photographer Eugene Smith, wandering off the main road into the village, found that its ways had advanced little since medieval times.

"Many Deleitosans have never seen a railroad because the nearest one is 25 miles away. The Madrid-Sevilla highway passes Deleitosa seven miles to the north, so almost the only automobiles it sees are a dilapidated sedan and an old station wagon, for hire at prices few villagers can afford. Mail comes in by burro. The nearest telephone is 12½ miles away in another town. Deleitosa's water system still consists of the sort of aqueducts and open wells from which villagers have drawn their water for centuries. Except for the local doctor's portable tin bathtub there is no trace of any modern sanitation, and the streets smell strongly of the villagers' donkeys and pigs.

"There are a few signs of the encroachment of the 20th Century in Deleitosa. In the city hall, which is run by political subordinates of the provincial governor, one typewriter clatters. A handful of villagers, including the mayor, own their own small radio sets. About half of the 800 homes of the village are dimly lighted after dark by weak electric-light bulbs which dangle from ancient ceilings. And a small movie theater, which shows some American films, sits among the sprinkling of little shops near the main square. But the village scene is dominated now as always by the high, brown structure of the 16th Century church, the center of society in Catholic Deleitosa. And the lives of the villagers are dominated as always by the bare

and brutal problems of subsistence. For Deleitosa, barren of history, unfavored by nature, reduced by wars, lives in poverty –a poverty shared by nearly all and relieved only by the seasonal work of the soil, and the faith that sustains most Deleitosans from the hour of First Communion until the simple funeral that marks one's end."

This is how Eugene Smith described his work in Deleitosa: "These photographs are pictorial paragraphs from a portrait of a modest village. I went away from the publicized historical attractions, the unrepresentative disproportion of the main cities; far away from the tourist landmarks. Spain is to be found. Spain is of its villages, simply down to the poverty line.

"Its people, unlazy, in slow pace, striving to earn a frugal living from an ungenerous soil. Centuries of blight, of neglect, of exploitation, of the present intense domination weigh heavily–yet they, as a whole, are not defeated. They work the day and sleep the night, struggle for and bake their bread; believing in life, they reluctantly relinquish their dead."

When the story was published, few in Deleitosa were happy about it, particularly the village authorities. Even today, Internet pages carry comments by Deleitosa residents complaining about Smith's reporting and accusing him of exaggerating the poverty. Yet they recognize that, because of the *Life* story, the town became famous and tourists visited it for many years. Accordingly, one of Deleitosa's streets now bears the name Calle W. Eugene Smith.

PORTRAIT OF A PLACE AND ITS PEOPLE. On ten pages the essay showed, through individual stories, the life of the town. Each character contributed to Smith's photographic feat. Edited as a whole, the photos attained great emotional impact.

THE PHOTO ESSAY:
From eugene smith to sebastião salgado

Through the years the photo essay became even more popular, and the work of almost every well-known practitioner of the genre appeared in *Life's* pages. One such was the celebrated Brazilian photographer **Sebastião Salgado**, perhaps the best-known photographer in this field in the late twentieth and early twenty-first centuries. Salgado, who was born in 1944 and got a doctorate in economics in 1971, took up photography in 1973 during a trip to Africa with his wife, Lélia. Since that time his work has attained worldwide recognition, including *Other Americas*, a book and exhibition of photographs taken between 1977 and 1984 in rural areas populated by descendents of indigenous peoples in Mexico and Brazil; *Sahel: End of the Road,* a 1986 piece that depicted that African region's devastating drought and helped to create Doctors without Borders; *Workers*, a photo essay on the end of mass labor, done between 1986 and 1992 in twenty-six countries; *Terra: Struggle of the Landless*, a 1997 study of aspiring home-steaders in Brazil; and in 2000 the twin volumes *Migrations: Humanity in Transition* and *The Children*: *Refugees and Migrants,* exploring the harsh conditions of the displaced in forty-one countries.

One of the jobs he did for *Life* was published in 1998 in issue number 2,000 of the magazine, and a Salgado photo had the distinction of serving as background for the index of this extraordinary issue. The nine-page article, titled "A Tribute to a Vanishing Way of Work," depicted the automotive and iron and steel industries in Zaporozhye, a city of some 863,000 residents in the Ukraine. In six photos, three of them double-page, the magazine published a masterful photo essay that Salgado had done for his *Workers*. This book was then just in its early stages, and Salgado planned also to visit Cuba's sugarcane fields, Germany's chemical plants, China's cotton fields, and Bolivia's tin mines, among others. "What I hope to achieve," –he told the magazine then–"is a world portrait of a disappearing race, the working-class man." In fact, the factory he had photographed started to install robots a few weeks later.

Salgado acknowledged Eugene Smith as one of the main inspirations for his photojournalism work. "He had an enormous respect for people," Salgado said in 1998 when his story was published in *Life*, precisely fifty years after the noted "Country Doctor" by Smith in 1948. *Life* thereby celebrated not only 2,000 issues but also a whole career and thousands of pages of what is now known as its journalistic legacy: the photo essay.

BUTE TO A VANISHING WAY OF
WORK

to Soviet factories, a photojournalist embarks on a labor of love

STORY AND SEQUENCE. One of the photos shot by Salgado at the steel plant was used as background for the issue's table of contents. The story started on page 119.

THE DISPLAY. After a first page in which text and headline predominated, the photos showed the factory's last few days of work, a study in sentiment and nostalgia.

the 1930s, recently began to modernize. "It employs thousands of people. If it suddenly needs only 500, where are the rest of the workers going to go?"

THE END. Salgado finished his act with a tender image of a couple embracing during a break on the assembly line. He thus highlighted the human aspect of a factory that was about to close.

sinatra's camera, mailer's pen

Like any leading publication, *Life* committed itself to permanent innovation in magazine journalism. It always sought to stand out, particularly in covering the events that attracted journalists and media from across the country. The question at story meetings was: Everybody will cover the subject, *but how will we do it?* When an event of this importance loomed, the whole staff– photographers, writers, editors, section editors, and top brass– were convened to hear and analyze all proposals. Such was the case of the boxing match in 1971 between Muhammad Ali and Joe Frazier. For weeks the whole country had awaited the fight, one of the most publicized in the history of boxing. All the national media and many from abroad would cover the event. TV planned a spectacular evening, with cameras in the dressing rooms, wherever the boxers went, and at ringside among the celebrity spectators. What was left for *Life*, then? What could it do differently? How could it touch and surprise its

readers? The idea the editors put into play was highly creative and an example of the originality with which the magazine tried to treat any subject. In the end, Ali-Frazier was covered for *Life* by the duo of singer Frank Sinatra and writer Norman Mailer, a find that the magazine's editor, Ralph Graves, explained in an editorial in the issue that published the report:

"For this week's cover story on the fight, we had some help from people who are not on our staff. Norman Mailer, a part-time fighter who has made more of a name for himself in other fields, was challenged by the idea of writing a 4,000-word article under our deadline. The fight would end around midnight Monday, and we would have to go to press Wednesday evening. He saw the fight, got a night's sleep and started writing–in longhand, as usual. Wednesday morning he called in to report, 'I wrote 5,000 words yesterday, but I threw out 2,000. How much time have I really got?' We exchanged predictions of

SINATRA'S PHOTOS. After the opening text, headline "Ego," came a spectacular photo on a slant, taken by Sinatra. One of his shots also made it to the cover.

SPECIAL "CHRONICLERS". An editor's note introduced Sinatra and Mailer, the two celebrities that *Life* placed at ringside to achieve a different news angle.

A DIFFERENT ENDING. For the finale of the story, *Life* had planned a photo to show the defeat of Ali's ego. But it was not to be: the only photographer allowed in the dressing room, Gordon Parks, was a friend of the boxer's and was so sorry for him that he hadn't the heart to shoot.

Gestures of defiance—and derision

Ali faces the final round, and is slammed down

disaster: a) if he didn't get it in on time, b) if he didn't have more time to write properly. As so often happens in boxing, the predictions were inaccurate. Mailer's stunning article, which finally came out at over double length, begins on page 18F.

"For our pictures of the action, we were relying on the magazine pool photographers at ringside, especially *Sports Illustrated's* Neil Leifer and Tony Triolo, who delivered outstanding pictures. But it never hurts to have a horseshoe in your glove. Six years ago Staff Writer Tommy Thompson and Photographer John Dominis were doing a story on Frank Sinatra. Sinatra was fascinated by Dominis's equipment and admitted he had been interested in taking pictures for 20 years.

"Shortly before the fight Tommy learned that Sinatra had wangled himself a ringside seat and was going to take pictures with a battery

of cameras. Tommy went to work wangling Sinatra into letting us have a look at his film. We didn't expect to get anything the professional photographers didn't have, but it might be worth inspecting. Indeed, Sinatra wound up getting the cover, a memorable full-spread picture (yes, he held his camera at that angle on purpose) and two other shots in our story. We are offering him a job.

"But we did not get one set of pictures we had been expecting. Gordon Parks, who has been a good friend of Muhammad Ali for years, explains why: 'Mine was the only camera allowed in Ali's dressing room right after his defeat. And I was ready, I thought, for what I had been assigned to record: his reactions in case he lost. As I entered Bundini nudged Muhammad. "Look who's here," he said. "Now we know who's really with us." Ali lay prone, doubled in misery. I bent over and we

touched cheeks. "Hi, champ," I said. "We had bad luck tonight." He answered slowly, "Yup, I got whupped—just got whupped." Bundini and Angelo Dundee began pulling on his underwear and his socks. Then they pulled his sweater carefully over his head. He seemed helpless, like a kid who has tumbled off his bicycle while showing off in front of his best girl. There he was, wordless at last, suffering more through inner pain than the swollen jaw—a situation so many critics had been waiting so long to describe. Now, the opportunity was mine, but suddenly my friendship for him outdistanced my journalistic chores. I couldn't bring myself to release the shutter.'"

The story was published on March 19, 1971. Mailer's report took up six and a half pages, and the photos, which included Sinatra's, eight pages.

WHY LiFe FAILED

One by one, the causes of the most talked-about closing in the publishing world. The role of advertising, television, postal rates, and newsroom costs.

Can a magazine go under when it's selling more than *5 million* copies a week? When it's reaching *40 million* people who read it every seven days? When, to boot, it's the most popular magazine in the United States? And, if that's not enough, when the magazine is a true institution in international journalism? All these questions were answered on December 9, 1972, when the *International Herald Tribune* published a front-page story with the headline: **"Life Magazine Is Dead at 36."**

The news spread around the globe and shook the whole publishing market. Although the decision taken by Time Inc. spoke only of a suspension and not of a definitive shutdown, the truth is that on December 29, 1972, *Life*–a leading magazine in the general interest sector and the American pioneer in the genre of photojournalism–stopped publication as a weekly, putting an end to a whole era. The last issue carried, below the date and price, the single word **"Goodbye."** Throughout the world, members of the media saw *Life's* demise as the death of a close relative.

But once the mourning for such a loss was over, and as Time Inc!'s stock shot up on the New York Stock Exchange after the company shed the deficits that *Life* had been running, publishing professionals started asking themselves new questions: What went wrong? What mistakes had *Life* made? What had happened with the magazine that just three years earlier, in 1969, had reached a circulation of 8.5 million? That in 1966 had sold 3,300 pages of advertising for some $170 million?

That in 1970 was charging its advertisers $64,000 a page?

The search for answers to these questions gave rise to all kinds of studies and analyses. Some blamed the crisis on the TV boom, others on aging content and minimal innovation, others on advertising billing, according to the angle of whoever was in charge of the investigation. The fact is that *Life's* fall was and still is a paradigmatic case for publishing professionals when they analyze the ups and downs of today's publishing business. At the same time, it seems misguided to attribute the magazine's fall to a single reason. In our opinion, after thoroughly examining everything that has been written and said about the fall of *Life*, there was no single cause; there were many, and all of them were interconnected, as if they were parts of a machine.

DECEMBER 1987/$2.50

LIFE

MERYL STREEP

On Top– and Tough Enough to Stay There

MONTHLY EDITION.
The magazine appeared regularly again beginning in October of 1978. This time it was a monthly, with a larger logo, a price of $1.50, and a circulation of 700,000. It targeted a more select public, the American middle and upper middle class.

During this period Meryl Streep was on the cover in 1981 and in 1987 (above).

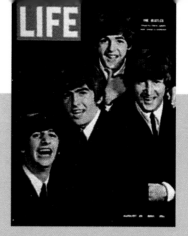

FUNDAMENTALS OF
THE PUBLISHING BUSINESS

It makes sense, though, to examine the machine one part at a time. To fully understand the way the gears worked at *Life*, we must first succinctly explain the workings of the American magazine publishing business. As in other countries, periodicals in the United States were financed mostly by advertising, and their profits depended on that. Advertising, in turn, needed the national mass media to promote its products and reach the greatest possible number of people. In that sense, magazines with a national circulation fulfilled their mission much better than newspapers, whose sales and reporting efforts were rooted in local interest. This being so, the magazines with the greatest reader penetration–that is, the largest circulation–were the most desirable to advertisers, who paid rates in accordance with that circulation. But of course these magazines, to achieve the highest revenues, had to corroborate their circulation figures. Here another crucial factor came into

play: subscription sales by mail. Given the large territory, national circulation magazines in the United States had always depended on the post office to distribute their issues, which they'd sold in advance to their readers through subscription campaigns.

That was the machinery that drove the publishing business and, therefore, the machinery that drove the business of *Life*. Schematically, *Life* the business was based on:

1. A big, ambitious, unique editorial product that could bring its readers an unmatched world every week. It was printed on the best paper and in a size that allowed it to emphasize its spectacular visual qualities.

2. The large number of readers who received the magazine every week. Most of them had been enrolled through impressive promotional subscription campaigns.

3. An agile and efficient distribution network through the mail, which guaranteed advertisers its immediate delivery to millions of potential buyers all over the country. This circulation was certified by the post office and served as a guarantee for advertisers who were paying rates predicated on the number of subscribers.

4. Outstanding ad revenues driven by the above three factors.

What happened in 1972, then, for this spectacular business to crumble? Each of the causes is explored here, in an attempt to explain why there's reason to believe that–apart from external factors, such as the advent of television–*Life* was a victim of the very business plan that had led to its success.

In principle, all the reports and analyses agree that 1959 was the year when *Life* started to notice it was vulnerable. For reasons that will be examined later, this year was disastrous and affected even subsequent years. Until then, the magazine had been a prosperous business, even though it never attained the earnings goal set by Luce: 15 percent of gross income. Only in 1956 did *Life* reach its highest level, with a pretax profit of 12.5 percent.

Still, during good times and bad, there was one area of *Life* that the company did not neglect: its editorial budget. This was the factor that allowed it to maintain its notable supremacy over its competitors, which translated into excellent series, done in all parts of the world, by prodigies of photography that no other magazine could match. Nor could the competition equal the excellence of *Life*'s 275-person staff, the breadth of its international coverage, its technical excellence,

and its speed in delivering the news. According to inside estimates, the editorial budget amounted to $10 million, twice that of the *Saturday Evening Post* and four times that of *Look*, its closest competitors. This difference was evident in the quality of the product and was used by the company's various departments to attract both subscribers and advertisers. *Life* knew full well that its business was based on the way it practiced journalism, and it put its money on the line.

LOOK, THE RIVAL

Two months after *Life*'s debut, the magazine that would become its greatest competitor hit the American market: *Look*. Its first issue was dated February 1937, but it went on sale on January 5. The founders of this publication were brothers Gardner and John Cowles, who had gotten their start in journalism with the *Register* and the *Tribune,* Des Moines newspapers that belonged to their family.

The cover was devoted to Hermann Goering and the story inside was titled "Will a Former Drug Addict Rule Germany?" Other offerings ranged from "A Psychologist Reveals Roosevelt's Popularity Secrets" through "A Car Kills a Woman Right in Front of You" to articles on Joan Crawford and Dolores del Río. The full-color back cover carried a sensual image of Greta Garbo. The initial run of 400,000 copies quickly sold out. And then an unexpected development made sales shoot up immediately to 700,000 copies. A man discovered that, owing to a strange optical effect, Garbo's photo when folded in half yielded an image of the female sexual organ. As can be imagined, the news spread quickly and the newly printed copies of an additional run were also snapped up.

The extra publicity that *Look* thus received immediately made the magazine popular. The March issue ended up selling 1.2 million copies, and a month later the Cowles family decided to change it from a monthly to a semimonthly publication. Before it was a year old, *Look* carried advertising, and by March of 1938 its circulation had reached 2 million. For more than thirty years *Look* and *Life* fought their own editorial battle to win readers and advertisers. They both lost it in the mid-seventies.

SPECIAL FLIGHT.
The February 5, 1965, issue devoted twenty-two pages to Churchill's funeral. For this story, the magazine chartered a special plane. In fact, the issue was put to bed aboard the aircraft between London and Chicago.

Life had acquired, early on, a well-deserved reputation for extravagance. Within the company, and outside as well, *Life* was said to throw money around with unseemly abandon. As Tom Griffith put it, "Even occasional attempts to economize were apologetic: there was waste-waste, which was to be deplored, but useful-waste was shooting 100 frames instead of ten, if doing so produced one great picture. *Life* opened its checkbooks to get the best pictures, the biggest memoirs. Once in 1958, when the *Saturday Evening Post* signed up the commander of the first submarine journey beneath the North Pole, managing editor Ed Thompson gathered every reporter and photographer he could find or fly to England to throw a party for the entire submarine crew on its arrival there, and in one night of booze-fueled interviewing of everyone present, got the whole story before the *Post* could." A year later, when NASA selected the first seven astronauts for Project Mercury and then marketed their personal stories, Thompson bid steadily up to $500,000 to secure the rights. He said: **"I thought men in space and the idea of Americans going to the moon was the biggest story around and that *Life* should somehow be identified with it."** Once, looking askance at *Life's* editorial budget, Luce had asked Thompson if

he could **"lop a million dollars off the top,"** to which Thompson allegedly responded, **"Harry, I could lop a million off the bottom for rent, light, heat, mandatory raises, that kind of thing. But I couldn't spare the top million. That's gambling money."**

Life never had any qualms about spending money to compete, to win, to show it was unique. Perhaps one of the best examples was its coverage of Winston Churchill's funeral services in 1965. In the issue placed on the newsstands on Monday, February 5, *Life* provided its readers with a color cover and, inside, twenty-one pages devoted to an event that had happened the previous Saturday. According to *Time Inc.*, "The coup was made possible only by taking *Life's* operations aloft in a chartered jetliner converted into a photographic laboratory and editorial office, and there, in the eight hours of flying time between London and Chicago, carrying out *Life's* entire editorial process—processing the film, selecting the pictures, laying out the pages, writing captions, text and headlines, editing, checking and fitting the copy—all to be ready for the printer on arrival." At the helm of the operation was Thompson's successor George P. Hunt, who wrote an Editor's Note at the beginning of the issue:

THE CONQUEST OF SPACE

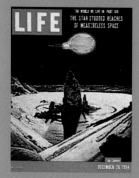

STUDY OF THE UNIVERSE
1954

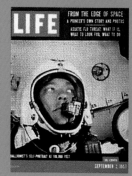

RECORD ALTITUDE
1957

SPACE TEST
1958

JOHN GLENN
1962

"   We are 33,000 feet up in the sky, traveling at 600 mph . . . [in a] DC-8 chartered from Seaboard World Airlines, fitted out as a flying editorial office to carry 40 busily working members of *Life's* staff. In the forward part of the plane is a photo laboratory in which, at this moment, six technicians are developing 70 rolls of color film taken of the service and ceremonies. Moving aft inside this airborne city room are layout tables and light boxes, where color transparencies already developed are being sorted out and arranged so that they tell the story of the memorable event our 17 photographers covered in London. Scattered through the seats filling up the rest of the plane, the writers are clattering away on their typewriters.... The concentration is furious, and only your voice raised over the sound of jets or your pencil slipping when the plane dips reminds you that this is not the Time & Life Building on a busy closing night. A cheer comes from the forward area just behind the lab. The pilot has sent back word that instead of expected snow at Chicago the weather is clear!"

The reportage was spectacular, touching, and unforgettable. The total cost of the operation was more than $250,000. However, the amount didn't seem particularly out of line, as the magazine's account books customarily reflected hefty expenses for major pieces— $1.15 million for Churchill's memoirs, for instance, and $1 million for General Douglas MacArthur's. In any case, *Life's* editorial expenses, although elevated, constituted only approximately 7 percent of revenues, a smaller proportion than at its sister publication, *Time,* and much less than in other business units. It was the printing and distribution costs and the promotions to boost circulation that caused a phenomenal imbalance in *Life's* ledgers. These numbers grew greater and greater with the advent of television, the medium that over the years would become the most important national competitor in the race for advertising dollars.

ROUTE TO THE MOON. The magazine kept step-by-step tabs on the space race, a topic that, through the years, it treated in many aspects and on many covers. It paid NASA $500,000 for the rights to Project Mercury.

VIEW FROM *GEMINI 10*
1966

TRIUMPHANT MISSION
1969

***APOLLO 11* SPECIAL**
1969

HOW TV affected LIFe

Interestingly, from their inception *Life* and television crossed paths. And, albeit coincidental and fortuitous, both took their first steps on the same month and year: as *Life* was launched in the United States in November 1936, the BBC started its regular TV broadcasts from London. Years later, when television had reached America, it would bump into *Life* again, and this time the encounter would create sparks, victims, and a fierce fight over the most valued prize: advertising revenue.

But was television really what led to *Life's* demise? It was and it wasn't. **It was,** because it competed directly with the magazine to get the ads: like *Life*, TV could offer advertisers instant national exposure for their products, every day and whenever ad agencies requested it. It was, because it forced the publication to undertake expensive promotional campaigns to gain subscribers and maintain a reader volume that was attractive to advertisers. **It wasn't,** because in terms of coverage—contrary to what many believe—TV turned out not to be a solid competitor. Initially it wasn't obsessed with news, nor were news programs a strong point.

In that regard, the corporate history of Time Inc. downplays the influence TV had on *Life's* ultimate destiny. The chapter "*Life* Seeks a Formula for Survival" points out:

To what extent *Life's* fall into deficit was caused by television was arguable…. As the average family's TV viewing hours increased, there was clearly less time left for magazine reading; there were other and growing demands on leisure time, as well, in the increasingly affluent American society. In picture coverage of the news, though, the competition to *Life* was not yet as formidable as it would shortly become. The network's evenings news shows ran only 15 minutes. . . . Television had to deal with the same physical handicaps of time and distance as did *Life*. Bulky cameras and sound and lighting equipment further limited TV's reportorial capabilities."

It went on: **"Television's impact on advertising was easier to gauge. Offering large, albeit undiscriminating, audiences at relatively low unit cost, TV was becoming increasingly attractive to the mass merchandisers who for years had been *Life's* mainstay."** In that sense, television had become the new star of Madison Avenue, with most advertising agencies boosting earnings on the strength of billings in the new medium. Perhaps some may remember that the media placement gurus of that era were recommending such shows as *Bonanza, Maverick,* and *The Flying Nun,* and that food advertisers, in particular, were delighted with the new medium that could reach consumers right before dinner, when their appetites were more sensitive to television's messages.

In the meantime, worries grew at *Life*. In 1959 the magazine's advertising director, Clay Buckhout, presented a report to management that said: *"Life's* basic competitive problem in relation to its past and its future advertising performance . . . is television. . . . Our biggest classifications are pretty much the same as television's—food, toiletries, tobacco, drugs."

GRACE
1954

GRACE
1955

CAROLINE
1957

GRACE
1961

CAROLINE
1986

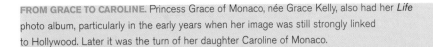

FROM GRACE TO CAROLINE. Princess Grace of Monaco, née Grace Kelly, also had her *Life* photo album, particularly in the early years when her image was still strongly linked to Hollywood. Later it was the turn of her daughter Caroline of Monaco.

A few numbers will give a sense of the dimensions of the advertising business in the United States and its influence on magazines. Gisèle Freund writes: "Between 1939 and 1952, the number of advertisers grew from 936 to 2,538, and the number of products advertised jumped from 1,659 to 4,472." It's worth stressing that, without a doubt, the main benefactors of that boom were magazines, just about the only national media at the time. And among magazines, *Life* set the standard. According to Freund, in the decade of the 1960s, of every dollar spent on advertising in all American magazines, fourteen cents ended up in *Life's* coffers.

It was natural that, as a national medium, television would become a fierce competitor of magazines in general, and of *Life* in particular. To be sure, this tough adversary did not emerge overnight in one fell swoop, but its presence did grow by leaps and bounds: while the United States had only sixty-nine television broadcast outlets in 1949, in 1970 it had more than eight hundred. This increase in TV stations started to tell on Time Inc. and its star publication. Freund reported the magazine's advertising pattern in the late 1960s: "In 1966, *Life* had sold 3,300 pages of advertising for close to 170 million dollars. Two years later it sold only 2,761 pages for about

$154 million, reflecting a loss of sixteen percent. In 1969, the deficit grew to $10 million, and losses continued in the following years." Thus in 1970 there was a decrease in advertising pages of 450, bringing that figure below 2,000 pages a year for the first time.

Further on, Freund did a comparison, perhaps the same one the magazine's managers did back then: "In 1970 a four-color full-page ad in Life cost $64,000 and reached a readership of 40 million. For the same amount of money, an advertiser could buy one minute of television time on one of the most popular programs, for instance *Laugh-In,* reaching 50 million viewers." Without a doubt, the equation still benefited *Life*. To hold on to its market share, the magazine had to hold on to its most important weapon for attracting advertisers: its great pool of subscribers, one of the gears that, as we have seen, sustained the great machinery of *Life* the business—a gear that by the late 1960s and early 1970s would start slipping and would turn *Life* into a victim of that same machinery.

a subscriber at any price

"I guess I still have in mind that *Life* can be and must be the outstanding magazine.... If a goal like that is still relevant and realistic .... 1) we would have our direct competition well licked and 2) we would get plenty of advertising $$$, no matter how many $$$ went to TV or skywriting or whatever... If [this] is the proper goal, then it seems to me that what we have first of all on our hands is a Circulation Battle with *Post* and *Look* and maybe *Digest*. This battle–and maybe it should be called a war–should be fought vigorously by every means. By all the editorial exertion and brains we can muster. And by Promotion. And by dollars.... Maybe we should cut back on newsstand price and subscription price. We would make things very expensive for *Post* and *Look* and sacrifice our own profit position in the process."

HENRY LUCE TO *LIFE* EXECUTIVES IN 1958

COUPONS. *Life's* promotions to get subscribers were an expense that became more and more onerous.

Luce's phrase best reflects the fierce competition that general interest magazines faced in the late 1950s. At that time, the struggle for circulation was fought between the *Reader's Digest, Saturday Evening Post, Look,* and *Life*. The four battled among themselves to get subscribers and advertisers. The former resulted in the latter. In addition, the four struggled head to head with television as they went after precious ads. *Reader's Digest* was on top with sales of 12 million copies by late 1959. But since it was a monthly publication and had a smaller page size, it was in a category by itself.

Life competed with the weekly *Saturday Evening Post* and with *Look,* a semimonthly publication. Each had a circulation of 6 million. In 1959 *Life* was still on top in terms of advertising revenue and, at Luce's urging, early that year it decided to increase circulation progressively to 7 million by dropping prices–the lowest in the decade–to retain that position. At newsstands, each issue ended up costing 19 cents compared to its 25-cent previous price. As for subscriptions, they went down by a dollar to $5,95 a year, with a 32-week trial offer of $2,98. **In the long term this strategy would put *Life* at the edge of the abyss.**

Because of that policy, 1959 ended with a record number of subscribers but with one of the worst balance sheets in the magazine's history. And the red ink continued for three years.

Only after 1962 would *Life* start showing a very modest profit of $1,4 million, which represented barely 1 percent of total revenues. The prospects for 1963 were not very attractive: according to that year's budget, an increase in circulation costs of almost $2,5 million was expected, even without going beyond 7 million copies.

With these projected numbers, the company understood that circulation couldn't keep growing indefinitely and took the decision to get out of the circulation race that three years earlier it had set out to win, no matter what the cost. The bimonthly *Look* took the lead with 7,4 million copies, while *Life* remained at 7 million and the *Post* at 6,5 million. *Look* took advantage of its lead and conducted a devastating campaign among agencies and advertisers. To counter this, *Life* spread the word that its decision to renounce "firstism" (the term used back then by the magazine's staffers) was precisely to strengthen its circulation base–not in quantity but in quality. Accordingly, it riposted with a campaign courting advertisers by emphasizing the superiority of both the magazine and its readers. And to be consistent with the promotion campaign and back up the notion of quality and selectivity, it returned in 1962 to the old pricing policy. It raised its annual subscription rate to $6.75 and increased the cover price to the 1958 level of 25 cents.

The recovery, however, would not last. Once again, the eagerness to increase circulation would only strengthen the

From left to right: **ROCK HUDSON** 1955, **HUMPHREY BOGART, WOODY ALLEN** 1969, **SEAN CONNERY** 1966, **PETER O'TOOLE** 1965, **FRANK SINATRA** 1965, **MARLON BRANDO** 1962.

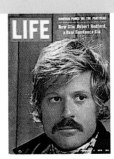

PAUL NEWMAN 1968

GARY COOPER 1940

PAUL BELMONDO 1966

ROBERT REDFORD 1970

GREGORY PECK 1947

CLARK GABLE 1961

causes of its collapse. After a prosperous 1966–operating profits at the magazine were more than $10 million on revenues of $165 million, the best results since the 1950s–*Life*'s executives made one of the biggest and most definitive mistakes for the magazine's future: they bought 50 percent of the *Saturday Evening Post's* subscribers in 1968. The *Post* had faced serious difficulties since 1966 when its advertising income had started dropping, so in early 1968 it put up for sale a list of 3 million subscribers. The publishing company that bought the roster would automatically deliver the magazine to the new clients that year and would gain the advantageous prospect of these subscriptions being renewed the following year. For *Life* and for *Look,* the opportunity of becoming the absolute leader was very tempting. And this time, *Life* had no intention of losing. In 1956 its executives had allowed *Look* to get its hands on the subscriber list that became available

when *Collier's* shut down, and they had always regretted it. In May of 1968 a deal was announced under which Time Inc. would put up $5 million for, among other things, half of the *Post's* subscribers. As it turned out, the deal was a poor proposition for both parties. The *Post* ceased operations the following year, and the *Time* executives who celebrated the agreement at the time of its signing would realize years later that they had made a huge mistake.

In October, with the first increase generated through the *Post's* subscribers, circulation increased to 8 million copies, and in January of 1969 came the announcement that it would grow even further: 8.5 million, an absolute record for the weekly.

Considering that the average copy was read by five or six people, *Life* had a total of 48 million readers, a number "larger than any other single communications medium in the world," as *Life* pointed out in a promotion piece distributed among agencies and

advertisers. Consequently, the magazine started to charge $42,500 per black-and-white page and $64,200 per four-color page, while *Look* charged $37,000 and $55,000 respectively. Although advertisers had no choice but to accept this increase, it was excessive for mass-product advertisers. In 1971 *Media Decisions,* the trade magazine of the advertising industry, pointed out in a retrospective study that "by 1966 page rates had passed some significant levels. A color page … was now over $50,000. It was also more costly than a minute on prime-time television …. As circulations, costs and rates rose… the same (advertising) dollars bought fewer pages. They were just about pricing themselves out of the market." Few could imagine what would happen after another of the gears in the *Life* business machinery broke: delivery. The *Life* case constituted a paradigm in that regard, since its experience showed publishers that **it's not always worth acquiring readers at any price.**

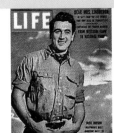

THE POST OFFICE
and a LETHAL BLOW

As early as 1965, in a report by executive Jerry Hardy, the company had been warned that increased production costs and postal rates could turn the *Life* business sour. According to the corporate history, Hardy pointed out that the magazine, sold at promotional rates of less than 10 cents in some cases, had such substantial production and delivery costs that it was losing 16 cents per copy. At the time, the newsstand price was a healthy 35 cents, and after some corrections in the "cheap" subscription system, the obstacles were overcome. But the situation became much more complex starting in 1969, when the magazine had to assume the cost of handling the many subscribers who'd come from the *Post*, along with rising prices for paper and printing, plus constant mail delivery increases.

Without a doubt, the toughest blow for *Life* came in 1971. It was delivered by the U.S. Postal Service when it announced in February a substantial rate increase for periodicals. Although the publishing industry foresaw the hikes, given the recent legislation mandating privatization of the old government agency, it never imagined they would be of such magnitude: **142 percent** over the five years from 1972 through 1976. In the case of Time Inc., it was estimated that they would be much higher (**176 percent**) owing to the magazines' size, the weight of their paper, and their national distribution patterns. The postal bill just for *Life* increased by $2 million in 1972, an amount that would grow progressively over the next few years.

The first magazine to feel the impact was *Look*, which stopped publishing on October 19, 1971. *Time* took advantage of the opportunity to harshly criticize the postal service with a corporate statement: **"It is always bad news for this country when a responsible journal is forced to close down. It is particularly bad news when the development is, in part, engendered by an arm of the government."**

Life held on for another year despite the fact that between 1969 and 1971 its losses surpassed $47 million. It did everything it could to stay afloat. It closed its international editions, *Life en Español*, *Life*

CORONATION. Elizabeth was one of the most popular princesses in the magazine. During the 1940s and 1950s, before and after she was crowned queen, she made the cover several times, including these.

International, and *Life Asia.* It decreased circulation to 7 million in 1971 and 5.5 million in 1972. It cut back on personnel and bureaus, increased the subscription price by 20 percent, and reduced ad rates by 18 percent. It projected a decrease in circulation to 4.5 million by 1973. But it was all useless. In the best-case scenario, the strenuous numbers game reflected a deficit of $17 million for 1973. And Time Inc., despite everything the magazine meant for the company, wasn't willing to continue losing money on it. There were other considerations in addition to the numbers: How would the advertising industry react to a new drop in circulation and another decrease in advertising rates? Wouldn't advertisers get the sense that the magazine was slowly retreating? Wouldn't the slow agony of its star magazine affect the company's overall image? Wouldn't it be better to close it down while it was still a leading product? Wouldn't that keep open the possibility of a future relaunching and the reasonable expectation of renewed success? *Life*, its executives ended up arguing, was *born Big, was Big,* and should end *Big* to keep open the possibility that it **would Become Big** once again. The decision to cease operations was taken in September, but was officially announced on December 8. The last issue, number 1,864, was published on December 29, 1972. It was the last installment of a weekly story that started in 1936.

Thus came to an end a wonderful magazine based on impressive, spectacular, large size images printed on quality paper with appealing stories and worldwide reports by top-notch photographers, writers, and editors.

It was also the end of a fabulous business that generated enormous amounts of advertising revenue, based on an enormous circulation of copies that, thanks to the postal service, were delivered to millions of reader-subscribers recruited through intense promotion campaigns.

After thirty-six years, the same virtues that had made *Life* the most popular magazine in the United States had become its worst enemy.

ROYAL WEDDINGS. Americans have always been interested in European nobility. And *Life* attempted to feed its readers' curiosity, as in the May 25, 1962, issue when the wedding of future king Juan Carlos of Spain and Princess Sophia of Greece was accorded the cover plus ten pages inside.

The editorial battle for survival

The question was asked then and it is still asked today in conversations about the *Life* shutdown: What was done from the editorial standpoint to avoid the magazine's fall? Plenty, perhaps more than was advisable, we may say today, given the magazine's popularity and circulation levels. Yet more than once those changes and innovations went unnoticed or were quickly cast aside because they affected one of the above-mentioned gears in the *Life* business machinery.

Such was the case with the first group of significant changes *Life* made, which appeared on June 2, 1961, in the first issue the magazine published in a slightly reduced size. One change that was immediately evident was a new cover design. Until then the cover had always sat atop a red bar; now it was totally clean, bare. This first issue showed Fidel Castro delivering a speech and, next to the photo, the headline announcing a new series: "The Crisis in Our Hemisphere." Inside, innovations were related to the incorporation of new features, such as the Article of the Week (a sensitive story about singer Judy Garland by *Life*'s first woman writer, Shana Alexander) and the new seven-page section Better Living (food, fashion, and furnishings for the California patio, including floor plans for a modest patio-style house that *Life* called its House of the Month).

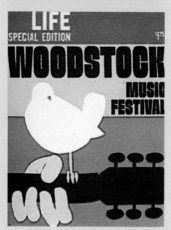

CHANGES AND NEWS. New cover, new size, and a new approach for a changing era. The massacre at My Lai, Castro, the Woodstock festival, and a montage of all the soldiers killed in Vietnam in one week were high-impact current events issues.

The publication's most visible inside innovation was the clustering of advertising pages to open up space within the magazine to display picture stories without interruption. The visual impact was fantastic. In addition, the editorial brass believed that it set *Life* apart and gave it a competitive edge to combat television. But it didn't last. The ad agencies of Madison Avenue rejected this "banking" of ads. Although *Vogue, Harper's Bazaar,* and the *New York Times Magazine* regularly ran their fashion ads clustered, the same move wasn't welcomed by *Life*'s advertisers. "Much of the past month," the advertising director wrote, "has been spent putting out fires started by the new *Life* format." A few months later, advertising pressures prevailed over editorial preferences, and ad pages were once again spread throughout the issue, at the expense of the magazine's picture displays.

These changes were a result of the constant worry over falling newsstand sales. Back in 1958 Luce had already asked *Life*'s publisher: "Are there not ways whereby *Life* can hold its audience without performing ever greater feats?" And in 1960 he came up with a document titled "*Life*: A New Prospectus for the Sixties" that was the basis for the changes made a year later.

The setback for the editorial sector over the banking of ads claimed the job of managing editor Ed Thompson, who was replaced by George P. Hunt. Under Hunt *Life* retained its focus on the news, but the style changed, not so much telling a pictorial story as delivering a pictorial punch. There was a trend toward using one higher-impact photo over a double-page spread instead of several in the same space. This single photo aimed to capture what Hunt termed the "frozen moment" of the story. Hunt felt that *Life* should communicate not just events but emotions. And that was his way of doing it. In the corporate history Time Inc., we read: "A *Life* editor later recounted how Hunt handled the bombing of a black church in Birmingham, Alabama, in September 1963. When he was brought a particularly poignant picture of one victim, a little girl blinded in the blast, 'We knew how George would react. He took one look at that picture and said, "That's it. It says it all." *Life* ran it as a double-truck in Newsfronts and that was it. It made a big statement!'"

During the Hunt years, through May of 1969, there were also more multipage spectaculars or "blockbusters." And there were special one-subject issues—four of them in his first year alone, on money, California, food, and the "takeover generation" of America's rising stars in a range of fields.

A paradox of this period was that, as the photo content got splashier, the word content got larger. For one thing, blocks of text made better use of awkward-shaped spaces left over by partial-page ads. Between 1960 and 1964 the average wordage per issue rose from about 7,000 to 23,000. Bylines likewise tripled. It had been a *Life* tradition that only major stories were signed, but now, in what Hunt called "the overthrow of anonymity," reviewers and columnists were regularly bylined.

It was also Hunt who initiated *Life*'s investigative reporting team. To head it he tapped William Lambert, a correspondent who already had a Pulitzer in his portfolio. Its first report, on the financial misdeeds of Lyndon Johnson's protégé Bobby Baker, was published in November of 1963.

Over the years, the team grew and so did the number of investigations. *Life* passed from merely covering the news to creating it.

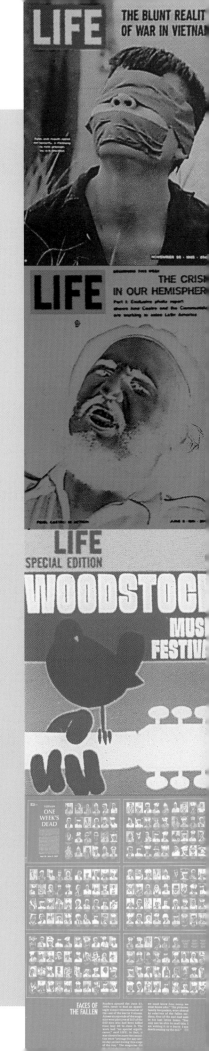

CHILDREN
October 20

**EDWIN LAND AND
THE POLAROID** October 27

JOE NAMATH
November 3

VIETNAM
November 10

RICHARD NIXON
November 17

"news that's in the air"

When Ralph Graves succeeded Hunt as managing editor in 1969, circulation was over 8 million and *Life's* advertising rates were the highest in its history, but the number of ad pages was dropping. Graves took over a magazine in a delicate and awkward financial situation caused by increases in printing and delivery costs as well as declining ad revenues, as we have seen. Management constantly complained about expenditures and also had begun to make severe cuts in personnel and bureaus. Despite all the editorial changes under Hunt, newsstand sales were flat. As this figure was considered a gauge of the interest the magazine generated, more changes were undertaken to improve it.

Graves's philosophy emphasized covering grassroots themes. In a meeting with the editorial staff, he conceded that big events created big interest: "An assassination, that first trip around the moon, Jackie's wedding . . . everybody cares." But the big news events numbered maybe ten a year, and, he said, "We are never going to make a living for 50 issues a year [on] our coverage of ten super news events." In the other forty

issues, *Life* had to give its readers stories that "touch their daily lives."

The new managing editor asked for more provocative stories and more emphasis on the American scene. "Maybe it is not the best country or the happiest, but it is where the action is. . . . the youth revolt, the Vietnam crisis, the Pentagon, the leisure age, the black militants, the good life and the bad life. . . . It is therefore *Life's* most interesting subject." And, like his predecessor, he gave priority to the photography: "We need to put more emphasis on pictures and less emphasis on text. *Life* is still a picture magazine. I seriously recommend that all reporters and young writers who are interested in their own bylines but don't really care about pictures should go look for a job somewhere else. . . . they have no real future on this magazine."

Such was the beginning of a new editorial approach at *Life*, the third in less than a decade that attempted to adapt the product to new readers in a country that was quickly changing. It first attracted notice with the issue of June 27, 1969, when *Life* published

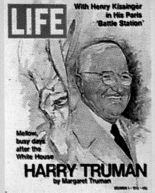

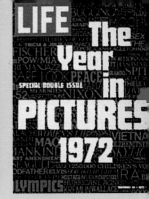

RGE WALLACE
mber 24

HARRY TRUMAN
December 1

DIANA ROSS
December 8

THE JOYS OF CHRISTMAS
December 15

THE YEAR IN PICTURES
December 29

THE LAST TEN COVERS. In 1972 *Life's* span as a weekly magazine ended. Since its launch and the Margaret Bourke-White cover, thirty-six years had gone by. Here are the last ten covers of this stage. They made history.

"One Week's Dead," a stark montage of photos of the 200-odd soldiers who had fallen in Vietnam during just seven average days. This hard-hitting story generated much comment and praise. So did the August 29 issue, which featured ten pages on the Woodstock festival–*Life* would later expand this coverage into a special issue–and an original and far-reaching literary-editorial venture: a 26,000-word piece by Norman Mailer, the first installment of three, about the Apollo moon shots, titled "A Fire on the Moon." A few months later, in the December 5 issue, *Life* again shook its readers when, in six pages of searing pictures, it recorded the massacre of Vietnamese civilians by American soldiers in the village of My Lai. The graphic reportage by an army photographer was supplemented by a staff investigation of the event, reconstructed by interviewing Asian survivors and American military witnesses.

However, all these editorial successes weren't enough to improve the magazine's financial situation, which forced further budget cuts. By March of 1970, the bureaus in Beirut, Miami, Moscow, Rome,

and Vienna were closed. Staff was reduced and several sections eliminated: Miscellany, Fashion, Sports. However, Graves was confident in the magazine's future and its new approach: "Instead of depending on pure news events, the kind that make daily headlines and appear on the Huntley-Brinkley show, we now concentrate on what Tom Griffith calls 'news that's in the air.'"

Unfortunately, the news that was starting to float in the air was the closing of *Life*. And this was not fanciful. Those who had been witness to the magazine's splendor, with issues exceeding 100 or even 150 pages, couldn't help but see it coming when they looked at the *Life* of the 1970s. It was a painfully thin publication that usually didn't go over 66 pages, perhaps 20 of them ads and the rest made up of six or seven stories plus a couple of fixed sections. That is what *Life* looked like during its last few years–a magazine that, despite the straitjacket the business side imposed on it, tried to maintain the appeal and editorial impact that had made it famous.

LIFE, THE magazine
THAT always returns

The announcement in December 1972 that *Life* would "suspend publishing" was so worded not only to keep alive the hope of its reappearance but also for legal reasons: to block the competition from using its name on a magazine, since it was part of numerous Time Inc. enterprises: Time-Life Books, Time-Life Records, Time-Life Films. Legal maneuvering aside, no more than a few weeks separated the closing of the magazine from the first talk of its relaunch. In October of 1973, just ten months after the suspension, Phil Kunhardt, a company executive and fervent advocate of resurrecting *Life*, sent to Otto Fuerbringer, editor of magazine development, a ten-page description of what **a new *Life*** would look like. At the end it said: "America needs *Life* again. Now they haven't got it, people miss it badly. Enough to make an audience for a new *Life* without hardly trying. *Life* should be part of the U.S. decor once more—an elegant, worldly, visually exciting, often passionate, always handsome part of the American home." This *new Life*, said Kunhardt, should:

1. be a monthly
2. have the same large page size as the old *Life*
3. cost at least $1 a copy ($10 a year for a subscription)
4. be printed on high quality, heavy paper with beautiful reproduction
5. have run-of-the-book color
6. contain advertising
7. be talking to an audience of between 1 and 2 million readers
8. be able to be produced by a very small editorial staff

The *new Life* had to wait five years. In the meantime, ten special editions were published to feed readers' interest. The first came out before the end of 1973 and commemorated the twenty-fifth anniversary of Israel. Available only on newsstands, it had moderate sales: some half a million copies. Only after 1978 did *Life* appear at regular monthly intervals, as Kunhardt had outlined five years earlier. It had a price of $1.50, a circulation of 700,000, and a goal of two million readers. Ad rates dropped to

THE JUNIOR KENNEDYS
November 1984

DIANA AND PRINCE HARRY
December 1984

BROOKE SHIELDS
February 1983

DEBRA WINGER
May 1983

BARBRA STREISAND
December 1983

a fourth of their 1970 value, with a color page costing $13,900.

Its first cover was devoted to the craze for hot-air balloons. In subject matter it was still a general interest publication and, as always, it emphasized photography. But unlike the old *Life*, it devoted itself more to issues and personalities than to news. It was very successful with the American upper middle class and, in contrast to the widely popular magazine of former times, it was attractive to a smaller and more select public. It came out as a monthly magazine for twenty-two years, until March 17, 2000, when Time Inc. announced that **"*Life*, the First and Most Famous Photojournalism Magazine"** would stop monthly publication with the May edition that year. At the time, it had a certified circulation of 1.5 million subscribers.

Thereafter the *Life* logo reappeared several times on special editions on different subjects: America Revealed: Tracing Our History Beneath the Surface and Behind the Scenes (2001); Our Call to Arms: The Attack on Pearl Harbor (2001); America's Parade: A Celebration of Macy's Thanksgiving Day Parade (2001); One Nation: America Remembers September 11, 2001; Rock and Roll at 50 (2002); Faces of Ground Zero (2002); Man in Space: An Illustrated History from Sputnik to Columbia (2003); and 100 Photographs That Changed the World (2003). Time Inc. thereby fulfilled the promise it had made to *Life's* loyal readers when it announced in 2000 the magazine's cessation as a regular periodical and yet its continuation through sporadic special editions: "*Life*, the magazine that recorded the world's great events in unique photos, is an invaluable trademark whose name must be preserved. However, despite the exceptional efforts of many talented editors and business managers, the magazine could not continue as a monthly. After much thought and deliberation, it was decided that this new strategy **would be the best way to keep the *Life* trademark alive forever."**

CHAPTER 4
PARIS MATCH

IT IS THE MOST POPULAR AND BEST-KNOWN GENERAL INTEREST MAGAZINE IN THE WORLD. IT UNERRINGLY COMBINES CURRENT EVENTS WITH POLITICAL PERSONALITIES, ROYALTY, THE FASHION WORLD, AND SHOW BUSINESS. THE Paris Match STYLE IS CHARACTERIZED BY VISUAL IMPACT, BY SPREADING ONE PHOTO OVER TWO PAGES, AND BY THE WAY EACH OF ITS PICTURES TELLS A STORY. IT IS IDENTIFIED WITH THE SLOGAN "THE SHOCK OF THE PHOTOS, THE WEIGHT OF THE WORDS."

HERE ARE ITS JOURNALISTIC PHILOSOPHY AND THE KEYS TO ITS SUCCESS.

Paris Match: a story in every photograph

Born in 1938 and reborn in 1949, the magazine imposed a new visual style in which the photograph occupied center stage. And, with its formula, it met the challenge of television.

Former editor Roger Thérond once said that *Paris Match* was one of the few magazines in the world, perhaps the only one, that had been reborn twice. And so it is.

In 1938 the French textile industrialist Jean Prouvost bought from Léon Bailby a sports weekly called *Match,* which had a small circulation although it had been in operation since 1926. Prouvost's aim was to turn it into a journal of current events. Starting in July 1938, *Match* was published under the subtitle **"the weekly of world news."** Although it wasn't a sports magazine anymore, the new owner decided to keep *Match* in the title because he thought that life is also always a contest. *Match* now came out every Thursday

with forty-eight pages. The cover said *Match, hebdomadaire de l'actualité mondiale* and it showed an unknown woman who smiled and raised her hand. Totally in black and white, the first issue had neither advertising nor editorials. Its contents were:

A double page with a sequence of sixteen photographs and the headline "September 1938, the most dramatic month that the world has seen in twenty years."

"Le Match de la vie, cette semaine" (*The Match* of life, this week): three pages with small photos and stories about the week's events.

A three-page article on peace, illustrated by a double-page drawing of Parliament in session in London, which announced the Munich summit meeting. Eight additional pages on the meeting's subsequent developments followed.

Four pages under the headline *"Paris se rallume"* (Paris revives), portraying the rebirth of the city with amusing casino photos.

Several two-page spreads on prominent personalities of the time, and a special story on odd Hollywood professions, such as creating sound effects, making cobwebs, and transporting plants.

Although the weekly emphasized political coverage, the section *"Le Match* de la vie, cette semaine" presented newsmakers in the round, against a background rich in detail, instead of imparting the information tersely in wire-service style. It aimed to show life in all its complexity. Each issue also had two full-page color drawings or caricatures. And there was usually a short fiction piece. But what best characterized *Match* was its display of photos and images in general. Therein lay its success.

When World War II broke out, Jean Prouvost briefly held the post of information minister in the Vichy government under Marshal Pétain, after which he was forced to shut the magazine down from 1945 to 1949. *Paris Match* died for the first time.

PARISH MATCH

BERLIN, 12 MARS 1949. LE PONT AÉRIEN. PREMIERS INSTANTANÉS EN COULEURS SUR LA VIE DANS LA CAPITALE ALLEMANDE (PAGES 18 A 23)

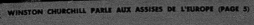

WINSTON CHURCHILL PARLE AUX ASSISES DE L'EUROPE (PAGE 5)   G. MILLER, AMÉRICAIN, EN QUÊTE D'AUTEURS FRANÇAIS (PAGE 35)

N°I - 29 MARS 1949   PRIX: 50 FRS

RENAISSANCE. On March 25, 1949, the French government authorized the reappearance of *Paris Match,* which had stopped publication in 1945 when it was called simply *Match*. This first edition of the new era featured four photos on its cover: the Berlin airlift, a smiling German girl, Winston Churchill, and an American theatrical producer. It ran forty-four pages, and its circulation reached 339,792 copies.

THE PICTURES AND COVERS THAT ILLUSTRATE THIS CHAPTER ARE COURTESY OF *PARIS MATCH.*

Issue number
one of a new era

Match would be reborn on March 25, 1949, when at last the French government authorized it to resume publication. One innovation was prefacing the title with the word Paris, to mark the publication's home. The first issue had forty-four pages, a circulation of 339,792 copies, and these distinguishing characteristics:

The cover carried four photos: a view of the ongoing Berlin airlift; an attractive German girl in a bar; Winston Churchill, shielding his face from the cameras, at the Council of Europe; and the American theatrical impresario Gilbert Miller, in Paris in search of French plays.

News stories dealt primarily with Winston Churchill and with Shanghai, at 5 million inhabitants the world's third largest city, then threatened by the advance of the Red Army and by the presence within its walls of 100,000 Communist infiltrators awaiting the signal to revolt.

A six-page section focused on Berlin and the airlift, with color photos of the war-ravaged city and its people, as well as articles on the city's military government.

Although the magazine didn't have a specific art section, there was an article in colour devoted to Raoul

DOCUMENTARY STORY. On pages 18 to 23, the magazine presented its first documentary article: "Berlin, March 12, 1949." Four of the pages were in color.

CHURCHILL. The English prime minister was among the inaugural issue's chief newsmakers and the subject of one of its cover stories.

Dufy, who in his seventies was painting with a brush tied to his hand because, like Renoir, he had rheumatism. Another story discussed the last painting done by Gauguin before his death, a scene of a snow-covered Brittany town.

The section *Paris Fashion* featured the season's haute couture shows, plus three more color pages, one devoted to the English photographer Dick Dormer, a special envoy from *Vogue,* one to the editor of *Harper's Bazaar*, and one to the artist and fashion illustrator Christian Bérard, sketching a model the very day he died.

The entertainment section included stories on the movie *Manon,* whose budget had swelled to 126 million francs; declarations of love by great lovers, with five photos of theater couples from 1902 to 1949; and an extensive profile of Gilbert Miller, America's great buyer of European theatrical pieces. It also told about the great success in New York and Berlin of *Les Mains sales* by Jean-Paul Sartre.

Prouvost faced an enormous challenge, and many people feared that the industrialist from northern France would not be up to it. But they were wrong. To begin with,

Prouvost had been interested in journalism and publishing ever since, as a young man in 1924, he had bought the newspaper *Paris-Midi* and raised its daily circulation from 4,000 to 80,000 copies. In 1930 his success led him to the purchase of the daily *Paris-Soir,* and within a decade he increased sales to nearly 2 million. In the midst of these achievements, Prouvost had also relaunched the women's magazine *Marie Claire*, with a circulation (apart from that of its sister *Paris Match)* of almost a million copies.

In short, before taking control of *Match,* Prouvost had become a true revolutionary in French journalism.

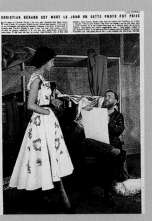

PARIS FASHIONS.
The season's couture showings were not absent from this debut issue of *Paris Match.* Fashion would be one of the magazine's regular sections.

ART. Though the magazine had no special art section, there were several articles on the subject, including one on Gauguin and this one on the interiors of the presidential residence, the Elysée Palace.

THE SPIRIT OF a magazine and an era

One of the great merits of this revolutionary figure in French journalism was to understand that color photography, which was in its infancy, had a great future and had to be exploited. Moreover, Prouvost always tried to offer readers objective political information, something they had lacked during the occupation and postwar years. On the assumption that people wanted not just information but also knowledge, Prouvost decided to start a series of well-written articles of a more intellectual bent, for which he eventually hired the best journalists of the time, among them Roger Thérond, Walter Carone, and André Lacaze. In addition, a team of young, untiring, enthusiastic, and talented photographers pivoted around these staff writers, willing to risk everything in this new profession called photojournalism.

At the center of this new wave was Roger Thérond, a liberal arts graduate who was to become, in time, one of the best editors in the world. He was known as *The Eye* because nothing could escape his gaze or curiosity. His passion for images in general, and for photos in particular, was insatiable. Thérond began his journalism career in 1945 as a movie critic for the magazine *L'Ecran Français*. In 1950, barely twenty-five years old, he began to work for *Paris Match,* first as head of the movie section and then as editor in chief. According to those around him then, Thérond had his finger on the pulse of the times. He would listen to what someone was telling him and immediately know whether it could become an article. He rejected no subject or social phenomenon. He tried not to have preconceived ideas about things, events, newsmakers. In short, he would first observe everything and then digest it journalistically.

RECORD SALES. This issue, on the death of King George VI of England, figures among the magazine's top ten best sellers, with 980,000 copies. It was published on February 16, 1952.

MATCH STYLE. The April 19, 1958, issue shows Fidel Castro in the Sierra Maestra, issuing an ultimatum to Batista. Faithful to its mission, the magazine would travel to the scene of all news events.

The decade of the 1950s, when *Paris Match* began to take off, was a time of great editors, people with strong personalities. The newspaper of record was *France-Soir,* led by Pierre Lazareff. This was considered the bible of the publishing industry: everyone watched to see what story led that day's issue. *France-Soir* was selling a million copies a day, and it had no competitors among French weekly newspapers. Then there was also Marcel Dassault's *Jours de France,* but that was born somewhat later and with a different perspective, so *Paris Match* was still the only current events weekly. Its great competitor worldwide was *Life.* Later on, *Look* would come out in the United States and *Stern* in Germany.

It was about then that President Charles de Gaulle received Gaston Bonheur, the magazine's editor in chief, at the Elysée Palace with the statement "Your magazine has national scope." The magazine covered all French news, from politics to economics, including show business and entertainment. Its prestige was such that readers would get in touch with *Paris Match* whenever something happened, whether insignificant village activities or events of national or international scope, which was of great help in getting "exclusives."

At first, *Paris Match's* main goal was to inform. The directors at that time had a paternalistic attitude toward the young talent. They didn't think in terms of profit, numbers, commerce. They were there to live an extraordinary adventure. There were no market studies or management controls. It was a totally different spirit. Journalists who worked for Roger Thérond said that they could call him in the middle of the night if they had doubts or problems with a story. He would ask them to send the article over and would respond within half an hour. A passionate man, Thérond was also untiring and insatiable: he would read everything that came to hand, listen to all the music he could, visit museums and galleries, see all the movies.

IMPACT. In issue number 2 of April 1, 1949, floods in southwestern France spill over the pages. The editing of photos was already aiming at a high visual impact.

WHEN THE ONLY SCOOP IS PHOTOGRAPHY

The first headquarters was established in the heart of Paris, in first-floor offices at the corner of rue François Ier and rue Pierre Charron, near the Champs Elysées. Thérond and his young journalists and photographers stepped out of the offices into a new and exciting adventure, reportage on a grand scale. One great help was that there was then no television, so visual scoops were exclusively the province of photojournalists.

Paris Match teams would fly on rickety planes to look for stories in faraway places, unknown and mysterious, for two, three, six months. In the public perception, the names of photographers such as Jean-Pierre Pedrazzini, Jean Roy, Tony Saulnier, and Jacques de Potier become intertwined with journalists like Jean Farran, Jean Diwo, Raymond Castans, Philippe de Baleine, Marcelle Ucliez, and Robert Barrat.

In these adventures, they gathered pictures and stories that would reveal the news through photos. An example: Henri Cartier-Bresson was the first Western photographer authorized to go to Russia after the war, and in 1955 *Paris Match* published twenty-four pages on that hitherto hidden world. They did it in two separate issues with the photographer's famous name on the cover and the strong heading *"Un témoignage sans précédent"* (An unprecedented report). Gandhi's India, the Brussels World's Fair, Indonesia, and the United States also made for great stories.

Thérond pushed his photographers toward irreverence, emotions, and improvisation, and away from the stiffness and posed photos that were frequent in the traditional French press.

Thus, when the photographer assigned to photograph Lionel Jospin learned that the prime minister loved basketball, he did not hesitate to hand him a ball, and got a unique shot.

To photograph André Malraux, the photographer asked him to lie down on the floor and strewed books around him. After Malraux's death, when his ashes were transferred to the Pantheon, the funeral organizer was inspired by the photograph in *Paris Match* and decided to surround the casket with photos of the life of the great writer and thinker.

To get distinctive shots of conductor Herbert von Karajan, *Paris Match* assigned the task to photographer Jean-Claude Deutsch, who followed the artist to his houses in Paris, St. Tropez, and Salzburg for six months.

"When you decide whether to publish a photo, you keep several criteria in mind," Roger Thérond would say later. "You think: Will I be overstepping limits? Who could feel hurt? Is the public eye going to accept this photo? Am I providing added information with it? All these questions put us in touch with ourselves, our readers, and society. We reject some photos to avoid lawsuits, but that's not the only reason. There is also an aesthetic criterion: if a photograph is ugly, we don't publish it."

In any case, as a result of these and other innovations in its approach, the magazine's circulation rose fourfold in just a few years, reaching 425,000 in 1951, 700,000 the following year, 900,000 in 1953, 1.2 million in 1954, and 1.4 million in 1955. Among other reasons, this boom was due to dramatic news events, such as Marshal Pétain's death, General de Lattre de Tassigny's shipwreck, and the death of George VI followed by the coronation of Queen Elizabeth of England.

HISTORIC ISSUE. Marshal Pétain´s death produced an issue dated August 4, 1951, that sold 580,000 copies, the highest figure reached that year.

CARTIER-BRESSON. The legendary French photographer came up with spectacular photo coverage of Russia, which *Paris Match* published beginning on January 29, 1955. Cartier-Bresson was the first Western photographer to go to postwar Moscow: his account filled twenty-four pages with a prominent teaser on the cover, reaffirming the magazine´s visual style.

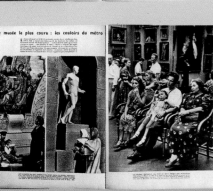

GRACE. *Paris Match* did not just follow the romance, it was instigator and witness of the first Grace-Rainier encounter. Thanks to the magazine, Grace Kelly was admitted to the palace.

BRIGITTE. Her first cover was in 1952. Bardot, who was just becoming well known, married Roger Vadim, a *Paris Match* journalist and aspiring filmmaker. Both would soon be famous.

journalists, reporters, and newsmakers

Quickly the staff started to make contacts and fill address books with important names. Journalists and photographers were becoming a part of Parisian life. They would meet in a small café called La Belle Ferronière, which nobody had ever heard of, right across the street from *Paris Match*. It became one of the "in" places, where people went to be seen, to rub shoulders with the *Paris Match* crowd and the city's most beautiful girls.

But journalists at *Paris Match* did not limit themselves to cultivating the rich and famous: they would go from mingling with *le tout Paris* to toiling a world away, bringing back unique photos and reportage. They often risked their lives, and some were killed. In 1956 two of their photographers died within days of each other. The first was Jean-Pierre Pedrazzini, shot ten times in Budapest while covering the Hungarian Revolution. Meanwhile Jean Roy went to cover the Suez Canal crisis and, with Magnum photographer David "Chim" Seymour, died in a fusillade after an armistice had been declared.

At first *Paris Match* had little money, and cleverness compensated for scarcity. When its journalists worked abroad, they had to do it on a shoestring and come up with good ideas to make up for the lack of technical equipment. As one former staffer defined the magazine then: "It's not orders that get handed down here, as in other companies, but rather enthusiasm. Without that enthusiasm, the best story ideas are worth nothing."

The dream team assembled by Jean Prouvost included future filmmaker Roger Vadim, Brigitte Bardot's husband. At that time Bardot was a young actress who would visit the newsroom each week and remain there, talking with people and sleeping in an armchair, while Vadim and his colleagues put the magazine to bed. Eventually Vadim would become a world-famous director and Bardot one of the most sensual and sought-after of actresses. This not only meant that *Paris Match* would always have easy access to the couple in general and to the actress in particular—she was often featured on the cover—but it also showed Prouvost's incredible nose for news and ability to quickly detect talented people.

Paris Match was also witness and prime mover when Grace Kelly and Prince Rainier of Monaco first met, another milestone in its history, which would result in prestige and millions of dollars for the magazine. Back in 1955 Grace Kelly, already an established Hollywood star, was attending the Cannes Film Festival for the first time. *Paris Match* had sent Pierre Galante, its movie editor and Olivia de Havilland's new husband, with a photographer to cover the event. Pierre Galante wanted to write a story featuring Grace Kelly, so he decided to organize a meeting with Prince Rainier at his palace in Monaco. But there was a small problem. Princely protocol demanded that women visiting the palace cover their heads, but Grace had no hats in her luggage because she thought they didn't flatter her. The photographer took Grace to a Cannes florist who improvised a hat from flowers. Grace went to the palace and met Rainier, romance was born, and the fairy tale began. And *Paris Match* was there to take pictures of it from the very beginning, giving new meaning to the title *Match*.

celebrities' cover appearances

Princess Caroline	83
Princess Diana	66
Princess Stephanie	62
Johnny Hallyday	58
Brigitte Bardot	35
Queen Elizabeth II	33
Alain Delon	32
The Shah of Iran and Farah Diba	31

(Source: Paris Match 2002)

MARILYN MONROE. 1953

GINA LOLLOBRIGIDA. 1954

SOPHIA LOREN. 1955

JANE FONDA. 1963

CLAUDIA CARDINALE. 1961

JEANNE MOREAU. 1958

LESLIE CARON. 1955

MONICA VITTI. 1963

GRACE KELLY. 1954

SYLVIE VARTAN. 1963

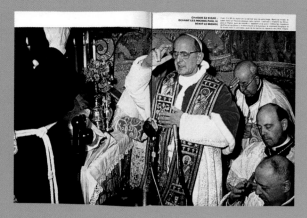

THe news IS KING

The place of photography was always the same at *Paris Match*: photos were fundamental. The magazine always strove for the shot that would make it stand out among its competitors. In France, it was the first magazine to use one picture in a two-page spread. At that time magazines considered photos mere illustrations of text. But *Paris Match* thought differently: the text should complement the photos. Besides, *Match* editors would say, sometimes a photo can be much more eloquent than words.

On that premise Roger Thérond coined the famous phrase "The news is king," which he explained thus:

"Time never ceases trapping us. We live it week after week in an intense and arbitrary way. Current events don't know where they're going and neither do we. We're rowers following the current, and suddenly a whirl-pool takes us and heads us toward a different horizon. You think of the coming issue, you imagine it and you feel it, and it's something else that's born—one word, one picture, one idea, and everything changes. The week isn't what it should be and what it fleetingly was in our dreams, even before it existed. Journalism is knowing that you're living it without thinking about it."

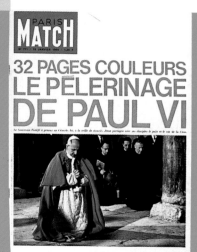

In January 1964 Paul VI became the first pope to visit Israel. The trip did not mesh with the magazine's closing date, yet *Paris Match* published a historic edition on the event, to which it devoted the cover and thirty-two color photos–a great milestone that showed the publication's zeal in covering current events.

A classic case of *Paris Match* being always on the alert for events and information was the visit of Paul VI to the Holy Land in January of 1964. This historic journey made the 262nd successor to Saint Peter the first pope to visit Israel. But the trip didn't fit well with the magazine's schedule. According to the editorial and production calendar, the coverage would be published ten days after Paul VI's return. Roger Thérond wouldn't settle for that. So, in order to cover an event that would change the history of Christianity, he leased and equipped a plane to follow the pope around during his visit. There were sixty persons aboard, including photographers, reporters, and layout people, plus a photo lab and a layout and pre-press

facility. Thérond watched the operation from Paris but in direct and permanent contact with his flying team, which developed photos, wrote, edited, and laid out all the material at 31,000 feet, on their way back to France. The plane arrived in Paris on Monday, January 6, and on that Wednesday the magazine was being sold on newsstands all over the country. The issue was a great success and confirmed readers' interest in the news *Match-style*.

By 1958 *Paris Match* had become France's leading magazine. But just a year later, it lost 300,000 readers. The formula seemed to be wearing out. In 1963, with circulation down to 1.4 million, Jean Prouvost ordered a market study. Based on its results, an attempt

was made to write livelier articles and to give the magazine a more European slant. And, as another survey found that 45 percent of its readers were women, it would have to "add a dose of princesses and divas" to the existing formula.

Paris Match then faced another challenge. Although on the one hand it was independent, in that it did not have outside ownership, on the other hand it was dependent on its middle-class public, which it had to please. About that time, the newsweekly *L`Express* wrote: *"Paris Match can be considered a mirror in which the French middle class is reflected."*

To cover the trip to the Holy Land and get the issue out on time, the magazine leased a plane and packed it with sixty staff members–photographers, journalists, layout people. A photo lab and design office were also installed on board. The plane returned to Paris on a Monday, and by Wednesday the magazine was on all the newsstands.

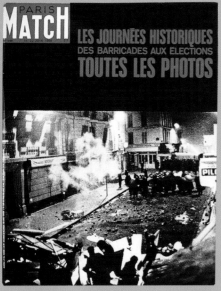

MAY 1968.
The magazine, which already had financial problems, was now in crisis. It didn't appear for several weeks, and afterwards several important journalists were gone, including Thérond.

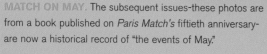

MATCH ON MAY. The subsequent issues-these photos are from a book published on *Paris Match's* fiftieth anniversary-are now a historical record of "the events of May."

At the start of the student uprising of May 1968, circulation had dropped appreciably, so the magazine faced a rather precarious financial situation. During the student demonstrations and the ensuing general strike, the staff worked daily, although the presses were shut down and, at night, St. Germain des Prés was barricaded. A mountain of photos piled up in the newsroom; these photos would eventually be the material for a series of extraordinary and historic issues, once the presses started rolling again.

But, like the rest of the print media, *Paris Match* could not hit the streets for weeks. The strikes and the threats of firings succeeded each other in an endless chain. The staff writers decided to form an association of *Paris Match* writers. At first Jean Prouvost agreed. In the preamble to the association statutes, the staff writers wrote: "The journalists are forming an association to express their willingness to sustain Jean Prouvost's editorial work according to the principles defined and applied by him in *Paris Match*." But on May 31, Jean Prouvost called a meeting of all editorial personnel and company employees and declared that the newsroom was only one of the pillars of the publication; that the other elements–management, sales, advertising–should not be forgotten; and that isolated initiatives should not be accepted. The journalists reacted by immediately activating their association of *Paris Match* staff writers. Jean Prouvost declared: "If you establish this association, you will do it without me and against me."

It was a period of orders and counterorders. On June 10, Jean Prouvost convened a meeting of the three top directors, Raymond Cartier, René Cartier, and Arnold de Contades (a Prouvost son-in-law). Most editors considered themselves fired; there was talk of fifty-four dismissals; decisions were delayed and no one wanted to assume responsibility for a break in communications. Everything ended in confusion, with a minimum of dismissals but nothing solved. As the unease continued, great magazine personalities left, among them Hervé Mille, Roger Thérond, André Lacaze, and Jean Maquet.

Circulation decreased even more in 1969. In September, Jean Prouvost, always with an ear to the ground, considered refreshing the magazine's formula to bring it up to date and put the focus back on photography, which had been affected by competition from television. *Paris Match* tried to get back on course by adopting a more encyclopedic profile, which didn't stanch the loss of readers: in 1972 circulation was under 900,000 copies. But Jean Prouvost didn't give up.

LOGO CHANGES

The *Paris Match* logo hardly ever underwent modifications, except for its colors. At the beginning, the word *Match* was in black and *Paris* in red. Later, whether in a box or on a banner, the two key words–*Match* in white and *Paris* in black–were always on a red ground, and the two were integrated, except in 1961 when *Paris* was written by itself over the letter M.

APRIL 1949
Number 2

NOVEMBER 1949
Number 33

APRIL 1961
Number 628

This cover, when the magazine was called just *Match,* appeared on the issue of September 7, 1939, in the first week of the war. From that time on, it wasn't published for five years.

new Design: in search of new readers

In 1972 Jean Prouvost consulted with several designers including the American Milton Glaser, *New York Magazine's* art director, about a new *Paris Match* format. Glaser went to Paris that November and quickly proposed several different variants for the *Paris Match* cover. Jean Prouvost was impressed and asked Glaser to completely redesign the magazine.

The only snag was that Prouvost was not willing to wait the three or four months that the designer foresaw for the job. Glaser himself wrote of the experience, a designer's dream, in his book *Graphic Design:* "I was in Paris on a business trip when Prouvost, who was already eighty-seven and was called *patron* by his employees, asked me to redesign the magazine overnight. He really meant the next day. I couldn't resist the challenge and began redesigning the magazine together with a very cooperative art staff and editors. It was five-thirty on a Friday afternoon. We worked through until ten, broke for a few dozen oysters, and continued until two-thirty that morning. We resumed early Saturday and worked straight through until eight in the evening. I started with the old logo, folded over the corner and put the word 'Nouveau' on it. I told the editors that in America, whenever the word 'new' was put on a package, sales increased by twenty percent. Using the modified logotype not only on the cover, but also on posters and promotional material, I aimed at institutionalizing the new formula. I advised the staff not to always bleed their cover photographs and to use a simple and consistent style for their typographical headings. [With] these changes, together with trimming three-quarters of an inch off the bottom (the new size of the magazine would be 27 x 31 cm), the magazine was strengthened. . . . The effect produced an impressive twenty percent increase in circulation. Of course, [the] difficulty would be to sustain it.

"The major difference in the old formula of *Paris Match* and the new page layout has to do with maintaining a consistent system. The old method varied from page to

page with no attempt at unity. The principle underlying the new design was to establish a consistent line style, using bold gothic letters, subheads on every page and a uniform way of dealing with layouts. In a magazine of this kind the essential objective is to help the reader understand the content easily, rather than to stress layout inventiveness."

Prouvost approved the mock-up, and they celebrated with champagne. "It was a drug for my self-esteem," Glaser said that day.

On the editorial side, two sections were added: one called "Vous" (You), which featured practical information and introduced the idea of service in the magazine, and the other called "La Semaine des

Parisiens" (Parisians' Week), which dealt with the problems of Paris and the region. The first issue under the new formula came out on December 9, 1972, and it was clear that the magazine was giving priority to information and news reporting rather than to photographs. Even though text and images now shared the magazine fifty-fifty, photos were being chosen more to complement an article than to dominate the accompanying text.

From then on, photos occupied a less important place in the magazine. That first issue had 160 pages, which included the event of the week, the man in the event, a long feature article, and a big color story. The results: in 1973 the magazine recovered somewhat but,

as its once and future editor Roger Thérond would later say, the change was ill-conceived from the beginning: "In 1968, Prouvost was convinced that television was going to win over the written press and that the photo was destined to disappear. I always had faith in photography. For me, an event cannot be separated from photojournalism. It cannot exist without pictures. Without them, current events or news items are reduced to a concept, a statistic. Daniel Filipacchi understood that we had to be the owners of the photo market even if this turned out to be expensive. *Match* is a very structured magazine, with strong periods and periods of light relief, like a movie script. My experience with the movies helped me in that."

THE COMPANY CHANGES HANDS: THE FILIPACCHI ERA

In June 1976, when the magazine was sinking fast, there came on the scene a man who wanted to buy *Paris Match* from Jean Prouvost, promising to restore its original luster, fame, and reader appeal. That man was Daniel Filipacchi.

After brief studies and a little time in the printing industry, Filipacchi had devoted himself to photography. In 1948 he joined what would become the mecca of European photo-journalism, *Paris Match*. "He was always successful at cards, with women, and in reporting," remembers Walter Carone, at that time one of the best photographers in the Prouvost empire. With a bit of luck and some exclusives on writer André Gide and Marshal Pétain, Daniel Filipacchi was appointed head of *Paris Match's* photo service and took part in the launch of *Marie Claire*.

Photography made him a lot of money, and then music made him into a businessman. In 1955 he met Frank Ténot, with whom he hosted a radio program. Four years later they would have a second show, *Salut les Copains* (Hey, Guys), which would become a real success. With the fame and money he earned, Daniel Filipacchi used his show to launch unknown rock singers with great potential, among them Johnny Hallyday and Sylvie Vartan, who became megastars. In 1962 his show had an audience of millions and received thousands of letters every week. The two partners came up with the idea of publishing a weekly. Though all their friends tried to dissuade them, they both decided to risk their savings, and in July of 1962 they launched the first issue of *Salut les Copains*, with Johnny Hallyday on the cover. It was such a success that the first press run of 100,000 sold out quickly and a second had to be printed. A record million copies was reached with the wedding of Sylvie Vartan and Johnny Hallyday. The magazine was also a hit with advertisers.

But Filipacchi was just starting. After that first success, the publishing house produced several magazines, some of them inspired by American models: *Lui,* patterned on *Playboy; Union,* an erotic-scientific monthly; *Mademoiselle Âge Tendre,* for teenagers; *Pariscope*, one of the first weekly pocket guides to the city; *Photo*, inspired by *Popular Photography.* By 1974 the company had impressive offices on the Champs Elysées, though it was still considered a marginal group that made its money from erotic and juvenile publications. *Paris Match* would help the company to diversify, something it needed to do.

Photographiée à 20 ans pour « Paris Match », en 1964, après « Les parapluies de Cherbourg ».

La star, fin 1983, va avoir 40 ans et a bientôt coupé ses cheveux pour jouer dans « Paroles et musique ».

LA BEAUTÉ DENEUVE

Son visage raconte au fil des ans la plus vraie et la plus magique histoire de la beauté. De l'adolescence à la maturité, Catherine Deneuve garde le même éclat et le même mystère, la même élégance et la même sensualité, mais chaque saison de son talent semble encore l'embellir. Elle n'inspire pas seulement des chefs-d'œuvre à Buñuel, Demy, Polanski et surtout Truffaut, dont elle est l'actrice fétiche. Marianne à ses traits dans toutes les mairies du pays, de 1985 à 1989, et elle demeure de film en film la star préférée du public. L'ancienne image romantique du cinéma français en est aujourd'hui l'incontestable diva. A 48 ans, elle trouve dans « Indochine » un rôle à la mesure de sa splendeur, de son métier et de sa légende. Le rôle d'une femme qui lui ressemble. Resplendissante et secrète, passionnée et troublante. Ce que j'ai aimé, dans ce personnage, c'est la félure », dit celle que le magazine américain « Vanity Fair » a qualifiée de « trésor national français ».

▲ Dans « Indochine » : Jamais elle ne s'était sentie aussi proche d'un de ses personnages. Le mythe Deneuve est désormais à son zénith.

▲ 1989, le brushing copié par tant de femmes magnifie la sérénité de ses 45 ans. L'inimitable « couleur Deneuve » n'a pas fini de séduire.

EN TRENTE ANS,
QUATRE ÉPOQUES, QUATRE
COIFFURES, QUATRE
VISAGES

CATHERINE DENEUVE.
Deneuve was a rather interesting case. She was on the cover several times, as in this issue devoted to the 1980s. But, according to the editors, the actress didn´t sell well. She´s a beautiful woman, they´d say, but there´s no mystery about her.

DELON AND BRIGITTE.
With their affairs and scandals, their covers always sold very well. As for Zidane, few football players have appeared on the cover of *Match*.

Paris Match and its Third Birth

Aware that the magazine had lost half of its audience in the previous five years and that the risk was enormous, Daniel Filipacchi faced the challenge and decided to ask Roger Thérond to be its managing editor. "Daniel and I were the only two people in Paris who knew exactly what we could do with *Paris Match,* with whom and how," explained Thérond. Before arriving in the newsroom, the two men had drawn up a list of dismissals: 70 of 170 journalists would have to go. After financial housecleaning, there followed a move to the Filipacchi group headquarters and a series of belt-tightening measures—among others, elimination of color, reduction in format, shutdown of foreign bureaus.

"In 1976, when we arrived, we found a dying magazine because our predecessors were convinced that television had won the battle and that the formula had to be changed," Thérond said. "We achieved success by going back to the origins: the photo, the story, the exclusive, the news, creating a new box of surprises with *Paris Match.* Television today does not cover the news better than it did twenty years ago and does not cause us

PHOTOS AND STORIES. For a photo to be published as a two-page spread, it needs to speak for itself, express an emotion, a feeling, tell a story. Definitely, the lead photo must be a summary of the article and support the headline, like the kiss in "The Wedding of the Century" or the intimate picture of "The King" Elvis Presley.

THE DOUBLE PAGE.
A feature of the design style that *Paris Match* imposed on the world is a double-page opening with a photo that says it all. This is a very clean and clear way of presenting a page. The headline, subhead, and caption are laid out so as to organize the way readers look at things. Later, continuity is added by the quiet accompaniment of the text.

particular problems. The demise of *Look* and *Life* did not occur because they lost their audience to television but because they lost advertising. The proof that there is still room for this type of magazine, despite the power of television, is evident in the results of *Stern* in Germany or of the *Sunday Times* magazine in Great Britain."

However, Thérond would not abandon political coverage. "Thanks to its new formula," he pointed out, "*Paris Match* has once again become a magazine that is full of life. But it still needs political credibility. With that in mind, we shall continue acting the same way with members of the majority or of the opposition when necessary. The objectives of *Paris Match* are to maintain the magazine's current intensity–impressive photos, scoops, unexpected stories–and general quality, but also to find once again that nose for the big story." The new approach hit the bull's-eye: by late 1977 *Paris Match* would stop losing money and regain its old prestige and circulation.

At a time when all newsmagazines were trying to attract more readers and major advertisers, *Paris Match* chose a much broader policy whose goal was to attract everyone from a company's directors to its doormen. Every week, *Paris Match* readers get their dose of cold sweat from the horrors of the world, as well as their dose of dreams with the successes of the rich and famous. When Roger Thérond was accused of lowering the magazine's standards, he responded by shrugging his shoulders. *"Paris Match* is becoming the magazine of the French people, with their virtues and defects."

CONTINUITY. Another trait of the *Match* style is the headline on the double-page spread that follows the opening. It gives the story clear continuity and is not necessarily a repetition of the title.

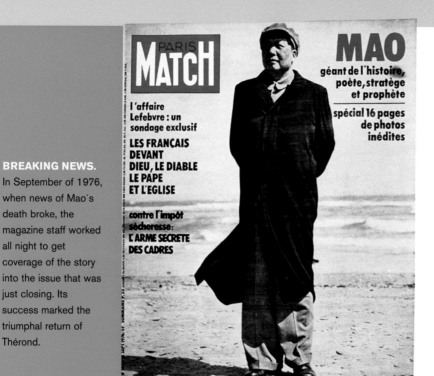

BREAKING NEWS.
In September of 1976, when news of Mao's death broke, the magazine staff worked all night to get coverage of the story into the issue that was just closing. Its success marked the triumphal return of Thérond.

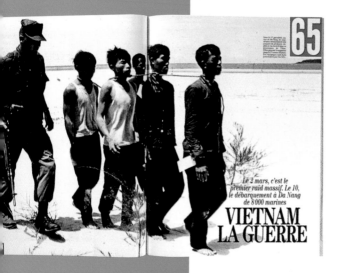

HISTORY. In 1998, to commemorate its fiftieth anniversary, *Paris Match* published a memorable 900-page book depicting in photos the history of the last half century, with its wars, *attentats*, and assassinations.

MITTERRAND AND THE 1980S.
The double life of this very attractive public figure captivated readers. The issue that presented Mazarine, his extramarital daughter, had high sales.

Thérond started off on the right foot in 1976. The very night his first issue as editor was being put to bed, Chinese leader Mao Tse-tung was dying. The newsroom worked all night to produce a special new issue whose cover featured a black-and-white photograph of Mao. With this issue, which sold more than a million copies, *Paris Match* rose from the ashes. Roger Thérond said of this day: "Our queen, the news, was with us."

Match continued to rise with the dramatic news events that followed, such as the death of Princess Grace. But Thérond did not stop there. He wanted to broaden the magazine's spectrum, rejecting nothing and no one: "Everything that surrounds us in our personal and daily lives becomes a subject for *Paris Match*. A child's words, a woman's secrets, a friend's opinion. *Paris Match* devours everything: family, relationships, avocations. It nourishes itself on our times. Our lives become a *Paris Match* exclusive."

The 1980s were superb for *Paris Match* because there were three particularly popular families generating news: the ruling family of Monaco, the French presidential family (with François Mitterrand leading a double life like a character in a novel), and the family of Princess Diana, with whom the French public identified since there was no monarchy in France. "Those people are either gone from the scene nowadays or are going," explained Alain Genestar, the magazine's current editor, near the end of the decade.

"Thérond's decision to eliminate the celebrity section was linked to this. It's a rule of news: when there's hard news, celebrities take a backseat. But in the eighties, when the news was less important–there were no wars, for instance–the rich and famous regained the spotlight. With the Tienanmen Square rebellion in China, the fall of the Berlin Wall, the advent of Gorbachev in Russia, important news events returned at the end of the eighties."

By contrast, in the 1990s celebrities and everything about the rich and famous would recover strength. A historic case for the magazine was that of Mazarine, the secret daughter of former president François Mitterrand. Although everyone in the press knew of her existence, no one dared broach the subject in print. Besides, father and daughter always took care not to be photographed together. Even when they went to lunch, each would enter and leave the restaurant alone. But then, one day in 1994, they surprised all the waiting photographers when they came out arm in arm. Mitterrand did not try to stop the photographers, nor did he ask his security personnel to do so. It was evident that he wanted to be seen with his daughter. *Paris Match,* however, faced an ethical dilemma: Was getting the scoop worth breaking an excellent relationship with the president? They did some discreet checking. No one raised a fuss or requested anything in exchange. Obviously they had a green light. They put the story on the cover and sold 1.13 million copies.

1981
June

1981
August

1984
September

1988
October

1989
January

eDITOrIaL Premises
THen anD now

The man most responsible for the great publishing landmark called *Paris Match*, the late Roger Thérond, set forth some editorial principles that are part of the philosophical foundations on which the magazine stands. Today they are as current and valid as when he issued them:

Politics: "*Paris Match* is an apolitical weekly. What's important for us is to cover the facts in our own way and not play politics."

Advertising: "Every week we're on the newsstands, and our cover is our best billboard. Our best publicity campaigns are those that we mount every week with our cover. So it's difficult to have an institutional advertising campaign. In 1984, when the Harmony agency offered the idea of tearing off the logo, it was a revelation: *Match* is the only magazine that's recognizable even when it's torn. The agency had come up with this concept that I'd already had in my head this way: governments come and go, *Match* remains. Beauty, experience, exploits, emotions, adventure, love, tenderness: all of that is in *Match*, and through seven photos extracted from one issue of the magazine, it produced a strong image of life." (This campaign featured seven covers with the logo scraped or torn off.)

Creativity: "A magazine that has to show weekly that it's liked by the public can't doze; it must be alert for the smallest event, while at the same time knowing how to respect the news hierarchy. In that sense, television stations have a lot to learn from magazines."

The future: "I believe that the next millennium's values will be tied to learning and knowledge. The public will be interested in crucial but quiet knowledge–medicine, architecture, painting, the arts, photography, philosophy–as well as economics, since the public is uneasy about what's going on and doesn't want it

TOP SeLLInG ISSUeS

DATE	COVER SUBJECT	COPIES SOLD
1970	Farewell to de Gaulle	2,114,000
1996	Funeral of François Mitterrand	1,665,000
2001	World Trade Center Attacks	1,500,000
1997	Death of Princess Diana	1,350,000
1996	Death of François Mitterrand	1,320,000
1952	Funeral of George VI	1,200,000
1997	Funeral of Princess Diana	1,150,000
1994	Presentation of Mitterrand's daughter Mazarine	1,130,000
1952	Death of George VI	980,000
1982	Death of Princess Grace	903,000

(*Source: Paris Match 2002*)

1956
April

1972
January

1983
July

1988
December

1990
October

ROYAL FAMILIES. Those of Monaco and Great Britain are closely watched in France, to such a degree that Caroline, her sister Stephanie, and Princess Diana are the three women who have appeared the most on *Paris Match's* cover.

to happen again. People are also going to be interested in the Earth, the freedom to live and breathe, and in nature, and in happiness. The future of magazines is that they will need fewer celebrities and more important articles that place a value on knowledge."

For the current editor, Alain Genestar, *Paris Match's* mission today is to be like television; that is, to alternate segments of entertainment with serious ones, as in a TV newscast. And its cover should always try to hook the public as much as possible, like a prime-time TV show. The mission is to mix information with entertainment, with the common denominator that both must be spectacular. "The idea is to apply everything we know to news reporting techniques. We're journalists and we have to bring back photos of what we see," Genestar summarizes. "For example, we're now finishing a book on the history of film. But these days, it's more and more difficult to photograph actors in their daily lives. (The best photos of Marilyn weren't taken when she was acting but when she was sleeping in her dressing room.) We try to convince the stars that these photos are necessary. When people are good and accept this reality game, it's even better. The future of *Paris Match* is to continue opening doors and winning people's confidence."

THE SHOCK OF THE PHOTOS, THE WEIGHT OF THE WORDS

This slogan defines *Paris Match´s* editorial philosophy and style. The editor in chief, managing editor, and art director explain how it's carried out and how the magazine operates today.

"

Everybody sniffs at *Paris Match* but everybody buys it," former editor Roger Thérond would say. This was true and still is, but for those producing the magazine it has become an asset more than a liability. Patrick Jarnoux, the current managing editor, says: "We don't mind if people read *Paris Match* at the beauty parlor or if they think it's a magazine for doormen. **My dream is that *Paris Match* be read by a million doormen.** It's true that people react like that, but it's also true that it's the most widely read magazine. Besides, we achieve quite a lot of things by being *Paris Match*. For example, when Lionel Jospin was elected prime minister, we went with him on a trip to the countryside.

En route, he decided to make a phone call. He got out of the car and the photographer got a shot of a man wearing a suit in the middle of nowhere. That's why it's so pleasant to work at *Paris Match*, because we dare to be different, to see men, whether politicians or philosophers or artists, as what they really are: men."

This philosophy and this enthusiasm are what open the magazine every Monday. The day starts early for the photo staff, because photo agencies submit material from the weekend, or from previous days on important events where it takes more time to find the appropriate pictures. A list is made of all the material available, and sometime around noon that day a meeting is held that generally lasts for about three hours. At this meeting are the top editors, the photo editor, a staff writer, and someone in charge of wire news who keeps track of developments abroad—some eight or ten persons in all. The photo portfolios are studied then, and the stories for the issue are chosen in terms of the quality of the pictures. Also selected

are topics that may be "intelligently" incorporated into the table of contents, so as to maintain a balance among the different sections—international politics, French affairs, political coverage, celebrities, the arts, show business, adventure.

The editorial meeting is usually held on Tuesday afternoon, when there already is a preliminary table of contents—the ideal issue the editors would like to have. That night, reporters and photographers receive their assignments for the week. Other meetings will take place from then on to see whether the selected story ideas are interesting, whether the editors want to go ahead with them, whether the photo coverage of the assigned stories is coming along well, and so on. Sometimes interesting stories fail for lack of photos. Events dictate the magazine's content. Occasionally, exceptional stories come about in unexpected ways.

PARIS MATCH

LA GUERRE

World Trade Center
Mardi 11 septembre 2001
9 h 03, heure de
New York

38 PAGES SPECIALES

www.parismatch.com
M 2533 - 2730 - 14.50 F

THE SHOCK. Perhaps the most impressive cover showing the Twin Towers attack. A *Paris Match* cover picture must meet several requirements, four of which are clearly exemplified here:

1. It must be a photo of current events.

2. It must not be retouched.

3. It must be authentic.

4. Deaths, births, weddings, and divorces, as well as catastrophes, make great stories.

THE MAKING OF THE MAGAZINE TODAY

As the week evolves, so does the situation. Some stories may gain in relevance and need help—in which case an extra team is assigned—while others become old news and fall by the wayside. The magazine's table of contents might change every day in consequence of breaking news. Often the biggest changes take place between Friday night and Monday because, generally, plenty happens during the weekend. Sometimes the magazine that was planned at the Tuesday meeting is completely different from the one that is finally published.

Wire editors, the magazine's managing editor, the section editors, the photo and art directors attend these and other daily meetings. The issue is analyzed then to see how it's evolving, and sometimes changes are made as events dictate. Those in charge of the weekend shift will keep up with all the news and read the American and British papers to see if they're carrying something the French editors might have missed. Part of the shift's mission is to stay in touch with journalists in the field where the news is happening.

How are the photographers chosen? The general policy is to assign the best possible photographer for a particular event or newsmaker, even if that person is not necessarily a great photographer. The best photographer is the one who will get the best photo. It might be someone who happened to be somewhere by chance. The magazine practices *la raflette,* a slang term loosely meaning "sweep" or "roundup"—when a team arrives at the scene of an event, its members always look for people who were there and who might have taken pictures. "Our starting point is that no matter what happens, there's always someone who took photographs and our mission is to find that person," explains managing editor Patrick Jarnoux. "To us, that photographer is the best one. Little by little, people have got used to this, and when they have a picture that might interest us, it occurs to them to call us."

The *Paris Match* formula tries to complement what is being done on television. "TV shows the instant; we show what occurs around it," Jarnoux clarifies. "That was what happened, for example, with the bomb that exploded on a bus in Karachi, Pakistan, with French naval engineers aboard. When a dramatic event like that occurs, we try to put the story together as we envision it. How is television going to cover it? Are they going to show us pictures right away or later? And we, what are we going to do? Are we going to think about the victims first? Who are they? Where do they come from? Later we'll link the Karachi disaster with the French Ministry of Defense: Is the attack directed against France? We assume

BEFORE AND AFTER. In the March 21, 2002, issue, six months after the attacks against the United States, the magazine published an exceptional story with Michel Setboun's photos: the city of New York before and after the Towers. This photographic "before and after" is a formula that *Match* uses frequently.

that the administration that has just been appointed is going to react. And we remember that the minister of defense is a woman, the first to have reached such a high level in government. And we immediately conclude that we need to be with her, Michèle Alliot-Marie, on the plane leaving for Karachi."

The magazine made arrangements with the French government, which finally authorized a *Paris Match* team to accompany the minister. From that point on, reporters and photographers from *Match* did not leave her side and came up with exceptional coverage, with all the intimate details of the trip and of her conversations with President Jacques Chirac.

The day of the first editorial meeting, a couple of options for the cover are chosen, although everything could change at any moment. In selecting the cover, editors keep one fact in mind: if readers wanted to select a magazine equivalent to *Paris Match*, they would have to buy several, since *Paris Match* is a mixture of many types. Its pages offer extensive reporting, sections for women, politics, economics, so there is material for all kinds of people. "As can happen with all magazines, *Paris Match* has issues that are not as good as others. Sometimes the news events don't help much, either," Jarnoux added. "So people buy fewer magazines. Nowadays it's hard to buy a magazine. Before, people would walk, stop at a newsstand, and take time to make their selection. That doesn't happen anymore. Most people go out in their cars or take the metro, and since it's packed, they can't read. Magazines are bought at airports or train stations when people have five minutes to stop and choose calmly. At that time, the cover plays a key role: it's what attracts the eye. This is why we have to be so careful about the cover photo and headline."

Currently, *Paris Match's* mock-up is divided into two large parts. One brackets the magazine in front and back–"*Match* de Paris" and "*Match* de la Vie" are its most important sections–and the other is located in the middle, where the news stories are. The outside sections comprise what is known in the newsroom as the "soft" part of the publication, while the hot news stories and those with greater impact are in the middle. At one time this block included a section called "Les Gens" (People), which was eliminated by Roger Thérond in 1997 because he no longer thought it worked. His successor, Alain Genestar, supports that decision. "The celebrity market fluctuates a good deal. It was a risk to eliminate that section, but reality was on our side," explains Genestar. "Today, after the September 11 episode and the advent of the extreme right in France, there are more news events."

NEWS WITH A DIFFERENCE. As its editors explain, *Paris Match* tries to complement television. TV shows the instant; *Paris Match* shows what occurs around it. Here the activities of the French minister of defense are added to reportage on the Karachi attack.

THE ATTEMPT ON THE POPE
May 1981

HORROR ON THE HIGHWAY
August 1982

PLANES CRASH
April 1977

TIANANMEN MASSACRE
June 1989

THE MARTYRS OF BEIRUT
November 1983

THE PREREQUISITES OF
a cover PHOTO

Genestar emphasizes the concept of "magazine" in *Paris Match*, instead of "photo album" like his predecessors. "*Paris Match* is not a picture magazine, but rather one that shows news events by means of photos," says its current editor. "We deal with current events on the international scene through their central figures, whether they are presidents, popes, gangsters, movie actors, theater audiences, war victims or heroes. Ours is a magazine without sections, which starts from scratch every week. The key to my management is maintaining continuity. To this I add my particular interest in excellent reporting."

Currently, the magazine's newsroom has a staff of a hundred, of whom half are reporters, about ten are editors, four associate editors, and some fourteen photographers. Unlike other magazines, *Paris Match* bases its work on the visual aspect, and each idea must be matched by a photo. Sometimes photos are even run as stand-alones, with no text. Since it has no commitments to anyone or anything, the magazine chooses its own subjects. Not all events make it into *Paris Match*. The first thing editors ask themselves is if they can do something that is exclusive or has a special angle or is different from other publications. "We're very demanding about the quality of the material," says Genestar.

"We're one of the few magazines in the world that can buy the visual material from the competition if our team did not produce the best photos. We always have to publish the best photo. This is our sacred rule. This may sometimes create a little tension in the newsroom, but it's also good because it motivates our photographers to constantly improve."

Consequently, *Paris Match* tends to produce about 60 percent of the editorial and photographic material it publishes, buying the rest from agencies. Partly this is because the independent photo agencies generate fewer and fewer photos, ideas, and special reports.

But what are the criteria in selecting photographs? "The only condition is that the photo be good," says the *Paris Match* editor. "Beyond the word *good*, several qualifications may be added: at the magazine, we believe that a photo must be informative, exclusive, striking, or simply beautiful. There are many selection criteria, but the most important one is that the photo be good."

This is why choosing the cover photo is crucial. The cover is first discussed on Tuesday, and ideas are exchanged throughout the week. These are the key commandments for selection:

BIRTH OF THE PRINCE
March 1958

FAREWELL TO JOHN LENNON
December 1980

SHIELDS-DELON ROMANCE
June 1986

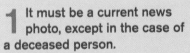

1 It must be a current news photo, except in the case of a deceased person.

2 It must never be a retouched photo.

3 It must not be a drawing or an illustration.

4 Montages are not accepted, that is, one or two pictures creating a single image to suggest an idea.

5 It must be an authentic photograph.

6 Ideally, the subject should face the reader and make eye contact, although this is not always possible.

7 Most important, the photo must tell a story; this criterion prevails over technical quality.

8 If the person is attractive, so much the better, but we must always remember that the most beautiful woman or most handsome man won't sell unless the photo tells a story.

9 It doesn't matter if the photo is in black and white.

10 Deaths, births, weddings, and divorces, as well as catastrophes, make great stories.

ACCIDENT INVESTIGATION
June 1998

THE DENEUVE MYSTERY
April 1992

JOURNALISTIC LIMITS and
THE PURCHASE OF EXCLUSIVES

In the war to find the best-selling cover or the celebrity with the most reader appeal, the question often arises of whether it's a good idea to pay for an exclusive, or to reach an agreement with a royal family when an article or photo threatens their prestige or integrity. "We sometimes pay for an exclusive story or make an agreement with the other party, but these are always private and specific deals, never general ones," Genestar explains. "Money is part of the negotiation; we can buy exclusivity. We can't talk about the amounts involved, because that's confidential information. We might do it more than other media, but it's not shocking. What's important is that the information be good and accurate. That we make agreements with the Monaco family is a myth. To be sure, we did do it before the birth of their children, so that we obtained exclusivity and they avoided being bothered by various publications. But those days are over now. We sometimes sign agreements with great actors' agents."

Anyway, the question remains: What determines what *Paris Match* would publish or reject? A clear example was the case of Daniel Ducruet, Stephanie of Monaco's former husband, who was photographed naked having sex with a

woman. The magazine refused to publish the photos, not because of any agreement with the royal family, as people thought at the time, but because the magazine considered the content of the pictures to be a "private act." "To us it's bad form to photograph people through their windows or to hide and catch them by surprise. We might be a bit daring, but we prefer not to be ill-bred," Genestar says. "Last summer I didn't accept a nude photo of the president on vacation. I thought it was in bad taste and counter-productive, since we would have unnecessarily antagonized the incumbent before the elections. At *Paris Match* we feel that when public figures use their private lives for their work—to sell albums and movies and so forth—their private lives belong to the public. But when public figures don't showcase their private lives, we're very discreet about them."

Another interesting case to illustrate the same limits, but on the political level, was the growing popularity of the extreme-right presidential candidate Jean-Marie Le Pen. *Paris Match* adopted the editorial position of not giving unnecessary publicity to the candidate, whom it considered an enemy of democracy. Since he was a political figure, it treated him as

such—it interviewed him, and covered his meetings and debates—but it did not promote his family, and it showed him only once with his wife, in an article that tried to portray him as he really was. The magazine did nothing to give him prominence: it didn't publish a story about his wife as it did with the other two candidates, Lionel Jospin and Jacques Chirac, nor did it photograph him playing golf or riding a bike.

But the ethics-versus-aesthetics equation is a very subtle one full of gray areas. What attitude should be adopted if there are good photos of a famous person's marital infidelities? What if the legitimate spouse might learn of the infidelity from the article the magazine published? In this last instance, *Paris Match* would opt not to publish the photos, since it takes

32. That's the number of times Alain Delon has appeared on the *Paris Match* cover. But it was always with a story to tell: a separation, a new love, or in this case his relationship with his young son.

Alain Delon
Il revient... à la télévision. A partir du 3 janvier, il incarne Fabio Montale, un flic solitaire de Marseille, dans une série sur T.f.1. Parmi les acteurs, un petit garçon de 7 ans nommé Alain-Fabien
"TU SERAS UN ACTEUR MON FILS"

TO WOMEN. This article targeted female readers with the relationship between the actor and his small son Alain-Fabien, who had been very ill and who also wanted to be an actor. The photos show an ideal relationship between father and son.

Vingt-quatre heures dans la vie de Delon

only measured risks, assuming responsibility in all cases. "But we'd always be inclined to be harder on cynical and high-handed celebrities, and to be more considerate of simple, well-bred, and courteous persons," explains Genestar. At any rate, the present editorial director and a number of his editors consider that the law is evolving in a way unfavorable to them, tending to favor protection of privacy over freedom of expression. They feel that it's a mistake to limit photos, because this is a step toward an overprotective government, which can be very dangerous. "To impede photographing people also means banning photographing the victims of an accident or a terrorist attempt. In society, you have to be able to see attack victims. And the laws now prohibit our taking this type of photo." Genestar says. "When this law came out, I wrote an editorial in which I stated that in the hypothetical case of a terrorist attempt, *Paris Match* would opt for skirting the law."

A 21 ans,
ça baigne pour
le joueur le
mieux payé du
monde

LA FUSEE RONALDO

URGENCE !
JOSPIN EN LIGNE DIRECTE
AVEC PARIS

HOW TO achieve
THe VISUaL STYLe

One of the great architects of the *Paris Match* visual style is Guy Trillat, who has been with the magazine since 1970 and has been its art director since 1976. Trillat, like Roger Thérond and Daniel Filipacchi, dismisses the myth that magazines such as *Paris Match* were destined for extinction after the appearance of television. For them, the two media complement each other instead of being adversaries. "By its very nature the television image is fleeting, while photography is a more permanent testimony," he explains. "They need each other."

From this premise it follows that the magazine needs a distinct visual style. Thus were born the two-page photo—which had never before been used that way in magazine publishing—and the slogan "the shock of the photos, the weight of the words," which, according to

Trillat, appeared in 1976 when a campaign was being organized to relaunch *Paris Match*.

"At the time, there was an advertising agency working with us. And that slogan came out during a creative meeting, as often happens, in a brainstorming session," Trillat explained. "Now we don't use it anymore because it's already public domain and everyone uses it, although the original philosophy of the magazine was to find the best photo and narrate the most interesting events by means of photos, but always accompanied by good stories. Now I think that it's the photo that gives weight to the words."

But how do you apply this formula to the cover selection? Says Trillat: "A week ahead, we already have a possible idea for a cover, if nothing important happens

in the meantime. In general, we prefer to give priority to stories about the rich and famous: for example, the birth of an artist's baby, a wedding, an exposé, some event in the lives of royalty. A folder is put together and then, during the Monday meeting, choices are made among the different photo portfolios, as long as these subjects continue to be current. Or perhaps we're talking about unposed photos, because people tend to resist posing. In that case we try to find current photos of them or talk them into a studio shoot. Among two or three options for the cover, we always choose whatever achieves the best results from the visual standpoint."

Trillat continues: "The problem with *Paris Match* is that we're not like other French newsmagazines—*L'Express, Le Point, Le Nouvel*

GRAPHIC SURPRISE. Readers should find celebrities in unexpected situations in *Match,* such as soccer player Ronaldo fishing, Prime Minister Jospin on the phone by the highway, Michel Platini very enthusiastic over the soccer World Cup in 1998, or Woody Allen doing something unusual for him: posing for a photo.

Observateur. They can do, if they like, a cover on executives' fortunes or Frenchmen's aching backs, and it works. But on our covers, readers have to find a newsy piece. We give priority to stories featuring female celebrities, since most *Paris Match* buyers are women. While the magazine is read by the whole family, it's the woman who buys it. So we must find stories that have a feminine sensibility. To show how hard it is to know whether a cover is going to work, we just need to cite a very concrete example: when we did one with actress Catherine Deneuve on it, we were basing this on a poll that named her as the French public's favorite artist. We came up with several covers featuring her, with the best photographs and the best photographers. However, since she never grants interviews and always refuses to talk about her private life, we end up showing the public a flat and purely aesthetic picture of a beautiful woman. Covers with Catherine Deneuve don't work, don't sell, because generally there isn't a story to sustain them."

What changes have occurred since 1976?
"Instead of drastic changes, an evolution has taken place. We never wanted to erase what had been done before and start from scratch. This isn't part of our policy. *Paris Match's* transformations have happened gradually. To begin with, a different typeface is chosen, a change that might be imperceptible to readers but that transforms some aspect of the magazine. But the thing that didn't change was the *Paris Match* philosophy. The *Paris Match* style is inalterable: we use pictures, we do two-page spreads, and through these double pages we tell a story. An important event will be covered in five double pages. The first is the opening, and each of the next ones will tell a story. Each double page is like a chapter in this narrative. And the text is an element that rounds off the photo coverage. This was always so and will not change. Some people say the magazine used to have more stories on great discoveries, but that's not true. The distribution among the various topics has always been the same."

DOCUMENTARY STORIES. These are published in the magazine's first few pages, after the first section, *"Match de Paris."*

THE PHOTOS MUST TELL A STORY

What share of the magazine is assigned to each section?
"The balance changes every week as a function of current events. One week it carries more celebrities, another week more topical events or issues. The proportion in every section depends on the weekly news. *Paris Match's* peculiarity is that when you get to the last advertising page, you get to the central section, where there is no advertising. We never interrupt a central article with a page of advertising, which is one of the advantages that *Paris Match* has over its competitors like, for example, *Le Figaro Magazine*, which cuts articles up to insert ads. Advertising is found at the beginning and at the

end in *Match*. In the central part–which contains two segments, one of forty-eight pages and the other of thirty-two–there is no advertising. A special supplement might be inserted in the center of the magazine, but these are rare because they are very expensive. After this central section, there are ads again, but they always go with the different sections, so that for every full-page ad there is a section on the opposite page–*Match* Travel, *Match* Money, consumerism, tourism, fashion, beauty, health, all the sections called *Match de la Vie*. These sections change every week –for example, one week may have beauty and travel and money–and they are part of an editorial strategy

planned over several weeks. The *Match de Paris* section highlights the trends of the times and is planned a week ahead. Every week there is a documentary piece that generally is at the beginning, but sometimes at the end. It all depends on advertising space. According to the amount of advertising, we will choose to place it in the front or the back. The sections depend on the amount of advertising, since every one-page ad must be accompanied by a one-page article. The body of the magazine never varies: it's always made up of the two segments, which add up to eighty pages. In an exceptional case, eight pages might be added if the news event is quite important or if there is a lot of advertising. Ad pages

HISTORIC AND DIFFERENT.
The event was covered by all the media. But *Paris Match* did it its own way: it told the story as if it were a documentary movie that would take readers from yesterday to today. That is its way of competing with television.

and sections are printed before Tuesday. What's printed Tuesday night are the current events sections. It's always been like that."

Were there mock-up changes?
"Yes, because one's style evolves. From 1976 until now, it was always I who gave *Paris Match* its style, although sometimes we had to adapt to circumstances. At one point there was a section called *People*. It doesn't exist anymore because celebrities have been integrated into the news coverage. I chose to simplify some elements – for instance, with the photographs. Before, I would use three photos to explain a situation, whereas now I try to choose only one because that

seems enough to me, especially if it's a good one. Evolution has occurred at various times because of external forces, because of the reportage. I'm sure we dealt with the events of September 11 in New York in the same way we would have done it twenty years ago. Still, there probably would have been minimal differences in the type choice, in the framing of the photos. The important thing today is to simplify the magazine and make it as clear as possible. My central premise in this sense is to be clear, simple, and clean so that people don't complicate their lives. We don't always succeed. Sometimes after printing, an issue doesn't come out well: the captions can't be seen

because they're printed in black on dark gray. The big changes are in the graphic use of type. I'm an interpreter of what people give me: photos, texts, captions. Of course, there is something more expected in the case of *Paris Match*: our weekly must be made to look like a monthly, more polished than a regular weekly. At many weeklies, there is a set mock-up that's full of blank pages. We don't want to just fill pages up, we want to tell a story. A photo is not an illustrative picture but a picture that tells the story. Sometimes it's difficult for me to accept that, in the one-page sections, the photographs may be merely illustrative."

BERLIN 1961-1989. In fifty photo pages in the issue of November 23, 1989, the magazine showed the history of the Wall—its construction in August 1961, the first escapes, and the most emotional moments of its destruction. This was a collector's edition.

OPENING. Photography is quite symbolic for the French. Chirac looks ahead to the future. After the anguish generated by the rise of the extreme right in the presidential elections, the image of Chirac represents hope and tranquility in the future.

SPECIAL EDITION. Chirac and his wife, in the gardens of the presidential palace, are featured on the cover for May 16, 2002. Art director Trillat used this issue to explain to the book's authors the magazine's editing style.

THE CELEBRATION. Each page tells a story. Celebrations, a greeting from the presidential couple, and the colors of the French flag accompany the victory. Close-ups are alternated with group shots.

TENSE WAIT. Chirac sits in his campaign offices before the election results are in. The photo transports readers to the candidate's intimate world and makes them feel close to him while he waits to learn his destiny.

RETURN. The news section ends with a symbolic return to the Elysée Palace. The article continues with its political and family album, and an image of opponent Le Pen's headquarters.

THE KEYS
TO THE EDITING STYLE

Did *Paris Match* dictate a style for the rest of the press?

"Whatever the case, there is a *Match* style that is known all over the world, to the point that I once designed a book jacket and people told me it was a *Match* cover. *Paris Match* is unique. People have tried to copy us, but badly. At one time we were considered a competitor of *Le Figaro Magazine*, which never managed to have a style like ours, which is a marriage of depth and form. *Paris Match* has a rhythm, the photos have meaning, they're not just aesthetic. When *Paris Match* devotes ten pages to a topic, that is, five doubles, there are going to be four two-page photo spreads and one for the text at the end. The four photo spreads are going to be quite rich in content and aesthetics, and afterwards the double one with the text, which will be relaxing to the eye, will tell the story, over a gray background, of what you have just seen in the pictures. This balances the photographic impact.

"Let's take as an example the article that we published about Chirac's victory in the presidential elections. The order was this: **1** a big photo, Chirac at the Elysée Palace, looking toward the future, large headline, lead; **2** flashback: Chirac at campaign headquarters before the results were announced; **3** victory, with him saluting the people who are celebrating it; **4** Chirac's supporters with the French tricolor; **5** the presidential couple (the idea in this case was to alternate close-ups of the main characters with group shots); **6** people who voted for the National Front of Le Pen; **7** island of text; **8** Chirac at the Elysée; **9** Le Pen with his family; **10** Le Pen at home, barefoot; **11** Chirac on a balcony, a reminder to readers of his victory in 1995; **12** his history, in black-and-white photos, when he was a young member of Parliament; **13** photos with Mitterrand and with Jospin [two political enemies]; **14** another island of text; **15** in his youth with his wife: he's fixing the car, she's serving drinks at an election meeting; **16** with his two daughters, Claude and Laurence; **17** his adoptive daughter; **18** text; **19** the art of grandfatherhood, with his grandchildren (two-page spread); **20** in his office, ready to return to work, surrounded by photos of his daughter and grandson; **21** photos of the Corrèze, Chirac's region. Also, there's a whole story on the painter Van Dongen in this issue."

Couldn't the magazine be reproached for having a display of Van Dongen's pictures next to a subject as serious as the presidential elections?

"No, because after forty pages of elections we needed something that was timeless. It did not have to be news. It did have to be justified by its beauty, since it was painting. It could have been a story on Egyptian archaeology. In that same issue, there was another timeless subject that made people dream: Ted Turner with his French fiancée in Patagonia—a man who achieves everything in life, in the wide open spaces of Argentina."

Does *Paris Match* have a preference for certain people?

"They don't always have to be good-looking and rich. We choose stories that we like. Some seem quite interesting to us, but the public doesn't find them attractive. It's difficult to satisfy five million readers. *Paris Match*'s profile is very broad!"

What about political opinions?

"We're considered pretty much a center-right magazine. But we gave Jospin a lot of coverage, for example, following him for a month. Besides, if a survey were done in the newsroom, I'm sure that most of the staff would be on the left. The magazine is not meant to have a political line but to be for the French as a whole. We try to distance ourselves from all that. If Chirac lets us do a pleasant story on him and his family, we don't hesitate to publish it."

In your opinion, what are the challenges that *Paris Match* must face in the future?

"The greatest will be to carry on with a similar magazine, with a continuation of what we're doing now. We'll probably have to reduce circulation and produce a denser and more expensive magazine. I think that in the next few years, press circulation in general is going to decrease, but prices are going to increase because people are not going to read as much. My sense is that they're going to be interested in more things and will have more free time, which they will probably use to travel and to improve their quality of life rather than leaning toward reading.

"If *Paris Match* wants to continue to sell well, it must still be a medium for original expression. It's the only magazine where you can find a variety and diversity of topics such as Van Dongen's paintings, Egyptian archaeological finds, the war in Afghanistan, Yann Arthus Bertrand's photos, scientific discoveries, and so many other things. The important thing is to continue being a magazine that people can keep and collect."

IN OCTOBER OF 1888 THERE APPEARED THE FIRST ISSUE OF THE NATIONAL GEOGRAPHIC MAGAZINE, WHICH OVER TIME WOULD BECOME THE MOST PRESTIGIOUS PUBLICATION FOR THE DISSEMINATION OF SCIENTIFIC KNOWLEDGE IN THE WORLD. ITS JOURNALISTIC HISTORY DEVELOPED WITH MAN'S PASSION FOR EXPLORATION, DISCOVERY, ADVENTURE. HERE ARE PRESENTED ITS EVOLUTION, ITS MOST IMPORTANT CONTRIBUTIONS, FROM PHOTO-GRAPHIC MILESTONES TO AMAZING ILLUSTRATIONS, AND THE WAY IT'S PRODUCED TODAY.

GEOGRAPHY in action

Its distinctive journalistic style, in which it is not only witness but participant in what it reports. Its first photo stories, its changes, and its evolution.

Their beards were long and dark, or gray, or very white. Their mustaches were bushy. They wore long ties, vests, stiff collars, and heavy suits. The thirty-three men who congregated on January 13, 1888, at the Cosmos Club in Washington looked like an odd mix of intellectuals, adventurers, and scientists. And their looks were not deceiving. They were geologists, geographers, meteorologists, cartographers, biologists, naturalists, topographers, and inventors by trade. They were also bankers, military men, lawyers, educators, and engineers. They were gathered to establish a society devoted to geography. The goal: to turn the nation's political capital into its scientific capital as well. Thus was born the National Geographic Society, and with it the *National Geographic Magazine*, which with time would become the world's foremost publication devoted to the dissemination of knowledge.

Two weeks after this historic gathering, the Society's founding members chose Gardiner Greene Hubbard as its first president. Hubbard, a wealthy lawyer who specialized in patents, had financed the experiments of Alexander Graham Bell, renowned as the inventor of the telephone, who had also become his son-in-law. In addition, Hubbard was fanatical about the exploration of Alaska. In his inaugural speech, he said that he wasn't a scientist nor could he claim any special knowledge that would entitle him to be called a geographer. He then underscored one of the main principles that would govern the Society down through the years: "By my election, you notify the public that the membership of our Society will not be confined to professional geographers, but will include that large number who, like myself, desire to promote special researches by others, and to diffuse the knowledge so gained, among men, so that we may all know more of the world upon which we live."

With this in mind, just nine months after its creation, the Society published the first issue of the *National Geographic Magazine*. The magazine, edited by Hubbard, came out in October of 1888. Long and thin, with an austere cover in an unattractive shade of terra cotta, it had the look of a dry scientific journal. Two hundred issues were printed and distributed among the Society's members, who paid annual dues and, in return, received the magazine at no additional charge. In the initial pages of the first issue, the publication explained its purpose and the Society's:

"The National Geographic Society has been organized to increase and diffuse geographic knowledge, and the publication of a Magazine has been determined upon as one means of accomplishing these purposes. . . ."

"It will contain memoirs, essays, notes, correspondence, reviews, etc., relating to geographic matters. . . . its pages will be open to all persons interested in geography."

Vol. I.   No. 1.

T H E

NATIONAL GEOGRAPHIC

MAGAZINE.

PUBLISHED BY THE

NATIONAL GEOGRAPHIC SOCIETY.

WASHINGTON, D. C.
REPRINT

Price 50 Cents.

FIRST ISSUE COVER. The first issue, now a collector's item, looked more like a scientific report than a magazine. It was published in October of 1888 and had a run of 200 copies, which were distributed among the National Geographic Society's members. Its editor was Gardiner Greene Hubbard, the body's president; in the introductory note, he said the magazine was published to "increase and diffuse geographic knowledge."

From issue number one to the first adventure

In that first ninety-four-page issue, a total of five articles were published, plus an introduction to the Society, giving its rules, norms, and procedures, and listing its members. Most of the stories were long, with few illustrations, and written in language that only specialists could understand. One of them devoted sixteen pages to geographical methods of geological investigation, and another of eight pages was titled "The Classification of Geographic Forms by Genesis."

The most readable story in the first issue was perhaps "The Great Storm of March 11–14, 1888." The storm, now known as the "Great Blizzard of 88," hit the northeastern United States over four days with forty inches of snow, freezing temperatures, and gale-force winds.

In addition to its twenty-five pages, the story offered the first illustration: a group of weather maps with isobars and isotherms and feathered wind arrows.

Seven months after the first issue, in April of 1889, a second issue of the *National Geographic Magazine* was published. It was paginated in continuation from issue number 1, and its main story, "Africa, Its Past and Future," was written by its editor and the Society's president, Gardiner Hubbard. Visually it was much like the first issue, with plenty of text and few illustrations. Subsequent issues presented stories considered milestones, such as "The Rivers and Valleys of Pennsylvania," the first in a series of reports on the American states (issue 3, July 1889) or "Across Nicaragua with Transit and

Machete" (issue 4, October 1889), a story that included some of the first illustrations and a map in pastel colors. This article's author was none other than Robert Peary, a young naval engineer who would go on to lead the first expedition to reach the North Pole.

The innovations continued in April 1891 when the magazine reported on what is considered the Society's first "exploration adventure." The story was titled "Summary of Reports on the Mt. St. Elias Expedition" and recounted the experiences of a group of ten men who reached the highest point along the Alaska-Canada border, discovering Mount Logan and a huge frozen river they called Hubbard Glacier after the Society's president. It is recognized as the first instance of the magazine

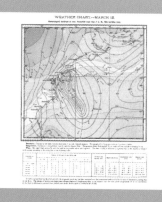

THE FIRST ARTICLES.
The issue was ninety-four pages long and had a total of five stories written by specialists. The one on the Great Blizzard was complemented by weather maps about the phenomenon.

FOUNDING MEMBERS.
This painting, in the Society's current headquarters, depicts the first meeting in 1888.

being witness and protagonist at the same time, perhaps one of the key elements of the publication's future success.

The expedition, mounted in 1890, was cosponsored by the National Geographic Society and the U.S. Geological Survey. In 1963 Melvin M. Payne, then chairman of the Society's board of trustees, wrote: "In several ways, this first expedition set a pattern for the Society's 200 explorations and researches that have followed over the years. It triumphed over the forces of nature. It added to man's knowledge of his world. And it established a tradition of close cooperation between the National Geographic Society and agencies of the United States government."

In the May 1891 issue the story of the expedition was augmented with a first-person narrative written by its leader, geologist Israel C. Russell, in a vivid style that would set the standard for future reports on explorations. Here is one passage:

"Darkness settled and rain fell in torrents, beating through our little tent. We rolled ourselves in blankets, determined to rest in spite of the storm. Avalanches, already numerous, became more frequent. A crash told of tons of ice and rock sliding down on the glacier. Another roar was followed by another, another, and still another. It seemed as if pandemonium reigned on the mountains.

"Looking out, I saw rocks as large as one's head bounding within a few feet of our tent. One struck the alpenstock to which the ridgerope was fastened. Our tent went by the board, and the rain poured in. Before we could gather our soaked blankets, mud and stones flowed in upon them. We retreated to the edge of the glacier and pitched our tent again. Wet and cold, we sought to wear the night away. Sleep was impossible."

FROM THE FIRST NUDE TO THE FIRST CHANGES

In January of 1896 the *National Geographic Magazine*, published irregularly until then, became a monthly. In its first years, the Society's and the magazine's only funding had been the dues paid by its members. As recounted in The *National Geographic Society: 100 Years of Adventures and Discovery,* by C.D.B. Bryan, the Society decided to publish the magazine at regular intervals and sell it on newsstands for 25 cents per issue, hoping to increase its limited income. It also decided to include ads. And the first noticeable design changes in the magazine's history took place. The terra cotta cover was replaced by a yellow one. Not only that, the cover now carried the editor's names and a table of contents, as well as the subtitle *"An Illustrated Monthly"* superimposed on a globe with lines depicting meridians and parallels. The issue's main story, "Russia in Europe," was preceded by a detailed color map of that region. The issue also included photographs—something the magazine had been publishing sporadically since 1890—of an Arctic whaling voyage. But perhaps the year's most surprising development was found in the November issue, when the magazine published for the first time the image of a bare-breasted woman. The photo depicted a Zulu bride holding hands with her groom. The caption had little to do with the occasion or with the couple's wedding attire: "These people are of a dark bronze hue, and have good athletic figures. They possess some excellent traits, but are horribly cruel when once they have smelled blood." This critical and cryptic caption was perhaps due to the debate that had been generated in the Society over whether to publish that photo. Some saw it as offensive to the members. But the eventual winners contended that the organization and the magazine could not change reality—some had proposed covering the African woman's torso—but rather were obliged to present it just as it was found. So the Zulu bride photo ended up being tipped in between pages 356 and 357 of issue 11.

Despite all the changes—the magazine's new cover, the newsstand sales, the audacity of publishing photos of half-nude women—the expected improvement did not materialize. Circulation and income remained flat.

There were no changes in the magazine's scientific approach, with its decidedly academic vision of geography and general subjects, and it was still edited by committee. The most significant changes for the *National Geographic Magazine* would take place at the turn of the century.

Vol. VII   JANUARY, 1896   No. 1

The
National Geographic
Magazine
AN ILLUSTRATED MONTHLY

CONTENTS

Price 25 Cents

NAT. GEOG. MAG.   VOL. VII 1896. PL. XXXVI

ZULU BRIDE AND BRIDEGROOM

GARDINER GREENE HUBBARD. The first president of the Society takes tea with his wife (below). With the January 1896 issue the magazine became a monthly publication and accepted ads (above).

TWO INNOVATIONS. The first woman shown with a nude torso was a Zulu bride in the issue of November 1896. Earlier, the January issue had featured a detailed color map of European Russia.

NAT. GEOG. MAG.   VOL. VII. 1896. PL. I.

RUSSIA
IN EUROPE

FROM THE INTERNATIONAL CYCLOPAEDIA, BY PERMISSION OF DODD, MEAD & COMPANY, PUBLISHERS.

CHINA
November 1964

PERU
February 1964

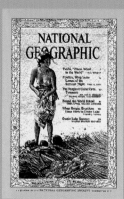

TAHITI
July 1962

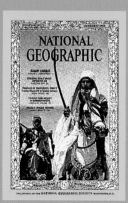

SAUDI ARABIA
January 1966

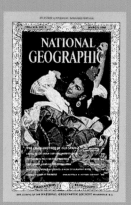

SPAIN
March 1965

ROME
June 1970

alexander Graham Bell:
a new course for the magazine

BELL, A REFORMER. Alexander Graham Bell succeeded Hubbard, his father-in-law and patent lawyer, as the Society's president. He soon decided to hire someone to work exclusively for the magazine—a good move.

Gardiner Greene Hubbard died in 1897, and his son-in-law, the inventor Alexander Graham Bell, was named Society president. Bell, by his own account, didn't want the job and accepted it only out of familial duty. He was more interested in his research —among his innumerable projects was trying to invent an airplane using tetrahedral kites—than in the Society. Thus, during his first year in charge, the membership rolls rose only from 1,140 to 1,400, the Society's debts amounted to $2,000, and the magazine was about to go bankrupt.

But Bell's perceptiveness equaled his sense of responsibility. When he took on the job, he'd resolved to rescue the magazine, and now he came up with a bold plan, which he presented to the board of trustees with these words: "Geography is a fascinating subject, and it can be made interesting. Let's hire a promising young man to put some life into the magazine and promote the membership. I will pay his salary. Secondly, let's abandon our unsuccessful campaign to increase circulation by newsstand sales. Our journal should go to members, people who believe in our work and want to help."

To Bell, the *National Geographic Magazine* was a way to build a larger organization that would welcome into Society membership everyone interested in the world, exploration, and discovery. Until then, the privilege of contributing to the grand private expeditions that fascinated the nineteenth-century public or to accounts of unknown peoples, inaccessible places, and stern trials to overcome had been reserved to men of science and men of wealth. Bell understood that, even for the simplest of men, supporting these investigations was a source of pride. So he set out to open the Society's rosters to all who were willing to contribute $2 a year for a magazine subscription, whether they were scientists or schoolmasters, aristocrats or artisans. Some members of the board of trustees opposed the proposal vigorously, but in the end it carried.

INDIA
May 1963

PHILIPPINES
September 1966

PACIFIC ISLANDS
December 1974

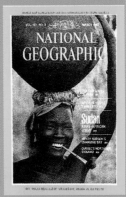

SUDAN
March 1982

More than anything else, this was the key idea on which the Society's phenomenal future growth was based. For it to work, though, it was necessary to produce an attractive and impressive magazine that was scientifically sound but also popular with all sorts of people, from experts to readers who were interested only in adventure stories. At *National Geographic*, the Society and the magazine had to grow together: the one depended on the other. So the *National Geographic Magazine* came to occupy an essential spot within the Society.

The first thing Bell needed to do was to find his hypothetical editor, someone who would work full-time at the twin tasks of producing the magazine and promoting membership—tasks that until then had been performed by Society members in their spare moments and without pay. Bell would later remember: "But in starting out to make a magazine that would support the Society, instead of the Society being burdened with the magazine, a man was of the first necessity; if we did not get the right man the whole plan would be a failure."

That man was Gilbert Hovey Grosvenor, who was hired in April of 1899 when he was twenty-three years old. The son of Edwin Grosvenor, a renowned historian and a friend of Bell's, Gilbert had graduated from Amherst College, where he had been an outstanding student and a champion tennis player. Now a graduate student and schoolmaster, he had no publishing experience whatever. But he was suggested for the job by Bell's daughter Elsie May, who had formed an attachment to the young man. So Gilbert "Bert" Grosvenor was hired provisionally for $100 a month. He would remain at the helm of the magazine longer than anyone—fifty-five years—and would turn the *National Geographic* into the world's most important magazine for the popularizing of scientific knowledge.

marketing and
the Grosvenor strategy

Bert Grosvenor's first few years at the *National Geographic* were not at all easy. He had begun as assistant editor for a three-month trial period, with the understanding that he would be hired permanently if he got a satisfactory evaluation from the Society's editorial committee. This was headed by John Hyde, the magazine's honorary (unpaid) editor, whose day job was as a statistician at the U.S. Department of Agriculture. The editorial committee was made up of twelve Society members, who also worked gratis and who were much older than the fledgling teacher, the first person on the payroll in the magazine's history. Grosvenor faced two main challenges: increasing the Society's income, and producing an attractive magazine out of subject matter that had to be submitted to a committee with little interest in popular or general interest articles.

The first task Grosvenor tackled was expanding the organization's membership and donor lists. He favored Bell's suggestion of recruiting members with a clever hook: offering not merely a magazine subscription but, therewith, membership in a prestigious society whose functions were to promote and spread knowledge of geography through conferences, monographs, bulletins, and the funding of expeditions of study and discovery. To do this, Bert started by asking the people he knew—among them his father and Bell himself—for the names of friends who might be recruited as members. He wrote each a personal letter, on fine engraved and embossed stationery, with the opening "I have the honor to inform you that you have been recommended for membership…." He sent a great many similar letters every week, and soon his simple and original marketing campaign started to pay off. As a reward, he was confirmed as the magazine's assistant editor for a year. By November, seven months after his arrival, Bert Grosvenor had managed to get 750 additional members for the Society.

The other task, popularizing the magazine's content and focus, wasn't as simple. Hyde's followers were unbending in their determination to continue publishing technical stories that were almost incomprehensible to general readers. And Bert knew that if he didn't change that philosophy, it would become very difficult to retain the new subscribers he'd signed up. In short, his fate and the Society's depended on his ability to improve the magazine. His best ally was Bell, who would soon become his father-in-law and whose definition of "geographic subjects" included "the world and all that is in it." Bell was known to be fond of reading encyclopedias, with their articles of manageable length, constantly changing subjects, always something new to learn.

Grosvenor thought along the same lines. He took his conception of geography from its Greek root: *geographia,* a description of the world. "It thus becomes the most catholic of subjects," he wrote, "universal in appeal, and embracing nations, people, plants, animals, birds, fish. We would never lack interesting subjects." In other words, a sort of encyclopedia.

The Bell-Grosvenor partnership thus resolved to pursue their project of solidifying the *National Geographic* as a popular magazine and further increasing the Society's membership and income. But they first had to defeat Hyde and the editorial committee, who were bent on Grosvenor's dismissal

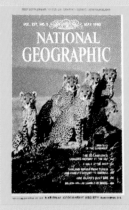

CHEETAHS
May 1980

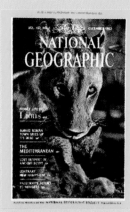

LIONS
December 1982

KANGAROOS
February 1979

INDIA'S WILDLIFE
September 1976

KENYAN ELEPHANTS
February 1969

LEOPARD
February 1972

WHITE TIGER
April 1970

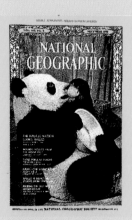

PANDAS
December 1972

and who, since their editorial arguments lacked weight, had gone so far as to complain of his attentions to the daughter of the Society's president. For his part, Bell wanted to get the direction of the magazine and its parent organization settled so that he could devote himself solely to his inventions and experiments. Returning from a trip to Europe, he urgently convened the Board of Managers, as the Society's governing body was then called. These men—scientists, professionals, explorers, businessmen—were disinclined to support Hyde and the editorial committee. In a resolution approved on September 14, 1900, they applauded Grosvenor's work, reaffirmed his permanent status with the Society, named him managing editor, and gave him a raise. Starting in 1901, his salary would be $2,000 a year—the $1,200 that Bell had been paying, plus $800 of the Society's own money.

THE BIG STORY THAT SET THE GEOGRAPHIC STYLE

"On the morning of May 8, 1902, Saint Pierre ceased to exist. At precisely 7:50 Mont Pelée exploded with a roar heard hundreds of miles away. An awesome blast of flaming gases and superheated steam raced down its flanks with incredible speed. In less than three minutes the beautiful city, its 30,000 people, all nearby country homes, and 17 out of 18 ships in the anchorage were annihilated." With these words, Robert T. Hill would tell *Geographic* readers of the disaster that had lately overtaken France's Caribbean colony of Martinique. The only survivors were a convict in a sturdy prison cell, two other people who shortly died, and the crew of the ship farthest from shore.

When news of the disaster reached Washington, soon-to-be editor Gilbert Grosvenor—John Hyde would remain the magazine's editor ad honorem—sent a telegram to the Society's president (then vacationing in Nova Scotia) asking approval to spend $1,000 to send a scientific expedition to the location of the eruption. Bell wired back, telling Grosvenor to go to Martinique himself within twenty-four hours to represent the magazine, and promising to cover his expenses. Bell's advice: leave the science to others and bring back vivid details, beautifully illustrated with photographs.

At the National Geographic Society, that telegram from Bell is nowadays considered the magazine's true charter. Bell's magisterial instructions would guide all the editors from Gilbert Grosvenor on, encouraging them to act with determination and promptness to send people and cameras throughout the world to bring back vivid details, beautifully illustrated with photographs.

In the case of Martinique, Grosvenor indeed acted quickly. Just six days after the first eruption, on May 14, 1902, the National Geographic Society dispatched a special three-man expedition: Hill, of the U.S. Geological Survey; Israel Russell, who had led the

explorations of Mount St. Elias; and Cmdr. C. E. Borchgrevink, an Antarctic explorer who had already studied Erebus and Terror, the southernmost volcanoes on the Earth.

The expedition was announced in the June issue, which prepared readers with a story about the eruption of Krakatoa in 1883, a brief essay on volcanoes in general, a map of volcanic islands, a story about the island and people of Martinique, and a couple of preliminary reports on the Pelée eruption.

But the major treatment came in the July 1902 issue with a cover title that said it all: "Martinique Number." Inside, the magazine featured Hill's forty-four-page main article, a ten-page story on the area's volcanic rocks, and three pages on the chemical properties of the "volcanic ejecta," plus two pages of "Reports of Vessels as to the Range of Volcanic Dust." And with its main course the issue offered a dozen photos of the destruction caused by the volcano's eruption. It was a stellar report and the beginning of the style that would give this publication its character.

THE BORDER THAT BECAME A BRAND NAME

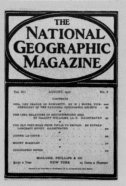

After those first few terra cotta covers, in 1896 the magazine chose a pale yellow. But between then and January 1901 it changed the cover's look several times. In June 1899 it kept the yellow color but got rid of the globe it had added three years earlier. In the first month of 1901 it again had a terra cotta cover, with a black frame and large logotype enclosed in a black oval. The title *The National Geographic Magazine* took up almost half the cover. The rest of the space was still occupied by the table of contents. And so it remained through December of 1903.

The fifth redesign of the cover was done in January of 1904, when the black box and oval border that framed the contents and title were eliminated. The most significant change was that the brownish background became lighter and the magazine's contents and logo were surrounded by a lighter art-nouveau frame.

That design was retained until 1910, when the yellow border of the magazine cover made its debut. With time, it would become the trademark not only of the magazine but also of all the products that the National Geographic Society would publish—maps, atlases, books, videos, CD-ROMs. The change took effect with the February issue, and the new border color was accompanied by another feature that, over the years, gave the cover personality and identity: a garland of oak leaves and acorns, topped by sprays of laurel and studded with four globes depicting each half of the two hemispheres.

Ten years later, in 1920, the original cover was slightly modified: the frame would become a stronger yellow while, inside, the table of contents would be printed on a white background.

YELLOW FRAME.
The magazine's cover underwent various changes during the first few years until the signature yellow frame appeared in 1910.

THE WRITING STYLE

In February of 1903, Gilbert H. Grosvenor was named editor with full powers to carry out all the projects he considered appropriate for the magazine's development. But he always maintained a strong editorial relationship with Bell, who was a fine mentor and sounding board. Thus, months after his appointment, Bert went to his father-in-law to ask his views on publishing a photo of Filipino women who were working in the fields bare-chested. Bell advised that he print the photo, and it was featured in the May 1903 issue. A story by Tom Buckley in the *New York Times Magazine* in 1970 would say that "so unquestionably genteel was the magazine, and so patently pure its anthropological interest, that even at a time when nice people called a leg a limb it never occurred to anyone to accuse Grosvenor of impropriety."

Still, Grosvenor and Bell agreed that it would be wise to establish some principles for the magazine, to offer guidance if similar cases should arise in the future. These principles, which dealt not only with nudes but with a range of other political and editorial matters, set the tone for editing the magazine over the next fifty years. These were the "commandments" submitted by

NUDES AND RULES. This photo of bare-breasted Filipino women was published in May of 1903. The magazine established guidelines shortly thereafter.

Grosvenor to the Society's board of trustees, according to Bryan's authorized history of the *National Geographic:*

1. The first principle is absolute accuracy. Nothing must be printed which is not strictly according to fact. . . .
2. Abundance of beautiful, instructive, and artistic illustrations.
3. Everything printed in the Magazine must have permanent value. . . .
4. All personalities and notes of a trivial character are avoided.
5. Nothing of a partisan or controversial character is printed.
6. Only what is of a kindly nature is printed about any country or people, everything unpleasant or unduly critical being avoided.
7. The contents of each number is planned with a view of being timely.

In general, there was an attempt to follow these principles to the letter. Exceptions were made only to numbers 5 and 6. In the case of principle number 5, interpretative subjectivity provided flexibility, and ultimately it was the editor who determined how far the magazine could go. Principle number 6 was followed rather strictly until the 1970s, when the magazine started to broach more controversial subjects, such as race and ecology.

Editorial style rules were also set at this time. They took into account the jaundiced opinion that, according to Grosvenor, most people had of geography ("one of the dullest of all subjects, something to inflict upon schoolboys and avoid in later life") and aimed to enhance the popular approach that the editor felt was best suited to overcome such preconceptions. He made a careful study of books with lasting appeal in which geography played a primary role: *The Voyage of the Beagle* by Charles Darwin, *Two Years Before the Mast* by Richard Henry Dana Jr., *Sailing Alone Around the World* by Joshua Slocum, and the travels of Herodotus, written two millennia ago. He concluded that the books were still interesting to readers because "each was an accurate, eyewitness first-hand account. Each contained simple, straightforward writing—writing that sought to make pictures in the reader's mind."

So Grosvenor set several writing rules, among them:
1. Avoid fuzzy language, which betrays fuzzy thinking.
2. Avoid urging a point of view. ("Stick to the facts. Our readers can be trusted to form their own opinions.")
3. Avoid long words and phrases when short ones will do as well.
4. Avoid lazy phrases such as "is said to." ("*The National Geographic Magazine* does not publish hearsay. Either it is a fact or it is not. Find out.")
5. Avoid pretentious language and foreign words without a translation. ("On the grounds that no one knows every language and it is our business to make ourselves understood," said editor Frederick Vosburgh.)

THe FIrST PICTUre STOry

More than once in the history of journalism, a milestone has come about as the result of pure chance, a random idea, a piece of luck. It happened at *Time* with the Man of the Year, and it happened at the *National Geographic* with the first picture story published by the magazine.

It was December of 1904. Grosvenor was in his office at the Society's new headquarters, Hubbard Memorial Hall, working alone as always, for the simple reason that he was the sole employee of the magazine and each issue depended on his ideas, plans, procurement of material, and editing. He did it all, from reading the submissions to closing the issue. The stories he had prepared for January had already been sent to the printer. But now the printer was on the telephone reminding him that the issue was still eleven pages short. Unless Grosvenor wanted them to appear blank, he needed to come up with more text. There was no suitable article to publish, and scant time to find or write one. As Grosvenor pondered how to deal with the emergency, he idly sorted the day's mail piled on his desk. A large, bulky envelope with foreign stamps caught his attention. He opened it and beheld

the answer to an editor's prayers: before him were no fewer than fifty photos of the mysterious Tibetan city of Lhasa, taken by two Russian explorers for the Imperial Russian Geographical Society, which was offering them to the *National Geographic Magazine* for free.

Grosvenor breathed easier. The photos—perhaps the first ever taken of the Tibetan capital—were so good that it was the work of a moment to select eleven for full-page reproduction. The captions virtually wrote themselves. Off the pictures went to the printer, and off Grosvenor went to his club. But relief soon gave way to worry: What would the Society think? What excuse had he to publish scenic photos in a scholarly magazine? And with no accompanying text except for the minimal captions? And at a cost for engraving that severely depleted the Society's slender resources? When he confessed to his wife what he'd done, he told her he was sure he would be fired. Yet once the January issue was published, his concerns vanished as Society members started congratulating him. They even stopped him on the street to tell him how much they'd liked the story.

This unprecedented editorial inspiration—published with a minimal introduction headlined "Views of Lhasa" and taking up pages 28 to 38 of the January 1905 issue—is considered the first picture story published by a magazine. Buoyed by its success, Grosvenor published a new photographic article three months later, this one devoted to the Philippines, with images provided free by the War Department, headed by his cousin William Howard Taft. In thirty-two consecutive pages titled "A Revelation of the Filipinos," Grosvenor presented 138 photos, from engravings prepared for the official report of that country's first census. Grosvenor would later say that no other editor would have published so many photos about a single subject in a single issue of the magazine.

The issue was so successful that it had to be reprinted for all the new subscribers. Thanks to the magazine and its photo stories, the Society went from 3,400 members in 1904 to almost 11,500 in late 1905 and ended the year with a substantial surplus on its books for the first time.

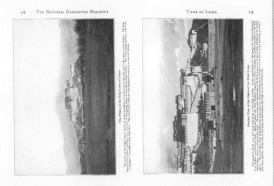

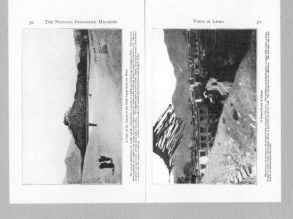

The magazine´s first picture story was published in January 1905 and took up pages 28 to 38. It was a resounding hit.

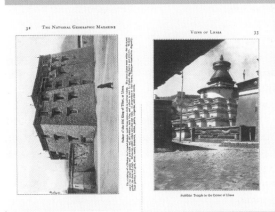

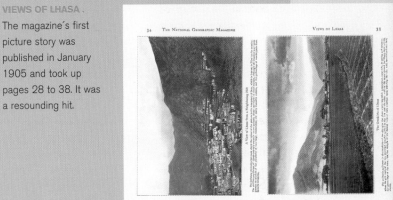

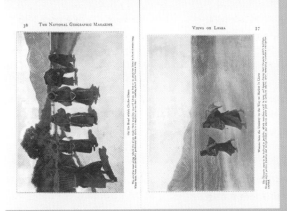

UP AND DOWN.

A common practice at the time was not to spread horizontal pictures over two pages but to print them vertically, so that to see them properly it was necessary to turn the magazine sideways.

expeditions that made history: the conquest of the north pole

VICTOR. Financially backed by the *National Geographic*, Robert E. Peary in 1909 led the first expedition to reach the North Pole. The magazine reported the feat in the October issue, devoting twenty-five pages to it.

In the early twentieth century the passion and curiosity inspired by far places, great heights, and unknown lands turned the *National Geographic Magazine* into a sought-after and ever more widely read medium. Nobody wanted to miss its adventures. Everybody wanted to participate in its discoveries. As we shall see, in 1911 the magazine surpassed 100,000 subscribers, and two years later it reached 200,000. The reason: the publication had actively participated in events of great popular significance. The first one was the conquest of the North Pole on April 6, 1909, by an expedition commanded by Robert E. Peary to which the Society had contributed $1,000.

To get a sense of what Peary's feat meant at the time, it's important to know that the Pole had been a goal for many years. In 1895 Fridtjof Nansen, a Norwegian, had made it to within 369 kilometers of the North Pole. In 1898 Peary himself made an attempt he had to abandon, during which he lost eight toes to frostbite. In 1900 Umberto Cagni, an Italian, surpassed Nansen's mark and stopped 334 kilometers short of the Pole. Peary made new and risky

attempts in 1901 and 1902, and in 1906 managed to beat the record and get to 286 kilometers from the northernmost point.

With that background, and backed by the National Geographic Society, Peary left in July of 1908 from the port of New York aboard his expedition's ship, the *Roosevelt.* The ship penetrated as far north as the summer thaw would permit. Five months later, when the winter freeze had taken hold, a base camp was set up 764 kilometers from the goal. From there on, the expedition –twenty-four men, seventeen of them Eskimos, and 133 dogs–had to cross on foot the frozen terrain and the pack ice with its treacherous fissures of open water. The advance started on February 28, 1909, in five teams, with Peary's own team in the rear. As C.D.B. Bryan recounts it: "Peary's method of moving men and equipment over the ice was revolutionary. His theory was to work the supporting parties to the limit in order to keep the final assault party fresh. The men . . . carved out a trail through the jumble of ice and pressure ridges for the main expedition to follow, built igloos for sleeping, and deposited supplies. It was an exhausting task."

By March 15 they had covered 160 kilometers. As foreseen, the support teams began to peel off one by one and return to base camp, until on April 1 only the team selected for the final assault remained: Robert Peary, his longtime friend Matthew Henson, and the four Eskimos Ooqueah, Ootah, Egingwah, and Seegloo. They and their forty dogs were 214 kilometers from the pole. Later, *Geographic* readers learned what Peary was thinking at the time:

"Now was no time for reverie. I turned to the problem for which I had conserved my energy on the upward trip, trained myself as for a race….

"Henson, with his years of experience, was almost as skillful at handling dogs and sledges as the Eskimos themselves. He and Ootah had stood with me at my farthest north, three years before….

"My 40 remaining dogs were the pick of the 133 which had left Cape Columbia. Almost all were powerful males, hard as iron, in good spirits. My last five sledges, fully repaired, were ready to go. I had supplies for 40 days. By eating the dogs themselves, we could last 50…

"I decided to strain every nerve and sinew to make five marches of 25 miles each, crowding them in such a way that the fifth march would end long enough before noon to allow an observation for latitude. . . .

"I hit the trail a little past midnight on April 2. . . . As I climbed the pressure ridge back of our igloos, I set another hole in my belt, the third since I started. Every man of us was lean and flat-bellied as a board, and as hard."

Peary, Henson, and the Eskimos reached the North Pole on April 6. It would be five months before the world heard the news, in September, when the *Roosevelt* finally reached Indian Harbor, Labrador, the first telegraph station on its southward journey. From there Peary wired his wife: "Have made good at last. I have the D.O.P. [Damned Old Pole]. Am well. Love."

The magazine published the story in its October 1909 issue. It ran to twenty pages and was a smash hit.

machu picchu:
chronicle of an
unexpected discovery

In the April 1913 issue, the 234,000 subscribers to the *National Geographic* were surprised by a story that would come to be regarded as historic. The photos published in the magazine revealed to the world for the first time the fabulous Inca city of Machu Picchu, just discovered in the Peruvian Andes. The author of the story and the discoverer was a young Yale historian named Hiram Bingham. The article took up a whole issue of the magazine titled "In the Wonderland of Peru." It was a formidable journalistic display: 186 pages, eight drawings, two maps, and 286 photographs.

In fact, the discovery had taken place two years earlier. Bingham, as he would

tell the *Geographic's* readers, had set out on a July day in 1911 to investigate the latest in a long line of rumors, "searching for the last capital of the great Inca Empire that had extended more than the length of Peru." He and his companions, two Yale colleagues and a Peruvian army sergeant named Carrasco, were in the deep and dangerous jungles of Cuzco province –a place to which he would return in 1912, 1914, and 1915, leading three expeditions sponsored by the National Geographic Society and Yale University—when, "camping beside the river [Urubamba] at the base of a mountain called Machu Picchu, we were told of another ruin on the ridge

above us." The informant, an Indian called Melchor Arteaga, agreed to take Bingham and the sergeant to the place for 50 cents.

"On all fours we pulled ourselves up through slippery grass, digging with fingers to keep from falling. Far below, the Urubamba snarled angrily. The heat was oppressive. Arteaga moaned that there were lots of snakes....

"Calling on every reserve, I clambered through thinning jungle to where the ground leveled. Drenched with sweat, I straightened and saw a grass hut. Indians approached with gourds of spring water....

"...Our Indian hosts said there were old houses 'a little farther on.' With a

IMPOSING. The photo was taken by Hiram Bingham, who discovered the Inca city in 1911.

SPECIAL EDITION. In April of 1913 the magazine devoted 186 pages to the discovery.

small boy to guide and Carrasco to interpret, I set out along the ridge.

"We rounded a knoll and suddenly faced tier upon tier of Inca terraces rising like giant stairs. Each one, hundreds of feet long, was banked with massive stone walls up to ten feet high.

"What settlement of Incas had needed a hundred such terraces in this lofty wilderness? Enough food could be grown here to feed a city!

"In my excitement, I forgot my fatigue and hurried the length of a wide terrace toward the tangle of jungle beyond it. I plunged into damp undergrowth, then stopped, heart thumping. A mossy wall loomed before me, half hidden in trees. Huge stone blocks seemed glued together, but without mortar—the finest Inca construction. I traced the wall and found it to be part of a house. Beyond it stood another, and beyond that more again….

"Down the slope, buildings crowded together in a bewildering array of terraced levels linked by at least 100 stairways. This beautifully preserved sanctuary had obviously never felt the tramp of a conquistador's boot. I realized that Machu Picchu might prove to be the largest and most important ruin discovered in South America since the Spaniards arrived."

At Machu Picchu, Bingham was sure, he had discovered the fabled city of Vilcabamba, the last bastion of the Inca monarch who had fled there to escape the Spaniards in 1537. The explorer drew a sketch of the place he'd found, then continued following rumors of other Inca cities along the Urubamba River before returning home to report his discoveries.

In the United States, he got in touch with the National Geographic Society. Hiram Bingham had already had dealings with the magazine and the Society, but the relationship had got off on the wrong foot. In 1908, when Bingham was conducting one of his expeditions, his wife offered the magazine two articles by her husband, with photos. Gilbert Grosvenor rejected the material, writing: "We have on hand a number of articles on South America and therefore cannot find room for them." But just a year later, when Bingham published his *Journal of an Expedition Across Venezuela and Colombia,* the admiring Grosvenor immediately asked him for an article "describing the least known section which you traversed with as large a selection of photographs as possible." He offered Bingham $25 for the text plus $1.50 for each photograph used. Bingham, nettled, reminded Grosvenor that this very material, his best, had already been seen and found wanting. Grosvenor affected not to remember.

But things were different now. It was no longer just a story or a few photos. The *National Geographic's* stamp of approval was crucial to uncovering Machu Picchu's archaeological relics. The place had been found, but the vegetation had to be stripped, equipment moved, the site dug, and the misgivings of an untrusting country, stung by previous plundering of its cultural treasures, overcome. Unless all these steps were accomplished, especially the last, the find could remain in oblivion. On February 23, 1912, after several conversations with Gilbert Grosvenor, Bingham requested in writing a letter from Society president Henry Gannett and another from Grosvenor himself, expressing their support and interest in his work. "The stronger the credentials which you can give me, the better able I shall be to persuade [the politicians in Lima] that

MAPS AND LANDSCAPES. The issue devoted to Peru's wonders published two orientation maps for readers and 286 photos along with the whole story of the adventure. Its impact was such that the magazine covered Machu Picchu again in 1915 and 1916.

our object is scientific and not commercial." A few days later, Grosvenor answered: "We find that there is considerable feeling that the work is archaeological and not sufficiently geographic, and I am afraid that we shall have to give up our plans for the present. I will write you again later. I am most interested in your work, and am doing all I can to put the proposition through."

Bingham was more than nettled this time. But he needed the magazine's backing to carry his project forward. On March 18 he wrote Gilbert Grosvenor again: "Your letter is very disappointing. I planned the work with special emphasis on the archaeological side because I gathered from my conversation with you that you were particularly interested in that field. You will remember that in my first conversation with you in your office I laid considerable emphasis on the fact that the map making begun by the Yale Peruvian Expedition ought to be completed at once, while the same topographer was available and willing to undertake the work. His work is purely geographical. You remember that you replied that you were not interested in that so much as you were in the ruins, the lost cities, and the bones. Accordingly it was in an effort to meet your interest in the matter that the plans were drawn up with so much emphasis on the archaeological side. If you wish to . . . have me alter my plans . . . I shall be very glad to do so."

The letter—along with the perseverance of Grosvenor, who thought that supporting this type of endeavor was fundamental to the magazine's growth—at last won the day, and the Society agreed to finance Bingham's return to Machu Picchu.

In the April 1912 issue, the magazine announced a $10,000 grant "to the Peruvian expedition of 1912." It was the Society's first contribution to an archaeological investigation. As mentioned, Bingham wrote the main story for the April 1913 issue. The subject piqued readers' interest, and the increase in subscribers led the magazine to publish new stories about Machu Picchu in 1915 and 1916.

BINGHAM. Below, outside his tent, stands the man behind the discovery, as published in the pages of the *National Geographic*. Without the Society as sponsor, Peruvian authorities would not have authorized the expedition that revealed the hidden city to the world.

ANIMALS AT NIGHT. George Shiras III was the author of the first night shots of animals, published in the July 1906 issue. The fifty-page story presented seventy-four photographs and explained the workings of the illumination system installed on the boat from which he worked.

PHOTOGRAPHY
national Geographic's new Language

If in its first years the magazine had filled its pages almost entirely with text, beginning in 1905 it drastically changed its concept. As Gilbert Grosvenor would later remember, that year marked a turning point for the Society, the end of the beginning. He said in 1951 about the stories on Lhasa and the Philippines: "Our members liked the pictures better than the manuscripts we had been feeding them. They showed their pleasure by sending in many new members. The incident taught me that what I liked, the average man would like, that is, that I am a common average American. That was how the *National Geographic Magazine* started on its rather remarkable career of printing many pictures, and later more color pictures, than any other publication in the world."

Indeed the magazine, a photography pioneer par excellence, offered its readers the first pictures ever taken at various places, times, heights, depths. And its subjects went beyond geography in the strict sense of the term, encompassing animals, birds, fish, explorations, discoveries, humanity, its past, its great works. In this retrospective of the *National Geographic's* photographic milestones and its contributions to the world of journalism, we must highlight one such important step for the magazine: the first night shots of wild animals.

The pictures, taken at night by George Shiras III with an innovative lighting system, were published in the July 1906 issue. In all, seventy-four photos were displayed over fifty pages, with only four devoted to text.

In the story, Shiras described how he'd set up his two cameras on the bow of a boat and focused them between thirty and forty feet, then placed a spotlight above them. He would float down along the edge of a stream or a lake, transfixing the fauna in the lamplight until he was close enough to take a picture. When the night images of forest wildlife were published, *National Geographic* received hundreds of letters asking for more stories about natural history. "But two distinguished geographers on the Board resigned," Grosvenor wrote, "stating emphatically that 'wandering off into nature is not geography.' They also criticized me for turning the magazine into a picture book."

THE COLOR ERA BEGINS

The first hand-tinted photos were published in the November 1910 issue. Grosvenor called them "color paintings." Taken by a wealthy New Yorker, William W. Chapin, who had made his money in Kodak during the company's first years, they were twenty-four black-and-white photos called "Scenes in Korea and China." Since color photography had yet to be perfected, Chapin had a Japanese artist color his photos on the basis of detailed annotations he had made about his subjects' clothing and the scenes he photographed. The chronological account of photographic milestones in the *National Geographic Magazine* follows:

First photo poster. In June of 1911, as a supplement to the regular issue, the *National Geographic* published a poster with an eight-foot-by-seven-inch panoramic photo of the Canadian Rockies.

First bird illustrations. The story was published in June of 1913, under the headline "Fifty Common Birds of Farm and Orchard." The fifty color plates, done by the U.S. Department of Agriculture, were a hit among subscribers.

First Lumière Autochrome. The Lumière Autochrome was the first commercial process in color photography, developed in France and marketed from 1907. Its first use in the *National Geographic* was in July of 1914, a single picture called "A Ghent Flower Garden" that had been taken in the Horticultural Hall at the World's Fair Grounds in Ghent, Belgium.

First color photo series. In April 1916 the article "The Land of the Best" was illustrated with color photos including a series of twenty-three Lumière Autochromes taken by the painter Franklin Price Knott. A second color series by the same artist was published in September. Because of the war there would be no more color pictures printed for five years.

First aerial shots of the United States. The July 1924 issue, which was entirely devoted to aviation, featured the first aerial photos of the United States, in black and white. It also contained a firsthand account of the first nonstop coast-to-coast flight, made by U.S. Army Air Service lieutenants John A. Macready (narrator) and Oakley G. Kelly in a single-engine, high-wing Fokker.

BIRDS. The first color illustrations of birds, plates depicting fifty different species, were published in the issue of June 1913.

COLOR PHOTOGRAPHS. Twenty-three of Franklin Knott's Lumière Autochromes were published in the April 1916 issue to illustrate a patriotic article titled "The Land of the Best."

THE MAN WITH THE BROOM
The old Portuguese geographers called Ceylon the "utmost Indian isle" during the days of their nation's ascendancy in India. For more than a hundred years it has been a British possession.

COLOR COMEBACK. After World War I, in 1921, the magazine published autochromes again, this time taken by photographer Helen Murdoch in India and Ceylon.

Color after the war. The postwar era of color photography started with the March 1921 issue, when eight autochromes of India and Ceylon by Helen Messinger Murdoch were used to illustrate the story "From London to Australia by Aeroplane." From 1921 to 1930, 1,818 autochromes were published in the magazine, and starting in September 1927, every *Geographic* issue included color stories.

Undersea innovation. The first underwater pictures were published in January 1927 and attracted wide attention. The work of photographer Charles Martin with ichthyologist W. H. Longley, they were taken fifteen feet under water, using a risky homemade flash contraption that ignited a pound of magnesium powder on a float and could be triggered from below.

Airborne innovation. The first aerial color shots were taken from a dirigible by Melville Grosvenor, the magazine editor's son, working with a group of technicians. *National Geographic* published them in September 1930 and they were very well received. Never before had Americans seen the Statue of Liberty, the Capitol, the Washington Monument, the Lincoln Memorial from above and in natural color.

First color photographs of moving animals. A fox-hunting scene featuring dogs and mounted horsemen was published in September 1935 as part of a story on Delaware photographed by Charles Martin's lab assistant B. Anthony Stewart, working in the Finlay process. The photo was quite an accomplishment for the times.

MAID AND A BRIDE OF KANDY: CEYLON

BENEATH THE SURFACE. The first photographs of fish taken under water by Charles Martin and ichthyologist W. H. Longley were published in January of 1927.

FROM ABOVE. The first color aerial photos (above) were taken by Melville Grosvenor in 1930. The first color photos of moving animals (below) followed five years later.

THE NATIONAL GEOGRAPHIC STYLE

Besides good reading and accurate information, the *National Geographic* imposed a style with its use of visual impact and set the course for future dissemination-of-knowledge magazines.

With the publication of the first picture story of Lhasa, the magazine's circulation skyrocketed. By the end of 1906 it had reached 19,237 copies.

In 1908 more than half of the pages were taken up by photographs every month. Their use, along with the Society's participation in significant events, stirred the interest of a public eager to learn about adventures, discoveries, and scientific advances. So the *National Geographic Magazine,* as a for-members-only publication, propelled its parent body's membership to an impressive climb. In 1911 it surpassed for the first time the 100,000 mark. Two years later, in 1913, there were 234,000 subscribers; in 1914 that number climbed to 337,000, and in 1915 circulation reached 424,000.

Associate editor John Oliver La Gorce, who had joined the magazine in 1905 and handled advertising, wrote in a promotional pamphlet that "the *National Geographic Magazine* has found a new universal language which requires no deep study—a language which takes precedence over Esperanto and one that is understood as well by the jungaleer as by the courtier; by the Eskimo as by the wild man from Borneo; by the child in the playroom as by the professor in the college; and by the woman of the household as well as by the hurried businessman—in short, the Language of the Photograph!" And this language metaphorically translated into issues and results: in 1917 the National Geographic Society reached 625,000 members, a number that rose to 668,174 in 1919 and 713,208 subscribers in 1920.

This rise was reflected in the dazzling and sometimes dizzying display of articles about diverse subjects for which there was only one requisite: photos. The magazine's pages became a stage for motor treks across deserts and continents, stories with unprecedented images of the life of insects or of pharaohs' tombs in Egypt. More and more, Grosvenor regarded text as an excuse to use photography. He frequently bought a manuscript, filed it away, and waited years to get photos that would justify publication.

When color photography was revolutionized by the advent of Eastman Kodak's 35-millimeter Kodachrome film in 1936, Grosvenor didn't hesitate to fill the magazine with images taken with this new process. Illustrations, he would say, make the *National Geographic Magazine*, and the magazine's life depends on getting the best possible photos.

By the end of 1929, the number of *National Geographic Magazine* subscribing members had passed 1.21 million, and the following year it would reach a total of 1.24 million. The magazine would not reach that number again until 1946.

VOL. 167, NO. 6   **JUNE 1985**

NATIONAL GEOGRAPHIC

GREAT SALT LAKE:
THE FLOODING
DESERT 694

U. S.–MEXICAN BORDER:
LIFE ON THE LINE 720

JAVA'S WILDLIFE RETURNS 750

Along Afghanistan's
War-torn Frontier 772

Haunted eyes tell of an
Afghan refugee's fears

FAIR SKIES FOR THE CAYMAN ISLANDS 798

SEE NATIONAL GEOGRAPHIC EXPLORER EVERY SUNDAY ON NICKELODEON CABLE TV

EMBLEMATIC COVER. The June 1985 cover is a milestone for many reasons: because it is a fine example of the impact of the magazine's photographic style, because it became an icon of the *National Geographic,* and because it showcased a change in subject matter dating from the 1970s. This photo of a young refugee was taken by Steve McCurry in 1984 to illustrate a story on Afghanistan. Since then her eyes have conquered the world.

FROM THE JUNGLE
TO THE BOTTOM OF THE SEA

From the moment they became aware of the impact that photos had on their readers, the *Geographic* editors turned photography into the magazine's trademark. Pictures also served to show that the magazine had been there and to disseminate news of its discoveries to the public. At a time when travel was infrequent, the photograph became an essential document to spread information and knowledge. Here are some of the photos that characterized the publication and its passion to unveil a faraway world, unknown and mysterious.

PHONOGRAPH.
PHOTO: **Charles Martin**, National Geographic Society
SUBJECT: Tribal chiefs in Lubuagan, Kalinga province, Philippines, discovering the sounds emitted by a phonograph in 1902.

OLMEC HEAD ON THE GULF OF MEXICO.
PHOTO: **Richard Hewitt Stewart**, National Geographic Society
SUBJECT: Dr. Matthew Stirling measuring one of the stone heads made by the Olmecs around 1200 A.D.

JACQUES-YVES COUSTEAU.
PHOTO: **Luis Marden**, National Geographic Society
SUBJECT: Cousteau with a school of fish in the depths of the Indian Ocean. The magazine began publishing stories on the French oceanographer's researches in 1952.

AFGHAN WOMAN.
PHOTO: **Thomas J. Abercrombie**, National Geographic Society
SUBJECT: An Afghan woman in 1967 hidden within her garments—caged, like the birds on her head.

PERU.
PHOTO: **William Albert Allard,** National Geographic Society
SUBJECT: A child, the son of Peruvian farmers, crying over his six dead sheep, hit by a taxi. Following the March 1982 publication of this photo, many *Geographic* readers sent money, and the boy got new sheep.

BAHAMAS.
PHOTO: **Bruce Dale**, National Geographic Society
SUBJECT: The magnificent waters of the Bahamas, a tourist paradise that attracts sportsmen and sun worshipers, photographed in 1982.

EVEREST.
PHOTO: **Barry C. Bishop**, National Geographic Society
SUBJECT: The first American expedition to climb Mount Everest, financed by the Society in 1963. Bishop was one of five to reach the top.

AIRPLANE
PHOTO: **Bruce Dale**, National Geographic Society
SUBJECT: The moment of landing of a Lockheed TriStar in 1977. From the cockpit Dale activated two cameras mounted on the plane's vertical stabilizer.

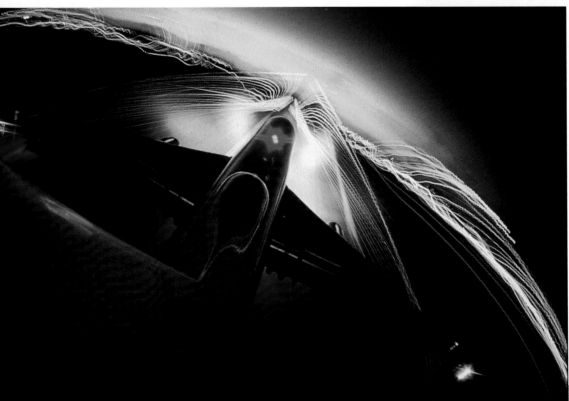

FROM MOSCOW
TO THE TITANIC

CAMELS.
PHOTO: **James L. Stanfield**, National Geographic Society
SUBJECT: Camels at the Imbaba market in Cairo in 1991. During breaks, the camels are hobbled to keep them from tiring themselves.

LION.
PHOTO: **Chris Johns**, National Geographic Society
SUBJECT: At the South Africa–Botswana border in 1996, a lion patrolling the dry bed of the Nossob River.

PEARS.
PHOTO: **Sam Bell**, National Geographic Society
SUBJECT: Lace curtains and ripening pears in a hotel window opposite the Kremlin. The 1983 image evokes the nineteenth-century Russia of Tolstoy's novels.

ROBOT CAMERA.
PHOTO: **Emory Kristof**, National Geographic Society
SUBJECT: The first test, in 1985, of an ROV camera operated from the surface. This camera would be used to take deep-water pictures of sharks and on other expeditions.

SHARK.
PHOTO: **Bill Curtsinger**, National Geographic Society
SUBJECT: A fearsome tiger shark in the waters off Hawaii, featured in the November 1999 issue.

TITANIC.
PHOTO: **Emory Kristof**, National Geographic Societ.
SUBJECT: The imposing bow of the *Titanic*, which sank in the North Atlantic on April 14, 1912. Kristof teamed with Robert Ballard in the expedition that located the ship in 1985.

THE NATIONAL GEOGRAPHIC MAGAZINE
MAP OF THE NEW BALKAN STATES AND CENTRAL EUROPE
PREPARED BY J. G. BARTHOLOMEW—GILBERT H. GROSVENOR, EDITOR.

GEOGRAPHY AND CURRENT EVENTS.
Two months after the beginning of World War I, in August of 1914, the magazine published a detailed map of the area where the conflict originated. And in 1916 it created its own team of cartographers. Ever since, the maps have been unsurpassed in quality, precision, and quantity of information provided.

maps, another of the magazine's trademarks

With the beginning of World War I came the beginning of a *National Geographic* tradition: the publishing of maps to be included with the magazine.

In just the second month of the war, the August 1914 issue was accompanied by a "Map of the New Balkan States and Central Europe" that Gilbert Grosvenor had ordered the previous year after traveling to Europe with his wife. During that trip they had been stranded in Edinburgh, unable to get money out of the bank for three days because a European war was expected. Upon his return, Grosvenor directed commercial cartographers to draw an updated map of Central Europe, which he distributed after the war started. Thanks to a "nose for news" that allowed Grosvenor to anticipate events, he brought to the Society in one year 100,000 new members eager to learn about the geography of the battle zone.

As a result of that experience, it was decided that the Society would set up its own team of cartographers, and in 1916 Albert H. Bumstead was named the first cartography chief. During his tenure, exceptional maps were drawn with unprecedented detail and information. The *National Geographic* maps were distributed with the magazine and were used everywhere from educational to military institutions. It was no surprise, then, that during World War II the maps printed by the Society would come to be true treasures for analysts and strategists. While other magazines covered the world-shaking war through photos, the *National Geographic Magazine* did so using maps. Thus, after the Germans annexed Austria in March of 1938, magazine subscribers received with their April issue a map of Europe and the Mediterranean. As the war unfolded, the maps published by the magazine featured other battle zones: "Europe and the Near East" was produced in May of 1940, "Indian Ocean Including Australia, New Zealand and Malaysia" in March of 1941, a map of the Atlantic Ocean in September of that year, and "Theater of War in the Pacific Ocean" along with the February 1942 issue. That same year, magazine readers received a map of North America in May, a "Theater of War in Europe, Africa and Western Asia" in July, a South America map in October, and in December a new "Asia and Adjacent Areas."

The maps became so popular that on January 15, 1945, the *New York Times* published an editorial praising the Society's collective cartographical production as "the most comprehensive atlas and gazetteer ever compiled" and saying, "The maps are to be found at the front, in the air, in our embassies and consulates, in business and newspaper offices, in schools." And so they were. Even President Franklin D. Roosevelt requested help from the *National Geographic*, to locate a town near Singapore that was under attack by the Japanese in late 1941. Years later, in his memoirs, Grosvenor wrote that the Armed Forces "drew heavily on The Society's collection of 53,000 maps from all over the world, many of them large-scale charts of strategic cities, harbors, railroads, air routes and caravan trails… Scores of Government agencies consulted The Society's research departments daily for elusive geographical information needed in war planning."

From that time on, in war or in peace, the *National Geographic Magazine* has been synonymous with cartography worldwide, thanks to its innumerable atlases and thousands of specialized books. And to this day, most of the magazine issues come with high-quality maps devoted to diverse corners of the world.

DINOSAURS IN ACTION.
The first dinosaur illustrations came out in the 1940s, done by Charles Knight. Those shown here are the work of John Gurche, a specialist in this type of drawing who also holds a science degree. For an illustration to work, he says, the scientific basis must be right.

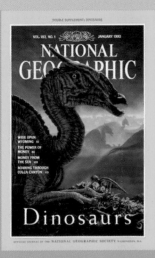

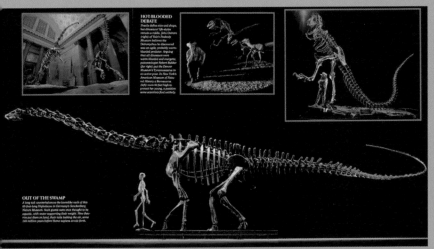

THE BEST-DOCUMENTED ILLUSTRATIONS IN THE WORLD

Before, during, and after the arrival of photography in all its splendor, the *National Geographic Magazine* has needed illustrators to portray the people, flora, fauna, places, and events that the camera can't reach. This job requires extraordinary flights of imagination such as only an artist can embark on—artists of the stature of N. C. Wyeth, James Gurney, Syd Mead, Jerry Pinkney (four-time winner of the prestigious Caldecott Medal), Andrew Wyeth, and many others who, in media ranging from pencil or watercolor or traditional oils through sculpture to computerized visual effects, have produced images of everything from the origins of the planet to the colonization of space.

The archives of the *National Geographic* now contain more than 12,000 such illustrations of great visual quality and high scientific value. Sixty-five of the illustrators are celebrated in the book *The Art of National Geographic: A Century of Illustration,* by Alice A. Carter. Her work proves that art and science are

NEW TERROR AFOOT

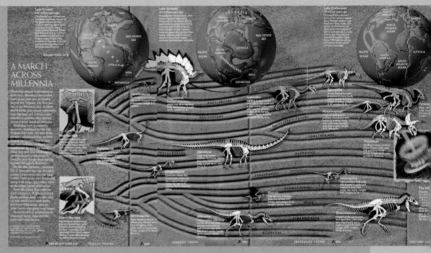

A MARCH ACROSS MILLENNIA

ARCTIC ATTACK

not antagonists but, rather, inseparable ingredients of human creativity, as is persuasively argued in the introduction by scientist Stephen Jay Gould.

Several of these illustrators, including John Gurche, who started working at the magazine in 1989 with a specialty in paleontological and anthropological sculptures and paintings, have science degrees. For an illustration to work, the scientific basis must be right; otherwise, illustrators would be creating fantasy,

says Gurche, whose dinosaur images are the best in the world. Another great *Geographic* illustrator is James Gurney, better known as the creator of the illustrated book *Dinotopia*. But the first to do a series of color illustrations of dinosaurs for *National Geographic* was Charles R. Knight in the 1940s.

When the magazine ordered an illustration, it would ask the designer to first investigate the scientific characteristics of the animal or plant in question before starting to draw.

Then the work had to undergo the scrutiny of scientific specialists and colleagues, and be open to constructive criticism. Thus it was not remarkable for an illustration to take six months or longer; for example, Canadian sculptor Brian Cooley spent two and a half months working on a model of a flying dinosaur, which he built using pheasant, partridge, and rooster feathers.

FROM DINOSAURS TO SPACE

Marvin Mattelson, creator of the excellent illustrations of the Cambrian Period published by *National Geographic* in October of 1993, once proudly explained that while other kids wanted to make it onto the cover of *Time*, he wanted to draw it. Although many of his illustrations and others'– among them, those by Jack Unruh– seem products of the imagination, nothing could be further from the truth: all these images have been thoroughly researched by experts.

In other cases illustrators become visual journalists, as Tom Lovell did in 1963, when his source was an oral account of an aerial odyssey. William Kepner, Orvil Anderson, and Albert Stevens had gone up into the stratosphere in the balloon *Explorer* in 1934 in a quest for the altitude record. At 60,000 feet they had seen their balloon start to rip. *Explorer* descended faster and faster until she was falling at a mile a minute, and the three narrowly managed to parachute to safety. Lovell came up with a splendid illustration published by the magazine in 1966, based on the three adventurers' dramatic account. By contrast, to create his memorable images of great moments in the American Civil War, he had to seek anecdotes about its protagonists in countless history books.

Around the same time, Jean-Léon Huens became known at the magazine

as the illustrator of scientists, painting those who had contributed to a better understanding of the universe. Perhaps the most representative of his portraits was the one of Albert Einstein in May of 1974. Ned Seidler did similar work with noted biologists. In these portraits the subjects were surrounded by icons that clearly showed their area of expertise.

At *the National Geographic,* visual reproduction constantly faced the challenge of making knowledge of the planet's flora and fauna accessible without diminishing its scientific rigor. This premise found great illustrators in Louis Agassiz Fuertes with his bird studies in the early twentieth century, and then in biologist Walter A. Weber, who at midcentury brilliantly combined scientific knowledge with painting skills. Weber collected, studied, and dissected more than 5,000 birds and some 2,000 mammals, as well as insects and fish, to do magnificent illustrations. Later artists, including John Dawson, Jay Matternes, and Ned Seidler, likewise had plenty of dedication and patience.

But none of them managed to surpass Hashime Murayama, who took four years (1921–1925) to make thirty botanical illustrations for the magazine. Murayama worked with magnifying lenses and microscopes to avoid missing details, to the point that one day he even counted the scales on a fish to be absolutely correct.

THE FACE OF THE PLANETS. These images were done by astronomy illustrator Ludek Pesek and published in the August 1970 issue. His work shows an aggressive planetary system, after the Big Bang theory became widely accepted. The magazine's illustrators are true researchers.

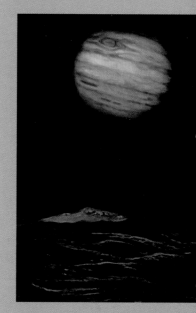

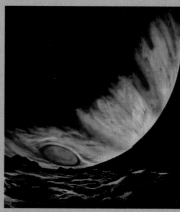

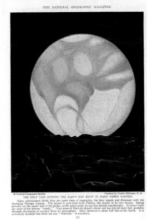

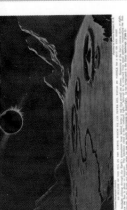

The visual portrayal of space was another of the magazine's great historical challenges. It took the editor, Bert Grosvenor, a long time to find a person who could paint the skies and stars credibly. But then he ran into Charles Bittinger, who had studied physics for three years at MIT before changing careers to devote himself to painting. Bittinger's eight illustrations of the solar system from 1939 were a milestone and, thirty years later, his illustration of the Earth seen from the moon was widely praised. His image of a solar system at rest greatly contrasted with astronomy illustrator Ludek Pesek's, which presented a more "threatening" vision of planets in 1970. Why such a divergence between the two? Very simple: from one issue of *National Geographic* to another, exploration and knowledge of space had advanced tremendously. For instance, in the decade of the 1930s little was said about the Big Bang, which suggests that the magazine evolved almost at the same pace as the new scientific theories and discoveries.

Together, all these artists and their works published in the *National Geographic Magazine* constitute a visual treasure of art and science, as well as a wonderful voyage around the world.

THe evolUTion OF THe cover

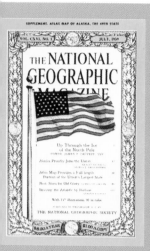

FLAG
July 1959

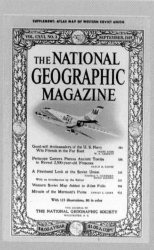

AIRPLANE
September 1959

VOLCÁNO
March 1960

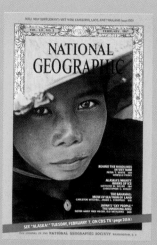

VIETNAM
February 1967

SHARKS
February 1968

In 1954, after fifty-five years in the post, Gilbert H. Grosvenor retired as editor of the *National Geographic.* He was seventy-eight years old, and his magazine was more than 2 million subscribers strong. He was succeeded by his friend John Oliver La Gorce for a short period; then in 1957 his son Melville Bell Grosvenor, Alexander Graham Bell's favorite grandson, took over. Melville had joined the magazine as a writer in 1924. Thirty-three years later he would become the editor of the publication that his grandfather had created and his father had managed, reinvented, and made successful. Melville, of course, would make changes of his own, many of them significant.

Like his father, Melville was a fan of photography and illustration. To exploit to the fullest the visual splendor of the pages, he increased the size of printed photos and started the practice of opening stories with a double-page image.

As for the cover, it can fairly be said that he changed the face of the *Geographic.* According to Bryan's history, Melville had grown tired of the magazine's "same old conservative covers." He called several colleagues into his office, picked up a pile of back issues, strewed them on the floor, and challenged anyone to pick out the latest. No one could. "You see!" he said. "They all look alike." Then he produced a dozen magazines with striking color photographs pasted on them. Holding up an issue with the image of a geisha on the cover, he said: "If you saw this on a coffee table in a friend's home, you'd think,

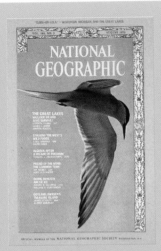

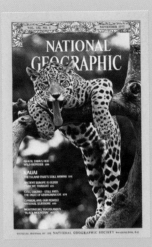

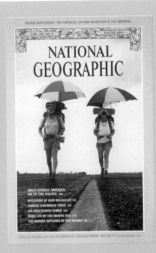

R SURFACE
ber 1969

SEAGULLS
August 1973

WILD BRAZIL
November 1977

WALKS
August 1979

JANE GOODALL
December 1995

oh yes, there's last month's *Geographic* with a story on Japan. Or you'd think, I haven't seen that one yet; it must be the new issue. Hereafter, there's going to be a color picture on the cover."

The cover of the July 1959 issue bore the new flag of the United States with forty-nine stars. The August issue had no illustration, but a small Navy fighter plane was on the September issue. Ever since, the *National Geographic's* cover has always carried a color picture. And that wasn't the only significant change that Melville Grosvenor made to the magazine's cover. In December of 1959 *The National Geographic Magazine* became *The National Geographic* and, in March of 1960, just *National Geographic*. He also narrowed the yellow frame and, in a decision that was highly controversial among subscribers, he started to do away with the garland of oak leaves. He had to move gradually to allow readers to get used to it; in fact, the leaves did not completely disappear from the cover until long after 1969, the year Melville Grosvenor retired as the magazine's editor. The process caused so much trouble that the elimination of the leafy border, begun in 1966, ended only in 1979, and many letters of protest were received. In 2000, the first year of newsstand sales, the cover would once again undergo changes to achieve maximum impact (see page 280).

COLOR AND CONTRAST. A *National Geographic* photographers practice, or "vice": to photograph places or people with strong colors standing out. This gave rise to all sorts of criticism, particularly from colleagues.

JUSTIFICATION. Editor Melville Grosvenor defended the "red shirt school." He said that everyone went on expeditions in khaki clothing, which made the photos monotonous. That was why his photographers resorted to colorful accessories.

Lake Superior Waves Carved the Helmeted Giant; Sunset Gilds the Pictured Rocks

"THE RED SHIRT SCHOOL"

Over the years, photography had become not just a passion but an obsession with the magazine's editors. In general, pictures were valued for their contributions as an educational element and a medium to inform readers of an endless procession of discoveries and innovations. However, with the unrestricted use of color photography, these values sometimes got skewed, with more importance placed on execution than on the subject itself. In the 1950s, as Bryan put it, "*Geographic* editors still believed color photographs were interesting as technical achievements, that… even being able to take such a photograph provided an end in itself. Therefore, the *Geographic* photographers were still taking color for color's sake, still taking perfectly composed and lighted, professionally challenging photographs–of often boring subjects."

We should remember that, right from the launch of *Life* in 1936, photojournalism had enjoyed great prestige. Once *Life's* photographers and editors had established the photo essay, people grew accustomed to seeing stories told through pictures. This new kind of photography, agile and spontaneous, gained more and more converts among media professionals every day–and the most highly regarded work was done in black and white. Without a doubt, this trend represented the opposite of *National Geographic's* colorful, yet posed and static, images.

Indeed, in 1962 the trade magazine *U.S. Camera* published the comment that "*National Geographic's* pictures, with rare exception, were all pretty much of the picture postcard type of idealistic beauty, rather than photojournalism."

The magazine's photographers strove for the most intense colors in order to achieve the most dramatic effect in print. They were conscious, and so were their editors, that color was the element that set *National Geographic* apart from other publications. They developed an array of standard stratagems, peopling their pictures with locals in native costume or tourists in bright attire, searching for backgrounds with a profusion of flowers or gateways in contrasting colors. Before long, critics began to call *National Geographic* photographers and photo editors "the red shirt school" in deprecation of their heavy reliance on red props–jackets, caps, sweaters–to perk up their images. In fact, the technique had been pioneered back in the 1920s when the *Geographic* published the autochromes of Gervais Courtellemont, a Frenchman who took with him on his travels through Europe, Asia, and Africa a supply of brightly colored scarves in which he wreathed his subjects or their surroundings. To him and to later *National Geographic* photographers, what was important was to ensure contrast in their photos.

Now, in an era of vastly improved developing and printing techniques, "the red shirt school" seems more an odd footnote than a photographic method. However, we must keep in mind the times and their editorial demands. As Melville Grosvenor once explained in defense of his photographers, "they'd go on these expeditions, and everybody would be in khaki, because that's the color of field uniforms. And they'd come back with the dullest bunch of pictures you ever saw! You couldn't use them editorially because they had no color. So, we decided to have people wear colorful shirts…You might as well be in black-and-white if you're all in khaki or dull green. There's no pep to it. But when a fellow had a red cap on–just a red cap–it would add a little color to the picture."

WITH ITS eyes on THe sea, space, and TeLevision

When Melville Grosvenor started working at the magazine in 1924, it had 905,700 subscribers, and when he was named editor in 1957, there were almost 2.2 million. Twelve years later, when he gave up the post, the magazine had reached a then-record circulation of 5.5 million. What did the junior Grosvenor do to achieve such success?

When he took over the magazine, Melville found that the *National Geographic* had almost run out of unexplored Pacific islands, journeys across deserts and through jungles, aerial panoramas, and unconquered high mountains. Accordingly, with the encouragement of the board of trustees, he expanded the Society's contributions to expeditions and research–from which the magazine could expect exclusives– and focused on the exploration and investigation of nonterrestrial frontiers: the sea and space. Thus the magazine took its readers to the depths of the ocean in numerous stories about Jacques-Yves Cousteau and allowed them to participate in the American

space program through the adventures of the astronauts about to reach the moon. Also under the Society's auspices, subscribers were able to share the excitement of "How We Climbed Everest" with Barry Bishop, learn of "Brazil's Big-Lipped Indians" with Harald Schultz, or unearth the hominid Zinjanthropus with Louis Leakey at the Olduvai Gorge. The new features that Melville Grosvenor managed to come up with were so popular that, in the early 1960s, the magazine was obliged to move its printing operation from Washington to Chicago, where the modern presses of Donnelley & Sons could print a greater number of full-color issues.

Nor did Melville Grosvenor limit his scope to magazines. He immediately instituted a Book Service Division, expanding the Society's sporadic efforts in that direction, and in 1963 published a three-hundred-page *Atlas of the World* that augmented the already unparalleled *National Geographic* maps with descriptions of

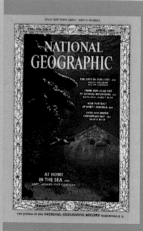

COUSTEAU
April 1964

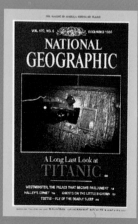

TITANIC
December 1986

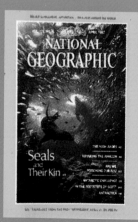

SEALS AND THEIR KIN
April 1987

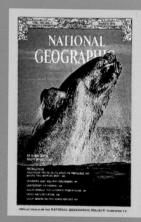

WHALES
March 1976

TITANIC
December 1985

every nation, flags, charts, tables, and an index of place-names with 125,000 entries. In 1961 a film department was organized, with the goal of producing four TV documentaries annually. Two years later Barry Bishop, a staff geographer at *National Geographic,* was among the first Americans to reach the summit of Everest–and also the first to ascend from the west and the first to film views from the peak. The TV documentary *Americans on Everest,* narrated by Orson Welles, was broadcast the night of September 10, 1965, to public and critical acclaim. More documentaries were filmed–*Miss Goodall and the Wild Chimpanzees, Dr. Leakey and the Dawn of Man, The World of Jacques-Yves Cousteau,* and the ratings-topping *Amazon.*

Thus *National Geographic's* "stars" became TV stars, while the magazine and the Society turned into one of the most popular dissemination-of-knowledge publications.

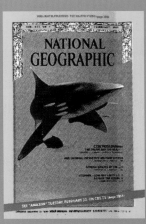

SHARKS
February 1968

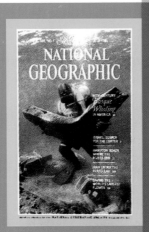

DISCOVERIES
July 1985

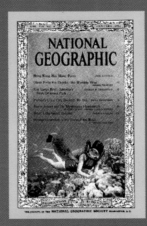

KEY LARGO
January 1962

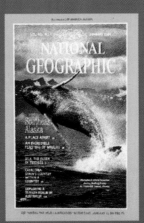

WHALES IN ALASKA
January 1984

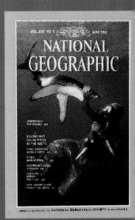

SHARKS
May 1981

UNDER THE SEA. *National Geographic* became an underwater photography specialist. It not only contributed to Cousteau's investigations, but it currently has oceanographers on its permanent research staff.

Facing the Critics,
Changing the Subjects

Despite his extraordinary energy and innovative editorship during the Society's "golden decade," there was one challenge Melville Grosvenor didn't manage to overcome: criticism of the magazine and its Pollyanna outlook by the rest of the press. The criticism was nothing new. Since well before World War II, the magazine had been the target of all kinds of accusations, particularly after 1937 when it published a story by Douglas Chandler titled "Changing Berlin" in which he said: "To develop boys and girls in body and mind, and thus insure a sturdy race to defend Germany in the future, is a policy of the present government… German youngsters now join an institution known as the Hitler Youth organization. Its emblem is the swastika, and its wide activities and political training are enormously popular with all classes."

All the criticism was directed at the fifth and sixth editorial principles that Gilbert H. Grosvenor had laid down at the turn of the century: "Nothing of a partisan or controversial character is printed" and "Only what is of a kindly nature is printed about any country or people, everything unpleasant or unduly critical being avoided."

By the mid-1960s, with the world in ferment in many ways, these outdated editorial rules came in for near-universal censure. For instance, when the New York Times evaluated Melville Grosvenor's successful work for the Society, it wrote: "Dr. Grosvenor did not dramatically modify the magazine's traditional tone of gentlemanly detachment from the ugliness, misery and strife in the world." Time magazine, calling the National Geographic Society "the least exclusive, farthest flung and most improbable nonprofit publishing corporation in the world," blamed the principles instituted by Grosvenor for "the unrealistic hue to the Geographic's rose-colored world." Even harsher was Newsweek, which in its issue of November 11, 1963, said that the seventy-five-year-old Society "thrives on a policy of daring serenity and a 'dear Aunt Sally style,' as staff members refer to it. The world of National Geographic is usually a sunlit Kodachrome world of altruistic human achievement in settings of natural beauty, a world without commercial blemish or political disturbance, even, it sometimes seems, a world without germs or sin." Still, despite the criticism, the magazine made no quick changes.

In August of 1967, Melville Bell Grosvenor retired from the magazine. He was succeeded by Frederick Vosburgh, who had been associate editor for ten years. Vosburgh was obsessive about accuracy and considered himself responsible for making National Geographic the most precise publication in the world. During his editorship, which ended in October of 1970, almost no changes in content took place. The most important modifications in editorial terms would be made by his successor, Gilbert Melville Grosvenor, whose name resounded with the family tradition within the magazine: he was the son of Melville, grandson of Gilbert, great-grandson of Alexander Graham Bell, and great-great-grandson of Gardiner Hubbard, all of them presidents of the Society and driving forces behind the magazine since its founding.

The first hint of the new Grosvenor's approach came in December of 1970 with the publication of "Our Ecological Crisis." The story signaled the magazine's altered direction by recognizing the existence of serious environmental problems, and even taking sides. Yet the third Grosvenor was not about to embark on a drastic overhaul. He took over the Geographic when it had 6.9 million subscribers, each of whom paid the Society, in advance, to receive at home every month a publication of prestige and predictable interest. So he had to make changes cautiously.

And that's what Gilbert Grosvenor did. He began by updating the writing style. The new editor then tackled subjects that he considered important to express the magazine's social conscience, with stories such as "Can the World Feed Its People?" illustrated by shocking photos of starving people in Bangladesh, or "East Germany: The Struggle to Succeed," which presented an objective view of a nation whose political system was openly opposed to America's. But these stories were a minority, published alongside such National Geographic staples as "Head-Hunters of Remotest New Guinea" or "Shy Monster, the Octopus."

"TO LIVE IN HARLEM":
When the story was
published in February
of 1977, the magazine
featured black
Americans for the first
time. The story, with an
upbeat tone, was
written by two black
freelance writers.

The core of the matter lay in maintaining a good balance—something that came into question in 1977, when the Society's board of trustees confronted the editor over the publication of such socially charged stories as "Cuba Today," an objective analysis in the January issue of life on the island under Fidel Castro, or "To Live in Harlem," a story written by two freelance black journalists and published in February of that year, a milestone because it offered a positive view of African-Americans, who had been ignored by the magazine up to that point. Grosvenor defended himself and won. "The magazine is not changing," he said then. "The world is changing."

Three years after the crisis, the last Grosvenor retired from *Geographic's* management. During his tenure, the number of subscribers had grown from 6.4 million to almost 10.8 million. The world had changed. And so had the magazine.

INSIDE FIDEL CASTRO'S CUBA.
Another unprecedented story, "Cuba Today," came out in January of 1977 with an objective analysis of life on the island under Fidel Castro. It too gave rise to controversy within the Society.

HOW IT approached newsstand sales

In 1999 National Geographic faced one of its greatest editorial challenges: selling the magazine not only by subscription but also on the street.

When the *National Geographic Magazine* first came out in October of 1888, it was a scholarly scientific periodical that reflected the interests of its small group of readers, most of them scholars and scientists. On its dull brownish covers there were no photographs. It was the nineteenth century.

Today, 116 years later at the turn of the millennium, the publication with yellow borders takes geography, in its broadest possible sense, to 10 million subscribers every month in every corner of the world. With long and varied stories, striking photos, and unmatched illustrations, the magazine reports and interprets the changes in the world through a unique and exclusive prism: the dissemination of knowledge through accurate, objective, accessible, and entertaining information. That is the key to its success.

In addition, *National Geographic* established the foundations and the philosophy for the whole of today's dissemination-of-knowledge sector, magazines such as *Muy Interesante, Quo, Discover,* or in its day *Conozca Más,* whose journalistic approach is to turn the most difficult subjects into easy, educational, and attractive ones. And its millions of readers are grateful.

At the same time, *National Geographic* transformed its subscribers into participants in the great exploits of mankind, as their annual contributions financed the most ambitious expeditions, whether conquering high peaks, penetrating uncharted jungles, rediscovering lost cities, diving to the depths of the ocean, or unearthing precious archaeological relics.

To this end, the magazine became both witness and protagonist. Its reader-subscribers –the only readers with access to the articles, since there were no newsstand sales– paid annual membership fees to receive the publication. With that money, the Society covered its production and editorial costs and financed research projects and expeditions. Then, month after month, the magazine was delivered to the subscribers who, through the stories, could follow the footsteps and adventures of scientists and explorers who had made one discovery after another, all owing to the readers' own monetary support. Readers felt they were a part of each significant contribution that *National Geographic* made to the sum of human knowledge.

And this formula lasted down the years. Currently the magazine has a formidable international presence thanks to the scientists, explorers, photographers, and writers who constantly travel the world, and to its score of international editions in nearly as many languages: English, Japanese, Spanish, Portuguese, Italian, Greek, Turkish, Hebrew, French, Dutch, German, Polish, Danish, Swedish, Norwegian, Finnish, Mandarin Chinese, Korean, and Thai.

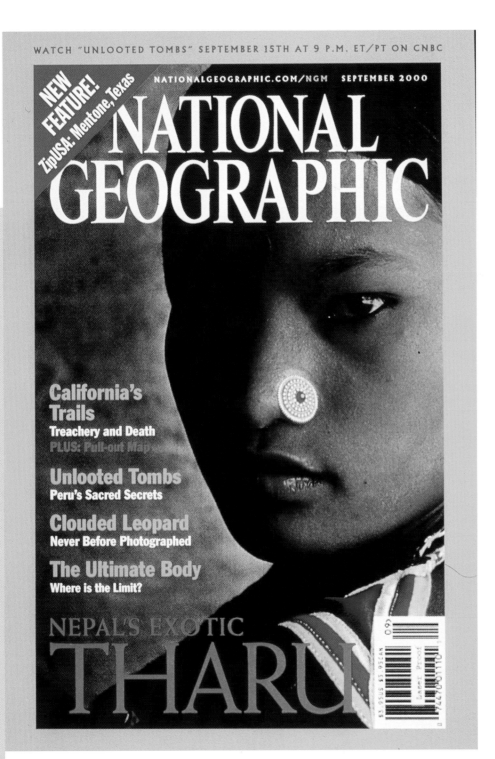

NEW FEATURE!
ZipUSA: Mentone, Texas

NATIONALGEOGRAPHIC.COM/NGM   SEPTEMBER 2000

NATIONAL GEOGRAPHIC

California's Trails
Treachery and Death
PLUS: Pull-out Map

Unlooted Tombs
Peru's Sacred Secrets

Clouded Leopard
Never Before Photographed

The Ultimate Body
Where is the Limit?

NEPAL'S EXOTIC
THARU

FACING THE NEWSSTAND. The cover of the first issue sold at newsstands (September of 2000) had undergone some changes.

Most important, the thin white frame that separated the photo from the yellow border was eliminated, mainly to make the magazine look larger.

Two different covers were printed, one for subscribers and the other with a bar code for newsstands.

THE BEGINNING OF
a new challenge

At the turn of the millennium, *National Geographic* had to face another crucial challenge in its evolution and history: the start of newsstand sales. For more than a century, the magazine had been only sold by subscription. That gave editors the comfort of not having to worry too much whether any given cover story would sell well or not: they didn't have to convince subscribers to buy the issue because they had already bought (and paid for) a whole year.

With the change in the sales system, the editorial parameters also had to change. The magazine now sells about 6 and a half million copies a month by subscription in the United States and about 258,000 issues in newsstands. "That forced us to introduce changes at the visual level, and in approach and content," the editor conceded.

The editorial staff faced the challenge in two ways. The first was to propose important design changes (see Keys to the New Design) "to make the magazine more visible." The second was to change the writing style.

An effective innovation for evaluating visual changes was the creation of a mock newsstand, located on the eighth floor of editorial headquarters, on which a variety of periodicals brought in by *Geographic* employees are placed on display. Members of the staff are responsible every day for rearranging the magazines in the racks. One or more dummy issues of *National Geographic* are placed among them, each bearing a new cover option, alternating with each other and changing position at irregular but frequent intervals. In this way, every

month more than thirty different potential covers are submitted to independent opinions. Since the newsstand is located at a high-traffic intersection, each cover option is subjected to the eyes and judgment of employees, visitors, and executives from other company departments. Every comment about the cover—positive, negative, or neutral—is briefly noted in a feedback book and later delivered to the editorial board to get "independent and varied opinions" about its visual material and text. "This method is incredibly useful because people look, then write down and say what they believe or think without limits or preconceived notions or prejudice or fear that their opinion will be singled out for reward or punishment," explained Connie Phelps, the publication's design editor.

THE NEWSSTAND. On the eighth floor of the National Geographic headquarters, a mock newsstand helps determine which is the most appropriate and attractive cover for each issue.

A Soggy Dry Run
Sending images home in the rain forest

BEHIND THE SCENES. In this interesting and entertaining new section, photographers and journalists who worked on the stories recount experiences from the trip or their coverage.

She and other in-house editors believe that the mock newsstand constitutes an excellent yardstick to gauge whether a cover image has visual power, whether a main headline is appealing or controversial, whether it is well placed within the yellow frame, or whether a subject is one readers are willing to pay for. "Experience has taught us not to place the headlines too low on the cover," Phelps said, "because the lips of the racks on the newsstands hide them or make them difficult to read. That helps us place the headlines strategically on the cover so that they don't go unnoticed or remain hidden."

ANECDOTES. Another journalist shares his experience in the same *Behind the Scenes* section, which tends to run about three pages (right).

BEHIND THE SCENES

■ NGS EXPEDITIONS GRANT
On the Inca Road

Behind in His Work

100 YEARS AGO

September 1900

FOR MORE INFORMATION

NATIONAL GEOGRAPHIC • SEPTEMBER 2000

nationalgeographic.com

The Yellow Border Gets Bigger
More to explore at the Geographic's redesigned website

DOT-COM. The section *national geographic.com*, also in the front part of the magazine, tells readers about the items found on its Web page.

National Geographic TV

In the Company of Lizards
Living among a unique menagerie of creatures

NATIONAL GEOGRAPHIC TV. This section provides information on scheduled broadcasts and on some of the shows the Society has in production.

Bear
BEGINNINGS
NEW LIFE ON THE ICE

NEW LOGO. When it hit the newsstands, the magazine enlarged its logo and introduced a new typeface on its cover. The Bartuska type, a variant of Times Roman, is used exclusively by *National Geographic*.

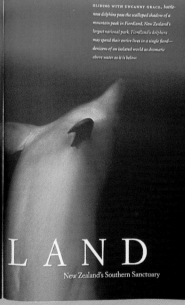

A SPECIAL PLACE

GLIDING WITH UNCANNY GRACE, *bottle-nose dolphins pass the scalloped shadow of a mountain peak in Fiordland, New Zealand's largest national park. Fiordland's dolphins may spend their entire lives in a single fiord— denizens of an isolated world as dramatic above water as it is below.*

FIORDLAND

BY KENNEDY WARNE   PHOTOGRAPHS BY ANNIE GRIFFITHS BELT

New Zealand's Southern Sanctuary

THE DAWN OF HUMANS

Hunt for the First Americans

By MICHAEL PARFIT
Photographs by KENNETH GARRETT

IN SEARCH OF PHOTOS.
According to photography editor Chris Johns, "Nowadays we want each shot to be more evocative. Photography has to go beyond mere information and connect emotionally with the reader."

CHANGES IN TEXT AND PHOTOS

The change in prose style was also significant after *National Geographic* started to be sold on newsstands. "We had to ask our journalists to write in a less distant style, with a stronger emotional connection with readers, although without losing our traditional seriousness and objectivity," Bill Allen explained. Since then, editors have allowed more first-person stories that emphasize individual experiences. "Before, we wrote with the head, and now we write in touch with the heart and all the senses," conceded an old and renowned text editor at the magazine. The best examples of that change are the magazine's recent stories on Afghanistan. However, the editorial staff tries not to fall either into excessive involvement or into dispassionate detachment.

The editorial approach has also evolved with time. Although some experts still criticize *National Geographic* for being the Disneyland of science, geography, and knowledge, and although there might be some truth to such criticism, the current approach is to make the stories "neither too rosy nor too depressing." A captions editor put it this way: "We show the dark side of places and things and people in the world, but we never make it totally black."

Important change also took place in the photography. One of the key professionals involved in this change was Chris Johns, who, after working for the magazine for more than thirty years as a photographer specializing in natural history, biodiversity, and ecosystems, was named illustrations editor of *National Geographic* in December of 2001. "The most significant change was in the photographic philosophy," said Johns. "Today we expect much more from the photographer than ever before: nowadays we want each shot to be more evocative. Photography has to go beyond mere information and connect emotionally with the reader. Today the magazine's photos have several levels of contact with the public."

Interestingly, despite having experimented with digital technology, *National Geographic* hasn't yet adopted it "because the quality still isn't up to our level," Johns said. However, several industry insiders say that the magazine's editors had a very bad experience with digital technology, which forced them to step back. A few years ago, the magazine wanted to put on its cover several pyramids at Giza in a single image but, since there was no perspective that permitted this, they digitized the shot and moved the pyramids closer together so they would all fit on the cover. This generated such a scandal among readers and editors for "having altered reality" that digital

photography was postponed for a while, until things settled down and the episode was forgotten.

The magazine's photographers continue to use Kodachrome, as they always have, but currently alternate with Fujichrome, Provia, and Velvia film.

Another recent change was the reversal of the traditional policy of sending journalists and photographers independently to cover a story. "In general, now they go out together because we believe that it's a complementary effort and therefore a cooperative one," said Johns, "although that's not always possible."

A further change: the photo department now has only three staff photographers, and the contract photographer no longer exists, although the magazine has a pool of twenty freelance journalists from which it regularly draws to find the appropriate professional for the subject and the circumstances. "Nevertheless, we're always looking for new talent," Johns said, "and lately we've even decided to contact famous photographers such as Sebastião Salgado, who have never had their work in *National Geographic* although it's first rate and has been published in books and magazines all over the world and has received international awards."

KEYS TO THE new Design

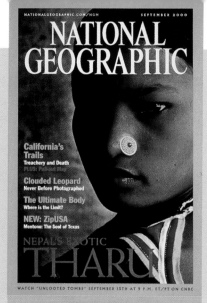

Connie Phelps, the current design editor at *National Geographic*, has spent a quarter century at the magazine and supervises nine people, of whom four do layout, one is a design editor, and three are type designers. Her say on the magazine's look is crucial, and therefore she is one of the members of the story team, along with the photographer, the illustrations editor, the captions writer, and the text editor. "Our great innovation is the practice of hiring the photographers on each story to work here with us for four to six weeks during the visual editing process. This is unprecedented in the business," Phelps said, adding, "That way, photographers contribute the ideas they had and have about the story, the difference between what they set out to capture and what they got, as well as their comments, impressions, and feelings during the job. This last

becomes part of *Behind the Scenes,* which is now a very popular section with our readers."

Regarding the redesign of *National Geographic*, it was not done all at once but rather gradually, "attempting to make it as imperceptible as possible to the reader." However, when the July 1979 issue completely eliminated the traditional leaves from the border of the cover, magazine aficionados protested, forcing editors to bring them back the following month. Later, as complaints died down, they were permanently eliminated in the December issue.

Something similar happened with the page numbers in the cover headlines. The magazine traditionally published page numbers to help readers find the story announced on the cover. With time, the editors considered that those numbers were unnecessary because the answer was more than obvious. But when readers complained, the editors had no choice but to include them again. "Our readers are very loyal and resist change," Connie Phelps explained.

Still, the new emotional parameters that applied when *National Geographic* was first sold on newsstands, as well as the visual modernization and certain pressures from the advertising side—for example, it was decided that the central part of the magazine, the editorial well, would not include ads—forced the editors to come up with a new, bolder design in the course of the year 2000. During this period, three fundamental changes were made, in addition to giving the publication new visual dynamics:

1 The logo was not only enlarged but it was printed in a typeface called Bartuska, a variant of Times Roman. Since other magazines also used it and *National Geographic* wanted to control it exclusively, the company opted to buy the rights to this type, so no other publication may use it nowadays.

2 The white inner edge of the cover frame was eliminated to achieve a "cleaner and fresher visual impression," said Phelps. Getting rid of the white border had another purpose: readers would get the idea that the magazine had grown in size, when in fact it remained the same. Readers' letters indicated that the desired effect was accomplished, as many congratulated the editors for "the decision to enlarge the size of the magazine without announcing it."

3 The magazine's table of contents was now set in Franklin Gothic type.

THe maGneTIC BOarD

Until his interview with this book's authors, nobody had had access to the "magnetic board" that the editor hides (and locks away) in his office on the eighth floor. "I'm going to show you something that nobody but my closest editors and assistants has ever seen," he said.

Reaching behind what looked from the outside like a decorative map, Allen deployed a gigantic board that bore a sort of "table of contents of the future" for the magazine, with articles planned up to two years in advance on the basis of an exclusive calendar of milestones and historical dates in science, geography, and knowledge.

Under each year, attached to the board and lined up vertically —using different colors according to the specialty or discipline— were cards with stories that were being planned or were in preparation for the next few issues. The categories were Geography, Natural History, Science, Exploration, and Adventure, and the stories ranged from "Dances of the World" to "The Sahara" or "Everest."

"A story's headline alone says nothing," Allen concluded. "But if we put it on this board it's because it's intimately related to a historical event or an important scientific milestone and the idea is to relate or compare the moment of the original story —or expedition or exploration or adventure or discovery— with the current coverage to see what comes out of the comparison."

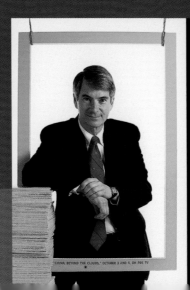

AN EDITOR'S CHALLENGE.
William L. Allen, the magazine's current editor, has faced the challenge of changing the editorial production structure to adapt it to a new, more competitive era with numerous editions in various languages.

HOW NATIONAL GEOGRAPHIC IS PUT TOGETHER TODAY

Spending time inside *National Geographic's* main office in Washington, D.C., watching the workings of the publication's editorial and pictorial machinery, is as amazing an adventure as reading any of its stories. "No other American or international magazine is planned and produced like *National Geographic*," Bill Allen, its current editor, told the authors. "I don't say this through arrogance or because I believe we're the best. We're simply different from the rest."

Indeed they are. To begin with, unlike most magazines, *National Geographic* doesn't conduct market studies to set its course or to select its editorial content or covers. "It seems hard to believe," said Allen, "but this is a magazine created according to its editor's judgment, knowledge, and experience."

Although the editorial principles that guided *National Geographic* for more than a century—accurate, objective, accessible, and entertaining information—are still in force, the publication is nowadays a combination of twenty to fifty other international general interest magazines. **"What's crucial is that in the formula there should be at least one story that gets the reader very excited,"** the editor said. Its genre is "journal" in both senses of the word, since as the voice of the National Geographic Society it traditionally publishes the travel journals of explorers, adventurers, scientists, and discoverers.

Its editorial framework has three parts: the front of the magazine, which is about 14 pages long; the "main editorial well," which encompasses six to nine long stories over some 120 pages; and the back, with about 10 pages.

Although the front and back sections are interchangeable, the front is generally the longer. The best example of their mobility is *On Assignment,* which was initially at the beginning and now is at the end.

The magazine's front section is more news-oriented than the back, with set sections—today they are not called **sections** but rather **departments**—that are very popular with readers. One such is *Geographica.* **"The spread of geographic knowledge is very important to our magazine, so we want to give it a constantly growing and more varied role. Now we are concentrating on educating readers about science without scaring them. The fact is, people know more about science than is generally supposed, and we want to tap into that. The news stories and sections in the front part, then, will be lighter and more humorous in tone without neglecting accurate information. So we are looking for a way to give readers the medicine with a fruity taste."** Its **departments** are *Forum* (letters to the editor), the aforementioned *Geographica, Behind the Scenes* (the experiences, emotions, and impressions of the professionals who worked on the issue's stories), *nationalgeographic.com* (notes on the magazine's Web page), and *National*

Geographic TV (notes on upcoming broadcasts or programs being filmed for TV).

Of the six to nine stories that make up the editorial well, the content usually alternates among geography, natural history, science, discovery, and adventure. "We don't start out with a specific idea for the cover ahead of time," Allen explained. "Any of those stories could be the cover. We don't limit ourselves from the outset. On the contrary, we ask the editors to think of two or three cover options for each story, and only at the end is one chosen."

The visual and editorial presentation of each of these longer stories is the "multimedia approach." That is, readers may get the story in three ways: 1 through the photos and the headline; 2 through the captions; or 3 through the story itself, along with captions and photos.

The sections in the back of the magazine are mostly lighthearted— *ZipUSA,* a feature about the life of an area or a city in the United States, chosen by postal code; *Final Edit,* a page devoted to a significant photo from the editorial well that, for some reason, didn't fit in the layout or eluded editors; *On Assignment,* profiles of the professionals behind the stories in the issue; and *Flashback,* which might offer a photo from a story published some time ago, so readers can look back.

One way and another, the editorial content today includes more subjects than ever before. For instance, two stories about food, a subject that was

not traditionally part of the table of contents, were recently published. But they were approached with "the *National Geographic* touch," that is, to examine how secure our food supply is (in connection with the terrorist threat after September 11, 2001, to contaminate the country's food) or the way our food is being genetically altered. This hitherto untouched area was incorporated to offer innovative looks at subjects of particular interest to readers. The category is called "commodity stories," and it has generated good feedback.

The content of the editorial well isn't chosen at random or capriciously. It not only follows a long and complex process, but the story selection must respond to these three editorial parameters:

1 Why should we cover this story?

2 Why should we do it now and not later?

3 How can we approach this story or what can we bring to it to make it memorable?

THE BACK. At the end, the magazine returns to short items. The longest tends to be the ZipUSA article, a commentary on the life of a town or area in the United States selected by zip code.

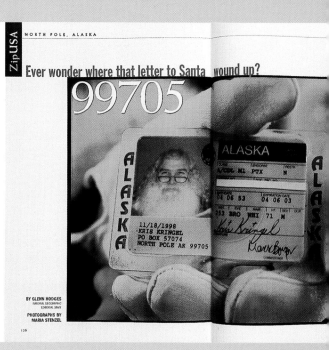

ZipUSA

NORTH POLE, ALASKA

Ever wonder where that letter to Santa wound up?

BY GLENN HODGES
NATIONAL GEOGRAPHIC
EDITORIAL STAFF
PHOTOGRAPHS BY
MARIA STENZEL

ITS EDITORIAL STRUCTURE

Editor Bill Allen isn't mistaken when he says that no other publication in the world is produced the way *National Geographic* is. However, there is a before and after in the magazine's editorial structure, and that change took place during the current editor's tenure.

Before, for many years, the publication relied on "area specialists," experts on a certain geographical area or subject matter. The areas were America, Latin America, Africa, the Near and Middle East, Asia, Biographies, Exploration and Adventure, Geography, Natural History, and Science. After someone proposed a story, that proposal was classified and submitted to an area specialist, who was responsible for evaluating it. If the idea was approved, the editorial process continued, while a rejection entailed returning it to the person who had originally proposed it for changes in approach, content, or execution.

If the area specialist okayed the proposed story, it was turned over to the Planning Council, which assigned a story team made up of an editor, the potential writer, the art director, a photographer, and the illustrations editor. This team would come up with a production plan for the story and turn a draft over to the senior editors and the editor in chief, so they would know in advance what topics the staff was working on. An estimate of expenses was simultaneously presented. If the story passed both filters—the story team and the budget—it went up to what was called the Post Planning Council, which included the magazine's editor. This council was responsible for approving the story and controlling its future development.

To produce a more dynamic magazine with a wider range of subjects, editor Bill Allen recently changed the internal organizational structure to "modernize it and put it more in sync with the new editorial direction."

Today there are only six area specialists: Natural History, Geography and the World, Science, Investigation and Exploration Committee, Adventure and Expeditions, and Photography. Each in turn may have one or more advisors. Any member of the editorial staff or the company as a whole may offer ideas, which also often come from readers' letters and suggestions.

Whatever the origin of the idea, it is first turned over to the area specialist, who may evaluate it or ask for more investigation by his advisors. If the idea is approved, it goes to the Story Development Committee, which meets every three weeks or so. This committee is made up of the section or department editor, the illustrations editor, the photography editor, the art director, and managing editor Robert Booth. They all express their views on the story and, if they agree, the story editor assigns a writer, the photography editor assigns a photographer, and together they decide on a researcher.

Among the decisions made at this meeting are the story's focus, its

QUESTIONS. This section, an interactive exchange of mail that used to go in the front or back, answered readers' questions.

WHO THEY ARE. Profiles of the professionals who prepared the issue's stories are published in the *On Assignment* section- yet another way to connect with readers.

REVISITING. The *Flashback* section at the end offers a story from the past on the same subject as a current one, for readers to compare.

deadlines, its art and photo and illustrative elements, and, if necessary, its maps. The story's length is also set, although it may later be trimmed or increased, depending on the quality of the story and photos or on problems that may crop up.

One recent innovation is publishing stories that span two or three issues. Another development is that, since the cost of sending special correspondents to various corners of the world is very high, stories that take more than sixteen weeks to do are unusual these days. "Most of our stories are produced in an average of two months," said Chris Johns.

At this same meeting, each member of the Story Development Committee except the art director is asked to come up with a viable budget that includes expenses, professional fees, travel, and lodging. When this last step is concluded, the proposal goes to the Story Conference, at which the article's final budget is analyzed, corrected as

needed, and approved. This budget will be analyzed separately by the writer and the photographer, with a flexible margin always provided to handle unforeseen expenses. Editor Bill Allen must approve the final budget before work on each story starts.

Those who participate in the story conference will continue to meet every two or three weeks to consider new stories and budgets, as well as to control the editorial, visual, and financial progress of those already in preparation. Bill Allen also attends and provides feedback during these meetings, often guiding the path the story is taking as it evolves.

After the photographer and the writer turn in the photos and text, and these are edited, the story development committee evaluates all the material once again and picks three or four options for its cover.

PHOTOGRAPHS
We are grateful for the cooperation of the National Geographic Society and its Illustrations Department, which provided the photos featured in this chapter, and whose credits or rights are: Charles Martin, George Shiras III, Robert Peary Collection, Gilbert Grosvenor Collection, Daniel C. Howell, Mark O. Thiessen, Thomas Nebbia, Dean C. Worcester, Peter Bissett, Melville Grosvenor, Sisse Brimberg, James L. Stanfield, William R. Curtsinger, Emory Kristof, Sam Abell, Chris Johns, Thomas J. Abercrombie, Michael Nichols, Edwards Park, Richard Hewitt Stewart, Bruce Dale, Barry C. Bishop, William Albert Allard, Luis Marden, Winfield Parks, Jerry Greenberg, Hope Alexander, Skeeter Hagler, David L. Arnold, Eric Valli, and Debra Kellner.

THE MOST MEMORABLE FACE IN NATIONAL GEOGRAPHIC

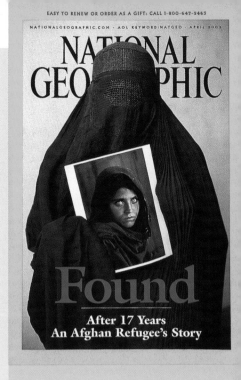

"Is it really her?"

With that question, editor Bill Allen started his letter to readers in the April 2002 issue. It was a fair question. For seventeen years the magazine had received letters, thousands of them, asking the identity of the young Afghan girl who, from the magazine's cover, had impressed millions of readers with her sad, beautiful, huge green eyes. In his letter Allen said:

"That was the first thing to run through my mind when illustrations editor John Echave told me that a crew from *National Geographic Explorer* had located the Afghan girl."

"The crew was in Pakistan, along with photographer Steve McCurry, looking for the subject of the most famous picture in our magazine's 114-year history: a young Afghan refugee photographed by Steve in 1984. The picture had run on several covers, including our June 1985 issue, our 1994 book *The Photographs,* and, just last fall, our special collector's edition magazine, *100 Best Pictures.* Over the years, Steve and the magazine staff had been besieged with requests for her name and her whereabouts. We knew neither.

"Now, perhaps, we had found her. She looked like the same person, but you can't always trust your own eyes."

At that point Allen didn't hesitate to set in motion the *National Geographic's* journalistic machinery and its basic guiding principles to verify the finding and to assure the magazine's readers of accurate, objective, accessible, and entertaining information. To examine the first point, the accuracy of the information, the magazine consulted Pakistani ophthalmologist Mustafa Iqbal. The doctor examined the young woman in person and compared her iris pattern and eye pigmentation with those in the original photo. The doctor said he was "100 percent sure" that it was the same person. Nevertheless, the magazine —fulfilling to the maximum its precepts of providing accurate and objective information—sought to corroborate with other sources the Pakistani ophthalmologist's verdict. So it hired three independent experts unknown to each other: Harry Quigley, an ophthalmologist at the Wilmer Eye Institute in Baltimore; Thomas Musheno, a forensic analyst for the FBI; and John Daugman, a Cambridge professor. The three agreed that it was the same woman photographed in 1984.

So, seventeen years later, *National Geographic* would present in its pages once again that Afghan girl who, we now know, belongs to the Pashtun tribe, is named Sharbat Gula, and is around thirty years old. To continue applying its guidelines and make sure the story was accessible and entertaining, Allen asked photographer Steve McCurry to tell the story of how he found her, in the first person, as if he were writing a letter to readers.

"Her skin is weathered," McCurry wrote, "there are wrinkles now, but she's as striking as the young girl I photographed 17 years ago. Both times our connection was through the lens. This time she found it easier to look into the lens than at me. She is a married woman and must not look at a man who is not her husband.

"Our conversation was brief. There was little emotion. I explained that so many had been moved by her photograph. I've received countless letters from people around the world who were inspired by the photograph to volunteer in refugee camps or do aid work in Afghanistan. When she saw the photo for the first time, she was embarrassed by the holes in her red shawl. A cooking fire had burned it, she said. She is glad her picture was an inspiration. But I don't think the photograph means anything to her. The only thing that matters is her husband and children."

News of her being found surpassed the magazine's expectations: just about every newspaper and newscast showed her before-and-after photos. For *National Geographic* it wasn't just a publishing coup. It was confirmation of the continuing vigor—as strong now as in its beginnings 115 years ago—of the *Geographic* formula of providing correct, objective, accessible, and entertaining information. A formula that has made it the most important magazine for the dissemination of knowledge in the world.

A LIFE REVEALED

Seventeen years after she stared out from the cover of National Geographic, a former Afghan refugee comes face-to-face with the world once more.

SHARBAT GULA TODAY.
Now we know her name and that she is around thirty years old. She is married and has two daughters. Her new portrait, after she was found, made its way around the world just as the first one did. It was published in the December 2001 issue.

She
remembers the moment.
The photographer took her picture.

She remembers her anger. The man was a stranger. She had never been photographed before. Until they met again 17 years later, she had not been photographed since.

The photographer remembers the moment too. The light was soft. The refugee camp in Pakistan was a sea of tents. Inside the school tent he noticed her first. Sensing her shyness, he approached her last. She told him he could take her picture. "I didn't think the photograph of the girl would be different from anything else I shot that day," he recalls of that morning in 1984 spent documenting the ordeal of Afghanistan's refugees.

The portrait by Steve McCurry turned out to be one of those images that sears the heart, and in June 1985 it ran on the cover of this

magazine. Her eyes are sea green. Than and now: As a girl labeled she was photographed by Steve McCurry in a camp in Pakistan for a story on Afghan refugees that ran in the June 1985 Geographic. Today she is the mother of three daughters, including one-year-old Alia.

and in them you can read the tragedy of a land drained by war. She became known around National Geographic as the "Afghan girl," and for 17 years no one knew her name.

In January a team from National Geographic Television & Film's EXPLORER brought McCurry to Pakistan to search for the girl with green eyes. They showed her picture around Nasir Bagh, the still standing refugee camp near Peshawar where the photograph had been made. A teacher from the school claimed to know her name. A young woman named Alam Bibi was located in a village nearby, but McCurry decided it wasn't her.

No, said a man who got wind of the search.

By CATHY NEWMAN
Photographs by STEVE McCURRY

ACCURACY STANDARDS. To make sure this was the same person that was photographed in 1984, the magazine had a Pakistani ophthalmologist examine the woman. The tests were then analyzed by a Baltimore ophthalmologist, a forensic analyst at the FBI, and a Cambridge professor. There was no doubt.

READER'S DIGEST WAS BORN IN 1922 AND, WITH A FORMULA AS SIMPLE AS SELECTING AND CONDENSING STORIES FROM OTHER PUBLICATIONS, IT BECAME THE BIGGEST SUCCESS IN THE PUBLISHING WORLD. YET IT HAS ITS SECRETS AND A SHADOWY HISTORY. PRAISED AT TIMES, CRITICIZED ALMOST ALWAYS, THE MAGAZINE CREATED BY DEWITT WALLACE IS, WITHOUT A DOUBT, A PHENOMENON WORTH ANALYZING TO DISCOVER THE KEYS TO A PRODUCT THAT IS SOLD IN SIXTY COUNTRIES AND NINETEEN LANGUAGES.

THE READER'S DIGEST PHENOMENON

The story of a success that goes on and on. Its evolution and how the magazine is produced. Its marketing strategies. The elements a story must have to be selected.

Historians of journalism seem sharply divided in their opinions about *Reader's Digest*. To some, it's a revolutionary twentieth-century concept. To others, it's barely a rehashing of an old concept, the eclectic magazine, created by reproducing a set of stories from other publications. In any case, after the Bible, *Reader's Digest* is the publication with the largest presence in the world: 23.5 million monthly copies, thanks to its forty-eight international editions in sixty countries and nineteen languages, a magazine that is read by an estimated 100 million people.

The truth is that both sides are right, in part. To begin with, the history of journalism reveals that almost 80 years before *Reader's Digest* was founded, the United States market already had magazines with the same editorial concept, such as *Litell's Living Age, Eclectic, Comfort, and Scrap-Book.* In 1922, however, the innovative contribution by *Reader's Digest* founder DeWitt Wallace was to condense stories to as little as one-quarter of their original length while attempting to retain their original style and substance.

Perhaps Wallace's greatest accomplishment was interpreting better than any other editor in the world the public's reading needs and preferences, providing practical and useful information at a time when all his predecessors offered fiction. On the premise that reading was meant to inform people and improve their lives, not just entertain them, Wally—as his wife Lila Acheson would nickname him—set out to sell, along with his magazine, a philosophy of a simple, innocent, triumphant, and all-powerful America. Its readers enjoyed his selection of easy-to-read stories, many of them about miraculous cures, others with enough inspiration to transform a tragedy into a triumph or to convey the message that there is no conflict or personal problem that cannot be overcome, no ambition or dream that cannot be realized.

DeWitt Wallace was born on November 12, 1889, in St. Paul, Minnesota, the fifth child of a Macalester College professor and Presbyterian minister. Before becoming an editor and journalist, young Wallace studied fitfully at Macalester and the University of California at Berkeley, sold maps door to door, and worked for the Webb Publishing Company, from which he was fired when he proposed extensive improvements to several of their publications. He also sold calendars and other advertising products.

But there was something that always entertained him: reading everything that came his way, trying to summarize each story's main points on index cards.

Unknowingly, Wallace had started planting the seeds of what would become the condensed stories in his future magazine.

THE READER'S DIGEST

THIRTY-ONE ARTICLES EACH MONTH
FROM LEADING MAGAZINES ❦ EACH
ARTICLE OF ENDURING VALUE AND
INTEREST, IN CONDENSED AND
COMPACT FORM

FEBRUARY 1922

THE FIRST ISSUE. The magazine was launched with this cover in February of 1922. Each issue cost 25 cents, and an annual subscription cost $3. The cover, printed on the same paper as the sixty inside pages, was illustrated with an art-nouveau-style drawing of a woman to attract female readers.

WE THANK READER'S DIGEST FOR PROVIDING THE IMAGES THAT ILLUSTRATE THIS CHAPTER.

ITS FIRST EDITORIAL STEPS

Although Wallace was a good all-around athlete and a semipro baseball player, sports did not attract him enough to devote his professional life to them. He was more interested in women, poker, alcohol, travel, and cars, almost all of which were against his Presbyterian religion and his father's advice. However, his extended trips throughout the United States yielded a discovery that would be the keystone of his career: that Americans were hungry for practical information and for an open window on the outside world, instead of the abstract academic and literary knowledge that his father wanted to instill in him and that every magazine in the country purveyed at the time.

The United States that Wallace had traveled was ready to welcome his offering: half the population was still rural, trains had opened up expansion to the West, many houses had electricity and telephones, and the radio was starting to put information within everyone's reach. Mail service was cheap and efficient, and with such advances as Ottmar Mergenthaler's 1886 invention of the Linotype and the advent of high-speed presses, printing was cheap and efficient, too. These were propitious times in which to produce a new national magazine.

Wallace got his start as a publisher with a 128-page booklet titled *Getting the Most Out of Farming,* a true forerunner and model for *Reader's Digest.* Interestingly, this project was financed by the Webb Publishing Company, the same company that had recently fired Wallace for suggesting editorial changes to the original material. It was 1915, and a $700 loan was enough for the young entrepreneur to set out on his own. His only edition managed to sell 100,000 copies. The publication's success was understandable: it informed farmers of the best and most useful information available, gratis from government sources, about agriculture; it advised their wives and families about clubs and community services; and it served up the information with a leavening of sketches and sharp one-liners. Wallace had it printed in Webb's shop and then sold it in bulk in Minnesota, North Dakota, Montana, Oregon, and Washington to banks and seed merchants which, in turn, handed copies out to farmers as a promotion. In material terms, Wallace did well enough: he was able to pay his expenses on the road, repay the loan from Webb, and move on. However, the greatest profit Wallace drew from the project was confirmation of his conviction that the American public wanted information, the more practical and useful the better. As he crisscrossed the United States the question on his mind became: What would happen if, instead of selecting only farming material, a magazine condensed the best of all U.S. publications for mass market?

The answer didn't come at once. Underemployed and bored a year after his initial editorial adventure, Wallace enlisted in the army as soon as the United States entered the war in 1917. Eventually shipped to France, he fought in the trenches and, in the Meuse-Argonne offensive in late September 1918, was seriously wounded in the neck, lung, and abdomen. During his long recovery in Europe and later in the United States, Wallace didn't waste any time: he read every magazine he came across and tried out different methods of extracting the essence of the stories, some of them ten years old.

His first office was the Minneapolis Public Library, where his aunt worked as a librarian. Here—as later at the New York Public Library—he had access to a full range of publications for free. For more than six months, Wallace worked there almost full-time, until in January of 1920 he managed to come up with the first full-fledged dummy of what would be *The Reader's Digest.* His working method remained the same: he wrote by hand on lined yellow pads.

The magazine's sample issue was a model of practicality, aimed unerringly at busy people who had little time to read and even less time to concentrate. To begin with, it was pocket-size, and

It became its readers' friend—for life

How a Little Magazine Went Around the World

THE EDITORS

First issue of Reader's Digest

WHEN ROUMYana Vekilov and her husband emigrated from Bulgaria in 1993 and settled in Huntsville, Ala., she wanted desperately to understand and become a part of the America she saw around her. But she couldn't speak English. Then her husband brought home a copy of Reader's Digest. Using her Bulgarian/English dictionary she began translating the magazine "word by word, sentence by sentence, article after article." Month after month she learned "not only the language but also about the American customs, traditions, history, problems, meals and to understand more the American people and the way they

look at life." She calls The Digest "my American life-style teacher, my English language textbook, my friend."

We like that. And especially those last two words.

Get past all the statistics—the 48 editions in 19 languages reaching 100 million readers around the world each month—and the real essence of who we are, the real fun of being Reader's Digest, is the friends we have made.

That's why, even as we celebrate our 75th anniversary, we feel so young. As we've grown, we've evolved and we keep making new friends. Funny thing is, we make new friends by remaining what we have always been—a magazine that connects with its readers.

That was part of the genius of our

12

PHOTO: © ARNOLD NEWMAN

Reader's Digest founders
Lila Acheson and
DeWitt Wallace

therefore totally manageable and portable. In fact, many people would call it by the subtitle it bore at its launch, "The Little Magazine." It condensed thirty-one stories into two pages each, one for every day of the month. These could be easily and quickly read during work breaks or on the way to the office or in any free time of the day or night. On the title page of the dummy Wallace defined the *Digest* as "the one magazine containing articles only of such permanent and popular interest that each issue will be of as great value a year or two hence as on the date of publication… no articles on purely transient topics and no articles of limited or specialized appeal." And it cost only 25 cents!

But when Wallace started to show his sample issue to publishers and potential investors, no one seemed very enthusiastic. Gertrude Battles Lane of *Woman's Home Companion* declared that fiction was what sold magazines;

the articles were there just to pacify advertisers. William Randolph Hearst was only slightly less negative: while he believed the *Digest* might someday approach a significant circulation, it would be too little for him to bother with. As John Heidenry put it in *Theirs Was the Kingdom: Lila and DeWitt Wallace and the Story of the Reader's Digest,* "A magazine with no advertisements, no fiction, no illustrations, and no color seemed a contradiction in terms, a formula for failure."

For the first time, DeWitt Wallace became deeply discouraged. After a few months in a meaningless job with a wholesale grocer, he went to work for the advertising department of the Westinghouse Electric and Manufacturing Company in Pittsburgh. He was the last employee hired for that department and, six months later as the recession of 1921 struck, he was the first to be fired.

In the midst of all this turmoil, Wallace would renew his prewar acquaintance with Lila Bell Acheson, sister of an old college friend, daughter of a Presbyterian minister, talented social worker, good dancer, and in short order DeWitt Wallace's fiancée and foremost ally in his editorial adventure. Lila not only helped him to pursue the project—the plan now was to solicit mail subscriptions from members of select organizations—but also helped with the financing. Wallace's father and brother Ben had been asked for a $3,000 loan but, whether from lack of money or lack of faith, had produced only $600, the same amount they had contributed to pay for the dummy. Lila got $5,000 from her brother Barclay, who had just married a millionaire. Lila also found the apartment where she would live with her new husband on Macdougal Street near Bleecker, in the Greenwich Village section of New York. With money so tight, they decided to sublet a room to a New York University instructor and his wife, sharing the kitchen and bath. For an office they took a basement room just up the street at 1 Minetta Lane. Before going on their honeymoon to the Poconos, the Wallaces sent out a particularly large mailing to prospective subscribers.

The first letters had gone to members of the Business and Professional Women's Club in Pittsburgh. Since Wallace felt the magazine should appeal to women, he and Lila got memebership lists of other women's professional organizations—teachers, nurses, social workers. Later, through family and friends, they would add lists of clergymen and academics, and they would recruit elderly ladies to write personalized letters for a modest stipend. Soon after the couple returned to New York, Wallace declared they had enough clients to proceed with a first issue of 5,000 copies.

BIRTHPLACE. The quintessentially Middle American *Reader's Digest* had its first home in New York's bohemian Greenwich Village (right). Lila Acheson, Wallace's wife (top) was listed as coeditor right from the first issue. The goal: to give women the sense that the magazine was made by and for women.

FIRST PAGE. The table of contents with thirty-one stories was next to an editorial, signed by Lila Acheson, headed "A Word of Thanks."

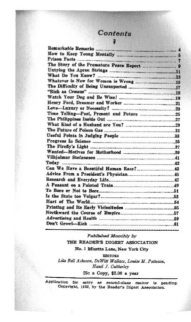

Finally, volume one, number one of the *Reader's Digest* was published in February of 1922. DeWitt Wallace and Lila Bell Acheson were cofounders and co-owners.

As the magazine especially targeted women, Wallace listed his wife, under her maiden name, and her cousin Hazel Cubberley as his coeditors on the masthead, although Lila had nothing to do with the day-to-day editing and Hazel, head of the women's physical education department at Columbia University, was never involved with the magazine at all. To reinforce the impression, the cover bore an art-nouveau drawing of an idealized woman in flowing garments writing with a giant quill on a scroll of paper. Under the drawing was a subhead explaining the new publication's philosophy: "thirty-one stories each month from leading magazines—each article of enduring value and interest, in condensed and compact form."

When the copies of the first issue reached *Reader's Digest's* makeshift newsroom at 1 Minetta Lane, Wallace and his wife hired extra hands from the speakeasy upstairs and a club down the block to help them wrap and label the 1,500 copies destined for the first subscribers. After loading them into mail sacks and whisking them by cab to the post office, the Wallaces opened a bottle of champagne to celebrate the magazine's future.

The first issue of *Reader's Digest* was simple and unpretentious. It didn't have illustrations, or color. It didn't have fiction, or ads. It was sixty-two pages long excluding the covers, all printed on the same paper. Each issue cost 25 cents, an annual subscription $3. The table of contents was on the inside front cover, opposite the first editorial page, carrying a message signed by Lila Bell Acheson (she would keep her maiden name until the March 1938 issue) and titled "A Word of Thanks."

THE FIRST TABLE OF CONTENTS

These are some of the articles in the first issue:
"How to Keep Young Mentally" condensed from the *American Magazine*
"Prison Facts" an exposé of abuses in the penal system, drawn from the *Atlantic Monthly*
"Watch Your Dog and Be Wise!" excerpted from a book by Albert Payson Terhune
"Henry Ford, Dreamer and Worker" and **"Vilhjalmur Stefansson"** inspirational profiles of persons Wallace admired
"Love—Luxury or Necessity?" condensed from the fashion magazine *Delineator*
"Wanted—Motives for Motherhood" condensed from *Outlook*
"Advertising and Health" an article by Royal S. Copeland, Health Commissioner of New York City, from *Printer's Ink*

Half a dozen of the selections were holdovers from the dummy issue prepared two years before:
"Remarkable Remarks" a long-running feature that, in the first issue, offered evangelist Homer Rode-heaver's pronouncement "One cigarette will kill a cat" and Billy Sunday's enduring "Try praising your wife, even if it does frighten her at first"
"Whatever Is New for Women Is Wrong" an arch look at women's rights, from the *Ladies' Home Journal*

"Useful Points in Judging People" summarized from a manual titled *The Art and Science of Selling*
"Progress in Science" drawn from two magazines, *Scientific American* and *Popular Science Monthly*
"The Firefly's Light" a straightforward nature piece excerpted from *Country Life*
"Is the Stage Too Vulgar?" condensed from *Theatre Magazine*

Some items that did not make it from the dummy to the first issue, yet reflected the range of *Digest* offerings, were:
"Is Honesty the Best Policy?"
"Men vs. Women as an Audience"
"The Shortest Route to the Top"
"The Art of Opening a Conversation"
"How to Regulate Your Weight"
"What People Laugh At"
"How We Get Our Styles"
A humorous column called **"The Spice of Life"**

All of the magazine's characteristic fare was present —women, nature, the art of living, ethics and morals, science, inspiration, sex, youth, self-help, humor, and a nonfiction book condensation —excerpted from a wide variety of publications.

1923
September

1929
March

1934
December

DeWitt Wallace gave part of the answer when he discussed the philosophy which he has imparted to every issue of the Digest since February 1922. At the dedication of The Reader's Digest building in Montreal, October 31, 1961, Mr. Wallace said:

"The Reader's Digest is the only truly international magazine, published in thirteen languages, and circulating in every free nation.

"There must be a reason for this phenomenal acceptance. There is! The Digest opens windows on the world. It discusses problems that baffle us all, and it publishes articles that cheer us—progress articles. The Digest promotes human welfare, promotes dedicated service to one's fellow man. The Digest imparts knowledge of stirring

DEWITT WALLACE

COVERS. The first changes took place in September of 1923. The image of the woman was out, the table of contents was in, and the word "Service" appeared after the title, soon to be replaced by "Articles of Lasting Interest." Later covers were printed on thicker stock with a colored background.

Wallace's Dark Side

With its inaugural issue, as Heidenry says, "the *Reader's Digest* established an editorial formula that it more or less faithfully adhered to for the next three-quarters of a century: three pleasantly patronizing tributes to women, two to animals; an inspirational profile of one of DeWitt's heroes, Henry Ford; useful pointers on how to get ahead in life and work; and assurances that common sense and a grasp of facts were society's best equalizers. The low proportion of humor… reflected his conviction that reading should be primarily informative, not entertaining. Only after success seemed assured did DeWitt open the floodgates of anecdotal Americana, jokes and… wordplay."

On the outside, the *Reader's Digest* looked like a portable primer on living, with upbeat advice including "Love—Luxury or Necessity?" which celebrated the therapeutic power of love, or "How to Keep Young Mentally" or "How to Regulate Your Weight." The instructional alternated with the inspirational and even the literary: in its first two years the magazine condensed works by such luminaries as Gabriele D'Annunzio and John Galsworthy, H. G. Wells and Bertrand Russell.

When the editorial content left extra space, Wallace filled it with promotional pieces that provide a window on the founder's philosophy. "Knowledge means power; the well-informed man is the strong man," said one. Wallace's heroes—Lincoln, Edison, Theodore Roosevelt—were held up as readers, questioners, searchers for facts.

But there was also a dark side to the publication. Wallace knew who his readers were, and how to play to them. As Heidenry put it, "The *Reader's Digest,* from its very first issue, became the secular Bible of [America's] deeply religious and immensely disaffected and fearful majority… [it] was a mass

149

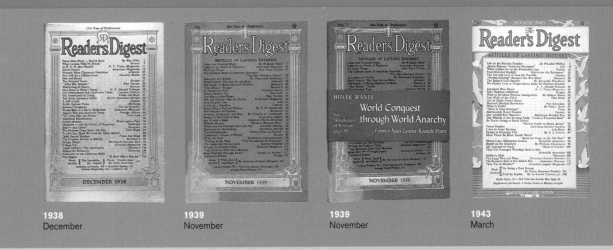

1938
December

1939
November

1939
November

1943
March

magazine in sensibility, taking the side of the vast conservative majority on almost every issue. Each month's selection of articles amounted to a personal credo, a manual for reinventing an older and better (namely, white Protestant) America. The mere fact that the magazine was a digest created the illusion that the editors were diligently culling the cream of the current magazine crop without regard for political content…. In actuality, though, the *Digest* from the very beginning had a reactionary bias." **Most sources of its selections—even such major magazines as the *Saturday Evening Post*, the *North American Review*, or *Scribner's*—were four-square for unfettered entrepreneurship and rugged individualism, and adamantly opposed to social programs of any stripe.** Wallace chose the stories to transmit not just the value he placed on reading but his personal values in the spheres of politics and religion. Over the years, an unsettling array of articles betrayed racial and religious prejudices against blacks and Asians, Jews and Catholics. When challenged, Wallace fended off such accusations by arguing that some of the magazine's best writers were Jewish and that he had published more favorable than unfavorable stories about blacks and Jews.

Wallace evinced a strange combination of conservative Protestant values (the legacy of his upbringing) and of liberal leanings in sexual matters (he had come of age in the twentieth century, and in college had declared his ambition to become "the playboy of the Western world"). The inner dichotomy was reflected in his magazine. Wallace supported sexual enlightenment, birth control, and divorce, and the *Digest* covered sex more often, more colorfully, and in greater depth than other magazines at a time when Puritanism and sexual taboos reigned. Yet such forward thinking was always firmly placed in a traditional context: the *Digest* defended marriage and monogamy as the untouchable foundations of society. And it continued to preach the benefits of poverty, prayer, and faith "which can move mountains."

In any case, the average American enjoyed *Reader's Digest*. The idea had been a successful one. As the publication's second year came to an end, the number of subscriptions had reached 7,000, which allowed Wallace, among other things, to buy a Studebaker convertible, which he often used to carry the issues from the press to the post office.

Since the Wallaces had been working nonstop for more than two years, they even found time and money to take a two-week vacation.

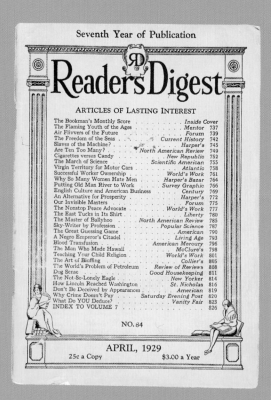

TO THE NEWSSTANDS. The April 1929 issue (the cover is shown above, the first story below) was the first to be sold on newsstands. It was a hit: of the 100,000 copies distributed, 62,000 were sold.

PROMOTION. For Christmas 1925 Lila suggested offering gift subscriptions, each to be announced with a specially wrapped free issue. The promotion was extremely successful.

KEYS TO SELECTING A STORY

Expansion became inevitable. The apartment and basement office in the Village were getting too small. One day Wallace saw a notice on a bulletin board for an apartment above a garage in Pleasantville, an aptly named town in Westchester County some forty-five minutes by train north of New York. The Wallaces went to see it and were delighted: they immediately rented it for $25 a month. For an additional $10 a month, they soon added a shed, without plumbing or heating, to use as an office. The homeowner, Pendleton Dudley, was surprised to see that the Wallaces' moving truck didn't carry much furniture. They mostly brought boxes of files and bundles of magazines.

Neither success nor expansion led Wally to waste any time. At thirty-three, he had made the *Reader's Digest* his life's project and, mindful that there's always room for improvement, he set out to polish the magazine. In the September 1923 issue, he made three key changes: he moved the table of contents onto the cover (a common practice at the time), eliminated the image of an idealized woman, and added beneath the logo the word "Service." As the number of readers grew, Wally also modified the sales slogan, which became "articles of lasting interest which will appeal to a large audience, articles that come within the range of interests, experience and conversation of the average person." With this foundation, Wallace would create a magic formula that went on to become the Four Commandments of the magazine. The selected stories had to meet these tests:

ITS OWN STORIES. The first stories *Reader's Digest* produced itself started coming out sporadically in 1930.

STRATEGY. The magazine decided to focus its energy on getting new subscribers with Christmas promotions.

BYLINED STORIES. The first signed stories written exclusively for the magazine were published in 1933.

1 Is it quotable? Is it something the reader will remember, ponder, and discuss?

2 Is it applicable? Does it come within the framework of most people's interests and conversation? Does it touch the individual's own concerns?

3 Is it of lasting interest? Will it still be of interest a year or two from now?

4 Is is positive? Does it offer the reader a solution, or an optimistic and uplifting message?

Lila contributed the last of the early innovations when, for Christmas of 1925, she proposed the gift subscription. The recipient would receive a handwritten announcement and a free issue in a handsome purple envelope. That December the tiny staff was swamped with orders. Another ploy to increase circulation was to give a free subscription to readers who managed to get ten new subscribers. Indeed, at one point subscribers were offered a free renewal for providing one new paid member plus the names and addresses of ten potential buyers.

The changes and innovations increased the magazine's circulation to levels the founders never imagined: 50,000 copies in 1926, 229,000 in 1929. Not only was Wally able to repay their relatives' loans, he also cleared more than $500,000.

Success brought new challenges. Competitors entered the market, raising the concern that if other magazines continued buying articles to condense, the material could run out and the very existence of the *Digest* be placed at risk. Wally reacted with a two-pronged strategy. On the one hand, he signed contracts with the major magazines, securing the exclusive right to reprint their stories. On the other hand, he looked into the possibility of selling his magazine on newsstands. To that end, he contacted the distribution firm S-M News and had discussions with one of its directors, the prodigiously talented Albert Leslie Cole, who was then president and publisher of *Popular Science.* Cole thought highly of the *Digest's* newsstand prospects, and Wallace thought highly of Cole—so highly that he tried to persuade him to move to the *Digest.* It would take a decade for Wallace to come up with an offer Cole couldn't refuse. Meanwhile they explored together the advantages of newsstand sales. Alone, Wallace contemplated the key disadvantage: such sales would raise the *Digest's* profile, inviting boycotts if not massive lawsuits unless he agreed to pay for reprint rights to all the stories he used, something he had heretofore done only in a selective and erratic fashion.

However, Wallace made the right decision once again. *Reader's Digest* distributed 100,000 copies to newsstands in April 1929 and sold 62,000 of them—a respectable proportion for any magazine and an impressive feat for a newcomer. At one stroke the *Digest's* sales shot up by almost 30 percent.

1957 August 1959 July 1962 July

a unique marketing strategy

The increase in circulation meant hiring more personnel. Before Lila and Wally quite realized it, the company had grown to occupy office space in a half dozen buildings in Pleasantville. Wally took an interest in improving employees' working conditions and schedules, and gave salary increases —some disproportionate—to his editors. Some of them, when revealed, not only scandalized the publishing world but also greatly angered Wallace's father and wife. Not that Wally was always throwing money away. Company lore tells of him going through the offices turning lights off after the workday, and sending memos to employees about leaving the lights on.

Wally not only showed he was his own best critic, he showed he had good business sense. For a long time he kept a low profile, in the press and among competitors, to keep secret his magazine's circulation. Wally was fully aware that if the public and the industry knew the company's real numbers, which were already among the highest in the country, the price he paid to reprint stories would surely increase. Yet he also knew that if he really wanted to

grow, the time would come when he had to accept advertising in his magazine and, with it, accept the auditing of his circulation. Since he wasn't ready for that step, Wallace took three smaller steps that would bring him millions in revenue with much less risk: he enlarged the magazine with a condensed fiction book in each issue; he began publishing original articles; and he expanded the pool of available "reprints" by financing the writing of stories to "plant" them in other magazines and then condense them in the *Digest*. This strategy made a story's content legitimate, although it was a smokescreen to meet Wallace's own demands, tastes, and beliefs.

As for the publishing of original material, as James Playsted Wood explains in his book *Of Lasting Interest: The Story of the Reader's Digest,* "Until he could gauge his readers' reactions, DeWitt Wallace went about the change very slowly." An April 1930 piece, "Music and Work," was presented as "a special compilation for *The Reader's Digest*"; in May came "Music and Health" and in June "Music and Animals," which was "a summary

especially prepared by one of our editors." Also unsigned was July's "A Worker Practices a New Art," about theater productions by workers' groups. The first original story with a byline, in February 1933, was "Insanity—The Modern Menace," written by Henry Morton Robinson, and others followed regularly, sometimes even two a month. But the much admired story that really had impact, that increased the magazine's circulation, and that earned the respect of the public was "And Sudden Death," based on a national tragedy: automobile accidents. The title was taken from the Book of Common Prayer: "…and from sudden death, Good Lord deliver us."

As might be expected, the idea originated with Wallace who, remembering accidents he had seen and hearing of others from his mechanic and friends, called upon writer J. C. Furnas to write a hard-hitting story to dramatize the need to drive carefully. His intention was to shock the public, to shake its indifference to the issue. So the text was full of blood, broken bones, and mangled bodies. Indeed, an editor's note warned that readers would find

LANDSCAPES. Color illustrations started appearing on the cover in 1948. The first were historic places.

many of the story's details sickening. Wally turned to his Pleasantville landlord Pendleton Dudley, owner of a well-known public relations firm, and asked if he wanted to promote the story. Dudley did so with great effectiveness: the story was sent to 5,000 media outlets before publication in *Reader's Digest,* inviting them to reprint it for free as long as it was credited. It appeared in newspapers throughout the country, it was read over the radio and in courtrooms, it was discussed in forums and conferences, it was turned into a comic strip and a film short. In one state it was distributed with every set of license plates.

The first result: In three months, the magazine had distributed four million reprints to more than 8,000 American companies.

The second result: In the six years following publication of the story, traffic fatalities—the ratio of deaths to miles driven—dropped by a third. What had started as a tactic by Wally to increase the magazine's circulation ended up also becoming a public service.

The practice of generating stories in-house for placement in other magazines

was also Wally's idea. The procedure was to approach a publication with a story idea and offer to pay the expenses and writer's fees in exchange for the right to reprint the story in the *Digest.* Invariably, the writer was chosen from among the *Digest's* authors or editors. While the ostensible purpose was to assure a supply of material for reprinting, the "planting" of stories had another purpose: if a story first appeared in a reliable and respected publication, that implied a certain guarantee of validity and accuracy, and eventually prestige when the *Digest* selected it to condense. Nobody at the *Digest* cared if a story that cost $1,500

between expenses and fees was placed in a magazine that might pay $15 for it. The benefit was not monetary but strategic: for a noted publication to edit and publish a story was the best way to earn prestige and legitimacy. Yet the practice did not meet with universal favor. One editor who rejected it as dishonest and unprofessional was Harold Ross of the *New Yorker*, who in a widely circulated letter argued that the *Reader's Digest* used it to exercise "indirect creative control, which is a threat to the free flow of ideas"— meaning that the *Digest* was using others to further its reactionary agenda. This, he said, "gives us the creeps."

IMPACT. "…And Sudden Death," a 1935 piece on car crashes, shook the country. Four million reprints were distributed.

BOOK excerpts

The Christmas 1934 issue included a third ingredient of the *Digest's* new editorial formula: the book bonus, which required a page increase from 112 to 128. In fact, it wasn't a brand-new practice for the magazine, which had already condensed several book chapters of fiction as well as nonfiction, by noted authors ranging from Robert Benchley to Stefan Zweig. The difference was that this time it was a condensation of an entire book. One notable incident in 1936 concerned a book by France's Nobel Prize-winning physician Alexis Carrel titled "Man, the Unknown," a mystical exploration of the sorts of racial theories with which Wally had always sympathized. Carrel believed in the superiority of the Nordic race and explained that blacks, American Indians, Latinos, and Asians had been so "burned" by the sun as to become inferior human beings. Wally offered $1,000 to Harper & Brothers for condensation rights. To his surprise, the publishing house declined, arguing that the excerpt would cut into the book's sale, which a year after publication still stood at 900 copies a week. Wally made a counteroffer: an initial check of $1,000 and another of $2,500 as deposit in case bookstore sales declined after the *Digest* condensation. Two weeks after the excerpt appeared in September, sales had quintupled; that second check went uncashed. Later

condensations had a similar effect. Some books were propelled to the top of the best-seller list. Wallace had gotten away with it once again. Anything he touched turned to gold.

Wallace's success seemed unstoppable. However, few knew that the magazine had reached a circulation of 2 million copies by 1936 and that the Pleasantville staff already numbered thirty-two people. Three researchers worked permanently at the New York Public Library. Ten women worked full time at the library in Cleveland. Altogether, every month, five hundred publications were read to select material for condensation, and five to ten original stories were "planted" in other magazines.

After considering and rejecting a move to New York City, Wallace decided to buy land and erect his own building some seven miles north of Pleasantville, between Chappaqua and Mount Kisco. Lila herself was in charge of the architectural design. The Georgian-style building cost $1.2 million.

ENLARGEMENT. The December 1934 issue included a condensed excerpt from a book. The number of pages increased from 112 to 128.

ONCE AND FUTURE HEADQUARTERS. The Georgian-style mansion is located near Pleasantville.

STYLE. The executive offices were decorated with fine furniture and artwork. Lila's idea was to create a "*Digest* style."

PAINTINGS. The works of Chagall, Cézanne, and Renoir (right) decorated Wallace's offices.

PARKS. These were landscaped for employees' breaks. The place was known as "the Wallaces' paradise."

The changes at the *Digest* went beyond architecture to include the editorial aspect. The first one was to eliminate "The" from the magazine's name, which would become *Reader's Digest*. Another was to replace the black-and-white same-paper-as-inside cover with a color cover printed on better-quality stock. In November 1939 the first black-and-white illustrations started to appear inside the magazine.

Before and after these changes, Wallace started experimenting with new sections, such as "Quotable Quotes," "Toward a More Picturesque Speech" and "An Album of Personal Glimpses." Some of them didn't make it; others would become well known, such as "Life in These United States," "Drama in Real Life" and "The Most Unforgettable Character I Ever Met."

Wally was never satisfied with the new story ideas brought to him. Once, tired of hearing stale ideas, he issued an offer of $15,000 to any author who'd write a great story and bring it to him. What Wally didn't know, or at least nobody was saying, was that great writers tended to stay away from his magazine because they considered it shallow, ultraconservative, and all written in the same voice. The great *New Yorker* writer and wit Alexander Woollcott, when he was invited to do a lucrative series for the *Digest,*

commented: "Mr. Wallace has destroyed the pleasure of reading; now he is about to destroy the pleasure of writing." Wallace was unperturbed, but sent out a memo asking his editors to make an effort to retain authors' styles in condensed stories.

For the purpose of creating new ideas, he created the position of "roving editor," a post that didn't require keeping regular office hours but could contribute to improving the magazine's content. A roving editor meant the reporter went where he liked and wrote what he liked, for a fresh approach.

Another important change was to increase the number of "fillers" used to round out an incomplete page. These could be jokes, anecdotes, proverbs, or sayings. *Reader's Digest* had had only two fillers in its premier issue but, as the magazine changed and expanded, many more became necessary. Wallace wanted to keep fillers from being commonplaces or simple information that lacked color or humor, so he opted for three techniques. The first one was to ask each staffer to contribute at least one a week (Wally took on the task of checking who did and who didn't). The second was to maintain, from 1929 to 1953, a special team especially devoted to that task at the Cleveland Public Library. The third was to offer $5–a considerable sum in the Depression era–to readers who sent in fillers that were selected for publication.

ILLUSTRATIONS. The interior pages began to carry illustrations, either black-and-white or single-color, in 1939.

INNOVATIONS. After the illustrations, new sections that are still remembered were added, such as "Drama in Real Life."

OUT TO CONQUER THE WORLD

The worldwide expansion of *Reader's Digest* was inevitable. The first international edition came out in Great Britain in 1938. Soon after, the first foreign-language version was launched: it was in Spanish and was published in Cuba in 1940. Called *Selecciones,* it was culled from back and current issues of the English *Digest* and translated in New York. Wallace thought it wouldn't sell more than 50,000 copies, but in only four months circulation had reached 250,000. The success of *Selecciones* in Latin America led to the 1941 launching of a Portuguese edition in Portugal and Brazil. New editions would follow in 1943 in Swedish and Arabic. The next frontier was Spain, where before allowing the magazine in, Generalísimo Francisco Franco demanded that nothing against him, his country, or the Catholic Church be published. Wallace acceded, and over the years would continue his European expansion with editions in Finnish, Norwegian, Danish, German, French, Italian, and Dutch. Japan would have to wait until after the war, but circulation there would quickly reach almost 1.5 million copies.

In 1941 *Business Week* magazine would confirm what the industry had suspected for a long time: *Reader's Digest's* total circulation, national and international, had surpassed 4 million copies. Less than nineteen years after its founding, the *Digest* had realized the American Dream.

Even before the international editions' success, the Wallaces had amassed an impressive fortune, and in 1935 they decided to build an impressive house. They bought a piece of land five miles from Pleasantville, near Mount Kisco, and gave orders for the construction of a Norman-style fieldstone mansion with twenty-two rooms, a magnificent stairway, and a massive tower. Other features included an Italian garden, a greenhouse, stables, and a swimming pool. The property was first known as The Tower and then as High Winds, from an inscription on an old English mantelpiece that was among the antiques Lila had acquired in anticipation of its completion. In addition to the Wallaces, a butler and two dogs lived there. In the corner tower Wally managed to get the office he always wanted. Only he had access to it, and at cleaning time he made sure to be present so nobody touched or moved anything.

Sensitive to criticism that his magazine read as if it was all written by the same person, though it had stories by various authors and in different styles, Wally in 1935 offered five $1,000 prizes to people who submitted pieces worth publishing. Each had to be a "true narrative of a personal experience in some specialized walk of life—dramatic, inspirational, humorous—and especially revelatory of human nature." The offer was so successful that more than 43,000 manuscripts came in. In the end, ten awards were granted instead of five. In 1955 the *Digest* increased the awards to $2,500, and more than 1,500 manuscripts would arrive in the newsroom every month. The first-person story became one of the magazine's most popular features, with titles such as "The Night I Met Einstein" or "My Japanese Brother" and authors ranging from professional writers and public figures to housewives, chauffeurs, and teachers. This was another smart move by Wallace to increase reader participation and interaction and the emotional connection between the public and the magazine.

By contrast, a class of articles that might be called the "new hope" genre, generally about revolutionary discoveries in medicine, didn't always go well. In his eagerness to avoid hopelessness and proclaim victory when faced with any challenge,

THE WALLACES AND THEIR INHERITANCE

Although Lila and DeWitt Wallace were healthy, as the years went by, they started to ponder to whom they'd leave the company after their death. Of one thing they were certain: it wouldn't be split up among their relatives. For these they made other financial arrangements—something that Wally's father and brother never forgave, since it was they who first loaned money to launch the *Digest.*

In October of 1964, the Wallaces selected Fred and Judy Thompson (left, in white) as successors. Judy was Lila's niece, and the four of them had an excellent relationship. A month later, Wally announced the creation of the post of president and named Hobe Lewis, who was also the magazine's editor in chief, to assume it.

But on Christmas Eve 1965, Wally suddenly announced a dramatic

EASTERN EUROPE. The Russian edition of *Reader's Digest* debuted in 1991. Later, editions would be published in Hungary, Poland, Slovakia and Germany (pictured left and below).

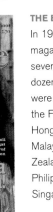

THE EXPANSION. In 1997, when the magazine turned seventy-five, half a dozen editions were launched in the Far East—in Hong Kong, India, Malaysia, New Zealand, the Philippines, and Singapore.

Wallace came up with an exaggerated version of the art-of-living approach that embodied the magazine's inflated optimism. Most of the time, the new hope was an experimental drug or treatment that was untried on humans or unproven, and therefore only raised false hope among readers and incurred the wrath of the medical establishment. A notable example was "A One-Day Cure for Syphilis." Other times, the stories were based more on faith than research and fact. For decades, staffers had joked that "New Hope for the Dead" would be the perfect *Digest* article. But then in 1974 the magazine offered almost exactly that, with "I Died at 10:52 A.M.," its first first-person account of the phenomenon newly known as a "near-death experience." This would be followed in 1977 by an excerpt from Raymond Moody's book *Life after Life*, a compilation of many such instances. As Heidenry put it, with these accounts "the *Digest* was finally able to guarantee its readers even immortality."

It was against such a background of ups and downs of principles and interests that the question of whether to include advertising in the magazine arose. To be sure, it would be restricted in some ways: ads for

tobacco and alcoholic beverages, for instance, were banned—which seemed inconsistent to those who remembered that, several years earlier, the *Digest's* international editions had been accepting such ads. Still, it wasn't an easy or quick decision for Wallace, who had entertained the idea since 1929 but had never brought himself to the point of implementing it for fear of hurting, or even losing, two generations of readers to whom the magazine boasted of being the only one on the market that didn't accept ads. But after an extensive survey in which readers opted for including ads instead of raising the cover price, Wallace made up his mind. In April 1955 an issue of 216 pages, barely 15 percent of them devoted to advertising, hit the streets. A black-and-white ad cost $26,000, as opposed to *Life's* $20,350. But six months later, the ratio of editorial content to advertising stood at sixty-forty. There was enormous pressure from advertisers to place ads in such a high-circulation magazine, and the *Digest* was able to set the highest advertising rates in the business.

piece of news: he was removing his right-hand man, Al Cole, to replace him with Paul W. Thompson, a former general whom nobody in the company liked. "This is the worst thing you've ever done to me," Cole managed to say.

The following day, Paul Thompson arrived early at the Wallace castle to impose three conditions for accepting the appointment: mandatory retirement for all company employees at sixty-five (which would guarantee for himself a five-year tenure and an orderly retirement), the title of executive vice president, and Al Cole's sumptuous office. Wallace accepted the three conditions. Cole, when he learned that even his office had been given to the Wallaces' surprise successor, emptied it of every last piece of paper over the weekend and vowed never to forget the injustice after thirty-three years as

a loyal and efficient employee. As for Fred and Judy Thompson, despite Judy's relationship to Lila, they and their two children were sent to Australia where Fred was assigned to take over the magazine's operations. The apparent motive: it was said that Lila had learned Wally was having an affair with Judy, her own niece. Her vengeance was to have Fred and Judy banished to the ends of the earth.

THe reader's DIGesT
as seen BY TIme

THE WALLACES IN *TIME*.
The painting is by Boris Chaliapin, one of *Time* magazine's most celebrated illustrators.

IN DEPTH. *Time's* reportage on the couple who created the *Digest* covered everything from the Wallaces' wealth to their home life.

CRITICISM. Although *Time* praised Wallace as a successful publisher, it also spoke of his magazine's "intellectual mediocrity."

Just weeks before their magazine turned thirty, on December 10, 1951, the Wallaces had the privilege of making the cover of *Time*, above the caption "The DeWitt Wallaces, with scissors, paste and sunrises, 15,500,000 customers." Inside, *Reader's Digest* was called "one of the greatest success stories in the history of journalism." It had a national circulation of 9.5 million copies, grossing $25 million to $30 million annually, and an international circulation of 6 million copies. Here is how Wallace explained the secret of his success: "I simply hunt for things that interest me, and if they do, I print them." In another paragraph *Time* described him as "the most successful editor in history," which was no small compliment coming from another publishing genius, Henry R. Luce.

The *Time* story took up eight pages and was titled "The Common Touch." Among its sources, it quoted Louis Bromfield, a frequent *Reader's Digest* contributor, in whose view the magazine essentially appealed to "intellectual mediocrity," adding that Wallace's own "strictly average" mind "completely reflects the mentality of its readers," who liked the magazine because "it requires no thought or perception."

After these comments, Bromfield was no longer hired as a writer by *Reader's Digest*.

❝ The formula has changed somewhat over the years, but it is still essentially the one Wallace hit on in 1920; simplified, condensed articles, most of them striking a note of hope, the whole interspersed with pithy saws or chuckly items," another paragraph added. "It tries to minimize the negative and accentuate the positive. The *Digest* has always been careful not to burden its readers with somber or brain-taxing articles."

Time also described Wallace as a "worrier, torn by inner doubts and subject to spells of melancholy," although it emphasized that he and his wife Lila loved to dance for fifteen minutes at home after dinner. Praise also went to Lila, of whom a source said: "Wally is the genius, all right, but Lila unwrapped him." As for their vast fortune, *Time* not only said that the couple was gradually donating it to a charity foundation which would run the *Digest*, but cited one of Wallace's more frequent sayings: "The dead carry with them to the grave in their clutched hands only that which they have given away." A few key points from the *Time* story follow:

In the *Digest* world, things are usually getting better, faith moves mountains, prayer can cure cancer and poverty holds hidden blessings. The *Digest* keeps a hopeful eye peeled for new miracle drugs and regards old age as nothing more than a state of mind. Even death is not fearsome ('It is not unpleasant to die'). It is a world of plants that act like animals ('Some Remarkable Carnivorous Plants'), animals that think and act like humans ('Seeing Ourselves in Our Dogs'), and humans who often seem more like saints ('God's Eager Fool, Dr. Albert Schweitzer'). 'The Most Unforgettable Character I've Met,' one of the *Digest's* most popular features, often tells about people dedicated to helping others. The wonders of nature are inexhaustible ('If there were but one sunrise in every century, all beds would be empty'), sermons are found in stones, and birds are God's own choir. *Digest* readers are left with a warm feeling about themselves, about life, and about the *Digest*."

Wallace thinks of himself as 'left of center'; he says most people are middle-of-the-roaders. But most middle-roaders would consider him well right of center. Not a deep or profound thinker, Wallace sometimes originates and runs glib, superficial articles on U.S. and world problems which other top editors would waste-basket…. In the main, his political outlook seems to be colored by a nostalgic yearning for the less complicated days of his boyhood, when every man could become his own master without help or hindrance from the Government."

Wallace's greatest contribution to the nation may be found in the cumulative effect of his overseas editions. Invariably, his readership surveys show that articles which U.S. readers like rate equally high with readers everywhere. The *Digest's* articles —depicting the innate decency, kindness and simple virtues of ordinary Americans, the triumphs of a George Carver or a Helen Keller— have probably done more than all the Government propagandists combined to allay the fears, prejudices and misconceptions of the U.S. in other lands."

Games and Lies

In 1962 *Reader's Digest* successfully tried out a new idea to attract more subscribers: sweepstakes, a type of legalized gambling. Each potential client received in the mail an invitation to participate in a contest with millions of dollars' worth of prizes. The invitation came with two stickers, one that said yes, the other no. All that was required to participate in the contest was to peel off the yes sticker and stick it onto the reply card. Whoever's card was drawn in the supposedly free contest received a check for the prize. The only problem: by attaching the yes sticker, the contestant also agreed to buy a magazine subscription, a condition that was buried way down in the fine print. The practice got exceptional results for many years. In 1979, national circulation surpassed 18 million copies, second only to *TV Guide*. Worldwide, the *Digest's* audience bordered on 100 million readers in thirty-nine editions and nineteen languages.

The game ended in 1999 after the Attorney General's office contended that the use of sweepstakes was unfair because it disguised as a game what in effect was a sales offering (the rules of the game were in almost illegible type). From then on, the Attorney General's office forced the *Digest* and many other companies —Time Inc. among them—to clarify in any sweepstakes mailing that: 1 buying a subscription didn't increase the chances of winning, 2 there was no need to buy anything to participate, and 3 the odds of winning were very low.

color and THE EVOLUTION OF DESIGN

During its first seventeen years, the *Digest* was purely a magazine of text. Moreover, at first, the paper of the cover was the same as what was used inside. Wallace wasn't embarrassed by this; quite the contrary: he presented it as a deliberate publishing decision. In his magazine, text was always more important than illustrations. Even when drawings or photos of people or animals were used, they were small in size and generally without captions.

This would start changing in the early forties, when the first redesign took place, although it was basically limited to type. The cover was now on thicker, colored stock —red, yellow, gray.

The use of illustrated covers, with watercolors that filled the back cover and wrapped around to the front, began in 1948. For the international editions, photographs were used. So many were needed that the *Reader's Digest* stopped buying photos from agencies and began taking its own. Lila became

the de facto art director at *Reader's Digest*, although her name didn't appear as such on the masthead. It was she who assigned a photographer to travel the world and bring back all kinds of images of monuments, landscapes, architecture, people, and customs in different countries. She also hired a second photographer to remain in Pleasantville and develop and print the pictures his colleague took overseas. This arrangement would last for six months, then the two would switch assignments for the rest of the year. Lila preferred that they both use the bigger format cameras to get images with a strong focus and contrast and with cover potential. In time, *Reader's Digest* would amass a collection of some 30,000 images from more than forty countries.

In 1955, after the incorporation of advertising, the magazine started using glossy paper for the ads and some stories, and embraced the significant use of color and illustrations. In 1957 Lila had the idea of putting a single illustration on the front and relegating the table of contents to the back cover, arguing that many readers had told her that they started reading the magazine from the back.

The first cover illustrations portrayed America's historical sites, but with time they encompassed scenes of rural beauty, urban industry, and everyday life everywhere in the country. These watercolors were commissioned from some of the best illustrators of the era. Lila personally selected them, as well as the covers and inside illustrations for the new *Reader's Digest* Condensed Book Club. Wallace never intervened in the visual arena because he recognized his wife's superior artistic sense and its effectiveness in furthering his own goals: making the magazine more attractive on the newsstand, increasing sales and circulation, and echoing the cheery chauvinism of its stories.

Lila's power over visual and artistic decisions was such that when Coca-Cola offered the magazine $18 million for the magazine's back cover for a year, Lila calmly told Wally, "I bid nineteen million." Coca-Cola was turned down; the back cover remained pictorial.

WHAT'S

Many times in the thick of fighti
has done a double take at the uni.
"What's a woman doing here?" In
Dickey Chapelle, one of the brave
porters and photographers in the bu
As always, what Dickey was doi.
story. Her determination to be wh
into some of the most violent act
for people in trouble has led her t.
She went ashore with the troops
II; she went into Hungary during
prisoner by the Reds; she went into
Castro's overthrow of Batista; pa
Vietnam.

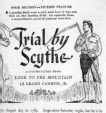

TWO COLORS.
Two-tone illustrations
to open the stories
became frequent in
the 1940s and 1950s.

FOUR COLORS.
Starting in 1960,
these color
illustrations paved
the way for
photos. Lila was
directly in charge
of the visual
aspect.

In 1962 the post of art director was given to Kenneth Stuart, whose professional ideas and personal style appealed to Lila. Stuart came from the foundering *Saturday Evening Post,* which during his two decades there, one critic sniped, "looked like a seed catalogue." But this hardly disqualified him with Wally, whose own journalism career had started with an agriculture magazine.

With Lila's blessing, Stuart made a number of changes including new fonts: Baskerville for display, Granjon for text. It became standard to illustrate stories with color photos or drawings. And the back cover sometimes bore, instead of an original watercolor, a reproduction from the Wallaces' superlative collection of Impressionist art. The visual alterations Stuart and Lila were making to the magazine were profoundly upsetting to traditionalists. One of these was Ken Payne, the magazine's executive editor and Wally's right-hand man, who was moved to do something he had never done before: he confronted Lila. His argument that *Reader's Digest* was a text magazine in which the visual aspects were only "a decoration or complement" sent Lila into a towering rage. Payne lost the battle and, like all those who dared defy Lila, ended up losing his job. From then on, the magazine underwent only minimal visual changes until in 1997 the editors decided to make a sweeping design overhaul, hiring Roger Black (see page 312).

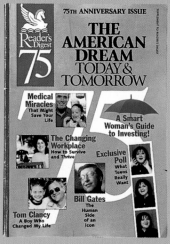

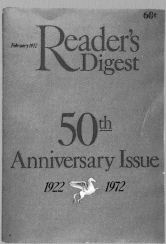

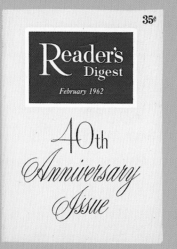

When the new offices of *Reader's Digest* were built in Pleasantville, Lila ringed the building's cupola with four statues of Pegasus, the winged horse of Greek mythology. As Pegasus was said to represent the poetic inspiration that must guide writers and literati, it would become the company's official symbol.

The magazine celebrated its fortieth anniversary in February of 1962 with a special issue that included letters of praise from such luminaries as President John Kennedy, former president Dwight Eisenhower, singer Marian Anderson, and Henry Ford II. Kennedy's letter said: "One of our major goals is to help people understand the complexity of the world in which we live and the variety of the problems we face. Without understanding, there cannot be intelligent action. Ignorance and prejudice—two of democracy's greatest foes—can be dispelled by the free flow of information and ideas. The *Reader's Digest* has contributed to this goal. I am pleased to send congratulations on the occasion of its 40th anniversary."

The late sixties and early seventies were a time of upheaval for the country and of distress at *Reader's Digest*. But, as Heidenry writes, "those years also witnessed the magazine's greatest triumph—its role as the mouthpiece of the Silent Majority and the single most powerful champion of Richard M. Nixon in the private sector." It condensed the presidential nomination acceptance speech that Nixon delivered to the National Republican Convention in 1968, and it deliberately omitted the Watergate scandal from its pages, in part to avoid tarnishing the spotless relationship that it had with the president at the time and in part because reporters Bob Woodward and Carl Bernstein had traced to

Pleasantville some undocumented cash contributions to Nixon. Before and after this incident, the more liberal media of the time suspected a connection between the *Digest* and the CIA, and accused the magazine of sending spies all over the world disguised as *Digest* photographers or reporters. Later, the *Digest* attacked Ted Kennedy to assist Republican Ronald Reagan's rise to power. Reagan not only was a devoted reader of the magazine but also considered it an excellent source of information about famous foreign heads of state. The *Washington Post's* Mary McGrory was moved to note his obvious reliance on the *Digest* and call it "the monthly for people who hate to read."

Aware of such criticism, Wallace always tried to strike a balance. A great coup was discovering and publishing novelist Alex Haley. After repeatedly, but encouragingly, rejecting his early articles, *Reader's Digest* published "The Harlem Nobody Knows" in June of 1954. Half a dozen years later came "Mr. Muhammad Speaks," which would lead to Haley's first book, *The Autobiography of Malcolm X.* Not long afterwards Haley met Lila at a *Digest* party, and she told him: "If I can ever be helpful to you, let me know." Haley had just then begun the delving into his family history that would result in his masterpiece *Roots.* After three years, he wrote to Lila about his progress and his plans; meetings were arranged, and the *Digest* offered Haley $1,000 a month for a year, plus travel expenses to wherever the retracing of his family's steps might take him. It took him to

England and France and, most important, to Africa for research he could not otherwise have done. Haley would win the Pulitzer with his novel, which became a bestseller and was, of course, condensed in *Reader's Digest*. In turn, the *Digest* would win Haley's heart.

In 1981, as Lila lay at home considerably handicapped by advanced arthritis, DeWitt Wallace died. He was ninety-one years old. Lila would follow thirty-six months later, at ninety-four. As they had promised each other, not a single relative inherited the company, which went instead to a number of charities, with control of the voting stock split among several top company executives, so nobody was able to function on his or her own or unilaterally make crucial decisions.

Before and after DeWitt Wallace's death, editorial control would remain in the hands of Edward T. Thompson, a man who during his eight-year command at *Reader's Digest* showed no desire to alter the magazine's basic philosophy or formula. He favored illustrated articles, which now comprised some 85 percent, but he also raised the number of reprints to about half, bringing the magazine back toward its origins. Thompson didn't want enemies, but he made no friends by traveling to Europe, Asia, or Latin America three or four times a year, something that didn't sit well with the company's conservative leaders, given the 1982 economic recession. In addition, Thompson seemed to have lost editorial control of the magazine. For instance, board member Laurance Rockefeller was shocked when he saw that a *Digest*-sponsored student art contest had been won by a drawing of the Statue of Liberty up to her neck in trash.

Rockefeller fired off a secret memo accusing Thompson of losing "consciousness of things religious and of the positive things of life." Rockefeller then joined forces with Al Cole and other company leaders to oust Thompson from the magazine. For appearances, he was offered a $1,6 million golden parachute.

His successor was assistant editor Kenneth Gilmore. But over time, it didn't quite matter who was the editor du jour: the formula created by DeWitt was so solid that nobody could break its structure. A revolving editorship didn't represent a hurdle for a company that, when it started trading on the New York Stock Exchange in 1990, had annual revenues surpassing $2 billion.

The Russian edition would be launched a year later, followed by Hungary, Slovakia, and Poland. In fact, from that point on, *Reader's Digest* would become a multifaceted corporation offering record clubs, condensed books, distribution services of records, videos, and other goods. *Reader's Digest* would turn seventy-five years old in 1997 with a special edition, followed by expansion into Hong Kong, India, Korea, Malaysia, New Zealand, the Philippines, Singapore, and Taiwan.

Today *Reader's Digest* is an empire worth more than $3 billion. Despite the death of its founder, it continues operating in the shadow of DeWitt Wallace, a man who was as contradictory as his editorial creation, but who has gone down in history as the great democratizing force of information.

SUMMARY OF GOD

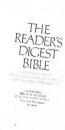

In 1976 *Reader's Digest* embarked on one of its most ambitious projects: condensing nothing less than the Bible, its only world competitor in terms of circulation. But what started out as an effort to honor God would end up three years later as a curse of the devil.

It was a huge task: cutting by 60 percent the 800,000 original words of the Holy Scriptures, a job that required a special team made up of editors and ecclesiastical experts from around the world. The estimated cost was some $4 million.

Wallace's scissors cut repeated words and thoughts, eliminated duplicate narratives, got rid of genealogies and geography, and did away with irrelevant historic or architectural details. The rules were steadfast: no editor could cut anything without first getting approval from at least three experts.

Despite being a masterpiece of condensation and possibly one of the most accurate and respectful excerpts of the Holy Scriptures' substance and style, sales were disastrous: some 500,000 copies, which in *Reader's Digest* terms was low indeed.

THE CHALLENGE OF CHANGING A WINNER

In May of 1998 the *Digest* changed radically. It came out with a new, strong design from cover to cover. Here are the reasons for that risk and the audience it targets today.

Surely there should be nothing harder for a publisher than changing a magazine from the ground up, particularly if it's a great success, and especially if that success crosses borders to make it the most-read publication in the world. In the case of *Reader's Digest*, something extra must be factored into that equation: throughout its seventy-five years as sales leader, the look of the magazine had remained unchanged, except for the few alterations mentioned. Did it need a redesign to change its image, then? Wasn't that too risky? How would its old devotees and readers take the change? Wouldn't it upset them? Would it help get new subscribers?

Should the changes be visual or deal with the content? And what if these changes didn't attract a new, younger audience? Despite all these questions, a *Digest* update was inevitable. And it became a model, since it involved visual modifications of the best-selling magazine in the world. It was a true challenge for those to whom it was entrusted.

After all, with the advent of the new twenty-first century, it was almost impossible to think that a magazine could retain its leadership position with the same attitudes and attributes that had attended its establishment several decades earlier. Thus in 1997 the company faced what would be the first major redesign in the history of the publication, to change it inside and out, and to adapt it to the new precepts of the image culture. To carry it out, the magazine hired prestigious designer Roger Black, a former *New York Times* and *Rolling Stone* art director, who had

also been responsible for redesigning *Newsweek, Esquire, Foreign Affairs, Fast Company,* and *Ad Age* magazines, among others. "The editors' diagnosis at the time was that it had become just a gateway for other products and services offered by the company," Black explained to this book's authors in 2002. "What they wanted was to make the magazine the company's focus once again."

After carefully studying the publication, Black proposed creating what he called a *"baby Rolling Stone,"* that is, a younger version of *Rolling Stone*. "Given that the audience's average age was over forty-eight years old," Black said, "and considering that the editors wanted to attract younger readers, I suggested emphasizing the 'book' concept to retain the original audience, and being more aggressive with evocative illustrations and photos to win over young people."

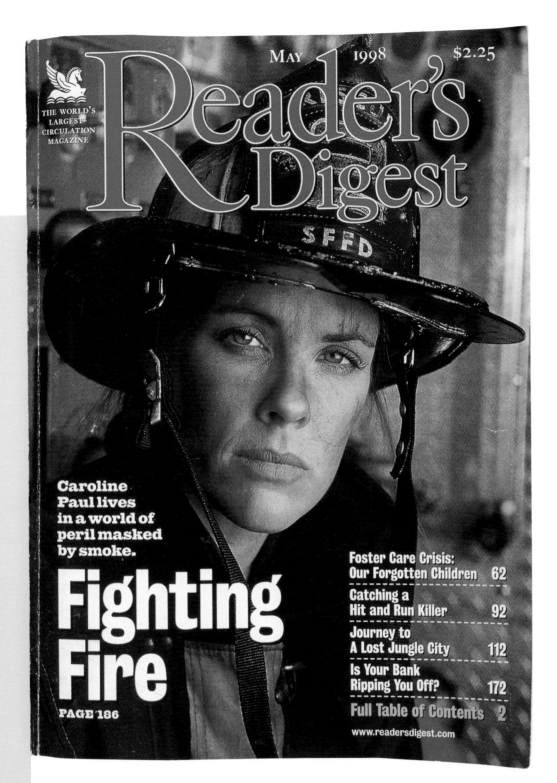

MAY 1998 $2.25

Reader's Digest

THE WORLD'S LARGEST CIRCULATION MAGAZINE

SFFD

Caroline Paul lives in a world of peril masked by smoke.

Fighting Fire

PAGE 186

www.readersdigest.com

VISUAL IMPACT. On the first cover of the new era, a photo of female firefighter Caroline Paul took up the whole space with the headline "Fighting Fire." The lower right corner featured highlights of the contents. "My aim," said Roger Black, the designer, "was to produce a baby *Rolling Stone."*

THE RIGHT MIX OF VISUAL STYLES

Black's most aggressive change took place on the cover. Instead of the traditional front with a table of contents and a small photo—its trademark before the redesign—Black suggested presenting a single large, strong image and, in a box on the right, the headlines of the issue's four main stories, along with their corresponding page numbers. "The cover of a magazine must be a poster," Black explained. "A single and strong image of a human being will always sell more magazines than

multiple photos or those that carry a list of story headlines. This has always been so and I think it will remain so." In May of 1998, the inaugural image of the redesign was that of Caroline Paul, a firefighter whose face could well belong to a model or actress.

The headline was forceful and suggestive: "Fighting Fire." Inside, Black had retained the original Granjon type for stories, although he added Giza for column heads and subtitles. "My redesign was wildly

visual on the cover and inside, but balanced enough for the magazine not to lose its book size, texture and appearance," Black said.

Black's other important contribution was to create strong two-page openings for some of the major stories by bleeding photos. In addition to the visual change that this represented in the history of the magazine, it was also an editorial accomplishment. By adopting different styles for the opening and design of original stories, he produced the

OPENINGS. The stories opened with a single full-page or page-and-a-half photo. According to Black, his design was "wildly visual," but balanced enough so that the magazine didn't lose the size or appearance of a book.

FOUR STYLES. Four covers, four periods. In the early 1990s, the table of contents over an illustration. Next, the table of contents retained, but with a celebrity added. Then the innovations of 1998. And now, with a smaller celebrity photo.

effect of "a combination of the different magazine styles on the market." This not only turned the *Digest* into a magazine with stories reprinted from other publications but, graphically, it made it a mix of their visual styles. It was a true revolution.

Black's redesign remained almost unchanged for a year, although it was progressively modulated by the editors that followed from 1999 on. For instance, on the dilemma of whether the *Digest* should publish

celebrity photos, Black advocated sticking to the rule of a single large image. But the new editors, uncomfortable with a drastic change in the magazine's traditional profile, chose another option. There was a place for celebrity photos, but it was to be a small one in the upper right corner, so the rest of the space could be used for other stories' headlines. The visual change still had an impact and didn't lead to a reader exodus.

INNOVATION. Never before had *Reader's Digest* published an opening with a two-page photo. The changes on a smaller scale were also drastic.

Age-Old Sentinels— For eight centuries, stone deities have stood guard over the temples in Angkor, Cambodia's forgotten city.

City Lost in the Jungle

I watched the saffron-robed Buddhist monks move by, oblivious to the stifling tropical heat. I had been to Cambodia before, but never to this place. Up I

By Fergus M. Bordewich
Photographed by
Jeffrey Aaronson

113

TABLE OF CONTENTS.
The changes were obvious, starting with the two-page table of contents, and became more evident in such sections as, for example, Medicine.

THE INS AND OUTS OF THE DIGEST TODAY

It's hard for the editors themselves to explain the way the magazine is put together today. "The *Digest's* formula is unexplainable if it's separated from the founder's virtues and defects," said one of the current top editors. Indeed, little has changed in the half century since Wood wrote: "Editorial communication at *The Reader's Digest* is carried on largely through osmosis and contagion. There are no stated staff meetings or scheduled planning sessions. There are few channels, and these are not direct. There is no taut chain of command. Except in the cutting and condensing process, there are few fixed editorial routines."

A story idea may come from many different places, from top management to the lowest editorial positions. An idea may be proposed over lunch. In Wally's day there were frequent lunches at the company's elegantly appointed Guest House with two or three editors and an author or literary agent, but these meetings take place less often today.

Over the years, the company's circulation and staff grew, but the editorial simplicity remains. Only one precept is crucial: that a story have universal appeal. Although a classification of categories that are of interest to the magazine may appear arbitrary and although many have changed over the years, several former editors came up with these: adventure and exploration, agriculture and the environment, art of living, automobiles and traffic problems, aviation, biographies (including the "Unforgettable Character"), business and the economy, civic and community issues, education and parenting, entertainment (show business, sports, television), fine arts, first-person stories and autobiographies, government, health, history, humor, industry and work, literature and journalism, medicine, natural sciences, rackets, religion, sex, and travel.

A number of current editors still point to a saying by Alfred Dashiell, the *Digest's* managing editor for several decades at midcentury: "The goal of this magazine is to inform, inspire, and entertain." Implicit in that second item is that the editors' mission is also to showcase in its pages a better, simpler, and happier world than the one outside. This is how the noted American journalist and scholar Martin L. Gross explained it to the authors: "Each issue of *Reader's Digest* is a balance between humor, celebrity stories, pieces about health and the art of living. Their common denominator is their usefulness. The magazine is also an exercise in idealism, an act of believing in the kindness of human beings."

Nobel Prize winner Albert Schweitzer said something similar in Africa when the magazine devoted a story to him: "The essential emotions in a *Digest* story are inspiration, faith, hope, and courage."

EDUCATION. Two stories with similar themes exemplify the visual differences between yesterday's opening —text only— and today's.

CELEBRITIES. Another section with more movement, more action. "The idea," said Black, "was to be more aggressive with illustrations and with evocative photos to win over young people."

HEROES. One of the classic sections that have lasted the longest in the magazine. To make all these changes entailed improving the quality of the magazine's photos.

THE SELECTION OF STORIES

Generally speaking, the *Digest* is still an "eclectic"magazine, but the ratio of condensations and original stories has reached an almost perfect balance: the magazine publishes an average of six excerpts plus a book condensation every month, and some seven original stories. Each of these editorial pillars has its own staff.

For the condensations, a group of editors and readers each go over fifteen to twenty magazines every month. Other readers pore over hundreds of newspapers, scientific journals, trade publications, and house organs.

Altogether, more than 500 publications are scrutinized every month.

Within this extensive editorial supply, stories are classified as NU (not usable), U (usable), or P (possible). Having read and classified the stories, the readers condense them, generally to one-fourth their original length. Beyond these markings, they write comments in the margins, such as "Needs punch" or "There's a good idea buried in here." The texts are then turned over to editors in charge of the reading and condensation staff, who act as yet another filter before they go

on to the editor in charge of the issue. During this process, each editor uses a different-colored marker to keep tabs on what was cut and by whom. Once a story is approved by the executive editor, it goes on to the research department for fact-checking, then to the copyeditors, and finally to the legal department, which looks for potential problems and lawsuit risks.

On the other hand, the hatchery of original stories is the magazine's own editors and correspondents. Some ideas also come from the international editions, adapted to the American

INTERVIEWS THEN. A comparison of this story on actor Michael Caine with the one on Jackie Kennedy clearly shows the evolution of the style and visual handling of celebrity stories. The *Digest's* "book style" gave way to a quicker read, to which younger readers are more accustomed.

Today *Reader's Digest* handles celebrity interviews and photos as if it were a general interest magazine or newsweekly. Nowadays, one might say, the *Digest* condenses not just the stories but also the visual styles of other publications.

public's taste. Journalists suggesting stories must do so in writing. In this complicated process, the "proposal" is often as long as the story itself. The proposal must discuss in detail the story's premise and tone, list the sources (pro, con, and independent) to be used to prove the thesis, and the research material (books, articles, documents, studies, and so on) that will be consulted.

Once the proposal is approved by the editor in charge, he or she chooses from among the magazine's usual collaborators the one most suited to write on the subject. Often a story is assigned a year in advance, and the writer is normally given two to three months to complete it. Once it is done, it is delivered to the fact-checking department, along with the original proposal, the entire transcription of every interview, a list of sources with addresses and telephone numbers, and photocopies of all print sources from which material for the story was taken. This department will meticulously check every one of the quotes, sources, and background data, and if there are significant changes, will go over the text with the writer to revise and correct it where necessary. Frequently, the whole story is submitted to the sources for review to make sure that the quotes are correct and reflect their ideas faithfully.

A different procedure is used with celebrity stories. A separate department is charged with getting these interviews, which are assigned to specialized journalists who travel the world to do them. The interview transcript is also submitted to the interviewee, who can approve or change the original.

WITH an eye to women

Editor-in-chief Jacqueline Leo describes the editorial makeup of the magazine as "a movie, with a beginning, a middle, and an end." It starts with the Upfront section, with set subsections, such as Close Up (a brief profile of a person), Turning Point (a crucial change in life), Attitudes, Well Being, You Said It (readers' letters and comments), Whatever Happened, News of Medicine, Word Power (a test of readers' vocabulary skills), Quotable Quotes, Everyday Heroes (ordinary people in extraordinary situations), Humor, and All in a Day's Work (funny stories told by readers themselves). "The common

denominator of these subsections is that they are short pieces that meet readers' expectations about diverse subjects, and in that way, they slowly prepare them to read the main stories in the issue," explained editor Leo.

The middle of the issue groups the main stories of the Features section under the subcategories *People*, Drama and Adventure, and the Art of Living.

The end tends to include a book excerpt—*Today's Fiction* or *Today's Nonfiction*. However, the back of the magazine underwent a fundamental change in 2001: the creation of the *RD Living* section, which groups short articles about health, money,

relationships, home, and work. The back cover was and still is a color photo of an everyday-life American hero, alone or with his or her family, under the heading American Heroes. "In a nutshell," Leo said, "the magazine now starts with short humorous articles and with personalized information of general interest, then comes the magazine's main body with longer and weightier stories, and it ends with service articles."

Since 2001, the magazine's table of contents has included the slogan "Stories about Life, Advice about Living."

1999. Covers with full-page photos. The editors considered the change too radical.

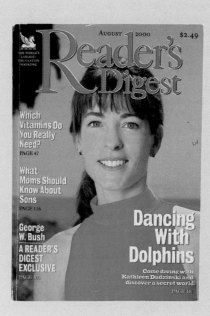

2000. Covers giving more on the contents. The celebrity photo, smaller, moved to the upper right corner.

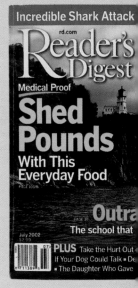

NEW CHALLENGES. According to *Reader's Digest* studies, 60 percent of its readers are women, with an average age of forty-eight. The goal is to appeal to younger women. The editorial work, the page style, and the textual content are all geared to that. Also, a woman is now the magazine's editor.

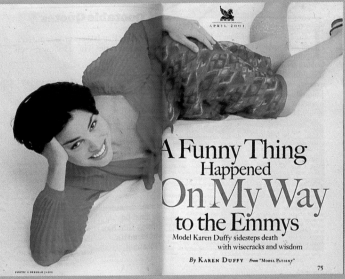

To some editors inside and outside the *Digest*, the magazine somewhat lost its direction after Wallace's death and has yet to find it again. According to its current editor, Jacqueline Leo, "The magazine faces a double challenge: first, to counter or do away with the criticism that the material offered is irrelevant and, second, the perception that it's not for young people." Bearing in mind that its audience is 60 percent female and has an average age of forty-eight, Leo feels the magazine should lean more toward women and, in fact, she has steered it in that direction.

Interestingly, in 2002 her perception was similar to that of DeWitt Wallace in 1922 when, on the first cover, he decided to use as the magazine's symbol an art-nouveau illustration that represented the "ideal woman." Back then, as today, the *Reader's Digest's* goal was to appeal to the female segment of the reading public. And barely eighty years have gone by.

celebrity
magazines

CHAPTER 7
¡HOLA!

Celebrity magazines, known in Spain as revistas del corazón–magazines of the heart–came to fame with ¡HOLA!, a weekly born in Barcelona in 1944. Although it wasn't the first, it firmly established a publishing sector characterized by lighter news, with many photos and brief text for a quick read. ¡HOLA! belongs to a magazine category that captivates millions of readers around the world. Here follow its history, its evolution, and the keys to a success that began in Spain and now extends to France and England.

THE HearT OF ¡HOLa!

It is the standard-bearer of a genre, the journalism of personalities and the famous, that encompasses many publications in the world today.

¡Hola! was born in Barcelona on September 2, 1944, in a Spain gripped by poverty and Franco's rigid censorship. Its founder: Antonio Sánchez Gómez, from Malaga, who was about thirty years old and who had already had nine years of journalism experience, as editor at the newspapers *Labor* in Soria, *El Día* in Palencia, *El Diario Vasco,* Granada's *Patria,* and now as editor of *La Prensa* in Barcelona. His intention: to produce a new magazine, aimed at women but with appeal for everybody. His idea was well received by the female public, bored with the politically restricted press of the time, which was packed with official proclamations and biased articles. Also, the publication's founder had realized that there was very little competition in this category.

Comments started flowing as soon as his colleagues at *La Prensa* found out what he was concocting: "Antonio, man, how can you afford to be a magazine publisher on your salary alone?" Antonio Sánchez Gómez knew that his colleagues were right. He had no financial cushion to support the publication, unless the almost miraculous happened and his idea managed to produce a profit right from the first issue. But while it's quite true that he lacked economic support, it's also true that he had self-confidence to spare. He believed blindly in his magazine and would summarize the philosophy of his project *¡Hola!* thus: "I had in mind a magazine that was entertaining, quite informative, and spectacularly graphic, with pictures taking a significant and central role seldom seen until then. What I proposed was a publication that would be diverting rather than raising concerns, without weight or density in its content, which through important current events would gather and present in its pages what at some point I took to calling 'the froth of life.'"

The formula invented by Gómez would coalesce in time: a cocktail of show business, local and foreign aristocracy, royal families, as well as the events in which all of them played the leading role, whether weddings, births, baptisms, divorces, funerals, exotic travels, or official visits to foreign countries. These topics would primarily be recorded in photographs, with short aseptic stories that expressed no opinion and did nothing to challenge Franco's moral strictures. Perhaps without knowing it, Antonio Sánchez Gómez was originating the global birth of a new magazine sector known in Spain as the *prensa rosa* (pink press) or *prensa del corazón* (magazines of the heart), and in the United States and other countries as personality journalism or celebrity journalism. *¡Hola!* was not the first in its field, but in its wake, magazines of the same type sprouted all over the world and eventually–thanks to their growing professionalism, their success, and their popularity– managed to climb a few rungs on the ladder of international journalism. Suffice it to say that, some years later, the prestigious Time Inc. group would introduce itself into the market by launching *People* magazine.

PRESENTATION. Cover of the first issue of *¡Hola!* for September 2, 1944. The color illustration, in sepia and blue, was done by Emilio Ferrer. The woman, the picture hat, a perky dog, the sailboat on the sea, as well as the smiling globe for the O in the logo, aimed to make it quite evident that this was an entertainment magazine. Sales reached 14,000 copies, the cover price was two pesetas, and the length was twenty pages.

WE THANK THE MAGAZINE *¡HOLA!* FOR FURNISHING THE PHOTOGRAPHS AND COVERS THAT ILLUSTRATE THIS CHAPTER.

THe FIrST ISSue

The magazine debuted as a weekly entertainment. It made its bow to the social world with twenty pages, a press run of 14,000 copies, and a price of 2 pesetas. The cover, very much in the style of the time, was a color illustration in sepia and blue signed by Emilio Ferrer: a woman, a picture hat, a perky dog, and a sailboat at sea. In the upper left-hand corner, in its first logo, was a smiling globe as the O in *iHola!*.

One of Sánchez's first concerns was securing the trademark of the magazine. Although the project was his baby, the name *iHola!* was conceived and registered by one of his friends and coworkers, cartoonist José Antonio Irurozqui Rivas, who would agree to sell it for 10,000 pesetas. Irurozqui was also the first editor of the magazine, although in name only: the law prevented one person from running two publications at the same time, and Sánchez Gómez was already the editor of *La Prensa*.

What was that first issue like? The paper, the ink, and the printing were of very poor quality. The content, which had no clear unity and organization, was rather chaotic. Nevertheless, what would become its fundamental feature was already in evidence: news about upper-class personalities.

The first table of contents included:

"Diagonal": announcements of weddings and baptisms, signed by a pseudonym, Hugo de Lys.

"Life Sentence": a serial love story.

"I Am Your Friend": an advice column in which readers got answers ranging from "what to do with your love letters" to "what to serve your sisters-in-law for dinner next Sunday."

A pictorial page by José Luis Pérez de Rozas titled "A Day in Sitges," full of photographs and names of the Catalán bourgeoisie enjoying the Costa Brava's fashionable beach resort.

Plenty of gossip, hobbies, and recipes.

A double-page spread of summer illustrations by Penagos, with two text boxes titled "The Water the Sea Contains" and "Famous Pearls."

Various clippings and reproductions of photographs, articles, interviews, and comics excerpted from foreign publications at no cost whatsoever, a habitual practice in the Spanish press at that time due to Franco's censorship.

A small editorial on the last page, devoted to women. Written in the male chauvinist style, it said: "Hasn't it ever occurred to you to wonder why a woman, by the mere fact of being one, occupies a privileged position in human dialectics? Such superiority is rooted solely in the fact that women have been, from earliest times, the repositories of moral treasure. This is one of their major functions and one of their most solid prerogatives. This custody confers on them personhood, the right to be respected and to be critical, the three essential attributes of participation in society. If women were to lose their morality, they would never be able to make up for it or remain on their pedestal a single day longer. They would be like men, but without the strength, ability, intelligence, and training. They would hardly be fit to meet their limited biological obligations."

In short, in that first number *iHola!* presented itself as a multifaceted weekly that included everything from amusing humor pieces to articles featuring society figures of the time, with a sprinkling of interesting facts—a graphic smorgasbord. In this debut issue, *iHola!* was already displaying what would become another of its permanent features: its absence of opinion and its kindly tone toward the personalities who inhabited its pages.

NEWS AND NEWSMAKERS.
Inside the magazine, eighteen
pages were devoted to articles
written in an easily identifiable
journalistic style: short,
enjoyable, easy-to-read
features offering news and
photographs of people who
represented "the froth of life,"
in the words of its founder,
Antonio Sánchez Gómez.

WHAT makes a CELEBRITY magazine

BARCELONA FAIRGROUNDS

MANHATTAN IN MARCH 1945

RECORD PASSENGER LOAD ON A HELICOPTER

PEACE MESSAGE IN OCTOBER 1944

THE CANINE FILM STAR LASSIE

The magazines that are part of personality journalism, including *¡Hola!*, are designed to appeal to the whole family, but their main target is women. Their editorial strategies are geared to women and seek ways to win them over, whatever the country of publication. And, although people often criticize and disparage this sector of the publishing world, we can say that magazines *del corazón* are one of the most studied and tested genres on the market.

This is not surprising: on its success may rest the fate of a whole media enterprise. For example, *¡Hola!* reached the enviable and prosperous circulation figure of 200,000 copies in the decade after it came out, securing the company's future. As for *People* magazine, it passed 2.5 million copies and generated profits hardly two years after its creation, in the 1970s, disproving the American "rule" that a magazine can be profitable only after five years of investment.

Now, what is the formula that has made these publications successful all over the world? They have some characteristics in common, independent of the country where they are published, while other factors are related to local trends, tastes, and customs. To under-stand the formula, we must analyze the two figures that have a central role in celebrity magazines: the celebrity and the reader. What are readers after when they buy such a publication? Invariably, they want to know the following about their idols:

1. What their domestic setting is like. How and where they live. What their houses, bedrooms, gardens, and pools look like. The reason: Readers hope that these magazines may be the key that gives them access to an intimate view of their idols, so they may witness their daily routine and home life. It's like going to the house of a friend and seeing the furniture, the carpets, the decoration. It also allows readers to copy fashions, tastes, and styles. This is the usual explanation given by women for buying this sort of magazine.

CHRISTMAS
1947

BARCELONA'S SOCCER
CHAMPIONSHIP IN 1951

HOLY WEEK 1944
IN BARCELONA

GALA NIGHT AT
THE LICEO THEATER

THE MARCHIONESS
OF SAMARANCH IN 1950

IN THE BEGINNING. The first covers had no definite style but were a mix of events, places, personalities, achievements, and celebrations. The photos were black and white or, in some cases, sepia.

2. What their lifestyle is like. What they do, how they dress, where they go. What kinds of cars they own. Whether they pursue a career, what things they have a taste or a weakness for. The reason: simple curiosity, or the desire of readers to know everything that might serve as a yardstick of what they should do, what clothes they should wear, how they can imitate their idols. These sometimes represent a role model, a goal to reach for, or a dream to realize.

3. What they look like. Whether they diet, play any sports, have had plastic surgery. What they do to stay in shape. The readers are seeking a mirror that will let them look at themselves and make them feel better about their bodies and about themselves. It's a sort of self-help, a way of telling themselves that they too can change or improve.

4. How they achieved success. Whether they started at the bottom, rising by chance or a stroke of luck, or through a lot of work, or because they inherited a fortune. In this sense, what readers are looking for is to prove to themselves that they can likewise succeed. Even without becoming famous, it is possible to advance, to grow in your work, career, or profession.

5. What their private lives are like. Their romantic relationships, their partners, their children, their illnesses. Aside from satisfying their curiosity and keeping up with what's going on in the world of the rich and famous, readers like to see that the same things happen to celebrities as happen to common people. Of course, to know these details is also to feel up to date, to have something to talk about with friends.

DOS aND DON'TS ON THE "FROTH OF LIFE"

LIZ AT THIRTEEN
1945

IN HOLLYWOOD
1948

LIZ AS MODEL
1949

WEDDING WITH NICKY HILTON 1951

LIZ AGAIN. Between 1944 and 1954 Elizabeth Taylor made the cover eleven times. This was a record she beat in *Life*, on whose cover she appeared twelve times.

Those five elements are in almost all celebrity magazines. Such publications also tend to present their articles and categorize the news in much the same way. Since most of them came into being in the television age, their editors created products that offered lavish photo displays and little text as a way of competing with the small screen. The idea is for the magazine to inform simply by being looked at. The pleasure comes more through seeing than reading. This, of course, varies according to the publication. *¡Hola!* and *People,* the two leading magazines in the celebrity sector, are not alike at all (as we shall examine in this chapter and the next), with the former focusing on European royalty, while the latter's realm is more in Hollywood than in Monaco or Madrid. Some of the dos and don'ts at *¡Hola!* are:

The news must be amusing, amiable, and appealing to the eye. It should never be hostile to the reader or the person interviewed.

The story must be told through pictures. If there are no photos, there is no article.

The subjects must always be well-known people. Exceptions are made only in the case of major events.

Generally, except for the cover article, the stories must be short.

Never must judgment be passed on celebrities.

Police stories and crime are of no interest.

Gossip or speculation that affects those interviewed or their emotional life must not be published, only information that has been confirmed or credibly verified.

In short: health, money, and love —the three wishes in the classic Spanish toast—are the three variables that are invariably present.

MOTHER ELIZABETH
1953

WITH MIKE TODD
1958

OSCAR AT LAST
1961

WITH EDDIE FISHER
1962

Thus it was not by chance that Mercedes Junco de Sánchez, the wife of the founder of *iHola!,* Don Antonio, played a key role in the publication's planning and execution. Doña Mercedes, daughter of a wealthy family of Palencia, contributed much more support to her husband than mere financial backing so he could continue publishing his magazine and paying his bills. She was a true partner, and a talented one. For example, Doña Mercedes was convinced that *iHola!'s* fans were women and she intended to connect with them through a means that was already in use at the time: a question-and-answer column about love and sex. In one of the publication's first issues, the magazine's advice column counseled a reader who faced family problems because she had a foreign boyfriend: "I hate to advise you to disobey your parents. Try to make them understand. If you don't succeed and you are old enough to act on your own, get married. This is a decision that you yourself must make, since you alone will be the one who will bear the consequences." It signaled a very modern attitude for 1944.

Mercedes also showed that she had the guts to face the economic rigors of the startup. When Don Antonio was tempted by an offer to sell the magazine, she made him give up the idea. Later he would say: "I remember that in those days, and under such circumstances, someone who wanted to buy his daughter a magazine was indirectly negotiating to buy it from me. After I talked it over with my wife, she, whose morale was better than mine, persuaded me not to do it."

And so the founding couple continued on their own. The first editorial office was the maid's room —barely eight square yards—in their apartment on the first floor of Muntaner 414. Don Antonio and his wife were the magazine's staff writers and editors. The product still had a long way to go. "I must confess that although the magazine looked as decent as it could back then, postwar paper and printing left a great deal to be desired," Don Antonio explained modestly as he evoked early times in an *iHola!* special edition to mark its issue number 2,000.

WHEN HOLLYWOOD SHOWS THE WAY

An economic crunch led the couple to make a change that would prove most beneficial. From the beginning, their covers had been the work of prestigious artists, whose fees ate up a large portion of their budget. They soon realized that they could save quite a bit if they took advantage of photos of Hollywood actors and actresses, provided by movie distributors for free. So on October 7, 1944, for issue 6 of the magazine, the cover drawing gave way for the first time to a photo: a picture of actress Ginny Simms furnished by Metro-Goldwyn-Mayer. This would become the norm starting with issue 52 on August 25, 1945. For the second time, the elegant and traditional drawings were replaced by a photo, this one of Clark Gable, sales immediately reflected the wisdom of the decision, and the course for *¡Hola!* was marked: fewer traditional sections and more visual display of the famous. At the same time, the space devoted to society stories, from Barcelona in particular, was augmented. "Enchanting young lady of extraordinary beauty and charm" was an exaggerated phrase often repeated.

As progress was made, the founders deciphered the secret keys to the publication's success. One of them was what they called the "HI factor," human interest. In that regard, the events recorded in those pages—with special emphasis on greater and lesser personages, as well as the usual famous ones and the members of royalty—aroused special interest in the most diverse female public, from humble housewives to ladies of high society.

Ever since Clark Gable's photo replaced the cover illustration, the Hollywood universe—the telling of the life stories and secrets of stars—has been not just an indispensable element of the froth-of-life formula but a magazine constant.

Movie star Liz Taylor led the ranking for the decade between 1944 and 1954, making her way onto eleven covers, followed by Ava Gardner, Rita Hayworth, and Virginia Mayo with eight each, and by Esther Williams and Lana Turner with five. During that time, 329 covers were devoted to Hollywood's famous. Actors also figured: Robert Taylor was featured on six covers, compared to Mickey Rooney's four and Clark Gable's three.

The actor Mario Cabré was the only Spaniard to break the Hollywood barrier. At that time, Spaniards were featured on about 5 percent of the covers of *¡Hola!*. With time, this trend changed. When democracy arrived in Spain and new politicians appeared, the Spanish presence on the cover would grow to 20 per cent in the magazine's third decade, and twenty years later to a record 51 per cent. The only person who managed to be featured on more covers than Julio Iglesias, who had a total of forty-nine in two decades, was Caroline of Monaco, with 101.

Romances between members of royalty or between a celebrity and a member of a royal house were part of a much relished variant of the froth-of-life formula, as in the case of Princess Margaret and Peter Townsend, or Soraya and the shah of Iran, or Rita Hayworth and Aly Khan.

CLARK GABLE

TYRONE POWER

MARÍA FÉLIX

INGRID BERGMAN

HOLLYWOOD 1940.
Between 1944 and 1949, Hollywood stars were the magazine's favorites. Actors and actresses occupied its cover 210 times out of 279 weeks in that five-year period.

GREER GARSON

MICKEY ROONEY

FRANK SINATRA

CLAUDETTE COLBERT

DEANNA DURBIN

HEDY LAMARR

JORGE NEGRETE

BARBARA STANWYCK

GINGER ROGERS

GREGORY PECK

CLARK GABLE

ROBERT TAYLOR

1952: THE EUCHARISTIC CONGRESS AND RECORD SALES

RECORD. The Eucharistic Congress broke *¡Hola!'s* sales record with 200,000 copies. At the time, the magazine included a "Weddings" section, a page for the contest of the week, and a section called "Panorama" devoted to local and international events.

While Don Antonio alternated his work as editor of *La Prensa* with *¡Hola!*, his wife Mercedes would work at home as editor, selecting photos and laying out stories from the EFE, Cifra, Mancheta, Logos, and Zardoya agencies. The two worked at the famous "stretcher table" which is always mentioned when people talk about *¡Hola!'s* early days. It was a long and narrow table, where the family members worked in isolation–three of them after the couple were joined by the owner's brother Rafael, who would eventually become assistant editor, highlighting the publication's family nature.

For the first few issues, they had several contributors. Del Arco, who would later be known as a great interviewer, wrote articles for a section called "Mano a Mano";

Antonio de Armenteras did movie reviews; Xaudaró, Penagos, and Gila drew illustrations; and Luis Marsillach and Eduardo Haro wrote stories.

At the same time, two sections that would become a trademark were added: "Weddings" and "Panorama." The first featured social activity in Spain, while the second included local and international news.

A month later, another section with the same tone would be added under the title "El lunes a las . . ." (On Monday at . . .) and the legend "Do you recognize yourself?" It featured candid shots taken on the street; the people shown circled in white in the photos could stop by the magazine later to pick up two tickets for a show. *¡Hola!'s* nets caught more and more readers every

GLORIA DE HAVEN

ESTHER WILLIAMS

LANA TURNER

time. Finally, the awaited breakthrough came with a special issue marking the first postwar International Eucharistic Congress, held in Barcelona in May 1952. This raised the publication's sales to nearly 200,000 copies, and they never again fell below 150,000. Sánchez well knew the importance of such a step: it pulled in first-time buyers who then became regular readers. Even better, from then on *¡Hola!* surpassed its two direct competitors, both pioneers of the *prensa del corazón: Semana,* born in 1940, and *Lecturas,* dating from 1941. Thanks to that issue, the owner would later tell people, even the Vatican itself directly ordered copies of the magazine.

In addition to the Sánchez-Junco couple, an assortment of nephews, cousins, and in-laws soon joined the editorial team: this way, everything stayed in the family. When contributors arrived at the magazine with their photos and stories, they were all treated with exquisite courtesy, as if on social calls. "Would you care for a cup of coffee?" was the invariable opening question. A bell would ring, and a maid in uniform and cap would come down a spiral staircase from the floor above bearing a silver tray and would pour coffee in porcelain cups, to the astonishment of the paparazzi. Things remained the same until mid-1964, when the family business went public with an initial capitalization of a million and a half pesetas. *¡Hola!* average sales had risen to 300,000 copies.

VIRGINIA MAYO

JUDY GARLAND

SUSAN HAYWARD

AVA GARDNER

BETTE DAVIS

THE ROYAL WEDDING BOOM

It was always clear to Don Antonio that no editorial content could better reflect "the froth of life" than close-up coverage of royalty–especially if there were weddings to show.

"A wedding between celebrities is a journalistic event for *revistas del corazón,*" he would later say during a lecture in Spain about the magazine. "But if the people getting married are also members of the European royal houses, then the story becomes a fairy tale."

That was exactly what happened in December of 1960 with the wedding of the Spanish aristocrat Fabiola de Mora y Aragón to King Baudouin of Belgium. It was an event that definitely consolidated *¡Hola!'s* position on the newsstands of Spain. To cover the wedding with the most spectacular display, the magazine rented a hotel room in Madrid as a sort of improvised newsroom. It was issue 851 of December 17, 1960, with sixty-eight pages, priced at eight pesetas. The coverage was so

extensive that 50 per cent of the advertising space had to be eliminated. Furthermore, technical considerations forced them to leave Barcelona and hire the services of the printers Hauser y Menet in Madrid. The result was worth the trouble: more than 200,000 copies of the issue were sold.

This would be the first in a series of historic sales records generated by royal weddings at European courts. In a new trend, real queens would start displacing the Hollywood queens who had reigned during *¡Hola!'s* previous decade. The weddings that contributed the most to its circulation in this period were those of the current king and queen of Spain, then still known as Princess Sophia and Prince Juan Carlos, on May 14, 1962, and of the shah of Iran and his third wife, Farah Diba, on December 21, 1959. But within the royal panorama there was one family

that meshed, more than any other, with the magazine's interests: the Grimaldis of the Principality of Monaco, a dynasty that fused aristocratic lineage with glamour when reigning Prince Rainier wed actress Grace Kelly, a Hollywood star of the first magnitude. It was such an ideal combination for *¡Hola!* that it occasioned the magazine's first great rush-to-press operation. Antonio Sánchez did not think twice about chartering a plane so he could put on the newsstands, before anyone else, details of the wedding which his readers would avidly devour. The public responded so well to issue 608 of April 21, 1956, with its three dozen pages of enthralling material, that it was followed some days later by a twenty-eight-page special edition. A study later done by the magazine itself revealed that in the decade 1954 to 1964 there had been historic growth thanks to the great royal houses, with a ranking led by

Grace of Monaco with 28 covers, followed by 13 of Queen Fabiola and 12 of Farah Diba. On the masculine side, King Baudouin and Rainier tied with 11 covers each in the same decade, followed by the shah of Iran and the crown prince of Belgium, Baudouin's brother Albert, with 6. So it wasn't by chance that the "monarchies" category, with 183 covers, should grow by 35 percent over a decade.

The trend would not be reversed in succeeding decades. Another famous wedding, this time with political connotations, took place in 1972. On March 8 the head of state's granddaughter María del Carmen Martínez-Bordiú y Franco married His Royal Highness Alfonso de Borbón Dampierre, duke of Cádiz. The issue had an exceptional press run of one million copies, and then a special issue was published with more details of the event.

THE advent of color
and royal exclusives

A significant change was the arrival of color. On October 6, 1962, in issue 945, eight of the fifty-six pages were printed in color. The issue had a press run of nearly 300,000 copies—and it inaugurated a new way of dating the magazine, with only the publication date indicated, rather than the range of dates in which the magazine was current.

The new color printing also marked the magazine's definitive move to Madrid, since Barcelona then had no print shops with the necessary capabilities. After the relocation, thanks to a new distribution system, *¡Hola!* evolved from a local magazine targeting Catalonia almost exclusively into a publication with a national character and scope. It now occupied two huge stories in a rented building on calle Miguel Ángel. The upper floor was the family living quarters, with the new editorial offices below.

At that time the agency Europa Press was providing *¡Hola!* with a great deal of its reportage. Its star staff writer was Jaime Peñafiel, who was a master at reporting the royal weddings that were so dear to the hearts of the magazine's readers. The founders decided to lure away Peñafiel to be their editor in chief.

Photographer Juan Chávez also joined the staff, and later the reporter Santi Arriazu. With the hiring of several relatives, the staff was complete.

Peñafiel became part of the staff out of simple budget considerations: with what Europa Press charged for his stories, *¡Hola!* could afford to pay him a high salary and have him all to itself. "I wound up becoming the alter ego of the magazine," remembers Peñafiel. "I would be there on the cover with the celebrities, do the exclusives, the interviews, almost everything—not because I wanted to but because Antonio Sánchez would ask me to." With Peñafiel on board, the level of the magazine's exclusives rose considerably. When he visited the palace of Hussein of Jordan, he took several books on Gaudí as gifts, since the monarch and Queen Noor were great admirers of the Catalan architect. "I arrived at ten in the morning and at ten that night I was still there having dinner with them. I think that's the secret to doing a good interview: to manage to get them to see you not as an intrusive journalist but as a family friend." Among the royals interviewed by Peñafiel for *¡Hola!* exclusively, either for

SEVILLANA. Queen Sophia was featured on *¡Hola!'s* cover twenty times between 1964 and 1974. On May 11, 1968, she wore the traditional costume of Seville.

ROYAL ALBUM. The magazine has followed step by step everything that happens to the Spanish royal family, and continues to do so: births, baptisms, first communions, birthdays, engagements. These are news and require an article.

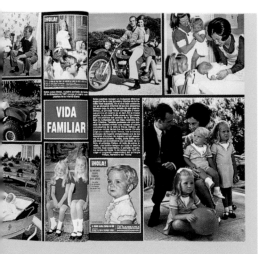

the cover or for long articles, were the prince and princess of Monaco (April 5, 1967), the shah of Iran (May 9, 1981), King Hussein and Queen Noor (October 30, 1982), Farah Diba (May 22, 1986), Princess Margaret (December 1, 1988), and again Queen Noor (December 15, 1988). But no celebrity was able to match the continued success of Caroline of Monaco, who made the cover 39 times in the decade 1974-84 and 53 times in the following ten years. She was not surpassed even by that other gold mine for the magazine, Diana, Princess of Wales, who in 1984-94 was on the cover 34 times. Interestingly, in the sixth and most recent decade of *¡Hola!*, Spain's own crown prince Felipe, who played a major role over the previous two decades, was joined by his sisters, the infantas (royal princesses) Elena and Cristina, thanks to their weddings and the birth of their children. They generated such a degree of interest that the issues covering the infantas' weddings were two of the four issues that sold more than a million copies.

As this book goes to press, *¡Hola!* is gearing up for the wedding of Felipe himself. Clearly, a print run of a million copies will hardly suffice.

coverage of the famous
–for a price

Little by little, along with royal weddings, the problems of princes and princesses, and the politicians of the day, *¡Hola!* turned to recording famous personalities' marital adventures and misadventures. A couple that filled an endless stream of pages were the singer Julio Iglesias and his first wife, Isabel Preysler. Everything was published: the courtship, the wedding, the singer's tours to Rio de Janeiro, New York, London, Tokyo, and Paris, and the family reunions that followed. The couple's divorce was also aired in *¡Hola!*; indeed, *¡Hola!* was the recipient of the communiqué stating that, after seven years, the marriage was over. The day they finally decided to split, Isabel shouted at her soon-to-be ex: "I will have more *¡Hola!* covers than you." And she would manage not only to do so but to become one of its staff writers, in spite of her lack of experience in the trade.

Jaime Peñafiel had established such a close personal relationship with the couple that in the spring of 1978 a female voice told the newsroom's answering machine about Isabel's alleged infidelities with the man who would become her second husband, the marquis of Griñón. This fact was the detonator of the couple's breakup, which became definitive less than twenty-four hours later. With this piece, the magazine would introduce a practice into "the press of the heart" that would become customary in this type of journalism: the purchase of exclusives and the sale of information.

¡Hola! was the first magazine to put a price on the life of a child before its birth. It happened on June 11, 1977, when a photographer traveled to London to get an exclusive on the birth of singer Massiel's child. The report took up four pages and the cover of the June 18 issue. (Seven years later, *¡Hola!* would buy an exclusive on the singer's wedding in Mexico to Pablo Lezcano, with writer Gabriel García Márquez as witness.) That same year, in another first, the magazine directly negotiated for the wedding of Merry Martínez-Bordiú, the third of Franco's granddaughters, to Jimmy Giménez Arnau, setting a new market standard in celebrity journalism.

"Don Antonio," Peñafiel said to his boss one afternoon in August of 1977, "Jimmy Giménez Arnau is here. He says that he wants to sell us the exclusive on his wedding to Merry Martínez-Bordiú."

"So how much is he asking?"

"He wants to know how much we'll pay him. . . ."

"I'll say hello now, and then you negotiate with him. But not a cent over a million."

As Peñafiel explained, "It was the first time that a personality negotiated and charged the magazine directly, without using any agency." Accordingly, in issue number 1,721 on August 20, 1977, that wedding occupied the cover and a thirteen-page color spread.

An unstoppable race had begun. The famous and pseudofamous would avidly sell off their privacy in a new era of "checkbook" journalism, which did away with the premise "You get the news, you don't buy it." From then on, the business had no limits. "Some women talk to their obstetrician to have their

delivery held up and, in that way, prevent it from coinciding with another famous personality's. If they were all to give birth at the same time, who would get the cover?" asked Jaime Peñafiel. Incredible as it may sound, such maneuvering undoubtedly has something to do with this kind of information: Rosario Flores, daughter of the renowned flamenco artist Lola Flores, and Rocío Carrasco, daughter of the singer Rocío Jurado, pocketed $130,000 each for presenting their respective daughters to society in the pages of *iHola!*.

Later the amounts were staggering. For example, Isabel Pantoja charged $200,000 for the first interview she granted after the death of her husband Francisco Rivera, the legendary bullfighter Paquirri. Their wedding, on February 16, 1973, had been a big draw. But the public was far more moved by the tragedy of September 26, 1984, when a 925-pound bull named Avispao stained Pozoblanco's sand with blood and mortally wounded the torero. The $150,000 that former

model Nati Abascal charged for posing with her two sons after the arrest of her former husband, the duke of Feria, did not go unnoticed, either.

These experiences would lead the magazine to create another well-received category: pseudomemoirs, like those of Julio Iglesias's former wife, Isabel Preysler, who was one of the first to dare to write them. On the strength of their success, *iHola!* hired Preysler as a "star journalist." Although she contributed only her presence, showing up at interviews with a list of questions prepared in advance by another journalist, Preysler would carry away a million pesetas for each report. But some of them wouldn't be such bargains. For example, when she interviewed Clint Eastwood, she asked him when he planned to make his first film as director, when actually the actor had already directed a dozen films. Furious, he got in touch with the Madrid office of Warner Brothers and reproached them: "What kind of *** journalist have you sent me?"

LEGACY. Isabel Preysler later interviewed celebrities for the magazine. And Isabel "Chabeli" Iglesias Preysler, daughter of Julio and Isabel, also appeared on the weekly's covers: for an exclusive interview, and at her wedding when her parents met again.

¡HOLa!, THe GeneraLísimo, anD THe POLITICIans

¡Hola! existed under the Franco regime for thirty-one years. The owner of the magazine never concealed the esteem in which he held Francisco Franco, about whom the magazine wrote often in laudatory and approving terms.

On the cover of issue 604 on March 24, 1956, the ruler was featured accompanied by his wife under the headline "Spanish Holy Week." On October 6, 1962, on page 3 of issue number 945, a celebratory piece on the twenty-sixth anniversary of his rise to power told readers: "Franco, leader in war and in peace, has lived and lives the needs and desires of the Spanish people every minute."

This loyalty was reciprocated by Doña Carmen Polo, Franco's wife, who was so enthusiastic about *¡Hola!* that she would send a chauffeur to the printing plant to bring her a copy hot off the presses.

Franco's death required a special issue titled "Franco Has Died," in addition to the cover story on November 22, 1975, four days after his death. The headline of this issue was "National Mourning: The Leader Has Died." And a legend read: "Doña Carmen and Franco, An Example of Fidelity and Love Entwined with Service to Spain." As was to be expected, Sánchez himself wrote this article.

With the arrival of democracy, *¡Hola!* remained faithful to its style. By rereading the magazine from then up to the present, it's possible to reconstruct the lives of King Juan Carlos, Queen Sophia, and the whole Spanish royal family, step by step. The birthdays of the prince and the infantas, as well as anniversaries and official trips abroad, were always celebrated by the magazine. Juan Carlos, crown prince at the time, would play photographer at family get-togethers and then deliver the film to the magazine, which would develop it and publish the pictures without his having any say in the selection.

Despite his clear sympathy with the Franco regime, Sánchez had more than one run-in with the censors back then. Some necklines or skirts above the knees would elicit the handwritten message "unauthorized for publication." Those inches of indecent skin were covered, with a firm hand, by the precise airbrush work of Rafael Sánchez, Antonio's brother.

With the death of Franco in 1975, the winds of democracy blew across Spain. A stage that would be known as the Transition was beginning, giving major roles to a formerly forbidden political class, while King Juan Carlos's role became ever more important. But each time someone suggested including the new prime minister Adolfo Suárez in the magazine, Don Antonio would shout: "But no, but no! This man, who brought communists to Spain, is not going to appear in my magazine. I assure you of that: he will not appear in my magazine."

The pressure of some colleagues and Suárez's charm would finally work the miracle. The article ran on the eve of the first democratic general elections, when the magazine's circulation had reached 600,000 copies. Aboard a small jet rented for a campaign trip to the Canary Islands, Suárez told the reporter about his whole life, right down to family problems. That first appearance would be followed by many others: between May 1977 and January 1982 the magazine would devote ten covers to him. In issue 1,710, for June 4, 1977, the publication allotted him five color pages and three in black and white. Suárez with his family was featured in twenty-two photos, sexy, smiling, casually dressed. That cover was shared with Prince Felipe, who had just been named soldier of honor in the King's Ancient Regiment. There was a total of four interviews with Suárez up to August 16, 1980. More would follow: during the Christmas holidays that year, in February 1981 upon his resignation, and on the island of Contadora in April 1981. The fourth time, as former head of government, he welcomed the magazine in his new home in January 1982. Result: Suárez would occupy second place among Spaniards most featured on ¡Hola!'s cover between 1974 and 1984, surpassed only by Julio Iglesias. Suárez and Amparo Yllana, his wife, ended up being very good friends of Antonio Sánchez and Mercedes Junco. The two couples would spend many weekends at the editor's country estate, El Retortillo.

King Juan Carlos's visits to foreign countries would always be featured in the magazine's pages. Politicians from all over the world would pose with him, many of them dictators—but never Fidel Castro or Pinochet, whom the editor of ¡Hola! rigorously excluded along with all members of the Spanish Communist Party.

Between the resignation of Suárez and the swearing in of his successor, an event took place on February 23, 1981, that would become known in Spanish history as "the 23-F Coup" or just "23-F." A coup attempt was led by Civil Guard colonel Antonio Tejero, gun in hand, in the middle of a session of the Cortes, the legislative body. After hours of tension—and a timely word from the king—democracy gained the upper hand. Then ¡Hola! devoted an institutional cover to the new head of government, Leopoldo Calvo Sotelo, and his wife. Over the picture of Suárez's successor was a small yellow strip with a headline in black: "At Press Time for This Issue: Photos of the Assault on the Congress of Deputies and a Chronicle of the Event." Inside there was no other commentary, no opinion or editorial. The headline was

"The Failed Coup, Minute by Minute," illustrated with eleven photos (ten from the official agency EFE) spread over four pages in black and white.

The magazine would give Felipe González a cover, for issue 2,000, only when he was already prime minister. The first member of his family to be featured in ¡Hola! was his wife, Carmen Romero, in 1977 when Felipe became the opposition leader.

Things changed when he took office on December 2, 1982. The magazine did the first article on the new prime minister and his family at the Palacio de la Moncloa, the official residence. The number, which was also a Christmas special issue, turned out to be a significant one. In terms of the story's length, González beat Suárez by four pages: he had twelve compared to the eight that were devoted to the postwar era's first democratically chosen head of government, although there was a tie in the total number of interviews.

THE DEATH OF THE PATRIARCH
AND CONTINUITY

Mercedes Junco, with reddened eyes and wearing deep mourning, sat as usual at the newsroom desk. Her son Eduardo, until then responsible for evaluating and purchasing exclusives—a key task at *iHola!*—sat next to her. It was 1984, the fortieth anniversary year of the magazine, and Antonio Sánchez had died. There was no doubt about who would carry on his work: Eduardo took the helm of *iHola!*.

But a conflict was about to break out —open opposition between the new editor and the magazine's star, Jaime Peñafiel. Eduardo Sánchez Junco had a very clear vision of the magazine: he had watched it grow, literally, as he himself grew up. Peñafiel's role as a personality was a problem. Finally the conflict exploded. Peñafiel came back from a royal visit to Russia in early January and ran into a surprise on the magazine's cover: "I saw it as soon as I arrived at the airport. 'Mrs. Reagan Welcomes *iHola!*,' the headline said. It was I who had done the interview and, logically, it was for me to write the story. I turned in my resignation."

Some say that this was just an excuse, since Peñafiel already had an offer to edit a new publication in the celebrity sector. For his part, once free of Peñafiel, Sánchez Junco rapidly demonstrated that he had very definite ideas. He followed to the letter his father's advice and his mother's guidelines without changing the magazine's essence at all. He hired Tico Medina, but did not accord him the starring role Peñafiel had had, and then he brought on board the highly experienced Javier Osborne from the magazine *Diez Minutos* to take charge of day-to-day editing.

Once his staff was realigned, Sánchez Junco continued working toward a clear objective. His father, proud of being "much more a journalist than an entrepreneur," had deliberately not concerned himself with advertising or distribution, entrusting the former exclusively to Publicitas and the latter to the Sociedad General Española de Librerías—a convenient solution but an ineffective one. Sánchez Junco hired a business genius, Javier Riera de Prada, a close friend and indeed a relative by marriage, to bring the budget into line and give the *iHola!* empire—whose circulation now exceeded 500,000 copies—the economic structure it needed. In this manner, the company's profits improved spectacularly. Eduardo managed to boost sales from

half a million to 670,000 copies. In spite of its traditional "well-bred" stance, *iHola!* now allowed itself routinely to talk about divorce, until then a taboo word. Not anymore: "Everything about the Separation of the Prince and Princess of Wales," the headline of one of its best-selling issues read.

In the meantime, familial continuity is assured. The current owner's wife, María del Carmen Pérez Villota, secretary of the Hola S.A. board of directors, is herself a journalist, and the couple's three children are also in the trade, so the editorial succession seems guaranteed. Even better, Eduardo has achieved what seemed to be impossible: to improve on his father's management style.

Just as Mercedes Junco had an active role ever since the first issue of the magazine was published, editing articles and doing layout, she still works there, although to a lesser degree. "She's my permanent advisor, above everything," says her son Eduardo. "Then for star reports, like certain weddings or exclusives in the homes of the famous, my mother still does the layout as she did on day one. Besides this, one territory is exclusively hers: fashion specials. There she makes all the decisions."

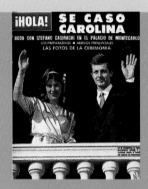

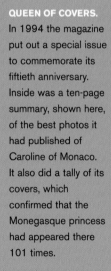

QUEEN OF COVERS.
In 1994 the magazine
put out a special issue
to commemorate its
fiftieth anniversary.
Inside was a ten-page
summary, shown here,
of the best photos it
had published of
Caroline of Monaco.
It also did a tally of its
covers, which
confirmed that the
Monegasque princess
had appeared there
101 times.

THe extension of THe name

On June 29, 1988, the English version of the magazine was launched. *Hello!* was the literal translation of the Spanish greeting, immortalized in white on red by Antonio Sánchez, who did not live to see the birth of his first international creation. On the cover of issue number 1 of the English edition were—how could it be otherwise?— Prince Charles and Diana, princess of Wales. The occasion was a polo match at Windsor Great Park.

Between the two editions, the Spanish and the English, weekly circulation would surpass a million copies. The first editor of the English version was a British newspaper-woman, Maggie Goodman, who was succeeded in 1993 by Sally Cartwright.

Hello! opened a new niche in the personality magazine market. In the wake of its success *OK!* was born, an obvious copy in terms of design, despite a decided difference in content. While *Hello!* preferred to feature anything about royalty and aristocracy, *OK!* leaned more toward celebrities. The struggle between the two periodicals pushed the price of exclusives up, and an absolute record was reached with the wedding of Spice Girl Victoria Adams to the star of international soccer, Manchester United's David Beckham. *OK!* reportedly paid a million pounds for the exclusive in 1998. Sales justified the investment: that issue sold twice the average of 400,000 copies.

The competition broadened the market, and *Hello!'s* growth was so significant that logistic adjustments had to be made. This task was entrusted to José Gilarranz, who spends the whole weekend glued to his mobile phone. The drivers of six 25-ton trucks can rely on that telephone in case of any kind of emergency. Every Saturday the entire print run of the British edition of the magazine is loaded on the trucks. "Transporting 600,000 copies weekly to the United Kingdom is quite a military operation," explains the business brain of the magazine, Riera de Prada. "Incredible though it may seem, we publish *Hello!* in Spain because there are no printers in the United Kingdom able to work with the speed that we get here. Over there, they would require us to deliver segments as much as three weeks ahead of time, and for us that is just not possible."

Hello! is the pride and joy, the crowning success of an enterprise that could not grow much more in Spain and had to consider expansion. "The reason," Riera said, "for extending a brand name toward that market is obvious: a universal language, a potential public of 600 million readers, and a high reading rate and high advertising investment."

Having conquered the English market, in 1998 the expansionist adventure turned to France. But in this case a lawsuit resulted, as Juan Caño describes in his book *Revistas* (Magazines). When the first issue of *¡Hola!*, titled *Oh La!*, hit the French newsstands on September 14, 1988, it ran into an unexpected and surprising competitor: the magazine *Alló!*, published by Prisma Presse. Two months before, when Eduardo Sánchez Junco had tried to register the name *Alló!* in France, he found it had already been registered as part of an operation involving Prisma, which then published two celebrity weeklies, *Voici and Gala,* evident rivals of the French *¡Hola!*. The idea was to poison the market, so the case went to court. It was a tough battle that lasted nine months, during which time neither magazine sold much more than 120,000 copies, far below the usual average.

Finally the court ruled in April of 1999, ordering Prisma Presse to change the name of its publication within four months and to pay 1.5

Su estilo y personalidad innatos la convirtieron en embajadora universal de la elegancia

Noblesse Oblige

million francs as compensation. The judge held that Prisma had imitated and competed unfairly against the Hola Group, owners of the Spanish weekly and its English version *Hello!*. Three months later, *Alló!* would close down.

Today, as *iHola!* approaches its sixtieth anniversary, it is positioned as the best-known celebrity magazine in the world, selling more than half a million copies in Spain each week, a like number in Great Britain, and nearly 200,000 in France. Apparently the "froth of life" that Don Antonio created has just started bubbling. Few have managed to summarize the social meaning of *iHola!* as aptly as the respected writer and intellectual Francisco Umbral, who said upon the magazine's fiftieth anniversary: "The chronicle of this half century was not recorded by the daily press nor by … historians, but rather by *iHola!*… Three generations of Spaniards have conducted their businesses, their work, their weddings, their yachts, their country houses, their hunting, their divorces, their children, their parties, and even their mourning in *iHola!*. None of what we have is true until we see it in that photo."

While most of their competitors never had second thoughts about revealing the darkest and most sensationalist secrets of any marital conflict of the rich and famous, *iHola!*'s editors always preferred to keep these quiet and to limit themselves to exclusive accounts from one of the parties involved, always preserving the integrity of the characters. The example that best illustrates the magazine's philosophy concerns the "favor" that *iHola!* did for the princess of Wales. In the early 1990s Diana was unfortunate enough to be photographed topless by a paparazzo while on a cruise. Those pictures were worth a fortune: they could have been the subject of a cover for any publication in the sector. Eduardo Sánchez Junco wasted no time in buying them, for a price that remains unknown, in order to file them away in a drawer. They never saw the light. It was a sort of counter-rendering of services to someone who had given so much to the magazine. Without citing concrete cases, Javier Riera, the company's business manager, explains why this is an acceptable practice. "Noblesse oblige. Since we have lived off some celebrities a ton of times, it's logical that, on special occasions, we pay back with this sort of gesture."

According to the magazine, the princess was on the cover sixty-one times up to 1994. After Caroline, she was the most frequently featured individual in that spot. Naturally she was also there on June 29, 1988, when the English version of the weekly, *Hello!*, was launched. The photos shown here were published in *iHola!*'s fiftieth anniversary issue.

HOW ¡HOLA! IS PUT TOGETHER

The editors' rules to make the magazine. How "the froth of life" is achieved today. Changes, new formulas, and new topics according to the present managing editor.

The scene has repeated itself punctually every Monday for years. Starting at 6 a.m., representatives of local agencies that specialize in celebrities, as well as the large international agencies, stand in line on the fourth floor of the building at 1 calle Miguel Ángel, *iHola!'s* editorial headquarters. It's closing day. From eight o'clock on, the magazine's editor, Eduardo Sánchez Junco himself, starts dealing with the agencies. He decides what to buy and what to turn down after comparing, one by one, the different stories about the rich and famous, local or foreign. Sánchez Junco deals with the selection alone because the magazine doesn't have a photo editor. On Monday appointments are not made, nor can a place in line be saved for anyone. It's first come, first seen, and when the material is fairly similar, being seen

first might be the key to scoring a scoop. The cover of *iHola!* and much of the late-closing material—which fills fifty-six pages—are among these snapshots of the famous and glamorous taken by paparazzi and by the most experienced photographers in the world.

So it is during this session that a decision is made about the hottest items in *iHola!.* Contrary to what some people might think, content is decided on the spot without a set plan for the issue. Eduardo Sánchez Junco explains: "Since we work with agencies so much, a particular characteristic of *iHola!* is that the mock-up gets produced quite spontaneously according to the material as we receive it. There is little story planning in *iHola!*"

The magazine comes out on Thursday, as it has for a decade (in its first half century, it appeared on Saturday). To meet that schedule, the editing of each issue proceeds in the same manner. The closing is done on Monday, from early in the morning until nighttime. "Only if something quite valuable turns up at the last minute can we add anything on Tuesday morning," says Sánchez Junco. "Otherwise, we close on Monday."

Thus every number is begun on a Tuesday. The editor, along with assistant editor Javier Osborne, divides the magazine into two large blocks. "The first segments, the beginning and the end of the magazine, include the least time-sensitive material, our own productions, and things that didn't get into the previous issue. This is where articles on celebrities' houses go in or anything else produced ahead of time. In the back portion are the fixed sections, such as recipes, beauty, fashion. Then, as we come to the center of the magazine, we find material on current happenings, which the agencies provide and which are therefore unexpected every week. In this area, of course, as in any other journalistic activity, the key is the sources we have, to keep us up to date with what is happening in the world of the famous. We manage this with two channels: with our own sources, who are close to the newsmakers we're interested in, and with the good work carried out by agencies on their own, which we benefit from simply because most of them prefer to come out in *iHola!* rather than in other media."

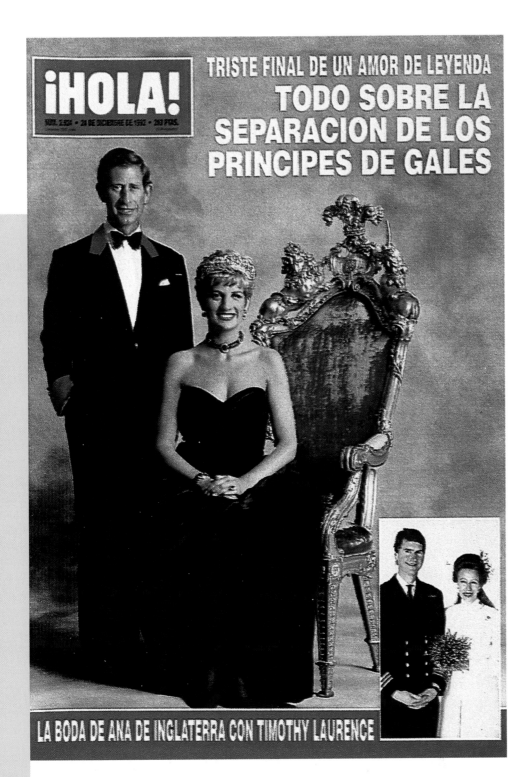

¡HOLA!

NUM. 2.524 · 24 DE DICIEMBRE DE 1992 · 240 PTAS.

TRISTE FINAL DE UN AMOR DE LEYENDA
TODO SOBRE LA SEPARACION DE LOS PRINCIPES DE GALES

LA BODA DE ANA DE INGLATERRA CON TIMOTHY LAURENCE

NEW LANGUAGE. Although *¡Hola!* continues to hold steadfastly to the editorial values of "good taste and good breeding," today it gives itself some latitude not found in its pages before. This cover's headline is a good example, and a milestone: it deals quite openly with a married couple's *separación*, a word the publication would not use before. At the same time, the weekly maintains its policy of not publishing nude photos and of not criticizing celebrities.

rules OF THe Heart

Eduardo Sánchez Junco starts by quoting his father, Antonio Sánchez Gómez, in listing the commandments that summarize the philosophy of *¡Hola!*, the most important *revista del corazón in Spain,* which is sixty years old in 2004. "My father, who conceived it and directed it until his last days, would always define *¡Hola!* as the 'froth of life.' That is, what is not heavy, what will let the reader pass time enjoyably. And that is basically summarized in two words: good taste."

These commandments have been observed for years:

Photos of topless women or naked people are generally not published. Undoubtedly, the most definitive example of this was the set of pictures taken of Princess Diana without her bikini top during a summer cruise in 1994. Those photos, which in any newsmagazine could have made a cover and a great article, were purchased in exclusivity by *¡Hola!'s* editor Eduardo Sánchez Junco—but not for publication. While the editor won't comment on the matter, one fact remains clear: those photos never saw the light of day.

There has to be an interesting story to go with the photos. "The rest is what wraps the report up, because there is no doubt that *¡Hola!* is a very graphic magazine. This is why the quality of the photos in each story needs to be defended," explains Eduardo Sánchez Junco. "It's all about having each photograph speak for itself, show something that may be of interest to the reader. It could be showing a house's decoration or other details, or the shoes a woman is wearing. Whatever detail it shows, each photo must contribute something."

The photos and material must be genuine and current. This is something the editor of the magazine considers "the ABCs of serious journalism."

The stories must be well written and serious. "Another feature that we pay attention to is the literary aspect: care is given to the writing."

Persons always come before things or issues. "What matters most here is human interest stories. We don't reflect only the happiness in life. As in life itself, in *¡Hola!* all the nuances are present, the happy moments and the sad, although always with good taste, I insist."

The celebrities must not be criticized. "In fact, we don't do editorial journalism. We reflect the reality of what can be seen, but without issuing value judgments. We don't speculate on people's attitudes; we leave that up to readers, who draw their own conclusions."

SOCIAL LIFE. In addition to royals, *¡Hola!* always makes room for the rich and famous, such as Carmen Martínez-Bordiú (later Rossi), Rocío Jurado, Alicia Koplowitz, Marta Chávarri, and model Claudia Schiffer.

LIFE CHAPTERS. The magazine follows every step in the lives of the famous, such as Isabel Sartorius (who was linked to Prince Felipe), Queen Fabiola, or Carmen Rossi.

Another distinguishing trait of *¡Hola!* is Eduardo Sánchez Junco's zeal in supervising directly the content of the Spanish edition, as well as of its sister publications in Great Britain and France. Given his tendency not to delegate, the purchasing of material is centered on his decisions and those of the assistant managing editor. "This is an area that I've divided in two: I handle purchases for international stories and Javier Osborne deals with local ones."

A related matter is the absence at *¡Hola!* of a photography editor, a key role in magazine newsrooms, given the extensive photo displays since the 1980s. "Yes, undoubtedly it's an important function in this sort of magazine. This brings to mind a great foreign magazine that I won't name, which almost always published exactly the same photos that *¡Hola!* used, out of the material that wasn't bought as exclusives. I was curious to know who was choosing the

photographs. I did some checking and they told me: 'No, that´s done by the editor,' and so I felt more relaxed. In this kind of magazine, that decision is very difficult to delegate —which doesn't mean, as in my case, that you don't have three or four persons you can trust completely, who embody the magazine's style and its criteria for choosing this or that material for publication."

at Home with
the rich and Famous

Another genre inextricably associated with *¡Hola!* is the "En la casa de" or "At Home with" piece. Why do these articles have such an impact? "Among human interest topics," the editor says, "the house often reflects characteristics of celebrities themselves. A large part of their personality is reflected there. In that sense, houses are not chosen with any kind of special guideline. They are what they are. Some are very pretty, others are less so. The one factor that determines publication is good taste. The more style and good taste is presented in a house, the more there is to show, and thus the more display it will deserve." Another explanation is the natural curiosity that any famous figure arouses. "And who doesn't like to

go in and look at, actually to spy on, the houses of the famous?"

It's difficult to say when such articles actually began. According to Eduardo Sánchez Junco, the model became common in the early 1980s, when better printing technology and paper quality allowed emphasizing this type of reportage. In terms of sales, one particular issue was able, in a special way, to reap the benefits of joining two significant elements of the magazine's formula: a celebrity of interest to *¡Hola!* and her house. Thus "La casa de Isabel Preysler" became a classic. Issue 2,517 on October 29, 1992, announced on its cover: "The House of Isabel Preysler and Miguel Boyer, Room by Room."

at Home with Isabel Preysler

In fact, almost all its rooms were included in the thirty-two pages, although they were shown without people. In the whole article, the mistress of the house appeared only three times, posing with her daughters Ana and Tamara in a variation of the cover photo. It was a total success, with circulation reaching 935,164 copies.

More modest earlier versions had been published before the magazine was able to achieve such a display. "The House of Manolo Santana," for the Spanish tennis star, warranted three pages on January 14, 1984. Singer Julio Iglesias's Los Angeles mansion took up the cover and ten pages on February 18 of that year. And Baron and Baroness Thyssen-Bornemisza showcased their modern art collection in five pages on November 17, 1988. This type of article follows a set pattern: celebrities don't change clothes, and photographers often show empty rooms without the owners.

What criteria are followed in each photo production? "Since the focus of the article is the house itself, everything is done ahead of time so the celebrities can take care of the final touches, prepare and present the house according to their taste. But they are the ones who decide on this or that element of the decor. We don't interfere."

A HOUSE THAT MADE A SPLASH. In issue 2,517, for October 27, 1992, *¡Hola!'s* cover story presented the new house of Isabel Preysler and Miguel Boyer. The thirty-two-page article sold more than 900,000 copies. Thus "At Home with…" became one of the formulas for selling the magazine. Its editor concedes that "among human interest topics, the house often reflects characteristics of celebrities themselves. A large part of their personality is reflected there."

a FORMULA FOR WEDDINGS

"A wedding is an event that is surrounded by that something that we at *iHola!* call the froth of life," explains Sánchez Junco. That is why, for the magazine, this is a more successful genre than others. First, of course, come the royal weddings, since *iHola!* is the royalty magazine par excellence, and then come weddings of the merely famous.

The best proof: in its six decades *iHola!* has managed to surpass the million-copy sales mark on only four occasions, and three of those issues featured weddings. With 1,637,519 copies sold, the leader in this class was the wedding of the infanta Cristina to Iñaki Urdangarín (issue 2,775 on October 9, 1997). Next was the infanta Elena's wedding to Jaime de Marichalar, with 1,625,810 copies (issue 2,642 on March 23, 1995).

The third-best seller was not a wedding issue but the commemoration of *iHola!'s* fiftieth anniversary in a lavish special edition (issue 2,620 on October 20, 1994) with 1,210,739 copies. In fourth place with 1,168,492 copies was another wedding (issue 2,830 on October 29, 1998), this one the quintessence of the world *del corazón:* the wedding of Eugenia Martínez de Irujo, daughter of the duchess of Alba, the grandest of Spain's grandees, and matador Francisco Rivera Ordóñez, descen-ded on both sides from the aristo-cracy of bullfighting.

The rule here is show the wedding to readers as if they were privileged guests, who will always see much more than an actual guest. Two sacred corollaries: highlight what

cannot be seen, and provide a chronology of the occasion—in other words, start with the preparations, go on to the church, later to the reception, and finally show the couple departing on their honeymoon.

iHola! generally has the exclusive on these weddings, which gives an even higher value to the coverage. Sánchez Junco refuses to talk about figures. He says, "Exclusives have always been around, they're as old as journalism. When you want something that more than one person wants, there is no choice but to pay to have it as an exclusive." One of the most recent examples of the privilege represented by an exclusive is issue 3,015 (May 23, 2002), the wedding of top Spanish model Nieves Álvarez to Marco Severini: cover and thirty-three pages.

11 **LIZ** 1944-1954

Elizabeth Taylor was the actress featured on the greatest number of covers during the magazine's first ten years.

20 **SOPHIA** 1964-1974

In its third decade Sophia, then the crown princess, was the personality with the largest number of covers; in the next, Queen Sophia was in second place.

FEMALE AND MALE LEADERS IN COVER APPEARANCES, BY DECADE

1944-1954		1954-1964	
Elizabeth Taylor	11	Princess Grace	28
Ava Gardner, Rita Hayworth,		Queen (later Princess) Soraya	20
Virginia Mayo	8	Queen Fabiola, Gina Lollobrigida	13
Robert Taylor	6	King Baudouin, Prince Rainier	11
Mickey Rooney	4	Generalísimo Franco	
Clark Gable, Mario Cabré	3	Shah of Iran, Albert of Belgium	

MILLIONAIRES. These are the four covers that, in the history of the weekly, surpassed a million copies (Source: *¡Hola!* magazine 2002).

1 1,637,519
WEDDING OF INFANTA
CRISTINA October 9, 1997

2 1,625,810
WEDDING OF INFANTA ELENA
March 23, 1995

3 1,210,739
¡HOLA! FIFTIETH ANNIVERSARY
October 20, 1994

4 1,168,492
IRUJO-ORDÓÑEZ WEDDING
October 29, 1998

average annual sales

YEAR	COPIES	YEAR	COPIES	YEAR	COPIES
1944	7,000	1974	470,000	1990	594,012
1950	14,000	1977	36,181	1991	640,001
1955	90,000	1979	411,790	1992	640,001
1962	250,000	1980	442,375	1994	708,273
1965	312,000	1981	500,510	1995	648,321
1968	322,000	1985	587,787	1998	621,302
1972	456,000	1987	582,778	2000	587,650

53 CAROLINE
1984-1994

This princess holds two records: 53 *¡Hola!* covers in a single decade and 92 in a twenty-year span.

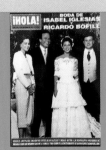

27 JULIO
1974-1984

The singer ranked first during this period; in the next, he was second to Prince Felipe.

34 DIANA
1984-1994

The Princess of Wales was the subject of 34 *¡Hola!* covers during this time, second only to Caroline of Monaco.

1964-1974		1974-1984		1984-1994	
Crown Princess Sophia	20	Princess Caroline	39	Princess Caroline	53
Carmen Martínez-Bordiú	17	Queen Sophia	26	Diana, Princess of Wales	34
Princess Grace	16	Isabel Preysler	18	Isabel Preysler	23
Crown Prince Juan Carlos	15	Julio Iglesias	27	Crown Prince Felipe	24
Alfonso de Borbón	12	Adolfo Suárez	11	Julio Iglesias	22
Prince Rainier	10	Crown Prince Felipe	10	Count Lequio	12

Like other magazines in its genre, *¡Hola!* has been the stage for romances, separations, and reconciliations. Yet in an area where rumor swirls, at the moment of deciding whether or not to publish something, this magazine follows its own rules. Sánchez Junco explains: "*¡Hola!* reflects the lives of a series of celebrities and everything that surrounds these lives, which includes their falling in love and out of love. But this is something that just happens and something that they themselves usually speak of in *¡Hola!*. That is, *¡Hola!* speculates little on affairs of the heart, except in the case of royalty, where there's simply no chance that the personalities themselves will comment on the situation. In such cases, we include the usual classic sort of speculations about the possible romances of a prince here or a crown princess there. The rest of the time, *¡Hola!* simply doesn't do it. It's the newsmakers themselves who speak out on their love lives. We don't like to function on rumors. And when a situation is presented as a crisis, it's because we're convinced that the crisis is a fact and will result in an almost immediate separation."

¡Hola!'s caution is such that in cases of infidelity, even when it has the privileged photographic proof as an exclusive (the editor won't name names), the magazine prefers to wait before casting the first stone. "**Of course. *¡Hola!* is quite discreet in all matters that revolve around celebrities' private lives, and we don't say anything about their good names, their reputation, or even their marital stability. It wouldn't be the first time that an infidelity revealed in the press had negative consequences in a relationship. . . . And in no case does *¡Hola!* wish to assume this responsibility. So we prefer to wait or verify with a very reliable source that the situation is already known to both parties, or that the facts will be learned relatively soon. But to reveal something like this to someone or someone's children, that just doesn't happen in *¡Hola!*.**"

FROM LOVE TO PAIN. *¡Hola!* and four stages of a love story that made people dream. The magazine showed all of them.

FROM JOY TO TEARS.
Another royal couple,
another prince, and a
story that unfolded
differently. Readers of the
prensa del corazón were
able to follow it step by
step in *¡Hola!*

**ANA DE INGLATERRA,
MADRE DE UN NIÑO**

THREE STAGES. This is the way *¡Hola!*
reported the courtship and married life of
Princess Anne and her first husband.

CLAUDIA SCHIFFER
Calendar girl

RAPHAEL AND NATALIA
Wedding

PRINCES AND PRINCESSES OF MONACO
Red Cross Gala

SARAH FERGUSON
Confessions

a magazine whose success doesn't depend on its cover

What prerequisites must a celebrity meet to be on *iHola!'s* cover? According to the editor, there are few weeks when the cover is produced ahead of time, since late developments —with the use of an agency photo—are generally decisive. "There are events for which there is a date, such as a wedding. But usually the cover of *iHola!* is pretty much an improvised thing."

The general parameters are:

1. People are given priority over topics or things.
2. The newsmaker should have eye contact with the reader.
3. Full-length pictures are preferred to close-ups, with as much background as possible.

However, at *iHola!* the cover doesn't have the same selling power as at other magazines in this sector. In other words, the cover is secondary, except to announce an exclusive or a wedding that everyone is awaiting. "I don't even know if our cover is our best feature. I believe that *iHola!* cannot reflect on its covers everything of interest inside, precisely because of the type of publication it is: our headlines are rather aseptic. That is, we don't use the cover

as a clamorous sales pitch," its current editor says. "In that sense, our covers are somewhat colder, more formal. Besides, it's quite difficult to reflect on the cover the volume of information in the magazine. I think our content generally is better than our covers. And luckily enough, we have readers who are very loyal and whose numbers keep increasing, who buy our product because it is in itself good enough."

This is also why *iHola!'s* management has felt no need to redesign the magazine over the years and no pressure to change the editorial formula or visual presentation. Says the editor: "Fortunately *iHola!* works so well that there's no indication changes are advisable. I must stress our readers' loyalty: if we've continued to be the leaders and continued to grow for so many years, why should we change?"

On the few occasions when the cover is assigned, the photographer gets very few guidelines. "Undoubtedly, visual contact is quite important. But unlike Americans, who use close-up pictures, we prefer a half-length or sometimes even a full-length figure, since I like the photograph to show to some degree the setting surrounding the subject, to give a bit of ambience if possible. But, I

BEYOND THE COVERS. *iHola!* is one of the few magazines in the world that doesn't depend on the cover's subject to sell an issue. According to its editor, the aseptic style of its headlines doesn't reflect the wealth of topics in its contents. Anniversaries, balls, fashion shows, weddings, or farewells to great newsmakers might be cover material for the weekly. Its articles reflect the social chronicle or "the froth of life" of an era.

repeat, those that we produce are a minority, because we can say without false modesty that *¡Hola!* publishes a very large number of exclusives at both the national and the international level. When you're able to achieve that level of privilege, the only thing you need to do is choose the best photo marking the news event in each case—photos generated by agencies. That's why we don't offer guidelines, we choose the best they offer, always following the style precepts we first discussed: good taste, no sensationalism, 'the froth of life' once more," the editor sums up.

Nowadays *¡Hola!* and its management don't spend much time worrying about the magazine's cover or content. These are known quantities. Editors and readers are clear about what *¡Hola!* is and what they will find inside. The future's main challenge is to pursue the international expansion started with *Hello!* and to extend its ventures into new territories. "As in all businesses," the editor explains, "*¡Hola!* wishes to expand and keep growing. We have no interest in publishing new or different products. Our policy has always been to promote what we have—that is, to take *¡Hola!* further, to promote or strengthen

it even in countries where we already operate. We started with the English version, *Hello!*, which is very successful and which has been a way of expanding the mother publication. We also are successful with the French edition, *Oh La!*. While these are our own projects, another challenge is to continue expanding into other languages and other countries that we're considering, but in such cases not as exclusive owners, as in England and France and Latin America, but as local partners."

Today *¡Hola!* produces nine different editions in the same week. The Spanish main edition has three variants, "with a segment and cover change according to the region": one version for Mexico and the U.S. Latino market, particularly Miami, another for South America, and yet another for Central America. In addition, there are *Hello!* and its three offshoots in Scotland, Australia, and Canada, and finally the French version, *Oh La!*. When asked about future challenges for the company, Eduardo Sánchez Junco speaks of a dream that is ever alive. "Man, there can't be any doubt that the United States market will always be running through my mind."

on march 4, 1974, THE FIRST ISSUE OF PEOPLE, and WITH IT THE FIRST magazine THAT TIme Inc. DevoTeD enTIReLY TO PeRSOnaLITIeS, came OUT In THE UnITED STaTes.
TO avoID COnFUSIOn WITH PUBLICaTIOnS THaT FOCUSeD On ScanDaL, PeOPLe USeD a veRY RIGOROUS FaCT-CHeCKING SYSTem. THe GOaL: TO DO SeRIOUS JOURnaLISm aBOUT FamOUS PeOPLe, even IF IT InvOLveD FRIvOLOUS SUBJeCTS. THe ReSULT WaS a magazine THaT WaS SUCCeSSFUL THanKS TO a meTICULOUS FORmULa OF UnIQUe eLemenTs.

THE PEOPLE FORMULA

In 1974 *People* added investigation and fact-checking to what is called celebrity journalism. These are the keys to the success of a magazine conceived to be sold on newsstands.

Nothing explains the *People* philosophy better than the introductory note in the premier issue on March 4, 1974. Managing editor Richard B. Stolley wrote: "*People* is a magazine whose title fits it perfectly. There is nothing abstract about our name. *People* is what we are all about. Journalism has, of course, always noted and dealt with people. But we dedicate our entire editorial content to that pursuit." The editor's note went on to lay out, in essence, a charter for the brand-new medium:

"Week after week, *People* will focus entirely on the active personalities of our time—in all fields. On the headliners, the stars, the important doers, the comers, and on plenty of ordinary men and women caught up in extraordinary situations.

". . . we will concentrate on individuals rather than issues, on the force of personality, on what's happening to human beings and how those human beings react. . . .

"Our attitude toward our subjects is amiable and perhaps a little skeptical. We hope to be fair, informed, informative. We hope never to be cruel or awestruck or gushy….

"We want *People* to be a magazine that is fun to pick up and both easy and worthwhile to read—page after page, cover to cover. We don't want readers to put *People* aside until they've got the time, because that extra time so often fails to arrive…. We aim to be the indispensable guide to those millions of aware Americans who cheerfully acknowledge that what interests them most is other people—especially the above average, the important, the charismatic, the singular….

"Editorially, we hope to come at everything fresh. To reappraise, to ask 'Who is this person' and give an honest, up-to-date answer. To reassess the old familiar faces. To welcome the new and eager. To peer into the lives of the hitherto undiscovered. And to do all of this with zest, sensitivity and good humor. Believe us, quote us, enjoy us."

The history of the magazine's birth goes back a couple of years before its launch. According to Stolley, the fundamental elements of *People* were already part of *Life's Parting Shots* section, which included brief bios of important people. Other Time Inc. editors believed that the true forerunner of the new magazine was the *People* section in *Time*. Still others equated the advent of *People* with an imitation of TV—a layout of large images and little type. Surely the true origin of the magazine was a combination of all these factors.

Whatever the genesis of the idea, in April of 1973 a team led by editor Otto Fuerbringer started to work out an editorial plan for the magazine that would be launched a year later.

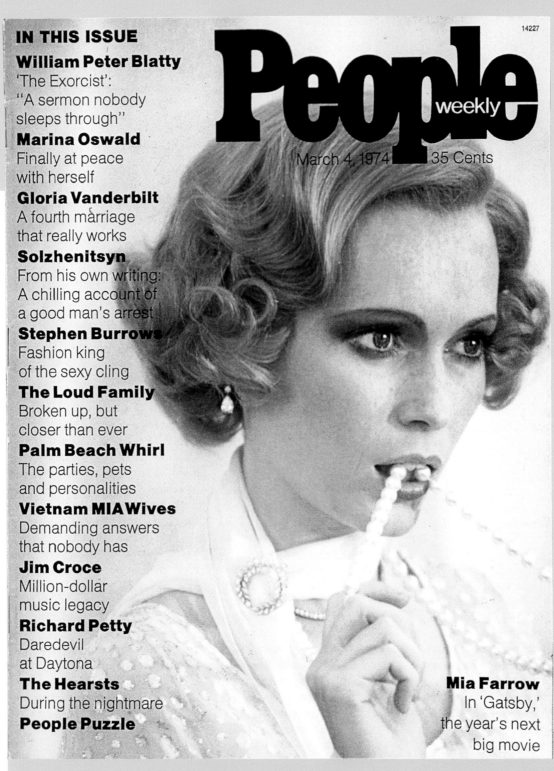

14227

People
weekly

March 4, 1974   35 Cents

Mia Farrow
In 'Gatsby,'
the year's next
big movie

LAUNCH. On March 4, 1974, *People* hit the U.S. magazine market with a cover featuring Mia Farrow, who was then starring in a remake of *The Great Gatsby*. Unlike other publications, *People* was meticulously put together in advance and tested on the newsstands before the launch. It presented to readers a very carefully planned formula.

THE Premier Issue

Fuerbringer's staff immediately began work on a business plan, which was presented in June. The magazine would contain between 51 and 54 editorial pages and, at first, would be sold only on newsstands, at 50 cents an issue. A *Camera Month* group made up of former *Life* editors Phil Kunhardt, John Loengard, Edward Kern, and Janet Mason put together a sample issue in paste-up form, which elicited much praise. According to an internal memo, the top brass loved it. The same group produced more pasted-up dummies, to make sure there would be enough visual material available from the wire services and photo agencies, and enough people to write about, every week.

After demonstrating that this was not a worry, the next step for the same team was to produce a fully developed prototype of the magazine. They were joined by Richard Stolley, an editor developing new product ideas for Time Inc., who wrote and edited some stories for it. This *People* prototype was called "the Liz-and-Dick dummy" because its cover featured the Hollywood couple that was always good for a story, Elizabeth Taylor and Richard Burton, who were on the verge of their first separation. The cover photo showed Liz looking to the side— that is, not making eye contact with the reader—over the headline "The Burton Split-up," with her husband behind her, somewhat out of focus.

To the left of the cover photo, under the heading "In This Issue," was a roster of the personalities featured inside, in some cases with the nicknames the public knew them by, in others with their full names: Liz & Dick (the Burtons), Ali & Steve (MacGraw and McQueen), Bobby Riggs, Ethel & Kids (Kennedy), Barbara Walters & Sally Quinn, Led Zeppelin, Joe Namath, Julie Eisenhower, Ari Onassis, Liza Minnelli, Lance Rentzel, Bess Myerson, Eugene Paul Getty II, Faye Dunaway, Paul Winfield, Brigitte Bardot, Sophia Loren, Naomi Sims, Jacqueline Susann. Princess Caroline was billed as "Grace's Daughter." The prototype's date: August 20, 1973. Its price: 35 cents.

As an experiment, a special type was used inside to make the stories look as if they were written with an old typewriter. The sections into which the prototype was divided—*Up Front,* with three stories led by "America's First Lady of Divorce"; *Winners*; *In Her Own Words; Bio; Star Tracks; On Stage; In Style; For a Song; Out of the Pages* (a book excerpt); *Over the Tube* (TV); *In Trouble* (famous people in difficult situations); *People in the Past; Chatter* —were so well thought out that many of them are still present thirty years later.

The main story's photos were blurry and grainy: Italian paparazzi had secretly shot them while Burton and Liz tried to reconcile at a mansion in Rome that Sophia Loren had loaned to them.

When the managing editors of Time Inc. were polled, the reaction was, to say the least, mixed. Bill Rukeyser of *Money* magazine dubbed the new product "journalistic popcorn" and forecast a solid success. To Robert Lubar of *Fortune,* the writing was "sprightly" but the appearance "somewhat grubby" and the personalities "drearily familiar." To *Time's* Henry Grunwald, *People* was "potentially very exciting" but needed "far more quality, information, variety, and thus money, than are evident in this issue." A report to the publishing group's chief editor Hedley Donovan on the range of opinions concluded: "The consensus was powerfully negative.... The words most often used were 'sleazy' and 'cheap.'"

However, as the corporate biography *Time Inc.* records: "A more upbeat evaluation came from Clare Boothe Luce, in Honolulu. [Board chairman Andrew] Heiskell had sent her a courtesy copy of the dummy. She had collected the opinions of a hairdresser, a manicurist, a friend, her two maids, her cook, her secretary, and the secretary's husband—all of whom liked it. Mrs. Luce for the most part liked it herself. She wrote to Heiskell: 'Please let me know how you make out with the advertisers. If you make out well, nothing can stop *People*.'"

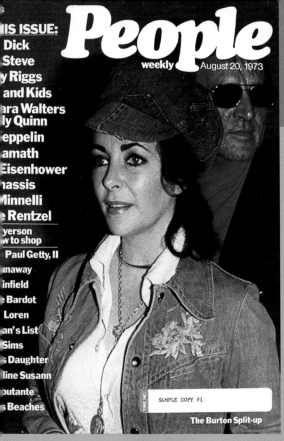

People

weekly · August 20, 1973

SAMPLE COPY #1

The Burton Split-up

"LIZ AND DICK." The main story in the test issue was the purported reconciliation in Rome between Elizabeth Taylor and Richard Burton. Next to the photo were listed the names of all the celebrities featured in the issue.

FRONT

Mrs. Elizabeth Taylor Hilton... Wilding... Todd... Fisher...

...Burton: America's First Lady of Divorce

INNOVATIONS. One of the most noticeable was the type. A special font was used to make it look as if the text were written with an old typewriter. But this typographic experiment was not retained in the premier issue.

People

weekly · August 20, 1973

newsstand testing

After testing the magazine in informal surveys and gathering personal opinions, the company offered the Liz-and-Dick prototype for sale in August 1973 on newsstands in eleven cities, in quantities calculated to approximate a million-copy national launch. The pseudolaunch was preceded by an intensive one-day advertising campaign in some cities, but unheralded in others. In one city where no advertising was done, the cover bore a price of 50 cents; elsewhere it was 35 cents. The sales were more than encouraging. In markets where the magazine was promoted, buyers snapped up 85.2 percent of the issues on the stands—a remarkable result given that, after allowance for copies that are lost, stolen, or damaged, 90 percent is considered a sellout. Even where there was no promotion and a price of 50 cents, sales reached 38.4 percent.

Extrapolating from the trial sales, circulation experts estimated that in three years *People* would be the fifth largest-selling magazine on American newsstands, after *TV Guide, Playboy, Penthouse,* and the *National Enquirer.* Profits were projected before the end of the second year. In executive circles at Time Inc., people realized that *People* would be a hit. So they wasted no time putting together a staff, starting with a managing editor.

After the Liz-and-Dick dummy went to press, Stolley went on vacation. He was at home in Greenwich, Connecticut, when Fuerbringer, who also lived there, invited him out to a popular watering hole and, with the approval of Time Group president Hedley Donovan, offered him the top job at *People.*

Stolley took some time to think it over. At forty-five, he had been in journalism for twenty-seven years. He had been *Life's* bureau chief in Atlanta, Washington, Los Angeles, and Paris before being named the magazine's deputy editor. He had also traveled throughout the world and was a man of endless energy and inquisitiveness. Now, as he debated a change of career, he realized that he'd rather run the new magazine. But before he did, he wanted to produce a second dummy.

Stolley's prototype had a cover featuring Billie Jean King and her husband, Larry, and fifty-three pages of editorial content divided into sixteen sections including *Up Front, In the Money, Jocks, Star Tracks, Chatter, Couples, In Her Own Words, Off the Screen, Out of the Pages,* and *Tube.* King's presence on the cover signaled clearly that the magazine wasn't just about Tinseltown. The prose style was a bit more polished and mature than in the first version. There were aesthetic adjustments, too. The obtrusive typewriter-style type of the Liz-and-Dick dummy was replaced by a sans-serif font that would remain in use for a decade or more. In general, *People* seemed somewhat better defined and more attractive. The editorial tone and the new look created the philosophical foundation for the publication: revisiting well-known people to tell something that was not known about them until then, as well as featuring unknown people in an interesting and provocative way. All of which made Stolley more comfortable with his new job. He pointed out then that there was no

FIXED SECTIONS.
Several of the sections
included in this first
dummy would remain
in future issues, for
instance, *Star Tracks*,
Bio, *In Style*, *For a
Song*, *On Stage*, *Over
the Tube*, and *Chatter*,
though *People in the
Past* would soon be
dropped.

other magazine like it on the market and, in the absence of any precedent, the editors had the luxury of doing whatever they liked.

People was brought before the board on October 18, 1973, and its launch was immediately announced for March of 1974. However, a worrisome situation soon arose. When the salesmen went out to solicit advertising, they found that the magazine's image on Madison Avenue was working against it. Like *Time* and *Life* and *Fortune* before it, *People* was sui generis. Since it didn't fit into any existing category, the ad agency executives were puzzled about how to "position" it—how to match their advertising clients with its target audience. What kind of magazine was *People,* after all? Was it more like *Photoplay* or *Playboy* or the *National Enquirer*—or perhaps a full-length version of *Time's* own *People* section? An additional problem, with ad execs who had seen the rather unsophisticated Liz-and-Dick prototype, was that *People* seemed below the quality of other publications of Time Inc. In Madison Avenue parlance it felt "downscale." Even clients who regularly advertised in the company's other magazines had to be persuaded to advertise in *People*. Fuerbringer himself got into the act, going down to Washington to convince the president of a supermarket chain that *People* would be a respectable

presence on the magazine racks. It seemed that Clare Boothe Luce was right to worry about "how you make out with the advertisers."

To address that concern, *People* arranged meetings with advertisers and point-of-sale people throughout the country. Stolley personally delivered many of these pitches. As Dick Thomas—who had just switched from *Money* to *People* as advertising sales director—later said: "Potential advertisers were always immensely impressed with Stolley. He never apologized or was defensive. If they thought *People* was garbage, Stolley would just say, 'Well, that's your opinion.' Since the downscale image was one of the things we were trying to beat, it was terribly helpful to have Dick Stolley talk about the magazine as he saw it. *People* never sounded downscale when he talked about it."

When he wasn't busy promoting the magazine, Stolley was looking for personnel. The plan was for *People*, like *Money*, to operate with a small staff and get its stories mostly from stringers, many of whom worked for newspapers and, when needed, could be called on and paid at the going rate of $7.50 an hour.

IN THIS ISSUE
Kissinger
Search for
a hostess
Elizabeth Taylor
Filming a
face-lift
Ellsberg Case
Shy psychiatrist
who got burgled
Amy Vanderbilt
Manners for
permissive people
Jackie Kennedy
Those White
House days
Howard Cosell
Is Congress
ready for him?
J. L. Seagull
The movie star
who flew away
The Pointer Sisters
Grandma told them
to take a chance
John Matuszak
Biggest thing
in pro football
Rebozo and Abplanalp
What it means
to be close
to Nixon
Bootsie and Jean
Two women fight
for a governor

People weekly
October 22 1973   35 Cents

Billie Jean and Larry King
"We'd be better off divorced
and living together"

THE FIRST ISSUE

It hit the streets on March 4, 1974. On the cover was Mia Farrow, star of the new movie version of *The Great Gatsby*—a choice that Stolley now considers a poor one. In the cover photo, he points out, Mia does not make eye contact with the reader, breaking what would become one of the generally sacred rules of cover-picture selection. Also, her film didn't open until after the week the magazine came out, breaking another sacred rule: the events that earn celebrities their place on the cover must take place during the week of the magazine's publication, no sooner and no later.

In addition, Mia Farrow's presence on the first cover made the ad sales people uncomfortable, since they had guaranteed potential clients that *People* wouldn't be just another movie magazine. However, the celebrity list on the left side of the cover proved the magazine's subject diversity:

William Peter Blatty. *The Exorcist:* "A sermon nobody sleeps through."
Marina Oswald. Finally at peace with herself.
Gloria Vanderbilt. A fourth marriage that really works.
Solzhenitsyn. From his own writing: a chilling account of a good man's arrest.
Stephen Burrows. Fashion king of the sexy cling.
The Loud Family. Broken up, but closer than ever.
Palm Beach Whirl. The parties, pets, and personalities.
Vietnam MIA Wives. Demanding answers that nobody has.
Jim Croce. Million-dollar music legacy.
Richard Petty. Daredevil at Daytona.
The Hearsts. During the nightmare.
People Puzzle.

The issue included twenty advertising pages, fewer than expected, and sold 978,000 copies, also somewhat fewer than expected, although neither figure was cause for concern. The editorial staff numbered only thirty-four, and at first it seemed that was enough. However, it was soon evident that the newsroom needed augmentation in a couple of major categories. For one thing, *People* found—just as *Life* had in its infancy—that it couldn't rely too heavily on photo agencies, but would have to come up with its own pictures. Stolley expanded the photo department, but not by putting photographers on the payroll. Instead he hired people who could select and supervise freelancers.

The other category, as Time Inc.'s corporate history points out, was equally important: "*People* also needed researchers. That became clear with the

SEVEN PARTIES IN A SINGLE DAY

PRESENTATION. The first cover story, with Mia Farrow as subject, ran only three pages. One of the longest, at six pages, was about Palm Beach; it led to the new magazine's first lawsuit.

People weekly

March 4, 1974 ⬛ Vol. 1 No. 1

first issue, which included an article by Sheilah Graham, the former Hollywood columnist, comparing Hollywood and Palm Beach. Buried near the end was a rather sensational line: 'The big difference between Palm Beach and Hollywood is that Hollywood is a working city. There you can open every door with talent. You can be illegitimate, as Marilyn Monroe was; a former call girl, as I was…:' [News editor Hal] Wingo cleared those last few words with Graham over the phone before publication, but when they appeared in print she threatened to sue. Two weeks later *People* ran an item in the *Chatter* section explaining that she had meant to say 'chorus girl.' Graham dropped her threat. The incident emphasized the critical importance of credibility for *People*. If it was to refute the critics who compared it with the supermarket tabloids, it would have to establish a reputation for solid accuracy. Stolley began adding research staff."

CONTENT. In all, the magazine had seventy-two pages, plus the covers. Ads took up twenty of them. It had a varied table of contents to guarantee diversity of subject matter.

EDITOR-IN-CHIEF   Hedley Donovan
CHAIRMAN OF THE BOARD   Andrew Heiskell
PRESIDENT   James R. Shepley
CHAIRMAN, EXECUTIVE COMMITTEE   James A. Linen
GROUP VICE PRESIDENT, MAGAZINES   Arthur W. Keylor
VICE CHAIRMAN   Roy E. Larsen

MANAGING EDITOR   Richard B. Stolley
SENIOR EDITORS   Sam A. Angeloff, Richard Burgheim, Robert Emmett Ginna
DESIGN DIRECTOR   Elton Robinson
NEWS EDITOR   Hal Wingo
PICTURE EDITOR   John Loengard
ASSISTANT EDITORS   Bina Bernard, Ross Drake, Jed Horne, Ralph Novak, Patrick O'Higgins, Jim Watters, Lee Wohlfert, Shirley Estabrook (Assistant News Editor), Clare Crawford (Washington)
REPORTERS   Curt Davis, James F. Jerome, Sally E. Moore, Joan Oliver, Ron Scott, Mary Vespa
PICTURE DEPARTMENT   Mary Dunn (Research), Kate Guardino
COPY DESK   Nancy Houghtaling (Chief), Paula Glatzer, Harold Rodgers, Catherine Radich, Nelida Granado
DESIGN DEPARTMENT   Daniel J. McClain (Assistant Director), Bernard Waber, Ellen A. Kostroff
EDITORIAL PRODUCTION   David J. Young
SPECIAL CORRESPONDENTS   Aspen, Nellie Blagden; Atlanta, Joyce Leviton; Baltimore, John Schulian; Boston, China Altman; Chicago, Linda Witt; Cincinnati, Bill Robinson; Cleveland, Richard Wooten; Dallas, Connie Hershorn; Detroit, Julie Greenwalt; Houston, Kent Demaret; Kansas City, Richard Mackey; Los Angeles, Barbara Wilkins; Louisville, Ed Ryan; Miami, Jane Rieker; Milwaukee, Tom Lubenow; Minneapolis, Daniel F. Wascoe; New Orleans, David Chandler; Orlando, Sandra Hinson; Palm Beach, Ed Dawson; Philadelphia, Gregg Walters; St. Louis, Jerry Curry; Salt Lake City, Nelson Wadsworth; San Antonio, Betty Dunn; San Francisco, Nancy Faber; Seattle, Jane Estes. (Overseas) Geneva, Robert Kroon; Hong Kong, June Shaplen; London, Fred Hauptfuhrer; Montreal, Laura Bell; Munich, Franz Spelman; Paris, Rudi Chelminski; Rome, Logan Bentley; Singapore, Carl Mydans
CONTRIBUTING PHOTOGRAPHERS   Harry Benson, John Dominis, Alfred Eisenstaedt, Bill Eppridge, Henry Groskinsky, Co Rentmeester, Stanley Tretick
EDITORIAL SERVICES   Paul Welch (Director), Norman Airey, George Karas, Benjamin Lightman, Doris O'Neil, Carolyn R. Pappas

MAGAZINE DEVELOPMENT
EDITOR   Otto Fuerbringer
PUBLISHER   Garry Valk

PUBLISHER   Richard J. Durrell
GENERAL MANAGER   Winston H. Cox
ADVERTISING SALES DIRECTOR   Richard B. Thomas
BUSINESS MANAGER   Paul E. Hale
CIRCULATION DIRECTOR   Austin O. Furst Jr.

Cover photograph by Steve Schapiro

PEOPLE is published weekly; $15 per year, by Time Inc., 541 N. Fairbanks Court, Chicago, Ill. 60611. Principal office: Rockefeller Center, New York, N.Y. 10020. James R. Shepley, President; Clifford J. Grum, Treasurer; Charles B. Bear, Secretary. Application to mail at controlled circulation rates is pending at Chicago, Ill. Direct all mail to PEOPLE, Time & Life Building, Rockefeller Center, New York, N.Y. 10020. Letters to the editors are accepted for publication but cannot be acknowledged. The editors assume no responsibility for unsolicited photographs and manuscripts, which must be accompanied by a self-addressed, stamped envelope if the material is to be returned. © 1974 Time Inc. All rights reserved. Reproduction in whole or in part without written permission is prohibited.

3

TIME GROUP'S BLACK SHEEP

Even in-house, *People* was hurt by the negative attitude it encountered. Few Time-Lifers wanted to work at the new magazine. According to Stolley, "They thought that for Time Inc. to put out a magazine like this was unseemly. Tacky. You'd be in the elevator and hear cracks like this all the time. Here we'd be, working eighty- and hundred-hour weeks, and then to get on the elevator and hear someone dump on the magazine— well, it wasn't pleasant. But it was all over the place." Beyond company circles too, *People* was at best dismissed as inconsequential, and sometimes witheringly ridiculed. Although the attacks abated over time, they were painful.

But nothing was as hurtful to Richard Stolley as a disparaging column William Safire wrote for the *New York Times* under the headline "Who Needs *People*?" Safire said that most of its "wealthy young" readers, whom he disdained as "page flippers," were "a collection of frantic, tasteless fadcats deeply concerned with social climbing and intellectual pretension, panting for a look at celebrities in poses that press agents staged back in the thirties." Safire shot several bullets at the stories in the first issue:

The magazine, he said, milked the craziness of exorcism with an interview that repeated what author William Peter Blatty's agent had been saying for months.

It exploited Solzhenitsyn's craziness with a tricky headline that led the page flippers to believe that the Russian author had written an exclusive for *People,* when in fact the story was part of a five-year-old book. "Palm Beach Whirl" was listed on the cover almost parallel to the mouth of Mia Farrow, who was chewing the pearls that *People* was throwing at its readers, a story with which the new magazine placed its readers' noses against high society's showcase.

Safire also commented that there were two photos of people in bathtubs, a grotesque story about overweight people who had their mouths wired shut, and a couple of full-page photos of U.S. senators acting dumb.

Only one story in the issue, the one on Marina Oswald, was spared. Safire said it was well written and its photos were reasonably good, a reminder of what the magazine could have been.

Safire's final verdict was deadly: "*People* fails on the tawdry terms it has chosen: The sex is not sexy, the gossip not current, the exploitation not with-it. Great effort is needed to lift it up to superficiality." Another paragraph called the magazine "an insult to mass audiences." Citing a phrase the magazine used in its ad campaign—"Tonight, plan to sweat

ss tomorrow"—Safire ended by
aying that he hoped that Time
c.'s many talented journalists
ould do precisely the opposite
nd reformulate the degrading
roduct until it became a
ublication.

Stolley clipped the column and
osted it on a cork bulletin board
his office as a "damned
eminder." Every night, before
rning off the office lights to head
ome after a long and exhausting
ay, he would read a paragraph to
ent his anger and vow to produce
better product. Instead of letting
get him down, the column
oaded him to get rid of the anger
nd improve the magazine.

Interestingly, many years later
tolley ran into Safire at a party.
When the former *People* editor
sked the *New York Times* writer
hy he'd written such a venomous
nd mean-spirited column, Safire
nswered that he didn't even
emember it. Indeed, said Safire,
e subscribed to the magazine and
ead it closely every week because
e considered it excellent. To this
ay Stolley has a hard time
elieving he was so upset for a
ecade for no reason!

TIME FOR CRITICISM. The stories in the magazine's first issue were harshly criticized by a *New York Times* columnist. The only story that escaped his scorn was an article on Marina Oswald, widow of the man accused of killing President Kennedy.

a magazine conceived
for sale on newsstands

At the beginning the *People* staff was stretched pretty thin, and the top editors wound up doing almost all the rewrites themselves. Cranston Jones, a senior editor who had come over from *Time* shortly after the launch, recounted Stolley's reaction upon reading a story Jones had just passed up to him. "God, we've finally got a good writer!" Stolley exulted. Jones shook his head. Stolley then understood that this piece too had been totally reworked, and quietly went back to his office.

In the development of the *People* writing style, one who was instrumental was Richard A. Burgheim. A former writer for the *Time* entertainment and TV sections, Burgheim had joined *People* when it first started and soon became assistant managing editor. Burgheim also turned out to have an uncanny instinct in the selection of cover stories.

If everyone put in long hours, Stolley put in the longest, personally reviewing every word of every issue. Once, Hal Wingo found Stolley in his office at 4 a.m. editing the *People* crossword puzzle. Sleep seemed a matter of indifference to him, and his staff took to calling him the "bionic editor." Perhaps he was too aware that, despite his own and others' efforts, the first issues of *People* had a certain inevitable unevenness. Still, if Stolley and his fellow editors at Time Inc. generally were dissatisfied, the readers seemed very pleased. The Cambridge Marketing Group, commissioned to study the public response,

presented its findings in late 1974. All the top executives of Time Inc. were present at the meeting. When the Cambridge analyst took the podium, his opening remark was: "Never in my twenty-five years of research have I seen a product with greater consumer acceptance than *People.*"

Reader acceptance, however, didn't automatically translate into success on the advertising front. Stolley had always expected that *People* would appeal especially to female readers, and studies confirmed that women constituted 60 percent of its readership. But advertising targeting women took a while to acquire; indeed, so did advertising of all sorts.

A separate problem was distribution. *People* wasn't getting good enough exposure on the newsstands–where, unlike the other magazines of Time Inc., it was designed specifically to be sold. And this didn't mean just the corner newsvendors. For a product like *People*, in the modern era, it meant the supermarket racks, where the largest proportion of sales are made and where the competition for favorable placement is fierce.

As Time Inc. depended chiefly on subscription sales, it had allowed Select Magazines, a cooperative distribution service formed by several publishers, to take care of all its newsstand operations. But happily for *People,* newsstand sales was an area in which its publisher, Richard Durrell, had once specialized. Before long Durrell decided that

MIA FARROW
March 4

MARTHA MITCHELL
March 11

J. PAUL GETTY
March 18

RAQUEL WELCH
March 25

GERALD FORD
April 1

TED JR. AND TED KEN
April 8

LORNE GREENE April 15

TATUM O'NEAL April 22

JOAN BAEZ April 29

GEORGE AND CORNELIA WALLACE May 6

Select was "spread too thin" and was not giving *People* the necessary push, both to get into the supermarkets and, once there, to get prominent display. By October of 1974, Time Inc. had established a new entity, Time Distribution Services (TDS), to work along with Select, and had tapped as its head Joseph Corr, once promotion director at *Life*. Corr broke with established practice and went outside the company to hire people with merchandising experience and a knowledge of supermarkets. In one short year at his post, Corr proved the wisdom of his strategy. TDS boosted *People*'s distribution so successfully that, in 1978, it took over newsstand distribution for the company's entire stable of magazines. In October of 1975, *People* was selling more than a million copies a week, advertisers were coming on board at a gratifying rate, and, to wide amazement, the magazine actually turned a profit. A balance sheet in the black within eighteen months of launching was an almost unprecedented feat. Another delightful surprise was the number of readers who asked for subscriptions, even though no discounts were offered. *People* did it as a matter of convenience.

Still, circulation consisted almost entirely of newsstands sales. Everyone knew that, on newsstands, the cover pretty much sold the magazine—and everyone knew that the selection of cover subjects was far from an exact science. At Time Inc. this had always been guided by company tradition and individual instinct. But *People*'s editors, again breaking with precedent, put money into market research. To be sure, the magazine was feeling its own way, too, and sometimes it found that the researchers' pronouncements didn't hold up. For example, one piece of conventional wisdom held that music personalities didn't sell, and at first *People* used them sparingly. "Then we put Olivia Newton-John on the cover, and pow—it sold like mad," Stolley said. "After that, music became a staple for us." Later, Stolley would encapsulate his years of experience in his own rule for selecting covers:

"Young is better than old, pretty is better than ugly, television is better than music, music is better than movies, movies are better than sports, and anything is better than politics."

Three decades later, Stolley still believes his law is valid, but he adds that nothing sells better than the death of a celebrity (something we shall see later in the table of *People*'s top-selling issues).

In the four years 1976-80, *People*'s profits rose more than fourfold to $17 million before taxes, a level of profitability that matched *Sports Illustrated*. Circulation reached 2.5 million, and the magazine had already become part of the national consciousness.

a Formula For SUCCESS For THE "me DECADE"

Unarguably, *People* had become one of the greatest hits of the 1970s. Stolley believes there were four factors that drove its success:

"First, it was a great idea. Second, it had no competition. Third, there weren't any picture magazines around when *People* was born; *Life* and *Look* were both gone, leaving us a vacuum to fill. Finally, there was a sociological, psychological climate that worked for us. This was the real beginning of the Me Decade. We found out that people in the news were quite willing to talk to us about themselves. They'd talk about lots of personal things—their sex lives, their money, their families, religion. They'd talk about things that a few years earlier wouldn't even have been brought up. The counterpart of the Me Decade was the You Decade, and that

meant more and more curiosity about other people and their lives.

"A lot of American magazines, especially the newsmagazines, had gotten away from the personality story; they'd become more issue-oriented. We intended to reverse that idea with *People*. We'd do issues, of course, but through personalities. I think the formula has worked and certainly has made an impact. More and more magazines and newspapers, and even TV, are now leaning toward personality journalism."

Those who believed that *People* would soon exhaust the celebrity list were wrong. "A bigger problem than adding names to the cover list was getting rid of them," Stolley explained. However, he and his team wouldn't take long to realize that some subjects worked better on the cover than others.

For instance, Cher sold well; so did Taylor and TV talk show host Johnny Carson. On the other hand, sports commentator Howard Cosell, who very popular during the 1970s, and John Paul Getty, a multimi-llionaire, hadn't sold well despite being rich famous. What was the deal? Stolle discovered what he called "the X factor." Putting someone rich and famous on the cover wasn't enough "There had to be something about person that you wanted to know."

It was an accurate observation. T cover on Burt Reynolds and Dinah Shore sold well because their love affair, which the actor discussed, w unknown until then. Henry Kissinge then the White House national sec advisor, sold well, not because he a brilliant and renowned diplomat,

JOANNA AND JOHNNY CARSON
November 23, 1974

GREGG ALLMAN AND CHER
September 8, 1975

LIZ TAYLOR
March 15, 1976

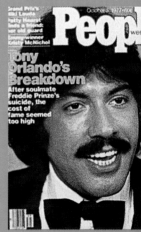

TONY ORLANDO
October 3, 1977

rather because he spoke about the beautiful women and actresses he was dating despite being a portly and unattractive man. Something similar happened with singer Tony Orlando, popular in the 1970s: his cover sold because he revealed his nervous breakdown, his slide into drug abuse, and how he'd managed to rise out of his emotional morass.

Altogether, in the ten months following that editorial insight, *People's* circulation increased by 25 percent to reach 1.25 million copies a week. It was at this point that *People*, barely eighteen months old, managed to climb out of the red and produce its first profits—quite a record, considering that it took *Time* three years and *Sports Illustrated* ten.

OLIVIA NEWTON-JOHN
July 31, 1978

LONI ANDERSON AND BURT REYNOLDS May 16, 1988

"THE X FACTOR."
To Stolley, having someone rich and famous on the cover isn't enough to sell a magazine. There has to be some mystique surrounding the newsmakers, something that people want to know about. What Stolley calls "the X factor" was clearly part of these covers, given the sales results. Most set records for the year.

THe VISUaL STYLe,
another element in the Formula

People would never have become such a success without the photographers it had along the way. Harry Benson, Mimi Cotter, Raeanne Rubinstein, Tony Costa, Dick Swanson, Ken Regan, Mark Sennet, Neal Preston, and Ben Weaver were much more than mere photographers. In time, they would become celebrities themselves.

All these photojournalists—along with photo editor Mary Dunn, who succeeded John Dominis in the post in 1978—were part of what is known as the "*People* visual style," a combination of shrewdness, humor, planning, and improvisation that still is its trademark.

Surely the best representative of this style is Harry Benson, who not only photographed celebrities—the Beatles, the Kennedys, presidents Richard Nixon and Gerald Ford, and thousands of personalities—but was a genius at getting them to do things they thought they would never do in front of a camera. Benson photographed famous people in their tubs, their beds, their swimming pools. Celebrities played for him, kissed each other, and stood on their heads if necessary, says Judy Kessler in *Inside People*, an excellent book about the creation and evolution of the magazine. An example of his great visual perspicacity: to protect the anonymity of a witness who had testified against the Mafia in court, Benson photographed him with a

stocking on his head. Another: to photograph Muhammad Ali outside the ring, he talked him into dressing as a slave (which his ancestors had been) for a special costumed celebrity issue on the occasion of the American bicentennial.

It was Mary Dunn who trained photographers in the use of their imagination to "produce" photos typical of the *People* style, which Stolley defined as "a sometimes elaborate setup that was not only refreshing and often funny, but which revealed something of the character and personality of the story subject." Some samples of that style:

Dick Swanson put on a bathing suit and jumped into the White House swimming pool to photograph then-president Gerald Ford in the water.
Harry Benson photographed Arthur Burns, the former director of the Federal Reserve, in his bath. He later talked Mark David Chapman, John Lennon's murderer, into posing with a finger pointing at his temple, as if he were shooting a gun.
Raeanne Rubinstein had actor Patrick Swayze put on the same costume he wore for the movie *Dirty Dancing* and dance in a field. In 1982 she also managed to get Dustin Hoffman to drop his pants to take "a different shot."
Steve Kagan sneaked into a concert by singer Lyle Lovett, who had just married Julia Roberts, to

"steal" shots of the couple onstage. When the film was confiscated, Time Inc. sued the actress's public relations firm and the MCA record company to gain access and publish the photos.
Mark Sennet got Robin Williams to jump on a tiny trampoline holding a rubber ducky.
Taro Yamasaki was the only one to get photos of the last days in the life of Ryan White, the hemophiliac teenager who died of AIDS, while his mother and musician Elton John stood a very painful vigil at his bedside.
Neal Preston shot a noted cover with actor Jack Nicholson holding a lit match in his mouth.
Oscar Abolafia accompanied Margaret Trudeau in 1977 when she left her husband, Canadian prime minister Pierre Trudeau, to tour the United States with the Rolling Stones. Afterward he escorted her

STYLISH SHOTS. A *People* photo must reveal something about the subject, such as Nicholson's fire or J-Lo's sensuality. Humor is another of its trademarks. With Roberts and Lovett there were problems about "stolen" images.

SLAVES AND LEADING MEN. Photographer Harry Benson had Muhammad Ali pose as a slave for an issue on the U.S. bicentennial. Pierce Brosnan was featured in a special edition.

THE SEXIEST MAN ALIVE 2001

Pierce Brosnan

Suave and sophisticated, caring and kind, he's also a total knockout—and a one-woman man. Who wouldn't bond with this breathtaking Irishman?

Last winter, Pierce Brosnan and a group of fellow nature lovers took to the choppy waters off the coast of Mexico's Baja California in inflatable boats for a close-up look at some gray whales whose birthing grounds they were trying to preserve. As the observers approached, the whales circled around, churning the water and spouting spray from their blowholes. "Most of the people looked a little pale and windblown," recalls environmentalist Ruben Aronin, a participant. "Then, as I glanced around, I realized that every one of us was covered with whale snot—everyone but Pierce. Not a hair was out of place. He just looked dashing, as always."

Cue the 007 theme music. It's Brosnan, Pierce Brosnan, acting very much like his alter ego, James Bond. Whether he's saving the world from evil in the movies or battling rocky seas in the environmental movement, Brosnan "has all the sensibilities of his character," says Bond coproducer Barbara Broccoli. "He also has the rugged good looks and the charm. He's manly."

Good deeds. Good looks. Charm. Manliness. Those happen to be the qualifications for this year's Sexiest Man Alive. Now is not the time for dangerous bad boys whom we wouldn't dare bring >>>

back to Quebec to make sure her husband didn't mistreat her.

In such cases, and in other photographic and editorial situations that entail divulging the ages, habits, vices, and intimate details of the lives of the rich and famous, *People* faces a difficult balancing act between the right to privacy and the public's right to know what's going on. "It is a complicated question for personality journalism," Stolley explained during a conference, "because every one of our stories is an invasion of somebody's privacy. Obviously we have a responsibility to the truth—in our case the most fragile of merchandise, the facts about another human being. But truth is sometimes an inadequate guide. I could tell you about the popular TV comedian who is a homosexual. The senator who drinks too much. The leading lady who has become a pill addict. This is truth, and we could undoubtedly find enough corroboration to print it and avoid libel or privacy suits. But here truth is cruel and reckless. Part of our responsibility at *People* magazine is to our story subjects themselves —not just to be truthful, but to be careful and tasteful and kind."

celebrities and tragedy

In 1980, with the issue devoted to Lennon, the magazine inaugurated the celebrity tribute editions it called Final Farewells.

The success of the Tony Orlando cover in October 1977, which featured his drug addiction, opened another door for *People*. Readers are powerfully attracted to a celebrity's troubles or tragedies, the ex-editor noted. That was the key to success also after Elvis Presley's death from a drug overdose in September 1977. But Stolley was slow to see that potential. Since "the King" died the day that week's issue was closing, Stolley decided to publish only a recent photo of the singer in the *Star Tracks* section. It was an omission for which Stolley had a hard time forgiving himself. "At that point we didn't realize that dead celebrities were going to be that hot," he said.

However, Stolley would soon learn the lesson. After Elvis's death, *People* did several covers on the singer, among them an interview with Linda Thompson, who had lived with him during his last five years. It would later publish a cover under the headline "Remembering Elvis" about the multimillion-dollar merchandising industry of imitators, fans, and swindlers. The first anniversary of his death was commemorated with "The Elvis Legend," and later the magazine got an exclusive interview with Priscilla, Presley's former wife and the mother of his only child. It was published on December 4, 1978, and still is one of the best sellers in *People's* history.

But Stolley's restoration to grace in the matter took place on December 8, 1980, when Mark David Chapman shot John Lennon in front of his New York home. Stolley pulled out all the stops to get the story into the issue. The magazine had plenty of photos and was offered hundreds more, Stolley said later, but the newsroom was trying to figure out how to cover the story without the cooperation of Yoko Ono and Sean Lennon. The answer soon came to Stolley: he remembered a long interview with Lennon that *Playboy* had just published, done three or four months before. It was written by journalist David Scheff, who had become so attuned to the singer and his family in the course of the work that he even decided to have a child himself when he saw the joy little Sean brought to the great British musician. Since Scheff was a freelancer and since *Playboy* allowed him to work with other media that weren't direct competitors, Stolley asked him to take the first plane from Los Angeles to New York, where *People* would postpone its closing and wait for him to write the cover story for that issue.

According to Judy Kessler's account, Scheff, unable to get a direct flight, put in a long and sleepless night of travel with several stops and arrived at the Time-Life Building in Rockefeller Center exhausted. When he got to the *People* newsroom, Stolley and

TRIBUTE TO LENNON. The issue showed intimate family photos, nostalgic moments with the Beatles, and even scenes of heartbreak in which his fans took center stage. Such tribute editions are collector's items to keep alive the memory of the idol.

By day and night, the mourners kept vigil

To tape-recorded Beatles songs, the crowd at Lennon's apartment house spoke its sorrow with wreaths and tears.

Burgheim met him in the hallway and, after a brief hello, stuck him in a private office with a typewriter. Every half hour or so, Stolley or Burgheim or someone would press an ear to the door, but did not hear typewriter keys tapping. Two hours went by and there wasn't a sound. The editors went in, Stolley remembers, and found Scheff frozen, his eyes fixed on the blank paper. Clearly, unless they did something soon, the magazine wouldn't come out. With only three hours left to write the whole cover story for the John Lennon tribute, Burgheim had to take over. As they pumped Scheff for information to produce the story, Burgheim said later, they realized he was not only worn out from the trip but overwhelmed by the news of his idol's murder. *People* managed to close the story by noon Wednesday, the tightest deadline in its publishing history. That issue not only broke the commandment against putting dead people on the cover, it also broke the sales record, with 2,644,000 copies, a figure that still stands as the fourth largest ever. It was another step in the unstoppable ascent of *People*, which in February 1978 had became the most successful magazine in the history of modern American journalism by climbing, in only three years, to ninth place in advertising revenue.

With that 1980 homage to Lennon, *People* discovered that readers were hungry for such parting tributes to their heroes. These became a full-fledged category known in house parlance as the Final Farewell. In 1993, however, while the death of actress Audrey Hepburn surely deserved a cover, her incredible life story demanded more. A special edition was produced in her name, the first of its kind in the history of *People*. Princess Diana in September of 1997 and Frank Sinatra in May-June of 1998 received the same distinction, as did the Tejano singer Selena in the spring of 1995.

There were other extraordinary cases. On June 24, 1987, actor Jackie Gleason died just as the tribute to dancer Fred Astaire was going to press. Honoring Gleason meant waiting until the magazine's next issue and publishing two stories about deaths back to back. The editors decided to take the risk: the cover with the tribute to Gleason came out on July 13, 1987, marking the first instance of publishing two consecutive Final Farewell covers.

celebrities in trouble

A variant of the Celebrities-and-Tragedy formula is Celebrities in Trouble, reserved for those who make the news when criminal or socially unacceptable behavior is uncovered. In the subcategory of sexual misdeeds is the case of Hugh Grant, the British actor who had a brilliant Hollywood career and a beautiful girlfriend, model Elizabeth Hurley, yet almost ruined it all by getting arrested for having sex with a prostitute, an event that made the cover of *People* on July 10, 1995. Or of film director and actor Woody Allen when he took up with Soon-Yi Previn, the adoptive daughter of his partner, actress Mia Farrow, all of whom were on the cover on August 31, 1992. Or of Senator Gary Hart when he cheated with the young beauty Donna Rice (cover of May 18, 1987), which ended his pursuit of the presidency of the United States. Or of President Bill Clinton, whom several women accused of sexual harassment (cover of February 9, 1998) while his wife, Hillary, stood firmly by his side.

Another, more gruesome, category within the tragic formula includes the case of O. J. Simpson, accused of murdering ex-wife Nicole Brown and her friend Ron Goldman (cover of July 4, 1994). Or the brutal killing of Jon Benet Ramsey, who was barely six (January 20, 1997). Or the hatred that exploded in Waco, Texas, where David Koresh opted to lead 85 of his Branch Davidian cult followers in committing suicide instead of surrendering to authorities (March 15, 1993). Or, two years later, the bombing of a government building in Oklahoma City by extremist Timothy McVeigh that killed 167 employees and children (May 15, 1995). This variant includes previously unknown people, such as Lorena Bobbitt (December 13, 1993), who gained notoriety for cutting off her husband John's penis, or teacher Mary Kay Letourneau (March 30, 1998), who lived an obsessive love affair with her sixth-grade student, had two children by him, and has been in prison ever since. "Famous people also can be infamous, and sometimes

IN THE EYE OF THE STORM. *People's* editors count on the class of story called Celebrities in Trouble, centered on scandals and infidelities, to round out the table of contents. It has featured subjects from actors to presidents.

DONNA RICE
1987

WOODY ALLEN
1992

ALI MACGRAW
1985

MICHAEL J. FOX
1998

MAGIC JOHNSON
1992

BREAST CANCER SURVIVORS
1998

CHRISTOPHER
REEVE 1997

CELEBS STAND UP AND FIGHT. Another approach at People focuses on medical issues, as famous people speak publicly about the private fights they face.

reality is stranger than fiction," says Landon Jones, who was managing editor for most of the 1990s.

A much more frequent variant among *People's* subjects is *Coping,* which presents a celebrity dealing with a difficult situation. When life gets tough, Lanny Jones explains, someone tough is needed to tell about it. That's what evokes the public's empathy, hope, and, at times, rage. That is precisely what happened with the 1974 cover devoted to First Lady Betty Ford, shortly after her doctor diagnosed her breast cancer. Instead of closing herself off and feeling sorry for herself, Betty Ford decided to come out publicly as a cancer patient. Almost twenty-five years later, on October 26, 1998, Betty Ford would pose again for the cover of *People* next to other survivors of the same disease—actress Diahann Carroll, chef Julia Child, skater Peggy Fleming, Supreme Court justice Sandra Day O'Connor—proving that there is hope after the initial diagnosis.

Actress Ali MacGraw and eight other women followed the same path, when they spoke about why they'd decided to have abortions and how they'd faced the emotional consequences, in the cover story of August 5, 1985. Judge Clarence Thomas and his wife Virginia told in *People's* cover story (November 11, 1991) how they managed to survive accusations of sexual harassment from his former assistant, Anita Hill, which almost cost him his U.S. Supreme Court post. Christopher Reeve and his wife Dana revealed on January 27, 1997, what they did to face the actor's paralysis after his riding accident. Actor Michael J. Fox disclosed for the first time in the cover story of December 7, 1998, his secret battle with Parkinsonism. It's unusual for a celebrity to take the initiative in speaking about a problem, said *People's* Los Angeles bureau chief, Jack Kelley. But many celebrities want the world to know that they're facing their problem or disease with courage and want to reach out to others who face something similar.

O.J. SIMPSON
1994

BILL CLINTON
1998

LORENA BOBBITT
1993

THe seesaw OF Love

GWYNETH & BRAD
1-13-97

GWYNETH & BRAD
6-30-97

BRUCE & DEMI
11-12-90

BRUCE & DEMI
7-13-98

PAUL & LINDA
4-21-75

LINDA & PAUL
5-4-98

JULIA & LYLE
7-12-93

JULIA & BENJAMIN
11-1-99

The formula for success wouldn't be complete without what *People* calls the Seesaw of Love, which is made up not only of romances, engagements, and weddings but also of breakups, falling-outs, separations, divorces, or the end of a partnership when one of the couple dies. While many publications chase after news the week or month it happens, Richard Stolley explains, *People* keeps up with all the cycles of love, its ending, and the birth of new relationships in the lives of the rich and famous. Take the case of Gwyneth Paltrow and Brad Pitt, whose romance made the magazine's cover under the headline "Engaged" on January 13, 1997, and returned there on June 30 when they announced they'd broken it off. Something similar happened with actress Julia Roberts and country music star Lyle Lovett, whose marriage made *People's* cover on July 12, 1993, but was over within the year; Roberts returned to the cover six years later with her then current beau, Benjamin Bratt.

The magazine did the same with actors Demi Moore and Bruce Willis, minimizing their marital woes in the cover story "Hollywood's Hottest Couple" on November 12, 1990, but announcing their "sudden split" on July 13, 1998. In the case of British rock star Mick Jagger and his second wife, model Jerry Hall, the separation took a while. *People* covered that story for seventeen years. The first announcement of a possible rupture made the cover on November 22, 1982, but the divorce took place on February 1, 1999; in the meantime the couple had four children, got married in Bali, and survived all but the last of Jagger's infidelities. *People* also covered the death that ended an intense love affair when Linda McCartney succumbed to cancer at fifty-six in May of 1998, with a cover devoted to the couple under the headline "Paul's Tragic Loss." They had first been on the cover on April 21, 1975. A *People* memo to advertisers explained its editorial philosophy by saying that, while love may or may not survive divorce or death, the magazine's mission is to follow it, whatever the case.

A month after its fifth birthday, *People* faced for the first time the challenge of a hot story without

THE CYCLES OF LOVE. *People* follows every stage in a couple's relationship, as it begins, unfolds, ends, or gives way to another. And the covers reflect all of those moments.

HARD NEWS. Cover and story on the nuclear accident at Three Mile Island in 1979. *People* aptly paired the event with the movie *The China Syndrome*, starring Jane Fonda and Michael Douglas.

famous people: the nuclear accident at Three Mile Island in April of 1979.

To his surprise, Richard Stolley discovered that no journalist wanted to cover the story for fear of being killed or contaminated by radiation. The only ones who accepted were reporter Rich Rein and photographer Michael Abramson. Later the magazine would send two women, Andrea Powyena and Judy Gurovitz, to the nuclear site. Their mission was to find and photograph human interest stories and stay away as much as possible from the strictly political and technological angles. Stolley's orders were to look for the people behind the story and tell it through them. Soon they would turn up "*People's* heroes": a couple who argued over whether to leave their home; volunteers who put themselves at risk to patrol the streets with Geiger counters to alert the community to danger; a tourist who made a detour to see the nuclear plant and be photographed there with his wife "before it disappeared." Rein took unending ribbing because most people involved in the story believed that *People* was interested only in celebrities. "The fact that we

covered ordinary people in extraordinary circumstances had not yet reached the readers, basically because the magazine was too young," the journalist said. The joking could be harsh. A plant manager asked Rein if *People* hadn't considered sending a raft full of celebrities down the Susquehanna so as to photograph them passing under the polluted nuclear plant. But *People* wasn't deterred. It ran a cover story headlined "A Disaster Movie Comes True," juxtaposing the nuclear reality at Three Mile Island with the release that very week of a —film with an eerily similar premise— *The China Syndrome*, starring Jane Fonda and Michael Douglas. *People* had taken a step to earn respect from those who believed that the magazine covered only celebrities and trivia.

The magazine's writing style was also maturing and its editorial formula growing stronger. Many *People* writers and editors recognize today that the magazine could not have become what it is without Dick Burgheim, Richard Stolley's right-hand man. Burgheim posted on the bulletin board a list of more than two hundred synonyms of the verb "say"

so reporters wouldn't repeat it in their stories. Moreover, during his tenure the magazine brought into common usage terms that didn't exist in the dictionary, such as "megabucks" and "altar-shy" and "bicoastal." Most important, Burgheim and Stolley raised to unprecedented levels *People's* painstaking fact-checking process. They could not run the risk of falling into the rumor and speculation of the tabloids. Thus, when the *Wall Street Journal* published a front-page story in 1981 that praised the magazine's fact-checking—in which $800,000 a year was invested— *People's* journalistic credibility was certified. "We proved," said Stolley, "that there was no need to speculate or stoop to gossip to do good personality journalism."

People and Princess Diana

Something happened in 1981 that would have great impact on *People* magazine and on the English monarchy, wrote Judy Kessler in her book *Inside People*. "Prince Charles finally found his royal bride. Luckily for *People*, she was Lady Diana Spencer, who would, by the end of the magazine's first twenty years, not only appear on its cover more than any other person in the world but also would be singularly responsible for an estimated seven million dollars in profits over the next twelve years." Indeed, from its first cover on the subject, headlined "Prince Charles Finally Finds His Royal Bride: A Shy Teacher Named Diana Spencer," the magazine would follow every step of her life from her engagement and wedding and children to her sudden and tragic death.

Recognizing that Lady Diana was a potential source of interest for *People,* Stolley set out to get "everything" about the royal couple and their lives. First, the London bureau was requested to clip and file daily every British and foreign newspaper and magazine with stories about them. Then, regular contact was maintained with Charles's physiotherapist, the princess's astrologer,

her hairdresser, her fashion designers, her advisors and chauffeurs. In 1981 and 1982 alone, Diana would be featured on the cover five times; she sold 11,786,000 copies.

The second story on Lady Diana came out in the issue of June 22, 1981, six weeks before the royal wedding. Headlined "A sneak preview of her Big Day: the wedding gowns (all 6 of them!), the gifts, guests and the royal pain of planning it all," it told of the invitations, the gift registry, the bridal couple's attendants, the cathedral where they would be married, the archbishop who would hear their vows, the dressmakers, the honeymoon plans. The issue sold 2,291,000 copies.

As the ceremony was scheduled for midweek, just when the issue of August 3 was due to appear, the editors took care to produce another elaborate story, headlined "Good Show" and timed to hit the streets that very day. True to its name, *People* offered an excellent behind-the-scenes look that focused on the event's supporting cast—the baker of the wedding cake, the driver of the glass coach, the choir director, the florist, the cathedral's cleaning crew,

and even the craftsman who built the lovebirds' king-size bed. Although the issue had no photos of the wedding itself, it sold more than 2.5 million copies. With the prince and princess of Wales, *People* had become a moneymaking machine.

Less than four months later, on November 23, another cover announced the princess's pregnancy, selling more than 2 million copies. For the baby's birth, the magazine designed two covers: a pink one in case it was a girl and a blue one for a boy. Prince William arrived in the world on July 5, 1982, just in time for *People's* closing of its next issue, which ended up selling 2,579,000 copies. Then came William's christening, the birth of Prince Harry on October 1, 1984, the princess's divorce, and finally her death. The coverage of the last event was unprecedented in the history of magazines. For the first time ever, *People's* cover bore no caption or headline—just the logo and the date and a vibrant portrait of the late princess. The high-impact issue sold 2,993,000 copies and still is the magazine's second best seller.

RECORD WOMAN.
Starting in March 1981, Diana Spencer's face appeared on the cover 52 times and her name 81 times more. The cover on her death was the only one in the history of People that bore no headline, and it was the second top seller.

Soon after he took over as *People's* editor, Landon Jones began to feel the magazine could use some design changes. An update had been done by Courtney Brown for Jones's predecessor James R. Gaines, but Lanny thought further changes were needed. To do the job, he hired Mary K. Baumann, former art director of the revived *Life* (1978), *Geo* magazine (1980), and the magazine development department of *Time Inc.* (1985). Baumann had successfully redesigned *Money* magazine when Jones was its editor.

Although the photos in *People* were not yet in color, Baumann explained, the magazine already used a red stripe with some section headings and red underlining with others, which was not only inconsistent but jumbled. The designer moved each section heading into a corner field of white space and did away with the red. She also gave greater emphasis to the magazine's visual punctuation and geography: until then, she said, it was never clear when one story ended and another started. Another change was no longer using white space to frame photos, particularly full-page or double-page photos, but rather bleeding them. This drew readers into the story instead of setting it off, she said, and helped carry them from one page to the next without interruption.

For the cover, Baumann suggested a large central image, and on the left a vertical strip of at least three minicovers, so that readers could know more about the editorial content. Another fundamental change was to color the logo. Although the editors loved the cover innovations, Baumann said, most of them were never carried out. The inside changes, however, were adopted starting on April 29, 1991, to wide approval, and remained in force for three years.

COVERS. The proposals by designer Mary Baumann included coloring the logo and stacking three additional photos to increase story offerings. The cover changes were well received, but they didn't see the light of day.

SECTION TITLES BEFORE. The section title was set on a colored ground and/or underlined in red, and the byline followed it.

SECTION TITLES AFTER. A new typeface and a cleaner and clearer style arrived, the colored ground and red underlining departed, and the byline was moved beneath the section title. This was now preceded by a small box, a design element.

CLEAR VISUAL IMAGE. Designer Mary K. Baumann changed the page's geography. Headlines were made more prominent and the columns of text pulled together, avoiding interruption by other elements.

From Sudden news to Story Series

In April of 1982, Stolley left *People* to take over from Phil Kunhardt as managing editor of the new version of *Life*. Stolley was succeeded by Patricia Ryan, who at age thirty-nine became the first woman to edit a Time Inc. magazine. Her greatest contribution was to counter criticism that the magazine seemed to be written by a single person. Ryan recruited great writers, offering a variety of styles that made the stories more interesting and varied. The new editor also improved editorial salaries and schedules.

However, Ryan openly disagreed with the other top editors on the direction the magazine should take. While she wanted to focus on social themes, such as working women, anorexia, abortion, or diet and exercise as a path to social acceptance, the rest of the management team favored a greater emphasis on news, without losing sight of celebrities. Ryan, for her part, hated movie stars. Once she even rejected an exclusive story about Mick Jagger and Jerry Hall smoking marijuana on vacation, arguing that it had all been set up by the couple to make money and generate publicity for themselves.

Besides, Ryan had started her job at the magazine on the wrong foot. She was enjoying her first vacation after her appointment when she learned of the death of Princess Grace of Monaco. It was September 14, 1982. Grace had died after a car accident while driving on the twisting roads above Monaco with her daughter Stephanie (it was later rumored that it was seventeen-year-old Stephanie who was driving). Landon Jones was filling in for Ryan when the bombshell landed on his desk. He decided right away that this was his next cover. Ryan disagreed and favored staying with the planned cover on Britain's Prince Andrew. Lanny decided to ignore her and follow his journalistic instinct. He pulled several stories that had already closed and set aside eleven pages for Grace's death, which he filled with a lot of photos and a little text. The cover image was the work of Harry Benson, who had photographed the princess a few months earlier with her children in Monaco. Lanny had to delay the closing, running the risk that the magazine wouldn't be printed on schedule for distribution by the fleet of waiting trucks, which could mean a

heavy monetary loss even if the issue sold well. But the risk paid off. *People* was able to put the issue to bed on Wednesday morning, one of its latest closings ever. The tribute to Princess Grace became the magazine's fifth top-selling issue, with 2,623,000 copies sold at the newsstands—and confirmed Dick Stolley's belief that nothing sells better than a celebrity's death.

Ryan was on vacation again in the summer of 1983 when a Soviet missile downed a commercial airliner, Korean Air Lines flight 007, killing 269 passengers and crew members. This time, the bombshell fell on the desk of Jim Gaines, since Landon Jones was also on vacation. Gaines was a talented journalist who'd started at the *Saturday Review,* gone on to *Newsweek* as a national politics writer, and then climbed the ladder at *People* to become assistant managing editor. As might be expected, Ryan didn't think the story was right for *People.* Gaines took a totally opposite view: he thought it was not only a great story but perfect for the cover. Internal differences intensified when the publisher, Dick Durrell, told Gaines he'd be nuts to pursue the idea.

The newsroom was also divided, because the story broke every single Dick Stolley cover commandment, particularly the notion that the cover personality should be known to 80 percent of readers.

Perhaps that is why Stolley choked on his lunch at *Life* magazine the day Gaines told him what he planned to do. But when he listened to the editor's arguments, Stolley changed his mind. When a staffer came up with the perfect headline for the cover, "Getting Away with Murder," Gaines had no doubt that this was the way to go: he assigned all available journalists in New York, Atlanta, Washington, Detroit, Philadelphia, and Tokyo to uncover the stories behind the disaster. Gaines produced a touching piece without celebrities but with brilliant writing that started right on the cover (along with a photo of the widow and children of one of the victims). The inside pages included chilling stories: a passenger who had switched his flight to the fateful 007 to spend more time with his children in Korea before a business trip; a woman who was booked on another flight and had to change to KAL 007

because she'd left her passport at home; U.S. Congressman Lawrence McDonald, who had missed a connection owing to bad weather and chose to spend another night in New York before heading for Korea. This was one of the few times that *People* opted for a cover story that didn't involve a celebrity. But once again it hit the mark: the issue was among the top twenty sellers in the magazine's history.

Gaines applied the same thinking in February of 1987 upon learning that Mark David Chapman, John Lennon's killer, had decided to reject the insanity-based plea bargain arranged by his own lawyer and plead guilty instead. Gaines set out to interview the murderer in prison and round it off with interviews with relatives, friends, and co-workers. The result was a three-part *People* series that put together a brilliant journalistic jigsaw puzzle of the killer. The success of the series helped legitimize the kind of celebrity journalism that had driven *People,* and it catapulted Gaines into the post of managing editor in 1987 as successor to Pat Ryan, who was transferred to the same position at *Life.*

FROM PAID COVERAGE TO SPINOFFS

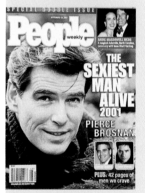

Under Gaines, coverage of the news through celebrities alternated with stories focusing on ordinary people forced to live in extraordinary situations. So AIDS was approached through Rock Hudson, the Hollywood star killed by the disease, but also through a small-town boy, Ryan White, who'd received contaminated blood transfusions and whose case was both educational and inspirational. During Gaines's editorship, the impossible was accomplished: photographing Michael Jackson in Tokyo for the cover and getting from him a poem, complete with misspellings, that read in part: "I was sent forth, for the world for the children. But have mercy, for I've been bleeding a long time now."

Gaines's reign had a dark side: the payment of large amounts of money to celebrities for exclusive reports in their own words about scandals—something that violated the *People* command-ments not to pay interviewees for stories and not to give them advance access to reportage or a say in the selection of photos. However, the magazine opted to pay Lynn Armandt to tell about the affair between her friend, model Donna Rice, and presidential candidate Gary Hart, as well as writers Kitty Kelley and Judith Campbell Exner to reveal details of the intimate relationship the latter had with President John Kennedy. *People* also opted to pay for exclusive photo access to the Liz Taylor-Larry Fortensky wedding

in 1991, although that payment went not to the actress but directly to amfAR, the charitable organization led by Liz that raises funds for AIDS research.

When the company decided to offer Landon Jones the job as Jim Gaines's successor, it could not have made a better choice. Jones had been a writer at the magazine right from its launch and had interrupted his ascent only to write a book and to run *Money,* another Time Inc. magazine, for five years. When he returned to *People* as editor, he found a gold mine: one in every ten Americans read his magazine.

With Lanny Jones at the helm, *People* used color for the first time and started publishing more stories tied to the news. During his tenure, the magazine stopped paying celebrities for stories, and the Los Angeles bureau hired more than fifteen reporters to improve the magazine's editorial quality. This era also saw the birth of spinoffs—special color issues published three or four times a year, long before the magazine started using color regularly—which not only strengthened the *People* name but also brought the company huge profits. Among them:

The Sexiest Man Alive. The name apparently emerged when photo editor Mary Dunn found a powerful photo of actor Mel Gibson for which there was no caption or story. She suggested publishing the photo just as it was,

under that headline, a suggestion that would evolve first into a story devoted to other "hunks" and later into an annual special issue. Some who later bore the title were John F. Kennedy Jr., Sean Connery, Tom Cruise, Harry Hamlin, Mark Harmon, and Brad Pitt.

The 50 Most Beautiful People. These special issues, the idea of *People* editor Susan Toepfer, were first published in 1990.

The Worst and Best Dressed. Having started out as cover stories in 1980, these too, with time, became successful special issues.

The 25 Most Intriguing People. This likewise originated as a cover story, in 1974, and then became a special issue. When Stolley was asked why twenty-five, he replied that ten were not enough: the magazine had a lot of pages to fill.

Celebrity Weddings. First published in 1990, a wedding issue comes out when events justify it—that is, when several celebrities get married in the same year or within a season.

Jones also led the *People Almanac* project, a celebrity encyclopedia with biographical information and anecdotes about the stars. Currently sold as a

book, it comes out annually, with more pages each year. On the downside, Jones experienced the magazine's worst times, when celebrities refused to cooperate unless money was exchanged and a story on *People's* cover was guaranteed. Jones frequently managed to sidestep these demands, using the writearound technique (see page 398).

On the plus side, Jones expanded the magazine's name when he came up with *Teen People,* which started making money about a year and a half after it hit the streets, something unusual in the magazine business; *People en Español* for Hispanic audiences, which now has a circulation of about 450,000 and contains only about 40 percent translated material from the parent magazine; and *Who Weekly,* the Australian edition of the magazine, which is very successful and combines personalities from the United States edition with those unique to Australia.

Jones was succeeded by Carol Wallace, who made her mark with an emphasis on crime stories. Martha Nelson, former editor of *In Style,* another Time Inc. monthly, then assumed the post with very good results.

WEDDING WITH A PRICE.
People has paid its interviewees more than once to get exclusives, such as Liz Taylor's 1991 wedding to Larry Fortensky. That time, though, the money went to an organization to fight AIDS, presided over by the actress.

WHEN FAMOUS PEOPLE SAY no

The technique of the "writearound," the formula used by the magazine when celebrities refuse to grant interviews. The required elements of *People's* covers.

Richard B. Stolley and Landon Jones, both former *People* editors, concede there was no set editorial formula for the cover to begin with; the principles developed along the way. There was one requirement, though, that all covers had to meet from the start: "celebrities who make or are news."

In any case, both say that show business editor Dick Burgheim was one of the main architects of the process of cover selection and formulation. Since Burgheim belonged to the show business world that many of the cover choices came from (because they were so popular), he started suggesting celebrity names from TV shows such as *Mork and Mindy, Laverne and Shirley,* or *Charlie's Angels.* A good move by Burgheim in 1975 was putting Telly Savalas, the star of the TV series *Kojak,* on the cover. This issue sold so well that, for the first time, *People* reached the goal of a million copies in guaranteed circulation for advertisers.

Although one of the few accepted premises from the beginning was that the magazine would devote half its pages to celebrities and half to ordinary people in extraordinary circumstances, in time it was established that, for an issue to sell well, the cover subject had to be known to 80 percent of the public. And not only that: the cover photos had to show the personalities wearing the same uniform or clothes their TV characters usually wore. Once, Stolley says, Alan Alda appeared on the cover in a jacket and tie and the issue sold poorly because people didn't recognize him as the army surgeon from the *M*A*S*H* TV series who made them laugh.

In addition, the editors soon realized that women worked better than men on the cover, and straight men better than gay men. Covers featuring people having affairs, such as film director Peter Bogdanovich and Cybill Shepherd, are riskier than those with settled married couples, Stolley says. Successful people have always sold well, but the editors soon noticed that "losers" also did well on the newsstand as long as the magazine explained their problems and tragedies and described how they overcame them, so that the story became an inspirational one. In *People* jargon, these stories—for instance, Tony Orlando talking about his depression, Carol Burnett speaking openly about her daughter's drug addiction, or Kelly McGillis telling how she'd been kidnapped and raped—were known as OPP: Other People's Problems.

PLUS:
MIRACLE SURVIVORS
A mom and her three kids come through a plane crash

Wills, Charles & Camilla: On the town together

FEBRUARY 26, 2001

People
weekly

Tom and Nicole square off
WHAT'S AT STAKE

The kids' futures

A $250 million fortune

Their reputations

$2.99

CANADA $3.99

0 72440 10227 9

09>

www.people.com (AOL Keyword: People)

WHEN THEY WON'T TALK. Cover on the separation of Kidman and Cruise. Neither would talk, so the magazine did exhaustive digging and interviewed everyone close to the couple—that is, it did a "writearound" and reported on them without their cooperation. This journalism formula was established by *People*.

cover story commandments

In 1980 Stolley came up with another commandment when he did the cover story on the death of John Lennon. The editors had never dared to put dead people on the cover, thinking that readers would consider this depressing and morbid and the issues wouldn't sell. But in the case of Lennon, Stolley explains, the subject was so newsworthy that he decided to take the plunge. The risk paid off: the issue sold more than 2 million copies and still occupies fourth position among the magazine's all-time best sellers (after the deaths of Princess Diana and John F. Kennedy Jr.). Stolley decided that his well-known Law of Covers– "Young is better than old, pretty is better than ugly, television is better than music, music is better than movies, movies are better than sports, and anything is better than politics"–needed an addendum: "…but nothing is better than a dead celebrity."

When selecting a story or a cover, *People* editors had to answer a series of questions. With time, the answers to some of them delineated the editorial commandments that are currently in effect.

When. The cover subject must not only be known to most readers but must also be newsworthy, for whatever reason, the week the magazine comes out–no sooner, no later. For instance, Stolley now concedes that, the first cover on Mia Farrow in March of 1974 was a bad choice because the movie starring the actress, *The Great Gatsby,* didn't actually premiere the week the magazine came out but later.

What. In general, the editors look for a certain balance among stories, so that the people featured are not all business people, or movie stars, or unknowns. The ideal magazine, says Landon Jones, is a mix of the predictable and the unexpected.

How. A key approach is to find the "home take," a *People* innovation that would become a model for other domestic and foreign magazines. The home take, says Landon Jones, is much more than just going into celebrities' homes. It's a technique that affords the magazine an intimacy and a unique access to the personality of the sort that close friends and family have.

First of all, the subject of a cover photo should have visual contact with the reader–in other words, should look at the camera. In addition, this photo and the others that accompany the story should show the "ambiance" or surroundings in which the person lives. There should be at least two changes of clothing to avoid giving the impression that the reporters spent little time there. In earlier days the celebrities were photographed by the pool, in the garden, at the front door, and in the living room. But little by little they've started to be shown in the dining room,

the kitchen, the bathroom, the bedroom. A constant factor in this type of shoot is a combination of planning and improvisation. Celebrities are prepped, Jones says, but generally the photos aren't set up. One day, photographer Harry Benson went to photograph actress Brooke Shields and found her wearing a Band-Aid on her ankle. Instead of asking her to take it off, he left it on and the magazine published a photo of her legs like that because the editors thought it made her look more natural, more flesh-and-blood.

Another crucial device that the editors learned with time and experience is a touch of humor in the photos. Sometimes it happens by chance and the photographer seizes it; other times it is deliberately created. In addition to the photos, Stolley explains, *People's* journalists are supposed to find out about the celebrity's wife or husband, the neighborhood where they live, their lifestyle, favorite pastimes, meaningful objects or accoutrements from their past or present, the books they read, the music they listen to, the cars they like, the paintings or decorations they hang on their walls—in short, everything.

People's Ten Best Sellers

DATE	COVER	COPIES SOLD
24 Sept 01	Terrorist Attack on the USA	4,100,000
22 Sept 97	Farewell to Princess Diana	2,997,000
2 Aug 99	Death of John F. Kennedy Jr.	2,800,000
22 Dec 80	Death of John Lennon	2,644,000
27 Sept 82	Death of Princess Grace	2,623,000
5 Mar 79	Readers' Five-Year Favorites	2,593,000
4 Aug 86	Famous Weddings	2,590,000
5 July 82	Princess Diana's First Son	2,579,000
3 Aug 81	Wedding of Diana and Charles	2,551,000
31 July 78	Olivia Newton-John	2,508,000

SOURCE: *PEOPLE* MAGAZINE 2002

AT HOME.

People has created a whole technique of photographing celebrities at home. The main thing is showing no conventional scenes. Michael Douglas was one of the first subjects of a family feature.

when celebrities
Get mad

Another key is making sure that a chosen celebrity always has some mystery to unveil. Stolley remembers that during his tenure, the magazine did three covers on TV actress Mary Tyler Moore (who also starred in the film *Ordinary People*, directed by Robert Redford). Though she was well known to readers and successful in everything she did, none of the covers sold well. With time, he realized that Moore had said it all in previous interviews and that there were no secrets left in her life. From then on, the editors made sure to look at that crucial factor in celebrity coverage.

Another key is to avoid approaching issues directly but to look instead for the people behind them. For instance, during the Watergate era, the magazine offered stories about many of the key players in the scandal, such as Judge John Sirica, who presided at the trials; Martha Mitchell, wife of the indicted attorney general; "plumber" E. Howard

Hunt; and presidential counsel and whistle-blower John Dean. Years later, on the occasion of the movie *All the President's Men,* the magazine also wrote a story about the journalists who had investigated the Watergate case for the *Washington Post*, Bob Woodward and Carl Bernstein. Likewise, while *People* didn't ignore AIDS, its coverage focused on the deaths of gay actor Rock Hudson, and of Ryan White, the hemophiliac teenager who received tainted blood transfusions. Sometimes, Stolley points out, two similar stories about the same subject help clarify each other.

An interesting variant, which often yields a cover, is to tackle events in which celebrities are the newsmakers. Such was the case with the "Hollywood Blackout" story, which spotlighted the shortage of black actors at the Oscar awards ceremony; only three of the 250 nominees were black that year. To Landon Jones this was an ideal

situation, a case of pure journalism in which celebrities were the central characters.

The tone of the story must not pass judgment on the interviewee. An internal memo from *People's* top editors instructed its journalists not to sound either too shocked or too enthused by what celebrities said or did, but rather to try to portray what they saw without falling into disdain or criticism. Thus there is no speculation or gossip in *People.* All published quotes are accurate and have been corroborated. And all the facts are meticulously verified by fact-checkers. Those interviewed may not like what is said about them, Jones says, but the information is always truthful and the magazine can back it up. A disputed case was an interview with actor Robin Williams, who was separated from his wife Valerie Velardi and also very much in love with Marsha Garcés, his son's former nanny, whom he would marry a year later. Williams complained that the story seemed to blame Garcés for the breakup of the marriage, which wasn't true. For five years Williams conducted a boycott of *People* among his friends and people in the industry to such a degree that the magazine had to work hard to repair its reputation in Hollywood.

At other times *People* broached subjects that were unexpected to its readers, such as its extensive coverage of the San Francisco earthquake and of the Gulf War, to which it sent its journalistic troops along with the American military. The pattern needs to be broken every once in a while, Jones points out. What's important is to always meet the challenge. And as challenges go, there probably isn't any greater one for the magazine than having to resort to a writearound.

COVER. Under the headline "Public Triumph, Private Anguish," the magazine told on February 22, 1988, about Robin Williams's separation from his wife Valerie.

BOYCOTT. The same story said that Williams had fallen in love with his son's nanny, Marsha Garcés. The actor was irate, since this made it seem she was to blame for his marriage breakup, and he started a boycott of the magazine in Hollywood. It was a terrible blow to *People*'s prestige.

julia Roberts

The ever-Pretty Woman is Hollywood's runaway hitmaker

Knock knock. Who's there? Madame. Madame who? M'dam foot's caught in the door!

Not funny? Well, it cracked up 9-year-old Scotty Leavenworth when he heard the joke from Julia Roberts, who plays the young actor's mother in her next film *Erin Brockovich*. "She's the nicest movie mom I've ever met," says Scotty. "She's very, extremely nice." He's not the only one who's just wild about Julia. Solidifying her status as America's most likeable—and bankable—movie actress, Roberts, 32, racked up two more blockbuster romantic comedies in 1999: the Hugh Grant cuddlefest *Notting Hill* (in which she was typecast as a famous screen queen) and *Runaway Bride*, which reunited her with her *Pretty Woman* romeo Richard Gere. Those films took in nearly $270 million combined at the box office, helping Roberts rake in $20 million—unprecedented for an actress—for playing a feisty legal secretary battling environmental pollution in the drama *Erin Brockovich*, due in March. "It's like watching Michael Jordan drive the lane," says the film's director Steven Soderbergh of Julia's performance. "She's at her absolute peak as an artist." Things are humming along on the personal front as well, where former *Law & Order* hunk Benjamin Bratt, 36, has been widening her megawatt smile since they hooked up in 1997. While Roberts was at work on *Erin* and Bratt was filming *The Next Best Thing* in Los Angeles, she playfully called him on the day he shot his love scene with costar Madonna. "She would report back to us after she quizzed him," says Erin costar Marg Helgenberger with a laugh. "'So, was it a good kiss? And did you like it? And how long was the kiss?' She talked about him all the time. They've got a real good thing going on." Roberts topped off her banner year by taking a decidedly nonstar trip to Mongolia, to film a PBS documentary on wild horses. "She went for a week with no bath or shower, no proper toilet," says her director Nigel Cole, "and yet she never complained." This, then, is why we like her: Roberts is the goddess-next-door. Oh, yeah, and that corny sense of humor. "She makes up a lot of good jokes," says young Scotty. "And she always gave me wedgies."

Photograph by Sante D'Orazio/Corbis Outline

JULIA ROBERTS. *People* has approached her frequently. She has agreed to do photo shoots sometimes, and declined at other times. Once, the magazine had to interview her mother in Atlanta to complete the story.

THE MOST SOUGHT-AFTER CELEBRITY. During the magazine's first twenty years, Jackie Kennedy Onassis was featured on the cover eleven times, even though she never granted an interview. The "writearound" technique was a must with her.

WRITING AROUND THE SUBJECT

A celebrity may cooperate with all requests from a magazine, some of them, or none. In *People's* case the challenge is even greater, since one of its sacred commandments is that if there is no home access, no intimacy, not even an interview, then there's no story.

So, what does a magazine that centers on celebrities—and has traditionally had access to them whenever it wanted—do when they refuse, partially or completely, to cooperate? That is a dilemma *People* has had to face right from the first issue and cover story, when actress Mia Farrow, star of the movie *The Great Gatsby*, couldn't or wouldn't deal with the magazine. Or when Tatum O'Neal, who had a leading role in the movie *Paper Moon* along with her father, actor Ryan O'Neal, asked the magazine to interview him instead of her for the eighth issue. The partial or total refusals happened not suddenly but gradually, says Landon Jones, who started out as a *People* writer and went on to become assistant editor and then, from 1989 to 1997, editor. Celebrities started to plead fear of robbery or kidnapping as the reason for not letting the magazine show their homes. Later they would offer to be photographed in restaurants or public places or their offices, often limiting the interview to their careers or professions and expressly asking the magazine not to touch on their private lives. Over time, Jones says, celebrities tried to grant interviews on condition they be guaranteed a cover story, a tradeoff that *People* has never accepted because it goes against its editorial policy.

To make matters worse, competing magazines began to fight over the same celebrities, with some editors agreeing to pay for interviews or guarantee covers to gain access to stars' homes and private lives. Often, Jones says, celebrities would demand a certain journalist or photographer of their choice, which blurred to an unacceptable degree the line between editorial principles and the journalistic goal of getting the story.

Since *People* opted not to give in to that type of pressure, the magazine seemed to be between a rock and a hard place: on the one hand, it needed access to the rich and famous, but on the other, it wasn't willing to break a sacred rule. How to solve the dilemma? the editors asked themselves. The answer was writearounds. It wasn't a new technique, says Jones; it had been used since the magazine was created, to compensate for a celebrity's lack of cooperation, or to write obituaries. When a celebrity died and could no longer grant interviews, *People* interviewed friends, relatives, co-workers, or schoolmates to build a mosaic of the life of the deceased. In this case, all they did was give a new dimension and a new use to an old technique.

THE MOST WRITTEN-AROUND.
Another factor accelerated the use of this investigative and writing technique. From the mid-1970s to the early 1990s, celebrities still needed magazines to make themselves known to the public and build their fame. Thus they would routinely accede to the demands of the publications that sought them out, asking for interviews and entry into their homes and private lives. However, with time and the advent of cable television and the Internet, following the end of the studios' exclusive control over their stars, celebrities reached a godlike status and didn't need magazines to showcase them.

Instead of celebrities seeking out magazines, magazines went after celebrities to increase their circulation, Landon Jones explains. It was then that celebrities adopted a more selective attitude and became more reluctant to open their doors and their hearts to magazines. The reversal of their openness coincided with a sociological trend, as the so-called Me Decade, which had eliminated the traditional reticence of the rich and famous to show their homes and belongings, gave way to an Us Decade that demanded moderation, modesty, and keeping a low profile.

Jacqueline Kennedy Onassis was one of the celebrities who made *People* resort to the writearound technique most often. During the magazine's first two decades, Jackie was the subject of eleven cover stories, although she never agreed to be interviewed. In 1983 *People* also published a cover under the headline "The Kennedys: 20 Years Later" that examined the lives of Caroline and John-John and provided an update two decades after their father's death.

Another case involved actress Julia Roberts. In 1990 her movie *Pretty Woman* had catapulted her onto magazine covers and marquees around the world. When Roberts declined to work with *People*, the magazine decided to work around her, interviewing her mother, Betty Motes, in Atlanta, who offered family albums; director Joel Schumacher, who'd worked with her in the movie *Flatliners*; Robert Harling, the *Steel Magnolias* scriptwriter; Peter Masterson, who'd given her one of her first breaks in the business; Garry Marshall, director of *Pretty Woman*; and Joseph Ruben, director of *Sleeping with the Enemy*. The story turned out as well as if she'd participated: that cover was one of the best-selling issues of the year.

WRITING ABOUT a CELEBRITY

The journalists assigned to each cover story must remember and respect the parameters of the *People* formula. This is how editor Roger Wolmuth describes what they are generally asked to keep in mind:

Physical description, not only of the personalities but of their surroundings. Tell us what's hanging on the walls in the interviewee's living room, what smells are coming from the kitchen, how strongly the wind is blowing off the lake the house overlooks. That is the type of information that can help a writer create an atmosphere, set the scene, and even pinpoint something distinctive about the personality being profiled.

Scenes. Let us see people doing things, not just saying them. The best scenes help paint profiles so that readers can get an image of the person. They show something instead of telling it.

Biography. Always provide the date and place of birth of every person interviewed, and other milestones in their lives or careers.

Quotes. The complete transcript of an interview is nowhere near as useful as three juicy quotes that are also relevant and accurate. Include a description of the speaker's delivery: we want to hear what they say but also the way they say it. Always remember that a good quote used properly can tell what the person is like without the magazine having to say it.

Other voices. In house parlance these are called "terts," or tertiary elements of the story. They are the voices of friends, enemies, rivals, descendents, acquaintances, and colleagues who have something to say about the person interviewed. They help to make a balanced story and neutralize the tendency of the interviewee to take over not only the reader's attention but the story's central voice.

Critical judgment. Don't be afraid of using it. We want to hear about the newsmaker's laurels but also about the warts on his hands and his athlete's foot. Always offer an evaluation of the character before you: is he or she credible, lovable, egocentric, a liar, a womanizer? Although it's not our role to judge people, we should still give our view of the subject.

A notable example of the application of these and other components of the *People* formula was the fleeting romance between actress Meg Ryan and Australian actor Russell Crowe, a *People* cover story on July 17, 2000. Despite the fact that neither cooperated with the magazine, fourteen journalists were assigned to the story. They managed to piece together a picture of the romance by interviewing friends, relatives, and co-workers of the two. They even managed to find a passenger who flew with them, first class, from Los Angeles to Australia to corroborate how the two actors murmured endearments, kissed, and held hands during the trip.

52 PRINCESS DIANA
June 22, 1992

13 SARAH FERGUSON
November 20, 1989

13 MICHAEL JACKSON
September 14, 1987

13 CHER
October 22, 1979

16 JULIA ROBERTS
July 7, 1997

9 JOHN TRAVOLTA
May 13, 1977

9 PRINCESS CAROLINE
August 30, 1976

11 MADONNA
March 11, 1985

Celebrities with the Most Covers

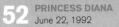

CELEBRITY	NUMBER OF COVERS
Princess Diana	52
Julia Roberts	16
Elizabeth Taylor	14
Jackie Onassis	13
Sarah Ferguson	13
Michael Jackson	13
Cher	13
JFK Jr.	12
Prince William	12
Madonna	11
John Travolta	9
Princess Caroline	9

SOURCE: *PEOPLE* MAGAZINE 2002

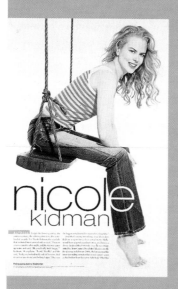

nicole
kidman

THE EARLY DAYS

"I feel
like I went
through
something,
and I really
went *through*
it. I didn't try
to hide"

AN AGELESS BEAUTY

nicole Kidman yes,
nicole Kidman no

With time, the writearound came to require more and better investigative reporters. In Los Angeles, for instance, the *People* bureau increased from the original four or five to a score of staffers. And the magazine started to devote a lot more people to researching a single article, particularly if it was expected to be a cover story. In such cases, Jones says, the magazine might assign ten people to a story. He underscores that the names of some

correspondents who take part in the research are not always printed, so the list may well be longer than those acknowledged in the byline. At *People* magazine this type of reporting team is known as The Swarm, a nickname that was first used after the excellent and exhaustive coverage of actor John Belushi's death in 1982.

In this respect, a unique case was the divorce of actors Tom Cruise and Nicole Kidman. *People's* reportage

early in 2001 included the bylines of ten journalists. This article, in which Kidman was the central figure, is also a good example of the graphic differences between a story where the personality cooperates and another where the magazine must write around the subject. In the issue of February 26, 2001, over six pages, *People* showed photos featuring the couple together with their children in different public situations, plus images of yachts, the

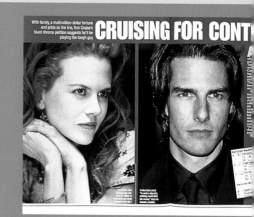

CRUISING FOR CONT

Yes

airplane, and other jointly owned
properties. To give the writearound
more character, *People* magazine didn't
use any studio productions or exclusive
posed photos, though it had a good
number of these on file.

More than a year later, on May 13,
2002, Nicole Kidman was on the cover
of a special issue devoted to "The 50
Most Beautiful People." In visual terms
the treatment could not have been
more different. The main photos were

shot by Andrew Macpherson in a
studio. Over the eight pages of the
story, along with these images, were
photos from her childhood, her acting
career, and previous productions by the
magazine that highlighted various
aspects of her beauty. Thus, on
People's stage, Nicole Kidman was the
star in two different scenarios, at two
different times in her life, with special
coverage in each case.

THE THREE ACTS OF A SMASH-HIT PLAY CALLED People

Whatever the variant of the formula —whether the celebrity is at the peak of stardom or on the seesaw of love, facing illness or troubles or tragedy— the events, says Richard Stolley, often come together into a three-act play: the rise, the fall, and the redemption. Just as people like to read about a star's successful climb or triumph and somehow recognize that this person is far removed from them, they also enjoy seeing their idols as real human beings of flesh and blood, with problems and sorrows and failures, just like any other mortal. That's why, he adds, the fall is as attractive as the ascent, and if it's followed by a redemption or inspirational outcome, so much the better, because then the message is that there's nothing that cannot be challenged or overcome.

The magazine has always followed the elements of this formula, although at times several years go by between acts of the play. A typical case is actress Tatum O'Neal. She became a child star with her Oscar-winning role in *Paper Moon* alongside her father, Ryan. *People* covered her climb to stardom, although in those days she would not grant an interview, forcing editors to do a writearound. This first act of the play continued through her teens, her marriage to tennis star John McEnroe, and the birth of her children.

However, the magazine also picked up on a long second act, with Tatum's fall into drug and alcohol dependency, her divorce, and the loss of custody of her children to McEnroe.

Then in June of 2002 the magazine moved into a third act with Tatum, at thirty-eight still beautiful, and trying to leave behind her cocaine and heroin addiction, for which she was attending Alcoholics Anonymous meetings twice a week. Tatum made the cover once again, this time without a writearound, because she welcomed *People* into her home and agreed to talk in an exclusive interview about what readers wanted to know. The circle came to a close with that third act that showed the actress trying to overcome her problem and put her life back together so she could win visitation rights with her children. *People* was along for the success (first act), the fall (second act), and the redemption (third act).

Regarding the magazine's formula and its philosophy, former editor Landon Jones concludes that the interesting thing about *People* is that it does not publish a single line of speculation or rumor. What sets it apart from the tabloids and the rest of the celebrity press is that *People* does pure journalism, interviewing each and every one of the sources and then carefully submitting the information to its fact-checkers and lawyers to avoid lawsuits or untruths. Now that the magazine is three decades old and has a weekly circulation of 3.6 million copies, *People* has shown that it can do journalism about the rich and famous with the editorial strength and credibility of all Time Inc. magazines. Its greatest contribution has been to conclusively legitimize celebrity journalism.

TATUM TODAY. This cover in June of 2002 showed readers the third act of Tatum's life. At thirty-eight, she talks about her efforts to overcome her drug addiction and about her attendance at Alcoholics Anonymous.

TATUM YESTERDAY.

In its coverage of the sad second act in the life of Tatum O'Neal, *People* showed images of happier times with her parents and former husband John McEnroe. The couple divorced because of her drug and alcohol addiction, and Tatum lost custody of her children.

TATUM, YESTERDAY AND TODAY. In this third act on Tatum, *People* draws a bridge —with images from yesterday and today— between the joys of the past and hope for the future. The coverage will not end there. Soon readers will want to know how Tatum's story continues.

BIBLIOGRAPHY

GENERAL

A History of American Magazines, by Frank Luther Mott. 5 vols. Cambridge, Mass.: Harvard University Press, 1938–68.

Magazines in the Twentieth Century, by Theodore Peterson. 2nd ed. Urbana, Ill.: University of Illinois Press, 1964.

CHAPTER 1

TIME

The American Magazine, by Amy Janello and Brennon Jones, for the Magazine Publishers of America and the American Society of Magazine Editors. New York: Harry N. Abrams, 1991.

Covering History: Time Magazine Covers, 1923–1997. New York: Time Inc., 1998.

Designer's Guide to Creating Charts and Diagrams, by Nigel Holmes. New York: Watson-Guptill, 1984.

Designing Pictorial Symbols, by Nigel Holmes with Rose DeNeve. New York: Watson-Guptill, 1985.

Faces of Time: 75 Years of Time Magazine Cover Portraits. Boston: Little, Brown, 1998.

Great People of the 20th Century. New York: Time-Life Books, 1996.

The Magazine in America, 1741–1990, by John Tebbel and Mary Ellen Zuckerman. New York: Oxford University Press, 1991.

Time Inc.: The Intimate History of a Publishing Enterprise, by Robert T. Elson et al. 3 vols. New York: Atheneum, 1968-86.

Time 1923-1998, 75 Years: An Anniversary Celebration. New York: Time-Life Books, 1998.

CHAPTER 2

DER SPIEGEL

The Spiegel Affair, by David Schoenbaum. Garden City, N.Y.: Doubleday, 1968.

Der Spiegel: 50 Years, 1947-1997, Hamburg: Spiegel, 1997.

Die Spiegel-Story: Wie alles anfing, by Leo Brawand. 2nd ed. Düsseldorf: Econ, 1987.

The Spiegel Story, by Leo Brawand. Translated by Anthea Bell. Oxford: Pergamon, 1989.

Die Spiegel-Titelbilder, 1947-1999, edited by Hans-Dieter Schütt and Oliver Schwarzkopf. Berlin: Schwarzkopf & Schwarzkopf, 2000.

CHAPTER 3

LIFE

The Best of Life. New York: Time-Life Books, 1973.

Eyewitness: 150 Years of Photojournalism, by Richard Lacayo and George Russell. New York: Time Books, 1990.

Let Truth Be the Prejudice, by W. Eugene Smith. New York: Aperture Foundation, 1985.

"The Life Photojournalism Essay Formula," by Caroline Dow. Paper presented at the annual meeting of the Association for Education in Journalism and Mass Communication, Houston, 1979.

Life: Sixty Years–A 60th Anniversary Celebration, 1936-1996. New York: Time-Life Books, 1996.

Life: Ten Years. New York: Time-Life Books, 1946.

The Magazine in America, 1741-1990, by John Tebbel and Mary Ellen Zuckerman. New York: Oxford University Press, 1991.

Photography & Society, by Gisèle Freund. Translated by Richard Dunn and Megan Marshall. Boston: David R. Godine, 1980. Originally published as **Photographie und Bürgerliche Gesellschaft** (Munich: Rogner & Bernhard, 1968).

Photojournalism. Rev. ed. New York: Time-Life Books, 1983.

Time Inc.: The Intimate Story of a Publishing Empire, by Robert T. Elson et al. 3 vols. New York: Atheneum, 1968-86.

CHAPTER 4

PARIS MATCH

La fabuleuse aventure de Paris Match, by Guillaume Hanoteau. Paris: Plon, 1976.

Graphic Design, by Milton Glaser. 1973. Woodstock, N.Y.: Overlook Press, 1983.

Paris Match: À 45 ans le roman de notre temps en 2354 couvertures. Paris: Paris Match, 1994.

Paris Match: 50 ans, 1949-1973, by Roger Thérond and France Loisirs. Paris: Filipacchi, 1998.

Paris Match: 40 ans. Paris: Éditions du Chêne, 1987.

Paris Match: Les 85 couvertures qui fait 35 ans d'histoire. Paris: Hachette-Filipacchi, 1984.

CHAPTER 5

NATIONAL GEOGRAPHIC

The American Magazine, by Amy Janello and Brennon Jones. New York: Harry N. Abrams, 1991.

The Art of National Geographic: A Century of Illustration, by Alice A. Carter. Washington, D.C.: National Geographic Society, 1999.

The Complete National Geographic: 112 Years. Collector's Edition, 1888-2000. CD-ROM. Washington, D.C.: National Geographic Society, 2001.

Great Adventures with National Geographic. Washington, D.C.: National Geographic Society, 1963.

"Inside the Geographic," by James Conaway. *Washington Post,* 1984.

The National Geographic Society and Its Magazine: A History, by Gilbert H. Grosvenor. Washington, D.C.: National Geographic Society, 1957.

The National Geographic Society: 100 Years of Adventure and Discovery, by C.D.B. Bryan. New York: Harry N. Abrams, 1987.

CHAPTER 6

READER'S DIGEST

The American Magazine: A Compact History, by John Tebbel. New York: Hawthorn, 1969.

The Magazine in America, 1741-1990, by John Tebbel and Mary Ellen Zuckerman. New York: Oxford University Press, 1991.

Of Lasting Interest: The Story of the Reader's Digest, by James Playsted Wood. Garden City, N.Y.: Doubleday, 1958.

The Reader's Digest Bible: Condensed from the Revised Standard Version Old and New Testaments, edited by Bruce M. Metzger. Pleasantville, N.Y.: Reader's Digest Association, 1982.

Reader's Digest: 40 Years. Pleasantville, N.Y.: Reader's Digest, 1961.

Reader's Digest: 50 Years. Pleasantville, N.Y.: Reader's Digest, 1972.

Reader's Digest: 75 Years. Pleasantville, N.Y.: Reader's Digest, 1997.

Theirs Was the Kingdom: Lila and DeWitt Wallace and the Story of the Reader's Digest, by John Heidenry. New York: W. W. Norton, 1993.

CHAPTER 7

¡HOLA!

Corazones de papel, by Alejandro Pizarroso and Julia Rivera. Barcelona: Planeta, 1994.

El imperio rosa: Poder e influencia de la prensa del corazón, by Pilar Falcón Osorio. Barcelona: CIMS, 1998.

¡Hola! 50 años. Special ed. 2 vols. Madrid: Ediciones ¡Hola!, 1994.

"¡Hola!" y el hijo de Sánchez, by Jaime Peñafiel. Madrid: Temas de Hoy, 1994.

Revistas: Una historia de amor y un decálogo, by Juan Caño. Madrid: Celeste, Eresma, 1999.

CHAPTER 8

PEOPLE

The Best of People Weekly: The First Decade. New York: Fawcett Columbine, 1984.

Inside "People": The Stories Behind the Stories, by Judy Kessler. New York: Villard, 1994.

The Magazine in America, 1741-1990, by John Tebbel and Mary Ellen Zuckerman. New York: Oxford University Press, 1991.

People Weekly: 25 Amazing Years! Collector's ed. New York: Time Inc., 1999.

Time Inc.: The Intimate History of a Publishing Enterprise. Vol. 3, **1960-1980**, by Curtis Prendergast with Geoffrey Colvin. New York: Atheneum, 1986.